# Knowing Books and Men; Knowing Computers, Too

# Knowing Books and Men;
# Knowing Computers, Too

## Jesse H. Shera

## 1973

## Libraries Unlimited, Inc.
### Littleton, Colo.

5/1974
Genl

LIBRARIES UNLIMITED, INC.
P.O. Box 263
Littleton, Colorado 80120

*Zusammengestohlen aus Verschiedenem
diesem und jenem. . . .*

Beethoven on his Quartet no. 14, Op. 131

# Preface

Despite the truth or falseness of the often-heard allegation that history repeats itself, there are few who would deny that journalists and other writers suffer from the sin of repetitiousness. To this fault the present writer must confess, for the *Lincei*, those lynx-eyed reviewers, will waste no time in pointing it out. The more generous among the critics may regard it as a commendable consistency in point of view, but for the others it will represent only a paucity of ideas and an excess of affection for the sound of one's own words.

This volume, then, it may be charged, is more of an addition to library shelves than to library literature, and one might properly question why it should have been put together at all. Was it mere personal conceit and the anticipation of royalties? Doubtless ego and avarice, supported by the urgings of the publisher, played some part in the decision. But might not such a charge be made against every author? Why does one publish a book; and once it is published, why does anyone review it?

This is not the place to engage in a philosophical consideration of the psychological motivations of authorship. We are confronted by a fact—the book is here, it is a reality, it exists. "The moving finger writes, and, having writ, moves on; nor all your piety and wit can lure it back to cancel half a line." A more important concern to the reader, perhaps, is not why the book was put together, but *how*. Many of the essays that comprise this volume were originally addresses, or speeches if that sounds less pretentious, presented to quite different audiences, and repetition was not a serious consideration; but when brought together under one cover the right of the reader to some variety cannot be ignored. Thus the editorial use of the blue pencil becomes mandatory, however painful the excisions may be to the author, and in the end some repetition has survived, either through oversight or because of the need for emphasis.

The perceptive reader will also find some anachronisms, references to events and publications that are dated long after the original essay was published; but these will be apparent only to those who note the date of the original and would seem to be of relative insignificance compared to the enrichment of the text or the strengthening of the argument. Some of the pieces have remained in their original state, notably "The Diagram Is the Message," and "The Beginnings of Systematic Bibliography in America." One, "The Literature of American Library History," has been so completely revised and brought up to date that the length of the original has been doubled. Most of the essays, however, have received some revision, and one essay, "For Whom Do We Conserve?" has not previously appeared in published form. All of this information, which will be of little concern to most readers, is a kind of gratuity given to the reviewer to ease the burden of his task and perhaps to elicit the reward of his mercy.

We wish to acknowledge with gratitude our debt to the many publishers who so generously permitted us to reprint the materials herewith included; not one who was asked refused. Appropriate acknowledgment appears at the beginning of each essay.

So now our book goes out into the world, its flanks exposed to the slings and arrows of outrageous critics. But that is as it should be in the world of authorship. We, for our part, can offer no apologies or make no excuses—*Quod scripsi, scripsi.*

May 12, 1973                                                          J.H.S.

# Table of Contents

# I.

# Toward a Philosophy
# of Librarianship

# 1

# What Is Past Is Prologue:
# Beyond 1984

*"So let us think kindly of those who would frighten us by slogans and catch-words about the great and growing mass of the world's literature, and of those who would take pity upon our benighted state to solve all our problems with machines they have not yet thought about."*[1]

With these words, the librarian of the Department of Agriculture won the esteem and devotion of the conservatives among librarians who looked with dread toward a day when they would be supplanted by a little black box. After all, had Ralph Shaw not invented the Rapid Selector? Who was better qualified than he to speak in Delphic tones of the future of the machine?

But reread today, after the passing of almost 15 years, Ralph Shaw's pronouncements, although sprinkled with wisdom, were, like the speech of most oracles, not always the outgrowth of a perceptive vision of the future; but they were tempered to the prevailing spirit of the times so far as most librarians were concerned. As the political sentiments of the Oracle of Delphi were generally aristocratic and pro-Dorian, so Shaw's sibylline words were conventional and conservative, though masked by a pretense of radicalism.

Yet almost 20 years before the appearance of "From Fright to Frankenstein," Frederick J. Keppel wrote with prophetic vision in his essay in *The Library of Tomorrow*:

> I blush to think how many years we watched the so-called business machines juggle with payrolls and bank books before it occurred to us that they might be adapted to dealing with library cards with equal dexterity. Indexing has become an entirely new art . . . and the modern version of the old Hollerith machine will sort out and photograph anything that the dial tells it. . . . We librarians must keep up with all these applications of science, and I admit it takes a fair share of our time to do so."[2]

Originally published in the *ALA Bulletin*, Vol. 61 (January 1967), pp. 35-47.

Again, this time in 1945, Vannevar Bush, who could scarcely be regarded as a weaver of science fiction fabrications, envisaged "memex," a device "in which an individual stores all his books, records, and communications, and which is mechanized so that it may be consulted with exceeding speed and flexibility. It is an enlarged intimate supplement to his memory."[3] Mr. Bush then proceeded to describe a mechanism that bears a striking resemblance to the on-line computer installation of MIT's Project MAC. Thus, by the time Ralph Shaw wrote his denunciation of the machine, tides were already running that his words could no more arrest than could the impotent commands of King Canute centuries before him.

## MINIATURIZATION

The advent of microphotography may probably be regarded as the harbinger of the Brave New World of librarianship. In 1935 the Bibliofilm Service was organized by three perceptive and visionary pioneers—Claribel Barnett, Rupert Draeger, and Atherton Seidell—all of whom were eager to extend the services of the Department of Agriculture Library to scientists throughout the country. It remained, however, for Watson Davis to take the initiative in merging those interests into a unified movement with Science Service as its focus.[4] At the 1936 conference of the ALA a symposium on microphotography for librarians was held for the first time, and in the same year Robert C. Binkley published his historic survey of methods for the reproduction of research materials.[5] Two years later the publication of the *Journal of Documentary Reproduction* was initiated under the auspices of the ALA Committee on Photographic Reproduction of Library Materials;[6] also in 1938, Eugene Power founded University Microfilms, and librarians began to talk glibly about the day when microfilm would supplant the book as the major repository of the printed word.

The popularity of miniaturization was given a substantial boost with the publication of Fremont Rider's *The Scholar and the Future of the Research Library*,[7] in which the author advocated the extensive use of microopaques (microcards) for the storage and dissemination of scholarly and research materials. Rider's book, which initiated the widespread use of Microcards, was, however, probably as important for the attention it drew to the exponential growth of research library collections as for its advocacy of microimages on catalog-card stock. For some years reduction ratios were thought to be limited by the "grain" of silver emulsions. Freedom from grain was achieved with the use of light-sensitive dyes, but recently Professor Richard P. Feynman of the California Institute of Technology has suggested that, since organic life is able to store its genetic information at the ultimate molecular level, it should be possible to approach such a degree of miniaturization with intellectual information by storing words at least near to the limits of magnification of the electron-microscope. John R. Platt, professor of physics at the University of Chicago, has pointed out that it is not beyond the possibilities of present-day technology to reduce printed text to the point at which the entire content of the world's literature, not just the holdings of the Library of Congress as has been frequently suggested, could be contained in a device no larger than the average office desk.[8] In Germany, G. Mollenstedt demonstrated that by etching on a thin metal film with an electron "pencil" 80 angstroms wide, letters could be produced some 100 times smaller than the limits of the optical microscope. Thus, Professor Platt envisages reduction ratios that would permit the "printing" on a sheet of standard letterhead of all the 20-million different titles that are supposed to represent the world's book production from the beginning of graphic communication to the present day. Whether such extremes of compression will ever be necessary is not now an important or serious consideration. The major problem that confronts the librarian today is not so much one of accumulation as of access to that which is accumulated. What will it profit a scholar if the entire Library of Congress sits on his desk, if he cannot select from it that which is living, vital, and relevant to his interests and needs? The library problem, like the problem of education, is not storage but retrieval.

## MECHANIZATION

The mechanization of library operations followed hard upon the development of microfilm, though what influence, if any, Keppel's prognostication of the future exerted is impossible to say. Certainly the basic idea of automated libraries was in the air. For a number of years prior to 1940 Ralph Parker had been experimenting with the use of tabulating equipment applied mainly to library housekeeping functions. During the Second World War, the Central Information Division of the now legendary OSS made a primitive adaptation of IBM equipment to the subject analysis of intercepts received in large volume from the U.S. Office of Censorship. In the late 1940s, Ralph Shaw, who was later to turn violently against machines, fabricated, with engineering assistance, a device known as the Rapid Selector, which combined coded microfilm with electronics in an unsuccessful attempt to produce a mechanized literature searching apparatus.

By 1950, however, Vernon Tate wrote in his opening editorial in *American Documentation*, "Studies ranging from those previously mentioned as the logic or philosophy of communication to concrete expressions in equipment, punched card machines, digital computers, 'electronic brains,' rapid selectors, and integrators have produced notable results."[9] One can say with assurance, however, that James W. Perry, first at the Massachusetts Institute of Technology, and later at the Battelle Memorial Institute and at Western Reserve University, was among the foremost of the pioneers in this rapidly expanding endeavor. His conference on the application of machines to the retrieval of scientific information, held at MIT in the spring of 1952; his volume on punched cards, written jointly with Robert S. Casey and first published in 1951; and his studies in machine literature searching laid the intellectual, and, to some extent, the technological, foundations of information retrieval as they are largely understood today.[10] At Western Reserve University a few years later he built, with the use of banks of telephone jacks and relays connected by untold miles of wire, a "Searching Selector." It would have made an admirable sound-effects device for a Hollywood battle scene, but it worked, miraculously, and it proved the soundness of the basic Perry thesis concerning the relation between semantic analysis and mechanized information retrieval.[11]

But at this same time much work was going on elsewhere, at IBM, Eastman Kodak, General Electric, Remington Rand, to name but a few centers. Mechanized information retrieval has progressed a long way since the pioneering days of J. W. Perry and Hans Peter Leuhn, and the production and searching of machine-readable records is no longer a novelty at the Library of Congress, the National Library of Medicine, the National Aeronautics and Space Administration. Substantial sums of money for exploratory work have been made available by the National Science Foundation, the National Institutes of Health, the Office of Scientific Research of the U.S. Air Force, and the Council on Library Resources.

At a symposium on the library of the future sponsored by the *Wilson Library Bulletin* and held in New York in June 1964, the future mechanization of the intellectual content of library materials was accepted as axiomatic and inevitable. Burton Adkinson spoke of the coming of facsimile transmission "at a very nominal cost." Again, he observed, "I predict that within the next 50 years, we will be able to sit in our own homes and dial our libraries to request certain information. When we are able to do this, the library will become a more integral part of people's lives."[12] Similarly, in his portion of the summation, William Dix, of Princeton, suggested, "The solution of many problems seems to be summed up by Mr. Greenaway's concept of a broader national network of libraries. For example, automated bibliographic control of materials, cataloging, acquisition of items from the remote, bibliographically unsophisticated areas of the world, should be considered as a national problem requiring centralized control as well as substantial investment."[13]

In 1961, the Council on Library Resources, having become concerned about the library of the future, turned to the firm of Bolt, Beranek, and Newman, consulting engineers with a primary interest in acoustics, for the preparation of a two-year study of the library of tomorrow that would focus attention upon "concepts and problems."[14] The investigation was placed under the direction of J.C.R. Licklider, an engineering psychologist and past president of the Acoustical Society of America. Despite the fact the Mr. Licklider obviously knew very little about either libraries or the future, his report on the research, if one can overlook his enthusiasm for "procognitive system," provides the discriminating librarian with considerable insight into the forces that will be acting upon his profession in the years ahead; and it also sets forth some indication of the role of mechanization in information storage and retrieval.

*Libraries of the Future* undoubtedly played an important role in stimulating the Intrex Conference sponsored by the Massachusetts Institute of Technology, at Woods Hole, in August 1965. The objective of this conference, which brought together librarians, engineers, information scientists, and publishers, was to develop the guidelines for a massive research program for the School of Engineering at MIT, to discover "long-term solutions for the operational problems of large libraries and of developing competence in the emerging field of information-transfer engineering."[15] Though the participants at the conference were careful not to espouse any special form of mechanization, it was very clear from the outset that the eventual use of some form of "machine-aided cognition" was assumed.

The approach to information retrieval, or transfer, that characterized the thinking at the Intrex conference, is clearly evident at the University of Chicago where plans are going forward for a multimillion dollar library which will utilize, as fully as existing technology permits, a multiple-access computer system in conjunction with closed circuit television, consoles, and related apparatus to bring to the individual faculty member the bibliographic resources needed for his intellectual work, whether he will be in the library, in his office, or at home. Such an installation on the university's Midway will make possible additional research in the experimental programs contemplated at MIT and will promote cooperation with present and future national and regional information networks.

The degree to which mechanization is infiltrating a wide variety of industrial and research libraries and information centers is clearly apparent from the surveys of such systems conducted from time to time by the Office of Science Information Service of the National Science Foundation.[16] Even in England, where resistance to machines has been considerably stronger than in the United States, a substantial amount of work is going forward in the utilization of machines for the organization of information, though progress there still lags behind similar experimentation on this side of the Atlantic.[17] Ben-Ami Lipetz, head of the research department of the Yale University Library, seems to have summarized admirably the present state of and prospects for mechanized information retrieval when he recently wrote in the *Scientific American*:

> There is great need for machines to take over significant portions of the intellectual work. Faster, larger, cheaper computers are not the complete answer, although they will certainly be necessary. The major contribution will probably come from enlarged understanding of how human evaluations are made and from increased effort to design improved programs of instruction that will endow machines with analytical abilities simulating human abilities. In a real sense the problem is one of learning how to educate machines efficiently. In humans the

educational process takes decades and requires the accumulation of vast amounts of experience, all of which is imperfectly, but quite effectively, stored. There is no reason to expect that advances in computers and programs will soon yield systems with the equivalent of a college education, but the trend will be increasingly in that direction.[18]

But the importance of machines to librarians is by no means limited to information retrieval. The early work of Ralph Parker, at the University of Missouri, in applying automation to library housekeeping functions, has already been mentioned. Photographic and edge-notched card systems for circulation control are now virtually commonplace. At Florida Atlantic University the application of the computer to circulation procedures has been extremely successful. The use of tabulation equipment for bookkeeping and other administrative operations in at least the larger libraries is widespread and is an obvious step from commercial practice. The generation of book catalogs and other bibliographic materials by computer is bringing back to the library a form of catalog that not long ago was supposed to have been completely superseded by the three-by-five card. Parker, in fact, confidently predicts that in a very few years the card catalog will be a relic of the past.

The big impetus to the adaptation of automation to library routines, however, probably came from a study conducted at the former Navy Pier Branch of the University of Illinois, Chicago, by Schultheiss, Culbertson, and Heiliger under a grant from the Council on Library Resources. The results of this pilot study indicated that electronic computers are capable of efficiently manipulating bibliographic data and control records (e.g., acquisition and cataloging procedures, circulation and overdue routines, and financial processes) provided that: 1) there has been a careful analysis of the library as a system in the light of its goals, objectives, and the services it is proposed to render; 2) bibliographic procedures have been standardized; 3) there has been a careful study of available machines, methods, systems, and forms for the selection of those most appropriate to the particular library tasks; 4) a progressive attitude of mind among all levels of the library staff has been fostered; and 5) decisions have been made as to the proper utilization of equipment.[19]

More recently, in the library of the Technical University in Delft, The Netherlands, Verhoeff and his associates have developed a highly mechanized system, known as Bibliofoon, for expediting circulation procedures and improving the efficiency of loan operations. Of this system, Verhoeff has written, "The Bibliofoon may prove to be a Trojan Horse to the library. It was brought in to speed up service, but when the statistics it gathers are analyzed, the whole approach to library operation may be changed."[20]

As one might anticipate, the automation of these library routines is moving forward at a rapid rate, and the pace may be expected to accelerate. The demands that such operations place upon the machine are much more akin to those for which they were originally designed, and the operations themselves are much more overt, repetitive, and easily standardized than are the subtle intellectual processes implicit in information retrieval and reference work. Ralph Parker's prognostications of the coming of automation could well prove conservative if one may judge from the progress that has been made during the past few years.

## THE FUTURE OF THE MACHINE IN THE LIBRARY

Up to this point we must plead guilty to the charge of having been more retrospective than anticipatory or oracular—it's safer that way—but we know no way of judging the future except from the experiences of the past. Moreover, we wanted to emphasize that the mechanization of the library, and the emerging information science that it rests upon, are not transitory enthusiasms. Librarians are confronted by a movement that has been steadily developing over the past 30 years and that, though it is very far from being immune from error, already has some impressive achievements to its credit. Librarianship is not going to be untouched by the machine.

"We would be underestimating the computer," insists Robert M. Hutchins in a recently syndicated newspaper column, if we treat it "as though it were just another invention, whereas it cannot be compared with any mechanical device in history. It adds a new dimension to the powers of men and to human life." Philip H. Abelson, in a recent editorial in *Science*, subscribes to the same view, though he enumerates the burgeoning powers of the computer in considerably more detail than does the former chancellor of the University of Chicago:

> A decade ago, use of computers seemed impractical for most scientists. Those conversant with the machines talked of frustrating hours spent in programming, compiling, and debugging. There were long delays between concept and fruition. . . . Usually the computers merely took advantage of the fact that the new devices were much faster than desk calculators. . . . Present-day models calculate $10^7$ to $10^8$ times as fast as man does. . . .
>
> Today, instructions to a computer can often be conveyed by typing simple English or abbreviations. Another means of easy access to the computer is through a console that employs something similar to an oscilloscope screen and a light pen. The computer converts a rough sketch into a finished drawing. . . .
>
> The computer can communicate with the user in new, simple forms . . . perhaps the most impressive development is the graphic presentation of data. . . . Today a glance at a curve on a screen or the plot of a thousand points can provide an almost instant summation. . . . Another impressive development is that of teaching a computer to talk. Through manipulation of controls, the investigator can change the character and emphasis of the speech. This would seem to speed the day when it will become possible to speak to a computer and to obtain quickly a spoken as well as a visible output.
>
> Improvements in computers and in the ease of using them portend a further great expansion in their use in all the sciences and in many of the humanities.

"After growing wildly for years the field of computing now appears to be approaching its infancy."[21]

There is a computer in your future, there is no doubt about that, and whether one regards it as the monster of a Frankenstein or the harbinger of a new industrial revolution will not change the course of events.[22] Men will continue to experiment with machines for the performance of intellectual tasks whether librarians approve or not, just as men continued to extend their physical powers with the aid of machines despite the opposition of the Luddites.

But, despite Marshall McLuhan's belief that the book is obsolescent and is having its last big splurge like the dinosaurs before their extinction, we are convinced that the book is here to stay. The capacity of a culture to accommodate and to absorb innovation is almost infinite. We well remember the day when it was widely believed that the new "movies" would make the legitimate stage obsolete, that the radio would put the newspaper out of business, that the "talkies" would really put the coup de grace to the stage, though it had stubbornly refused to surrender to the "movies," and that television would sweep all else before it, including the book. Even the automobile did not eliminate the horse; it raised him from the drudgery of the milkcart to a position of new social prestige in the paddock. So, too, the machine, if librarians will but prepare themselves for its coming, will raise librarianship to new levels of intellectual strength and attainment. Innovations are usually responses to new or altered social aims, needs or desires. Mechanization, by providing the librarian with powerful new tools, which admittedly he must learn to master, can open endless frontiers of new service unimagined and unimaginable when Poole and Winsor and their colleagues foregathered in Philadelphia 90 years ago.

## SOCIAL CHANGE AND THE FUTURE OF THE LIBRARY

But the library of tomorrow is not solely to be understood in mechanistic terms, spectacular and fascinating though they be. Of even greater importance than electronics to the changing pattern of librarianship is the social milieu in which it will exist. As surely as the library has been, and is, the resultant of social forces, just as certainly will it be reshaped by social mutation. Quite rightly, the emphasis of the Wilson symposium was social rather than technological; indeed, the latter received scant attention. The engineer is not the Messiah to deliver us from the wilderness.

In the space that remains, only the most pronounced threads in the merging social fabric can be identified. Most important of all are, of course, the demographic features. American society has moved from what appeared in the 1930s to be an aging population to a population in which the majority is under 30 years of age. But a recession in the birth rate has followed the drastic upsurge of births that characterized the 15 years following the Second World War, while dramatic improvements in medicine promise a steady increase in life expectancy. A time may yet come when youth will no longer dominate the American people.[23] To the librarian, the mobility of the population and the shift from rural to urban living are almost as important as the alterations in the fertility and morbidity patterns of the population. All of these influences will contribute in significant ways to the demands and interests of tomorrow's borrowers. Nor has society yet come to appreciate the meaning of increased leisure time resulting from the spread of automation, and the deterioration of the work-ethic. The social consequences of a work-free life may be even more powerful than the blast from nuclear fission. Eventually man may have to learn to live in a world, and with an economy, in which labor has been reduced almost—one is tempted to say "dangerously close"—to the vanishing point. If such a transformation does not place a heavy burden on the educational system, including the library, we know not what will. Prospects of a leisure-oriented society dominated much of the discussion at the Wilson symposium. "We are not really prepared," Emerson Greenaway observed, "for a situation in which many educated people will also have to face unemployment," and William Dix responded, "No doubt all of us will have to face the fact that any given person will spend more time in the future in formal education, but one hopes he will also spend more time . . . in informal education, in the whole process of continuing education outside the classroom."[24]

Second in importance only to demographic and occupational trends is the evolution of the governmental pattern, the eradication of old jurisdictional boundaries, the surrender of authority by local government to regional and national agencies, and the inescapable redrafting of the tax system. The time is fast approaching when libraries can no longer afford to remain isolated units, however much they may gratify local pride. As the school district was too small for library support, even in the 19th century, so the city may well be too small to provide for the libraries of the 21st. But reform follows the tax dollar, especially at the local level, and a largely archaic tax structure must be remodeled, not just for the benefit of libraries, though they will share in the rewards, but for all society. Whether we approve or not, the federal government must, in the very near future, increase its concern with the equitable allocation of public financial resources for all forms of human activity. The risk of excessively centralized power must be taken if chaos is to be avoided. Our society cannot progress in the face of its increasing complexity unless local initiative is harnessed, and a harness implies control.

But if the governmental structure must be built more rationally, orderly, and with increased clarification of responsibility, so the library system must be dealt with holistically as a network of interrelated and interdependent functions, responsibilities, and services. As librarianship moves away from local emphasis and the local plan, it will move toward a close working relationship among all types of libraries. But the distinctions that define the role and responsibilities of each type of library will be more sharply and clearly drawn than they have yet been. This system will be backed up by a national network of integrated regional bibliographic centers which in their totality, so Dix estimated at the Wilson symposium, will be equivalent to a library of 50 million volumes so stored and organized that their physical images can be transmitted to any desired point in the country; thus, greater and greater concentrations of original materials in fewer and fewer libraries will become possible and even desirable.[25]

Even locally, the apparent decay of the inner city may mean the dispersion of library facilities. "We have to get away from the idea," Adkinson warned the Wilson group, "that libraries are a series of isolated units. Libraries must become a network at all levels so that a reader doesn't think in terms of a public library versus a school library versus a university library, but of the library *system.* Then if a user goes to any one, he will have a connection with the others."[26] But to utilize fully the assets of this integrated system, much more attention than has been characteristic of the past must be devoted to the preparation of new bibliographic tools and to bibliographic organization generally, as regards both physical and content, or intellectual, availability. Whether such organization is achieved electronically or by more conventional means has no real bearing on the importance of the need.

As system is important to the totality of a nation's library resources, so is it important to the organization of the individual library. Perhaps one of the most important benefits to the profession that has resulted from its technologic revolution is the imperative forced upon librarians to define precisely their role and the role of their institution in society, to think through the philosophy of their profession, and to differentiate that which is truly intellectual from that which is only routine and clerical.

At long last a philosophy of librarianship is beginning to come into its own, and it is coming in, not through any ivory-towered pedagogy, but from the hard-headed rationality of systems analysis. We do not mean to imply that, in their hunger after efficiency, the systems engineers will reject outright the substantial virtues of much of conventional librarianship. "This may seem old-fashioned," Dix told the Wilson symposium, "but an attractive room and a wide-ranging collection of books, freely accessible, seems to me what a library is."[27] There will be plenty of space in the library of the future for Mr. Dix's attractive room, and, if we are not mistaken, the systems analysts have no intention of tossing the baby out with the bath. Serendipity has its place in librarianship, and the intellectual is often most efficient when he appears least so to others.

## PROFESSIONAL EDUCATION AND RESEARCH

"Each generation must define afresh the nature, direction, and the aims of education," writes Jerome S. Bruner, in *Toward a Theory of Instruction*, "to assure such freedom and rationality as can be attained for a future generation. For there are changes both in circumstances and in knowledge that impose constraints on and give opportunity to the teacher in each succeeding generation."[28] Education, therefore, must be in constant process of invention, for as the technology of a culture grows increasingly complex, in both machinery and human organization, the role of education becomes more central to society, both as an agent of socialization and as a transmitter of knowledge and skills. The basis for the redefinition of education, then, is the changing society. We do not mean to suggest that education must necessarily follow the lead of society; it can, and should anticipate change and prepare society for innovation. But whether education, at any given moment, leads or follows, certain decisions with respect to educational policy cannot be avoided.

The first, of course, has to do with what will be taught. In library education especially, a harmonizing of skills with fundamental theoretical conceptualization is particularly important. Skills will be important because they relate to the technology that is adding powerful new dimensions to the library enterprise. But librarianship must also move toward the sciences of human behavior. To paraphrase Bruner, it is the behavioral sciences and their generality with respect to variations in the human condition that must be central to the librarian's study of man in relation to his accumulated knowledge.[29] But it must be a behavioral science seen against a biological setting, for man is a biological organism that betrays his lineage at every turn.

In library education, as in other forms of education, one must recognize that the process of learning is cumulative, not in the sense of adding, or storing, increasing amounts of knowledge in the brain, but in the sense that mastery at one educational level strengthens the powers of mastery at a higher level. A curriculum, then, despite its etymology, is not a race to be run, but a ladder to be climbed, a ladder in which the rungs are increasingly distant from each other as the learner ascends. Unfortunately, up to the present, library education has not really exhibited this intellectual progression to the degree that it should.

Finally, if education for librarianship is to keep pace with, much less lead, social change, it will have to bring far greater resources to bear upon itself than has been true in the past. If the librarian's bright new world is to become a reality, the profession must not only prepare for, but must also invite, invasion from without. The growing dependence of society upon its graphic records is becoming too important to be left to the librarians, and the profession can no longer lift itself by its own intellectual boot-straps. No form of human activity, unless it be the profession of law, is more interdisciplinary than librarianship, and librarians, in their education, as well as in their practice, cannot afford to isolate themselves from the world. They must draw from other branches of scholarship new intellectual and human resources. If they do not, other disciplines will assume the responsibilities that rightly, by experience and capabilities, belong to the librarians.

Again the theme of interdependence interjects itself. Conventional librarianship alone leads to sterility, but science and engineering lack the essential bibliographic foundations that librarianship can provide. To acknowledge this lack of professional self-sufficiency is going to be painful to the librarians, but they must confess it or suffer dire consequences. Too long have librarians been brought up in the tradition that they can be all things to all men; they must recognize specialization and seek the assistance of mathematicians, engineers, anthropologists, political scientists, linguists, and a host of others. The humanistic tradition from which librarianship emerged has much to its credit, but humanism itself is slowly learning to accommodate to intellectual cross-fertilization from the physical and social sciences. The librarian's future may be a land flowing with milk and honey—we hope and believe that it is—but the road to it is as yet uncharted. The librarians are going to have to ask the way of many "strangers," and even then there will be times when the profession seems hopelessly lost. To change the metaphor, if the bright new world is to be burnished to its luster a lot of people are going to be rubbed raw.

Bruner argues vigorously for a restructuring of the educational process in terms that are directly applicable to librarianship. "It is plain that if we are to evolve freely as a species by the use of the instrument of education, then we shall have to bring far greater resources to bear in designing our educational system. For one thing, if we are to respond to accelerated change, then we shall have to reduce turn-around time in the system. To do this requires greater participation on the part of those at the frontiers of learning."[30]

In library education, the old core curriculum, over which so much ink was spilled during the past decade, is dead, and in its place must come an intensely accelerated program which will provide the student with the theoretical foundations of librarianship and launch him at the earliest possible moment into his specialty. The specialties must be enriched from a wide variety of course offerings taught, in part, by people who have never "met a library payroll." To this program of study must be attracted the best minds of the younger generation, men and women with distinguished undergraduate achievement who have the flexibility and toughness of mind that will enable them to see librarianship steadily and see it whole, to see it over and beyond the confines of their own specializations.

Gordon Ray of the Guggenheim Foundation, who can scarcely be accused of being an enthusiastic supporter of automation, was very right when he told the sweltering audience at the recent New York Conference of the ALA, "It is clear that the fascination of these developing electronic techniques is a vitalizing force in the library world, attracting many talented young people who otherwise might not be interested in the profession. But I do propose that you should remain librarians, not what Samuel Butler, in his vision of a mechanized future in *Erewhon*, calls 'machine-tickling aphids.' The country's great library schools would be ill-advised to stop educating librarians in order to train information retrievers."[3][1] His association of "education" with librarianship and "training" with information retrieval is significant. The greatest resource of librarianship is still its reservoir of human talent, and if this is properly nurtured the future will take care of itself.

Research in librarianship must, of course, be interdisciplinary and directed toward the solution of library problems, toward the solution of problems that now becloud the vision of what librarianship is and ought to be. Again to refer to Mr. Ray, "Books and libraries have not been granted immunity to change. They will prosper only as they adapt to the needs of a society that is itself changing more rapidly than ever before."[3][2] The profession does not need a "researcher" in every library, but it does desperately need a substantial body of skilled investigators capable of bringing to bear upon library problems the powerful tools that modern scholarship has made available, investigators who are not stricken with terror by a mathematical model or a page of computational linguistics. When the library process becomes an integrated system built upon a sound body of theory derived from precise knowledge of man's use of communication and recorded knowledge, when library service is the fruit of all relevant scholarship, then, and only then, can librarianship be said to have achieved professional maturity and quality as a science in its own right. It is we, all of us, who will invent the future, and if it is not as we would have it, the fault, dear Brutus, will not be in our stars.

If the above delineation of the library world after 1984 is less sharp and precise than one might wish, it is only in part because of the oracular predisposition to hedge one's bets with ambiguity. Civilization, and with it librarianship, must travel a perilous knife-edge into a paradoxical tomorrow of both menace and promise, a world about which there are no certainties except uncertainty. But for all the doubt, or perhaps because of it, we face a very exciting time to be alive, a time in which man's achievements will be limited by only his will to better his condition. We wish we were at least 20 years younger and a great deal smarter than we are, for we would like to see the world that lies beyond 1984 and be an active participant in it.

## FOOTNOTES

[1] Ralph R. Shaw, "From Fright to Frankenstein," *D.C. Libraries*, Vol. 24, No. 1 (January 1953), p. 10.
[2] Frederick J. Keppel, "Looking Forward, a Fantasy," in Emily Miller Danton, ed., *The Library of Tomorrow* (Chicago: American Library Association, 1939), p. 5.

³ Vannevar Bush, "As We May Think," *Atlantic Monthly*, Vol. 176 (July 1945), pp. 106-107.

⁴ Jesse H. Shera, "Mirror for Documentalists," *D.C. Libraries*, Vol. 27, No. 2 (April 1956), pp. 2-4.

⁵ Robert C. Binkley, *Manual of Methods of Reproducing Research Materials* (Ann Arbor: Edwards Brothers, 1936), 207p.

⁶ The *Journal* flourished from 1938 to 1943 when publication was interrupted by World War II. It was revived in 1950, with a grant from the Carnegie Corporation of New York, as the official organ of the American Documentation Institute under the title *American Documentation* with the editor of the original journal, Vernon D. Tate, still in charge.

⁷ Fremont Rider, *The Scholar and the Future of the Research Library* (New York: Hadham Press, 1944), 236p.

⁸ John R. Platt, "Where Will the Books Go?" *Horizon*, Vol. 5, No. 1 (September 1962), pp. 42-47.

⁹ *American Documentation*, Vol. 1, No. 1 (January 1950), p. 4.

¹⁰ Robert S. Casey and James W. Perry, *Punched Cards, Their Application to Science and Industry* (New York: Reinhold, 1951), 506p.; 2d ed., 1958, 697p. *See also*: Howard F. McGaw, *Marginal Punched Cards in College and Research Libraries* (Washington: Scarecrow Press, 1952), 218p.; and James W. Perry and associates, *Machine Literature Searching* (New York: Interscience Publishers, 1956), 162p. Most of the essays in this volume were originally published in *American Documentation* between 1954 and 1955.

¹¹ James W. Perry and associates, *Tools for Machine Literature Searching* (New York: Interscience Publishers, 1958), 972p.

¹² "The Library of the Future; A WLB Symposium," *Wilson Library Bulletin*, Vol. 39 (November 1964), pp. 234-41.

¹³ *Ibid.*, pp. 242-43.

¹⁴ Verner W. Clapp, "Foreword" in J.C.R. Licklider, *Libraries of the Future* (Cambridge: M.I.T. Press, 1965), p. viii.

¹⁵ Carl F.J. Overhage, "Plans for Project Intrex," *Science*, Vol. 152 (May 20, 1966), p. 1032. *See also*: J. H. Shera, "Librarians' Pugwash, or Intrex on the Cape," *Wilson Library Bulletin*, Vol. 40 (December 1965), pp. 359-62. The official report of the Intrex Conference has appeared as Carl F.J. Overhage and R. Joyce Harman, eds., *INTREX: Report of a Planning Conference on Information Transfer Experiments* (Cambridge: M.I.T. Press, 1965), 276p.

¹⁶ National Science Foundation, Office of Science Information Service, *Nonconventional Information Retrieval Systems in Current Use* (Washington: National Science Foundation, 1962), 209p.

¹⁷ *See*, for example, *Looking Forward in Documentation, Papers and Discussion, Aslib 38th Annual Conference, University of Exeter, 1964* (London: Aslib, 1966), 109p.

[18] Ben-Ami Lipetz, "Information Storage and Retrieval," *Scientific American*, Vol. 215 (September 1966), p. 242.

[19] Louis A. Schultheiss, Don S. Culbertson, and Edward M. Heiliger, *Advanced Data Processing in the University Library* (New York: Scarecrow Press, 1962), pp. 108-10.

[20] J. Verhoeff, "The Delft Circulation System," *Libri*, Vol. 16, No. 1 (1966), p. 9.

[21] Philip H. Abelson, "The Human Use of Computing Machines," *Science*, Vol. 153 (July 15, 1966), p. 253.

[22] "While prospects for machine information retrieval systems appear distant still, the extent of energetic talent and resources being applied to these problems, if only in experimental and preliminary phases of the work, would seem to insure ultimate modification of the traditional means whereby access to information is gained," Paul Wasserman, *The Librarian and the Machines* (Detroit: Gale Research Co., 1965), p. 144.

[23] For a prognostication that really went sour, *see* J. H. Shera, "The Librarian's Changing World," *Library Journal*, Vol. 58 (February 15, 1933), pp. 149-52.

[24] "The Library of the Future," pp. 230-31.

[25] *Ibid.*, p. 238.

[26] *Ibid.*, p. 232.

[27] *Ibid.*, p. 233.

[28] Jerome S. Bruner, *Toward a Theory of Instruction* (Cambridge: Harvard University Press, 1966), p. 22.

[29] *Ibid.*, p. 36.

[30] *Ibid.*, p. 37.

[31] Gordon N. Ray, "The Future of the Book," *ALA Bulletin*, Vol. 60, No. 8 (September 1966), p. 792.

[32] *Ibid.*, p. 784.

# 2

# The Diagram Is the Message

The diagram is a special case of picture-making. It involves the same representational condition: the mapping of a content in shapes which themselves possess—and transmit—a characteristic content. It is necessary to distinguish between the paradigmatic intent and the emblematic form of a diagram. In the Postscript the error potential implicit in the interplay of these properties is demonstrated by examples which include the book arts.

## PART I

From the grottoes of Combarelles and Altamira to the galleries of the Louvre the walls bear eloquent testimony to man's basic need for pictorial representation. First, say the historians of art, there was sculpture; "the object represented through all its profiles," writes Faure, "having a kind of second real existence." Sculpture was followed by the bas-relief, "which sinks and effaces itself until it becomes engraving,"[1] and finally there was pictorial convention, the representation of the object painted on a cavern wall. The modern archaeologist, armed with the tools of science such as carbon-14 dating, might disagree with this sequence, but the argument is irrelevant to our purpose. What is important is that man needed pictorial representation both for communication with his fellows and for self-expression. Pictorial representation, then, can not only be traced back to the Reindeer Epoch and the dawn of civilization; it shares with language, writing, kinesics, and all the variant forms of non-verbal communication a major role in that total process by means of which cultures came into being and evolved.[2] From the bison of Font-de-Gaume to the image from an overhead projector is quite a leap technologically, but the intervening

---

With Conrad H. Rawski. Originally published in *The Journal of Typographic Research*, Vol. 2 (April 1968), pp. 171-88, and *Library Resources and Technical Services*, Vol. 11, No. 4 (Fall 1967), pp. 487-98.

millenia have not altered the human compulsion to outwit time, as it were, by recreating to hold unchanged forever the fleeting image of a moment.

In the present essay, the authors are concerned with but one specialized form of the picture—the diagram. Diagrammatic representation is a skeletal form of graphic representation; in it extraneous detail is omitted, it is highly stereotyped and stylized. But it does not dispense with the pictorial *as if.*[3] It merely employs reduction. This reduction may eventuate in outline drawings of botanical specimens in a fieldbook for flower identification, the denotative devices of a picture language (e.g., Otto Neurath's Isotype), the abstract figures used to exemplify molecular structures in organic compounds, the schematic wiring diagram for an electrical circuit, or Charles Morris' graphic representation of the human action system.[4] The element of reduction that characterizes, and in a sense defines, the diagram may either facilitate or impede recognition, or even make recognition impossible. Its success or failure depends upon the extent to which it employs a form of signification that is meaningful to the viewer. For diagrammatic representation employs what may be regarded as a very special and often sophisticated form of *semasiography,*[5] and the solution to the problem of signification that it presents is quite different from that which attempts to invoke reality in more elaborate pictorial terms. But if that which is pictured cannot be recognized by the viewer, it matters little how it is pictured. As Abraham Kaplan has observed, "Appearance is what is to be known, reality what it is known as."[6] The object of the diagram is to reveal this reality. There is no other justification for its existence.

The diagram is a special case of picture-making: it bodies forth its subject in a pictorial way, in shapes which themselves possess a characteristic content, but are used to represent another. Any histogram in *Fortune* magazine illustrates this characteristic of the diagram.

The problem of symbolic significance presented by diagrammatic representation—one might say the semiotic of the diagram—have long occupied the most competent minds of Western scientific and philosophic thought. We do not propose to attempt to scale these precipitous paths, even were we competent to do so. Our objective is much more humble. Science is probably responsible for the extensive use of diagrams because the attributes of the diagram as representation fit so appropriately many of the concepts, phenomena, and processes of science. From the literature of science the diagram, which probably began in that shadowy realm of cosmology, or had, at least, philosophic origins, spread to other neo-scientific fields, the social sciences, management, history, linguistics, and eventually even librarianship. So recent has been its introduction into library literature that one will find few examples of diagrams prior to the 1930s, for it was during those years that librarians turned the corner and saw before them the vision of a new heaven and a new earth bathed in the light of the scientific method.

It may, therefore, not be altogether inappropriate for librarians to pause for a moment in their mad rush into scientific methodology to inquire into the nature of diagrammatic representation, to remind themselves of its proper use, and to ponder Alfred North Whitehead's remark that "the object of symbolism is the enhancement of the importance of that which is symbolized."[7]

## PART II

A simple diagrammatic situation obtains in the family tree reproduced in Figure 1. Correspondence with fact is obvious in this filiation scheme. It becomes much more subject to interpretation when used, for example, as a stemma in descriptive bibliography[8]—although specialists, who are painfully aware of the complexities behind the lines connecting texts A and B, may remind us that certain skeletons in family closets could also affect the stemmatic simplicity of family trees.

Similar relatively straightforward situations obtain in various kinds of block-diagrams, when they map synchronous or diachronic situations as in Figures 2 and 3. Both diagrams involve, as it were, implicit locus problems. In the case of Figure 3 this is duly accounted for by Professor Ash, when he refers to information theory as "an attempt to construct a mathematical model for each of the blocks" in the figure, and adds that "we shall not arrive at design formulas for a communication system. . . ."[9]

The diagrammatic situation recalls Clyde Coomb's insistence that the term *data* be restricted to observations which are already interpreted in some way and "are in part a product of the mind of the observer. . . . We buy information with assumptions—'facts' are inferences, and so also are data and measurements and scales."[9] Pictorial information likewise is bought with assumptions. If one would not understand that in Figure 4 the legends enclosed in blocks and the swirl of connecting lines between them signify steps, decisions, conditions, and circumstances that are considered to be situationally related significant determinants in accordance with present-day theoretical convictions, he would not benefit from P. J. Runkel's careful commentary.[10] As soon as we are not attuned to the inferential situation and, if you will, the style of thought which generate the diagram, we find it difficult to read the picture. Figure 5 is a representation of the mechanism of government, the wheels of state in the Holy Roman Realm. Iconographic expertise may bring us somewhat closer to the meaning of the diagram and contemporary modes of representation. But the hierarchial pattern, significant as it is, will surrender its message only if and when we understand the theory of state and government and, in this case, certain specific popular and regional ideas, traditions, and idiosyncrasies held by the 15th-century designer.[11] Modern organization charts are said to harbor similar intracacies. Conversely, Figures 4 and 5 do make explicit situations of complexity and articulate pictorially, at least, certain aspects of these situations which as such do

FIG. 1. THE ELZEVIR FAMILY

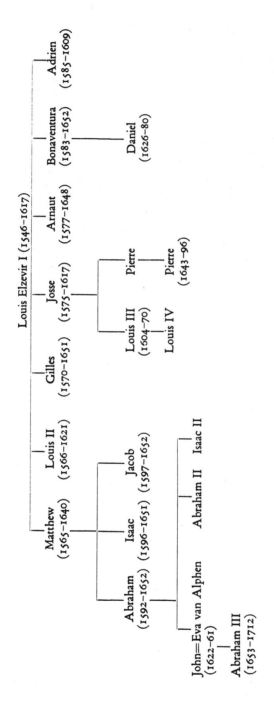

The Elzevir Family

From N. E. Binns, *An Introduction to Historical Bibliography* (2nd ed., London: Association of Assistant Librarians, 1962), p. 96.

FIG. 2.  THE CLASSIFIED CATALOG SYSTEM

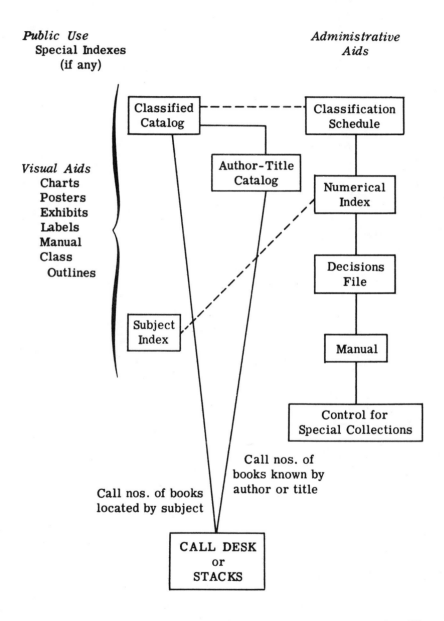

*Public Use*
Special Indexes
(if any)

*Administrative*
*Aids*

Classified Catalog ---- Classification Schedule

*Visual Aids*
Charts
Posters
Exhibits
Labels
Manual
Class
Outlines

Author-Title Catalog

Numerical Index

Decisions File

Subject Index

Manual

Control for Special Collections

Call nos. of
books known by
author or title

Call nos. of books
located by subject

CALL DESK
or
STACKS

From J. H. Shera and M. E. Egan, *The Classified Catalog* (Chicago: American Library Association, 1956), p. 67.

FIG. 3. COMMUNICATION SYSTEM

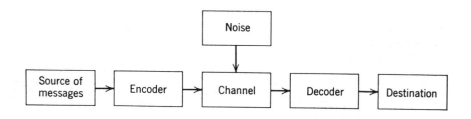

From R. B. Ash, *Information Theory* (New York: Interscience Publishers, 1965), Fig. 1.1.1., p. 1.

FIG. 4. A BRIEF MODEL FOR PUPIL-TEACHER INTERACTION

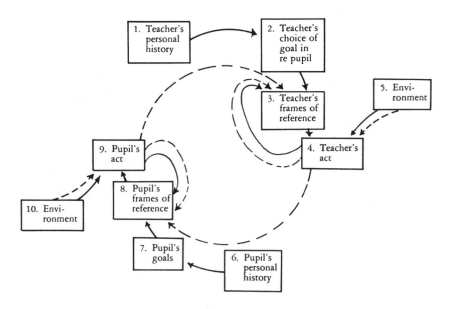

Solid lines represent intrapersonal communication via the nervous system, etc. Dashed lines represent interpersonal communication via vision, speech, etc.

From N. L. Gage, *Handbook of Research on Teaching* (Chicago: Rand McNally, 1963), Fig. 22, p. 126. Originally in P. J. Runkel, *Personal Communication*, 1958.

FIG. 5.

From W. L. Schreiber, *Holzschnitte, Metallschnitte, Teigdrucke aus dem Herzoglichen Museum zu Gotha. . . .* (Strasbourg: Heitz, 1928), Plate 15.

not seem to lend themselves readily to articulation.

S. R. Ranganathan uses diagrammatic representation for his modes[12] "by which the field of knowledge may throw forth new specific subjects:"[13] dissection; denudation; lamination; and loose assemblage.[14] These diagrams are well known to librarians. They have a long and interesting history as representations of class relations and syllogistic moods in formal logic. Schopenhauer, who used the familiar circle diagrams to indicate conceptual relationships in his *Die Welt als Wille und Vorstellung* (1818),[15] credited the "exceedingly happy idea" of graphic representation of these relationships to L. Euler (1768), J. H. Lambert (*c.* 1765), and G. Ploucquet (1763), "who used squares and probably thought of it first." Actually the use of the figures can be traced further back to J. C. Sturm (1661), J. H. Alstedius (1614), and L. Vives (1555).[16] Leibniz used both circles and straight-line figures to diagram the old mnemonic designations coined by Peter of Spain.[17] Syllogistic diagrams were familiar to the ancient commentators of Aristotle and the Megarian Stoic school. Their use during the Middle Ages is yet to be explored, although Medieval predilection for diagrammatic representation and, specifically the *pons asinorum* (a diagrammatic statement of the Aristotelian doctrine of the *inventio medii*), is well established.

Schopenhauer diagrams within the context of his presentation and with obvious reliance on the traditional Euler figures. He diagrams what we know and neglects the visual factors exhibited by his figures. This is amusingly demonstrated in his representation of "dissection" of a conceptual sphere including two or more concepts which "exclude each other," yet fill the sphere (Figure 6).

Euler's graphics of propositions and syllogisms in his *Lettres à une princesse d'Allemagne*[18] are much more elaborate. He is fussily concerned with the proper interpretation of his figures: one might make bold to state that Euler would not have let pass Schopenhauer's figure, above.

> These circles, or rather these spaces, for it is of no importance of what figure they are, are extremely commodious for facilitating our reflections on this subject, and for unfolding all the boasted mysteries of logic, which that art finds it so difficult to explain; whereas by means of these signs the whole is rendered sensible to the eye. We may employ, then, spaces formed at pleasure to represent every general notion, and mark the subject of a proposition by a space containing A, and the attribute by another which contains B. The nature of the proposition itself always imports, either that the space of A is wholly contained in the space B, or that it is partly contained in that space; or that a part, at least, is out of space B; or, finally, that the space A is wholly out of B.
>
> (Letter 103, February 17, 1761)

Euler uses these "emblems" to develop a veritable pictorial notation which, he hopes, would be "a great assistance towards comprehending more distinctly wherein the accuracy of a chain of reasoning consists" (Letter 102, February 14, 1761).

FIG. 6.

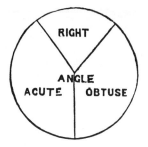

*A sphere includes two or more spheres which exclude each other and fill it.*

From A. Schopenhauer, *The World as Will and Idea* (New York: Charles Scribner's Sons, 1883), I, 56.

Euler, Schopenhauer, and Ranganathan use diagrammatic figures of great similarity. Ignoring the purposes for which each employs the figures, we may observe that a variety of situations is mapped with essentially identical graphic shapes. Euler's emblems "are" more explicit than Ranganathan's because of Euler's insistence on detailed contextual exploration, illustrated by the diagrams in Figure 7. The "lamination" emblem, for instance, appears as a paradigm for both affirmative and negative situations, and we are reminded to look, as it were, in more than one direction, beyond the shape of the emblem. In the case of syllogistic diagrams the figures for relations between more than two or three classes developed by J. Venn[19] and W. E. Hocking,[20] are the graphic results of precisely such "thinking beyond the diagram." On the other hand, the concrete pictorialism of the emblem as such may invite further interpretations resulting in clarification or extended application. Thus Peter Caws uses a series of "lamination" emblems to represent the relations between the world of ordinary

FIG. 7. EMBLEMS OF THE FOUR SPECIES OF PROPOSITIONS

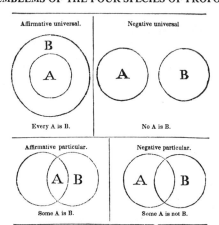

*Our author subjoins here the following diagram, with this short introduction: — "I shall once more give you a visible representation of these figures or emblems of the four species of pospositions."*

From *Letters of Euler on Different Subjects in Natural Philosophy Addressed to a German Princess*, ed. D. Brewster and J. Griscom (New York: J. & J. Harper, 1833), I, 341.

experience and scientific theory, and maps imaginatively the scope of argument in each part of his *Philosophy of Science*.[21]

## PART III

In our attempt to follow on a humble level Wittgenstein's advice to "treat of the network, not of what the network describes" we have traversed familiar territory. We all have long been aware of the fact that pictures depict as we look at them, that they are what we see and signify what we know. It does not take much intellectual effort to understand the implications of the diagrammatic situation that offers concrete, definite emblems and the attendant advantages of explicit relationships graphically represented, but that has to be clearly understood in its conceptual context in order to be properly construed as a paradigm.

Most of us, at one time or another, have been aware of the illusion created by certain forms of advertising, which shrewdly ring the changes on these properties of the diagrammatic situation as they present us with stunning graphic tableaux of "irrefutable objective scientific data gathered by an independent research organization." This is abuse, or more or less serious deceit, aimed at "them"—the unthinking public. But it is important to remind ourselves that essentially the same conditions obtain when we use diagrams in our attempts to ascertain the truth through reflective inquiry. If used properly, diagrams can explain and simplify, can reveal an underlying order, permit systematization, and point to gaps in our knowledge or our design. They enable us to set forth, for all to see, the essentials of a situation or what we consider these essentials to be. As a means of representation they are more elastic than quantitative techniques, and they allow us to map with considerable precision situations which otherwise seem to preclude such treatment.

As a medium for the communication of thought, diagrams are easy, direct, tangible—we almost said healthy. These properties, in turn, may beget undue affection for them, and we may diagram what cannot, hence should not, be diagrammed. The debit side includes the implicit emblematic pitfalls discussed above, the dangers of undue simplification, distortion or misrepresentation, and deceptive finality (present in any formalization). It is so very easy to conflate the diagram with what it is supposed to represent, and to accept uncritically as properties of the "real" subject those which, in fact, are the emblematic properties of the diagram.

"Ah," you say, "who would make the mistake of assuming some connection between the color green and the French, just because France is green on most political maps?" To which we can only meekly reply that whoever has thoroughly grasped this lesson obviously does not stand in need of our disquisition, which derives its justification only from the fact that, alas, we often know less than we think we know.

## FOOTNOTES

[1] Elie Faure, *History of Art: Ancient Art* (Garden City, N.Y.: Garden City Publishing Co., 1921), p. 13; also, J. Pijoan, *History of Art* (London: Batsford, 1933), Chap. 2: "Art in the Reindeer Epoch"; and R. Huyghe, *Ideas and Images in World Art* (New York: H.N. Abrams, 1959), pp. 104-24.

[2] I. J. Gelb, *A Study of Writing* (2nd ed., Chicago: University of Chicago Press, 1963); C. Cherry, *On Human Communication* (2nd ed., Cambridge, Mass: M.I.T. Press, 1966), esp. Chap. 7: "On Cognition and Recognition"; E. T. Hall, *The Silent Language* (Garden City, N.Y.: Doubleday, 1959); J. Ruesch and W. Kees, *Nonverbal Communication* (Berkeley: University of California Press, 1957).

[3] *Cf.* E. H. Gombrich, *Art and Illusion* (New York: Pantheon, 1961), Chap. II; and the same author's delightful *Meditations on a Hobby Horse* (London: Phaidon, 1963). *See also* Gelb, pp. 35ff.; L. Hogben, *From Cave Painting to Comic Strip* (New York: Chantecleer Press, 1949), pp. 179-83.

[4] *Toward a Unified Theory of Human Behavior*, ed. R. R. Grinker (New York: Basic Books, 1956), pp. 350f.

[5] A. Kaplan, *The Conduct of Inquiry* (San Francisco: Chandler Publications, 1964), p. 85.

[6] Quoted after C. Morris, *Signification and Significance* (Cambridge, Mass.: M.I.T. Press, 1946).

[7] *Cf.*, e.g., P. Maas, *Textual Criticism* (Oxford: Clarendon Press, 1958), pp. 42-49.

[8] R. B. Ash, *Information Theory* (New York: Interscience, 1965), p. 1.

[9] C. H. Coombs, *A Theory of Data* (New York: John Wiley, 1964), pp. 4, 5.

[10] *Handbook of Research on Teaching*, ed. N. L. Gage (Chicago: Rand McNally, 1963), pp. 126f.

[11] *Cf.*, e.g., T. Steinbuechel, *Christliches Mittelalter* (Leipzig: J. Hegner, 1935), pp. 208-72.

[12] R. S. Parkhi, *Decimal Classification and Colon Classification in Perspective* (New York: Asia Publishing House, 1964), pp. 415-18.

[13] S. R. Ranganathan in *Bibliographic Organization*, ed. J. H. Shera and M. E. Egan (Chicago: University of Chicago Press, 1951), p. 96.

[14] J. H. Shera and M. E. Egan, *The Classified Catalog* (Chicago: American Library Association, 1956), p. 30.

[15] i, 1, 9.

[16] I. M. Bochenski, *A History of Formal Logic* (Notre Dame, Ind.: University of Notre Dame Press, 1961), pp. 260f.

[17] *Opuscules et fragments inédits de Leibniz*, ed. L. Couturat (Paris: F. Alkan, 1903). Bochénski, p. 258, ascribes to Leibniz the introduction of the Euler diagrams.

[18]*Letters of Euler on Different Subjects in National Philosophy Addressed to a German Princess*, ed. D. Brewster and J. Griscom (New York: J. & J. Harper, 1833), I, 337-54.
[19]J. Venn, "On the Diagrammatic and Mechanical Representations of Propositions . . .," *London, Edinburgh and Dublin Philosophical Magazine*, 5th Ser., X (1880), 1-18.
[20]W. E. Hocking, "Two Extensions of the Use of Graphs in Elementary Logic," *University of California Publications in Philosophy*, II (1909), 31-44.
[21]P. Caws, *Philosophy of Science* (Princeton, N.J.: Van Nostrand, 1965), p. vi.

## POSTSCRIPT

(1) The error potential implicit in the interplay of paradigmatic intent and emblematic properties–J. S. Coleman distinguishes between endogenous and exogenous variables in a model[1]–is handsomely demonstrated in this passage by Carl G. Hempel. Speaking of simplicity and the problem of simplicity regarding scientific hypotheses Hempel suggests the following assumptions:

> Suppose that investigation of physical systems of a certain type . . . suggests to us that a certain quantitative characteristic, $v$, of such systems, might be a function of, and thus uniquely determined by, another such characteristic, $u$ (in the way in which the period of a pendulum is a function of its length). We therefore try to construct a hypothesis stating the exact mathematical form of the function. . . . Suppose further that concerning these systems . . . the following three hypotheses have been proposed on the basis of our data:
> $H_1: v = u^4 - 6u^3 + 11u^2 - 5u + 2$
> $H_2: v = u^5 - 4u^4 - u^3 + 16u^2 - 11u + 2$
> $H_3: v = u + 2$
> . . . Any criteria of simplicity would have to be objective, of course; they could not just refer to intuitive appeal or to the ease with which a hypothesis or theory can be understood or remembered, etc., for these factors vary from person to person. In the case of quantitative hypotheses like $H_1$, $H_2$, $H_3$, one might think of judging simplicity by reference to the corresponding graphs. In rectangular coordinates, the graph for $H_3$ is a straight line, whereas graphs of $H_1$ and $H_2$ are much more complicated curves. . . . But this criterion seems arbitrary. For if the hypotheses are represented in polar coordinates, with $u$ as the direction angle and $v$ as the radius vector, then $H_3$ determines a spiral, whereas a function determining a "simple" straight line would be quite complicated.[2]

(2) Conversely, we might consider this interplay and its effects as such. In the field of the book arts this has been done primarily in terms of artistic creation and its impact. When William Morris championed Emery Walker's "principles" of book design–at about the time Charles Saunders Peirce developed his pragmatic theory of signs–he may have had in mind systemic interpretations and their potential, although the products of the Kelmscott Press do not graciously corroborate such an assumption. Today we have a whole

literature on the design of books and the component parts of books. Yet when it comes to inquiry into the effects (and the intrinsic problems attendant upon these effects) wrought by the emblematic characteristics of books and related materials, we do not seem to have gone very far beyond the position held by early commentators, such as Polydore Vergil, who noted in 1499 the "new kind of writing, invented in our times," which makes it possible that one fellow prints in one day all that could be written by several scribes within a whole year.[3]

We coin terms such as *mis-en-page*, *Schriftbild*, etc., which designate but do not explain. We draw more or less appropriate analogies concerning typographic characteristics, letterform, and overall arrangement, and express expected and experienced effects in a metaphoric phraseology fully as naive, but seldom as charmingly compelling as Hogarth's "peculiarity in the lines . . . that *leads the eye a wanton kind of chace*."[4] We map page spaces and opening. But we do rarely probe for causes or implications and ignore the pertinence of history. After a century, Theodor Birt's *Buchbegriff* remains simply outside the "professional" literature and its concerns.[5] Even sophisticated approaches, such as tachistoscopic experiments, seldom question the status quo of traditional notations: syntactic and diacritic marks, letter width, word separation, etc., are treated as "data," i.e., as quasi absolutes of "the" printed page.[6] In the '40s and '50s we discussed the ideas of William Ivins.[7] Now we have exchanged them for the more buxom pronouncements of Marshall McLuhan. But, somehow, we do not get down to the specifics and reflective inquiry into the specifics of the problem of the book as an object which offers its contents in terms of its properties as an object—designed within a specific contextual field of purposes, conventions, assumptions, etc.

How did a 15th-century reader approach a page of tiny black letters crowded into compact double columns? What does the closely-spaced roman, unrelieved by paragraphs, or the simultaneity of text and surrounding scholarly commentary on a Renaissance folio tell us about the designer's intent; and what effects do these visual arrangements entail? Have you ever contemplated the unmitigated uniformity of a mid-16th-century duodecimo in italics and asked questions concerning the matrix of subordination supportive of interrelated contents, which most of us take for granted? We smile at the "allusive" printing of the 1800s, but may ignore, at the same time, allusive effects operative in the "standard" product of our time.

All these questions involve emblematic properties which are the *terms* on which the contents is offered. How intricately these terms may affect the "information" becomes crystal clear in situations involving contexts that are foreign to us or with which we have lost direct or imagined affinity, e.g., Chinese xylography, or ancient "books."[8] It seems that a generation concerned with electronic media, CRT terminals, KWIC and KWOC indexes, and computer printouts can no longer afford to ignore them.

(3) The following two items are offered by way of summary. We have found them easy to keep in mind.

"Well! I've often seen a cat without a grin," thought Alice, "but a grin without a cat! It's the most curious thing I ever saw in all my life."–Lewis Carroll, *Alice in Wonderland*.


## FOOTNOTES TO POSTSCRIPT

[1] "An Expository Analysis of Some of Rashevsky's Social Behavior Models," in P. F. Lazarsfeld, *Mathematical Thinking in the Social Sciences* (Glencoe, Ill.: Free Press, 1955), pp. 119, 122.

[2] Carl G. Hempel, *Philosophy of Natural Science* (Englewood Cliffs, N.J.: Prentice Hall, 1966), 40ff. For an interesting illustration of, as it were, the emblematic properties of terminology, see *The State of the Social Sciences*, ed. L. D. White (Chicago: University of Chicago Press, 1956), p. 44.

[3] Polydore Vergil, *De rerum inventoribus* ii, 7.

[4] William Hogarth, *The Analysis of Beauty* (1753), ed. J. Burke (Oxford: Clarendon Press, 1955), p. 42. Italics are quoted.

[5] The term relates to the semantics of graphics and is used by I. J. Gelb in *A Study of Writing*, rev. ed. (Chicago: University of Chicago Press, 1965), Chapter VI.

[6] Theodor Birt, *Das antike Buchwesen* (Berlin: W. Hertz, 1882); and "Abriss des antiken Buchwesens," in I. von Mueller, *Handbuch der klassischen Altertumswissenschaft*, i, 3.

[7] *Cf.*, e.g., L. Carmichael and W. F. Dearborn, *Reading and Visual Fatigue* (London: G.G. Harrap, 1948); and H. F. Brandt, *The Psychology of Seeing* (New York: Philosophical Library, 1945).

[8] W. M. Ivins, *Art and Geometry: A Study in Space Intuitions* (1946), and *Prints and Visual Communication* (1953), both published at Cambridge, Mass.: Harvard University Press.

[9] Note, in particular, the remarkable Chapter V, "Laterculis coctilibus," in A. Leo Oppenheim's *Ancient Mesopotamia* (Chicago: University of Chicago Press, 1964).

# 3

# Plus Ça Change

*The cult of relevance was made restless and frustrated by the hard work which it takes to master the disciplines and professions. Yet without such command there is little chance to have much leverage on many social problems. Most particularly, the demand for relevance was scornful of history. The paradox was that some of the students' most far-out faculty mentors were revisionist historians.*

—Kingman Brewster, Jr.

"Here was a new generation . . . grown up to find all gods dead, all wars fought, all faith in man shaken," wrote F. Scott Fitzgerald in *This Side of Paradise*. Except for the reference to the First World War, which to our sorrow we found was not Armageddon after all, Fitzgerald's words could have been written today. In many ways the '60s were not unlike the '20s. Our own parents blamed everything on "The War," as they looked with consternation and dismay across the generation gap of the "roaring twenties." Indeed, it must have looked that way to an America, exhausted with the dreary story of a brutal war and its sordid settlement at Versailles spread before their resentful eyes by such books as Sir Philip Gibbs' *Now It Can be Told*, John Dos Passos' *Three Soldiers*, E. E. Cummings' *The Enormous Room*, and, for those who had the determination to pursue it, John Maynard Keynes' *Economic Consequences of the Peace*. Forgotten was the excitement and adventure of Arthur Guy Empey's *Over the Top*, Coningsby Dawson's *Carry On*, Frances Huard's *My Home on the Field of Honor*, not to mention Edward Streeter's *Dere Mable*.

It is scarcely surprising that a generation which, during the years of the First World War, had discovered the ease with which legislation, propaganda, and even intimidation could be used to compel at least the appearance of conformity and acceptable conduct should have viewed the uninhibited '20s with a feeling akin to horror.

The revolt of youth against the restraints of a mid-Victorian childhood climaxed by a war "to end all wars" was in the making. World War I had brought with it, as all wars have, the proliferation of legislative controls for the regulation of conduct, and restraints were not difficult to maintain even after the signing of the armistice. Protest was almost inevitable. In April 1920, F. Scott Fitzgerald, just out of Princeton and, therefore, one who certainly should "be with it" so far as youth was concerned, published *This Side of Paradise*: "None of the Victorian mothers--and most of the mothers were Victorian—had any idea how casually their daughters were accustomed to be kissed," wrote the young Princetonian who, five years later was to establish himself as a writer of importance with the appearance of *The Great Gatsby*: ". . . Amory saw girls doing things that even in his memory would have been impossible . . . talking of every side of life with an air half of earnestness, half of mockery, yet with a furtive excitement that Amory considered stood for a real moral let-down. But he never realized how wide spread it was until he saw the cities between New York and Chicago as one vast juvenile intrigue." One well-nurtured Fitzgerald heroine brazenly confided, "I've kissed dozens of men. I suppose I'll kiss dozens more"; while a young lady observed philosophically, "Oh, just one person in fifty has any glimmer of what sex is. I'm hipped on Freud and all that, but it's rotten that every bit of real love in the world is ninety-nine per cent passion and one little *soupçon* of jealousy."

Such books as Warner Fabian's *Flaming Youth* and Percy Marks' *The Plastic Age* may have opened the astonished and disapproving eyes of our parents to the glitter of rebellious youth of the '20s—the gin parties, the petting, the sex, the "indiscretions" of cigarette-smoking "flappers" with their bobbed and shingled heads—but it remained for *Main Street* and *Babbitt*, and most of all, perhaps, Mencken's *American Mercury* to lay bare the real malise that was infecting society. For, if there was a flask in the hip pocket of every racoon-coated youth who cheered on "The Four Horsemen" or "Red" Grange, the green cover of the *Mercury* protruded from beneath every arm.

In his searing photographs of Gopher Prairie and Zenith, Lewis portrayed the superficiality and hypocrisy of the façade of American life, and in George F. Babbitt there was incarnated the arch-enemy of the enlightened and the stereotype of American free enterprise. If anyone doubted the essential validity of Lewis' sharp pen, it was given credence by the revelations of Senator Walsh's investigation into the financial dealings of Secretary Fall and the Teapot Dome scandals of the Harding administration. Nevertheless, despite such machinations within the Republican party, Coolidge was returned to office in 1924, and Oscar W. Underwood probably lost the Democratic nomination that same year because he dared openly to oppose the Ku Klux Klan. Nationalism, which had been glorified during the World War, assumed a particularly virulent form during the Harding-Coolidge era, when criticism became un-American. The spirit of "normalcy" manifested itself in a variety of ways: revision of history texts, insistence that teachers subscribe to loyalty oaths, denial of citizenship to pacifists, deportation of aliens, suppression of economic unrest through criminal syndicalism and criminal anarchy laws climaxed by the Sacco-Vanzetti trial, purging of legislative and other bodies of "Socialists," repudiation of liberalism in all the arts, celebration of fundamentalism in religion (which reached its peak with William Jennings Bryan and the "Monkey Trial" in Dayton, Tennessee), and legislative and judicial emasculation of federal and state bills of rights. Those were times that tried the souls of youth, and it is hardly surprising that youth reacted in protest and struck out in its own way.

The stage was indeed set for the advent of the "Bad Boy of Baltimore," whose *American Mercury* replaced the ill-fated *Smart Set*. The new journal began where its predecessor left off, and was an immediate success. By 1927 its circulation had soared to 77,000, a relatively small figure in comparison with today's statistics, but remarkable in the '20s for a journal so young. Its editor became, as Walter Lippman wrote, "the most powerful influence of this whole generation of educated people." The pages of the *Mercury* were filled with ridicule of religion, morality, patriotism, prohibition, prosperity (especially Coolidge prosperity), democracy, socialism, academic pomposity, Bruce Barton's revision of the Christian doctrine for the glorification of the higher salesmanship, and what Mencken himself called "the bilge of idealism." At the same time, its editor championed such writers as Willa Cather, Sherwood Anderson, Theodore Dreiser, Sinclair Lewis, and James Branch Cabell. He seriously questioned, as he said, "that civilized life was possible under a democracy," and again he declared that he was "against patriotism because it demands the acceptance of propositions that are obviously imbecile—e.g., that an American Presbyterian is the equal of Anatole France." He fought anything that threatened personal liberty, and soon became the darling of the young intellectual iconoclasts. The pages of the *Mercury* were fresh, startling, and delightfully destructive, and its popularity on scores of college campuses was unchallenged by any other publication. Yet much of Mencken's vindictiveness was little more than name calling—mountebank, charlatan, swindler, numbskull, swine, witch-burner, *homo boobiens*, and imbecile. It was not easy to be coolly analytical in the face of such a prose style as he commanded. Though the intellectuals had been on the offensive against the absurdities of the '20s, Mencken gave them added courage and such magazines as *Harper's*, *The Atlantic*, *The Forum*, began to reflect more boldly than they had in the past, and perhaps even more than they would admit, the views of the intellectually rebellious minority. In a curious kind of way Mencken stood to the youth of the Coolidge era as 40 years later the Kennedys and Eugene McCarthy were to rally the young of their generation. Though their styles were different (Mencken's voice was strident), each in his own way spoke to youth with spectacular success.

The *credo* of the intellectuals during these years of revolt can be summarized briefly as: belief in a greater degree of sex freedom than had been sanctioned in the past; defiance of the enforcement of morals, exemplified in the Volstead Act, by legislation; rejection of all forms of censorship; skepticism of religion, particularly organized religion; scorn for the great bourgeois majority; distrust of the military; "debunking" of the great and the near-great; fear of mass production and mechanization; opposition to capitalism and its economic and social hypocracies; and disillusion over the consequences of the Treaty of Versailles. Not all of the young intellectuals who subscribed to these tenets were willing to accept all of these propositions, but any who accepted none were suspect among the enlightened. As Frederick Lewis Allen wrote in *Only Yesterday*, "The prosperity band-wagon rolled on, but by the wayside stood the highbrows with voices upraised in derision and dismay."

By the wayside crying out with derision and dismay, indeed! The young rebels who vocally opposed standardization and repression, and who were so devoted to the cause of freedom, could not answer the question—freedom for what? Uncomfortable though the house of Babbitt was, there was little to be gained from having one's freedom but not knowing what to do with it. A few of the "lost generation" dashed off to Paris to be free of Buffalo or Iowa City, as Richmond Barrett wrote in *Harper's*, but after being excessively rude to everybody they met and after tasting a few short and tasteless love affairs and soaking themselves in gin, finally passed out under the tables of the Café du Dôme. It was the age about which F. Scott Fitzgerald wrote in *All the Sad Young Men*, but it was also an age in which many clung to the old values of the essential common decency of man.

> The mountain's steeple;
> The folk that people
>     The plains and valleys below,
> Are ten times nicer
> Than Lewis, Dreiser,
>     And Sherwood Anderson know.

Thus wrote Arthur Guiterman in a spirit that mirrored that of many during these troubled years. One may call it nostalgia for those far-off happy years before 1914 or one may call it wishful thinking, but there were a surprising number of people who believed in, or thought they believed in, this simple faith in basic human goodness.

But it was probably Walter Lippman in *A Preface to Morals*, who most keenly perceived and penetrated to the central issue: "What most distinguishes the generation who have approached maturity since the *debacle* of idealism at the end of the war is not their rebellion against the religion and the moral codes of their parents, but their disillusionment with their own rebellion. It is common for young men and women to rebel, but that they should rebel sadly and without faith in their rebellion, and that they should distrust the new freedom no less than the old certainties—that is something of a novelty." Lippman tried to lay the foundation for a new system of ethics and beliefs that would satisfy everyone, and for a brief time, humanism—under the leadership of such academicians as Irving Babbit and Paul Elmer More—enjoyed a degree of popularity among the intelligentsia, but no one quite knew what humanism meant or what brand of humanism was being discussed. There was also an attempt to find in the scientific philosophizing of Alfred North Whitehead, Sir Arthur Eddington, and Sir James Jeans the basis for a new ethic. Nor had the old liberalism been entirely swept away, a politically progressive Catholic was nominated for President in 1928, only to go down to defeat. But there was unmistakable evidence that a search for new values had begun, and a search that would explode in new and quite unanticipated directions on Wall Street on "Black Tuesday" of October 1929. Main Street would never again be the same.

To all of these currents and eddies in the life of a nation the librarians were largely oblivious. If they showed any concern at all for happenings beyond their own cloistered walls, it was in the establishment by ALA of its national headquarters and the "expanded program." Attempts to "professionalize" the craft were gaining some headway, especially as related to the training of librarians, and attempts were being made to determine exactly what it is that librarians do when they are working. Such concern as there was with the world outside was largely reserved to an interest in the re-establishing of European libraries devastated by war, and to efforts to spread library practice throughout the earth. But mostly the librarians devoted themselves to burnishing and tending the local lamp of learning, and if their libraries subscribed to the *Mercury*, the *Nation*, or the *New Republic*, their issues were probably kept in a file cabinet behind the desk where it was available on request. Many were grateful that the *New Yorker* was beginning to replace the *Mercury* in the required reading of the literati.

The crash of the stock market and the economic catastrophe that it precipitated was, in a sense, both a fulfillment and a refutation of youthful prophecy. Certainly it revealed the myth of eternal prosperity and the instability of its tinselled façade. The "higher learning" had been right in condemning the "higher salesmanship." Raucous gin-drinking youth of the '20s came face to face with economic hardship and met the challenge. The cigarette-smoking "flappers," over whom their mothers had agonized, had become mothers themselves; they were doing, by the way, a creditable job of rearing their own children in the face of economic deprivation, and frequently even in the face of the necessity of working themselves to support unemployed husbands and fathers. Youth had been right too, about the hypocrisy of prohibition and the futility of morality through legislation; that fiction was revealed in all its starkness in a blaze of gunfire in a Chicago garage on St. Valentine's Day of 1929.

But the youth of the '20s had also been tilting with a windmill or two: Fundamentalism in religion, and Babbittry (which would be reborn a generation later in "the ugly American" and, therefore, may not qualify as a windmill). Youth had been wrong, too, in excessive devotion to Mencken, whose negativism was really anti-intellectualism, and who was scarcely qualified to lead "the children's crusade." The Great Depression gave youth a new focus, and it may have been a kind of testing time for the holocaust of the '40s. The era of "debunking" had ended, and Elmer Gantry, Sinclair Lewis' hypocritical minister, was dead. Economic problems were the major concern of youth in the '30s, and if Lewis were read, it was *It Can't Happen Here*, rather than the earlier, and better, works. The corporation and the economic system that supported it were the *bêtes noires* of the era. From the ragged sleeve of the racoon coat, if any such had survived, there protruded, not the green cover of the *Mercury*, but A. A. Berle and Gardner Means' *Modern Corporation and Private Property*, or Thurman Arnold's *Folklore of Capitalism*.

Youth was steeped in "social significance," and it fought with all the undernourished vitality that it could muster against "big navies," the armament merchants, the rising tide of fascism polarized by the Spanish Civil War, the waste of natural resources, and the degradation of that third of a nation that was "ill-housed, ill-clothed, and ill-fed." Youth looked with hope to the Soviet Union, joined the Abraham Lincoln Brigade in Spain to fight against Hitler and Mussolini, and, at home, attacked the American Liberty League.

Yet for all our *Weltschmerz*, those of us who lived through this trying time found a certain joy in holding high the banner of the New Deal, like Eagle Scouts. What gorgeous, disorderly, far-off days they now seem. "Hope grew 'round us like the twining vine." Nothing seemed beyond the realm of possibility, and from 16th and Pennsylvania Avenue came that ever strong and reassuring voice, admonishing, challenging, inspiring. Youth followed the voice, as a generation later it was to follow the Kennedys and Eugene McCarthy, like mystics called to worship by the bell of a distant shrine, like Chaucer's Pilgrims on the road to Canterbury—and just as motley. The thoughts of youth are always "long long thoughts," but we were intoxicated with thinking.

The blast furnaces of Gary and Pittsburgh and Youngstown were cold, but there was a bright glow in the night sky over the industrial centers of Russia and youth looked to the east with hope. Looked to the east, but with eyes closed to the purges of Stalin and the suffering that the Soviets had wrought. By the end of the decade the thunderheads of war lay black and menacing on the eastern horizon. In Africa, a "sawdust Caesar" had lain low the Lion of the Tribe of Judah. In Austria, Seyss-Inquart had proclaimed *Anschluss* with Germany; and in Germany itself Hitler, with whom one really couldn't do business, had annexed the Ruhr, turning its industrial might to his own nefarious ends. In France, Leon Blum and Edouard Daladier were forcing the government increasingly toward the extreme Right. Across the Pyrenees, the battle-scarred fields of a prostrate Spain were a testing ground over which three mighty military machines had refined their techniques in mass homicide. And at No. 10 Downing Street an aging Neville Chamberlain, who had just returned from Munich, was brandishing an umbrella and crying, "I believe it is peace for our time." But almost as he spoke, the heavy artillery of the Nazis, with the British prime minister's sanction, was rumbling across the Czech border. On this side of the Atlantic, youth had been told that it had nothing to fear but fear itself, but in those dark days fear seemed quite enough to cause anyone concern, and disillusioned youth was ready to admit that it had been lying to itself about Russia. That admission may have been the bitterest pill of all.

Drastic reductions in income which compelled shortened hours of library service, curtailment of book funds, and reductions of salaries and staff, all brought the librarians to the realization that "no man is an island," and that the bell was tolling for them, too. This revelation of the library as a part of the social fabric, of the public sector, undoubtedly helped prepare the way for the arrival of Louis Round Wilson at the University of Chicago and his insistence that the library was a social phenomenon and should be studied as such. The Great Depression having rekindled interest, particularly among the youth, and a certain sympathy for the Soviet experiment, once again the threat of censorship and the witch-hunt flourished. In the face of these threats, the ALA pursued its generally placid way. Of course these events were regrettable, the Establishment admitted, but the profession would have to tailor its garments to conform to the available fabric, and in those days the ALA was short of yard-goods. The association was a tightly closed corporation in the days of the consulship of Carl H. Milam. If there were a sword suspended above the head of this "Damocles," he would not look up and eventually it would probably disappear. A decade later that sword was to come crashing down, but that is another story.

But within ALA, there was a militant band of Young Turks, few in number, geographically dispersed, and pitifully weak in economic resources, who knew what it wanted and set forth with determination to achieve its goal. Fortunately, there were on the side of the young three figures whose names will be etched forever in the minds and hearts of the youths they encouraged—Charles Harvey Brown, distinguished director of the Iowa State University Library, and a recognized leader in the academic world; Marian Manley, librarian of the pioneer Business Branch of the Newark, N.J., Public Library and disciple of John Cotton Dana, that iconoclast of an earlier day; and Stanley J. Kunitz, poet and progressive editor of the *Wilson Bulletin*, the name of which was later changed to its present familiar title as an implicit denial that it was for the birds. Kunitz stood to the Young Turks of the '30s much as *Library Journal*'s Eric Moon and John Berry have to the young activists of the present generation. The *WB*, like the *Mercury*, had a green cover in those days, a coincidence into which one can read nothing of significance, but its pages were always open to protest, and it gave its youthful contributors a rallying point and a voice.

Despite the slamming of bank doors and the general financial panic that marked the last year of the Hoover administration, enough young librarians were able to scrape together sufficient funds to attend the New Haven convention of the ALA in 1931, and there organized the Junior Members Round Table. What the group wanted was "involvement," but the problem of how to become involved was one to which no one seemed to have a valid answer. Projects, rather than direct action in the politics of the association, seemed to offer the greatest prospect for success, and accordingly, the group undertook two activities: the compilation of a subject index to library literature that would carry forward *Cannons' Bibliography of Library Economy, 1876-1920*, and a survey of opinion concerning the effectiveness of library training. The first was brought to successful fruition under the able leadership of Lucile Morsch, and was published by the ALA under the title *Library Literature, 1921-1932*.

The critique of library training was far less satisfactory in execution than was the bibliographic undertaking. The survey of opinion as reported in *LJ* for July 1933 (pp. 585-89) was based on a very limited seven-point questionnaire sent to a "highly selected" sample of recent library school graduates. The results indicated that, in general, the 77 students who replied tended to favor: 1) the selection of students from those who held the baccalaureate degree and had some previous experience in library work, and had indicated in an interview that they possessed such desirable personal traits as adaptability, sense of humor, intelligence, and calm temper; 2) approval of existing faculties as being well qualified by virtue of diversified experience, though "their teaching could be made more practical, broad, and inspirational"; 3) emphasis upon broad principles rather than a "mass of technical details to be mastered"; 4) existing methods of teaching cataloging, while criticizing the teaching of reference work and library administration for being overburdened with detail; 5) the making of courses in children's work, story-telling, and advanced cataloging "optional"; 6) the continuation of practice work as a requirement, though improvement in the enrichment of the student's experience would be desirable; and 7) the interrogation of library school directors concerning their policies regarding restrictions on enrollment, standards for faculty appointment, objectives of their schools, teaching methods, and alumni contacts. When one rereads, a generation later, the results of this inquiry, it is difficult to avoid the uncomfortable feeling that, except for minor variations, a comparable questionnaire would produce much the same responses if given today. How very familiar it all sounds: the battle between theory and practice; the relevance of the curriculum; admission policies, standards for faculty appointment, evaluation of teaching methods, and relationships with alumni. Is it the schools or is it the students who have not changed, or is it both?

Whether such undertakings as these were appropriate to the desires and needs of the Junior Members was questioned by many. Among such skeptics were Leon Carnovsky and E. W. McDiarmid, both of whom were at that time students in the University of Chicago's Graduate Library School. They urged strongly that the newly-organized group should set itself to the task of formulating a social philosophy of librarianship. In the January 1934 issue of *Library Journal* (pp. 32-33), they wrote, in part:

> If ever there was a time when a philosophy was needed it is the present. Today when librarians are faced with the necessity of proving the library's importance to the community, they are rarely able to relate their activities to the social process. What librarian is not faced with the problem of presenting evidence to validate his claim to continued support in the face of greatly reduced municipal income? . . . The Junior Members' Round Table amply makes up in range what it lacks in length. Among its members are numbered representatives of all types of libraries, and all branches and departments of library activity. . . . Whether a definite philosophy of librarianship would ultimately emerge from the group's deliberations it is impossible to say; but there can be no doubt that from a sincere effort to determine "whither librarianship" the profession would immeasurably benefit.

Because of the criticism that the new group lacked a program, six objectives were adopted at the 1933 Chicago conference of the ALA; these were set forth in the *ALA Bulletin* for March 1934 (pp. 139-40) by Foster E. Mohrhardt:

• To sponsor special meetings to discuss professional problems of concern to the younger librarians.

• To increase the participation of young librarians in ALA conferences and other professional activities, including membership on ALA committees and participation on conference programs.

• To promote studies that would benefit the profession of librarianship.

• To encourage young librarians to join the ALA.

• "To plan various social activities."

• To cooperate with the ALA in promoting its programs, plans, and activities.

Such statements were certainly general enough, and it is to be noted there were no "demands," no threats of secession, and no particular suggestion of social consciousness. Rather the program was largely self-serving; the young outsiders wanted some of what the "in group" had. Expressed or not, economics was in the background, and what the Young Turks really wanted was something that would increase upward mobility and earning power. Thus, Arthur Berthold, writing in "What of the Junior Members?" in the December 15, 1933, *Library Journal* (pp. 1039-40) raised the question of whether the newly formed Round Table was not actually an organization paralleling ALA itself, and urged a further clarification of the group's objectives, a cohesive program of action, and representation on important ALA committees so that the goals could be realized. The present writer, in his valedictory to the Juniors (*ALA Bulletin*, March 1938, pp. 181-84), took much the same position as that of Berthold, and attributed much of the failure of the Round Table to form an adequate program and set of professional goals to the great diversity of disparate interests represented in the group.

In 1928 Stanley J. Kunitz, *summa cum laude* from Harvard and distinguished young poet in his own right, assumed the editorship of the *Wilson Bulletin*, a position which he held until 1943. In 1943 he invited Arthur Berthold to edit a monthly column entitled "The Young Librarian," and thus established his journal as something of an official voice for the young dissenters. In these columns were discussed such topics as: library training; librarianship as a science; the objectives of the public library; the impact of the National Youth Administration on the young librarian; the librarian's use of leisure (of which it might be said, parenthetically, that he, or she, had plenty in those days). There was also the department called "The Roving Eye," which was available to any who wished to unburden himself concerning the problems of youthful professionalism, and not a few did. Sandwiched in among special contributions dealing with school and small public libraries were features such as: Gretchen Garrison's "Public Libraries and the World View," Ortega y Gasset on "Man Must Tame the Book," and William Fielding Osborn's "The Library and the New Social Order." After reviewing the social role of the public library in the decade of the '30s, Osborn concluded with a statement from H. G. Wells, that colleges and universities should have "professorships of foresight," as well as professorships in history, and Osborn adds, "We might have in our libraries many chairs of foresight as well as in our universities the better to feel our way and be prepared for the problems of the future" (April 1934, p. 447). Thus was the plight of youth in the decade of the depression reviewed again and again by many voices, young and old, under the sympathetic editorial eye of Stanley Kunitz.

Two "battles" stand out in the memory of this writer as arousing particular concern: the segregation of Negroes at ALA conventions, and the famous case of the discharge of Philip O. Keeney, for alleged "communist" activity, from the post of librarian at Montana State University in Missoula. The Keeney case became something of a *cause célèbre* among the young dissidents, for, despite the fact that the defendant had been cleared of any wrong-doing, in published and widely distributed reports of investigations by both the AAUP and the American Federation of Teachers, the ALA refused to intercede, using the excuse that no funds were available for such defense. We still recall the sting in the observation by both teacher associations that, in view of the failure of the American Library Association to conduct its own inquiry, the two investigating teams were compelled to assume that Mr. Keeney was professionally competent.

Struggle against the Establishment's indifference to the library's relation to the problems of the world continued until the *Wehrmacht* swept all else but global war before it and library professionalization seemed by contrast puny indeed. When the decade of the '40s dawned, youth was indeed becoming involved, but not in the politics of ALA.

With the surrender of Germany and Japan came a time of renewed hope and belief, marred only by the terror of the Bomb, that the lights would go on again all over the world and that there really would be bluebirds over the white cliffs of Dover. In the years that followed, young librarians were much too busy advancing their professional educations with the largess of the G. I. Bill to worry much about the Establishment. Nevertheless, the Milam dynasty was overthrown, and many former Juniors were coming into power. In the world outside, there was a brief rekindling of the old spirit with the third-party candidacy of Henry Wallace in 1948, but he was betrayed by some unfortunate associates, and anyway, Harry Truman—"good old Harry"—was doing quite all right, except, perhaps, for Korea. In '52 and again in '56, youth fought vigorously for Adlai Stevenson, but the country was weary of internationalism, even as it had been at the close of Woodrow Wilson's career, and was ready for retreat to "normalcy" with Eisenhower and the "father image."

With the election of John Fitzgerald Kennedy to the Presidency, the dream of youth seemed to be on the point of realization. The mystique of this dynamic young Irishman who had promised to get the country moving again was the very personification of the spirit of reform and innovation. But the dream was ended with three rifle shots in Dallas, and what had begun in hope ended in tragedy and frustration. "For a time," wrote Walter Lippman (or was it "Scotty" Reston?), "the worst in American life seemed to have prevailed over the best," and it was to be a different time, a sadder time, after Dallas.

In large measure Johnson repeated the harvest of which Kennedy had sown the seed. Never before had the country seen such a massive outpouring of social legislation as that which was placed on the federal statutes between 1964 and 1968. But Johnson's social program also wrote *finis* to the New Deal, for his administration saw the realization of the social goals of Roosevelt and we found that they were not enough. It was the unnecessary and miserable war in Vietnam that brought Johnson down, yet history has within it a self-correcting force and, if we read the record aright, he, like Truman before him, can await the verdict of posterity with considerable confidence. Perhaps the year 1968 may be seen as the climax, the watershed of the decade—strife in the city streets, the meteoric rise and collapse of the McCarthy campaign, the dream of Martin Luther King and the youthful promise of Robert Kennedy both terminated by the assassin's bullet, and the defeat of Hubert Humphrey—indeed it was a different time, a sadder time, after Dallas. So the '60s came to a close; they were sad, sassy, and sexy, or as Clifton Daniel characterized them, a time of "morals, manners, money, and the moon."

The paradoxical '60s, with all their inconsistency and internal contradic-
tions were poetically eulogized by at least one scientist, John Walsh. He wrote,
in part, in "A Not Too Fond Farewell" (*Science*, December 26, 1969, p. 1605):

> Engendered on the New Frontier,
> Change was in the atmosphere;
> With Berkeley, Watts, and Vietnam
> Turbulence succeeded calm.
> On the campus things grew hotter.
> Up against the wall, O. Alma Mater!
> Teach-ins, sit-ins, power grabs
> Penetrate the ivory labs. . . .
>
> And looking back, as on a graph,
> The Sixties rate this epitaph:
> For science, big and little both,
> An end to exponential growth.

The 20th century had begun in the naive belief that science and its burgeoning
technology would solve all social problems, and that the realization of social
justice would be possible without sacrifice of personal freedom, but it hadn't
worked out that way. "We are a society bemused in its purpose yet secretly
homesick for a lost world of inward tranquility," wrote Loren Eiseley in *The
Unexpected Universe.*

Against such a backdrop of paradox, instability, and ambiguity it is not
difficult to see a generation of youth frustrated, alienated, and in some quarters
despised. Because youth today is economically more secure than it had been in
the '30s, it has more time now to indulge in its social consciousness and
*Weltschmerz* with more real freedom than ever before (though youth never
regards itself as being free), so one may expect an increasingly intensified
polarization in our social and political life. It is this latent sense of economic
stability—security, one might even call it—that has engendered in the youth of
today an indifference to money that makes the single great difference between
the youth of today and their counterparts of the '30s. With unemployment and
misery on every hand, one did not, in those days, lightly cross swords with the
Establishment; instead, one recoiled from anything that might jeopardize his job
if he were fortunate enough to have one. Thus, there is something reassuring
about the emergence of reform from opulence rather than from those "shirtless
ones" who had nothing to lose but their poverty. The shift in concern from
economic to social values must be regarded as a healthy sign, even though the
elders may complain about the ingratitude of a generation that would bite the
hand which has fed it. Was an earlier generation too much aware of the parental
sacrifices that made its education possible? The question is not an easy one to
answer. Conformity may not necessarily be the highest expression of gratitude.
What parent, at one time or another, has not learned to his chagrin or
embarrassment that Papa doesn't always "know best"?

The "happenings" at Bethel, New York, in Texas and California, and on the Isle of Wight, and the Washington Peace March against involvement in Vietnam, were expressions of youth glorifying itself, seeking its own identity in the companionship of its contemporaries—its own kind. One may deplore its tactics and its excesses, but its determination to realize a better, more honest, less hypocritical world than that in which it finds itself should not be discounted and dismissed as adolescent naiveté. If we of an earlier generation deplore boys with beards and long hair, we must not forget that *our* elders looked with stern disapproval upon girls with lipstick and short hair. Such aberrations in tonsorial convention are but the symbols of protest, and though those of us who have come out of an earlier age may not find them appealing, they are basically unimportant. We of the '20s certainly did not regard the "flapper" as being physically repulsive or her smoking of a cigarette as an open invitation to seduction. "Why is a flapper like a bungalow?" our elders were wont to ask, and the approved response, "Because she's painted in front, shingled behind, and has no attic." In those days, too, it was not always easy to "tell the boys from the girls."

Once again the shock-waves of youthful frustration, discontent, and protest have reverberated in the smug little world of the librarians. The profession in "one of those periods of testing out of which either good or evil will come," observes William Dix, the newly-elected president of ALA, in his inaugural address at the 1969 Atlantic City convention. He went on to say, ". . . many people, most of them young, have realized that there are a number of wrongs in our society, have determined to right them promptly, and are in the process of attacking a number of our concepts and institutions which they believe, correctly or incorrectly, share some of the blame for the present situation. They have done a great service in disturbing our complacency. In the process, some of the revolutionaries have adopted tactics of ideological positions considerably at variance with what we used to believe were basic liberal positions." But "liberalism" for the newly elected president was little more than an echo of the once vibrant spirit of the New Deal, and his key to the current problems of change was "understanding." The business of librarians, he said, is understanding. "This, I submit, is the real objective of all our techniques, and programs, and projects . . . for all kinds of people . . . to bring them understanding of man and the nature of the universe, of the means of livelihood and the uses of leisure, of human dignity and fallibility, of justice and humility."

The address was a sermon rather than a call to action, and despite his appeal for "understanding," and the obvious sincerity in his desire to sympathize with the problems of youth, there was in his peroration little real evidence that he understood the changes taking place either in society or in librarianship. "I submit that the most effective response to the challenge of these difficult and exciting times may be to do better—much better—what we have always tried to do."

As we listened to the demands of the young activists, the new constituency, and the response from the new leader of the Establishment, we were back once again in Chicago in 1933, along with the other "Sons of the Wild Jackass," pounding at the doors of, not 50 East Huron Street, but, as it was in those days, 520 North Michigan Avenue, demanding involvement and participation. "To do better what we have *always* tried to do." *Hang yourself, brave Crillon, we fought at Arques, but you were not there!* The issues of yesterday and today—one could almost pair them off—Spain and Vietnam, little navies and ABMs and MIRVs, and some of the issues were identical—peace, involvement in the activities of the ALA, Negro (now black) segregation, library unions, condemnation of library education, intellectual freedom, the right to preserve the integrity of acquisition policies. The actors are different, but the script is much the same.

Recently a very close friend of ours, who is young in years but rich in wisdom, wrote to us, "There is a great need for a rebirth of professional dedication and enthusiasm." Professional dedication and enthusiasm—she might well have added "a sense of humor," though, blithe spirit that she is, there is no need to remind her of that. The younger generation does seem to lack a sense of humor, a sense of relationship of values. It is all very well to wear a crown of thorns and, indeed, every sensitive person carries one in secret, but in public it should be worn, if at all, cocked over one ear. In the same communication, our friend also observed that she was a "little weary of having so much of the blame laid at the door of the library schools," but that may be a consequence of having graduated from a school of very special excellence, a possible explanation that we shall not pursue. There is no doubt that library education in general has many shortcomings for which it must accept responsibility.

But there are, it seems to us, three important differences between the position of the young dissidents in the profession today and the position of our earlier generation. Today there is in the youth a conspicuous lack of a sense of history, a feeling that they are the first to pound their fists against the pillars of the Establishment, whereas in the '30s we were painfully aware of history, especially the socio-economic history in the continuum of which we saw ourselves. "In our streets and on our campuses," wrote Eiseley, "there riots an extremist minority dedicated to the now, to the moment, however absurd, degrading, or irrelevant the moment may be. Such an activism deliberately rejects the past and is determined to start life anew—indeed, to reject the very institutions that feed, clothe, and sustain our swarming millions." Those who would remain ignorant of history are, indeed, bound to repeat its errors, and we can see little evidence that the new constituency has profited from the mistakes we made, indeed we doubt that they even know we made them.

Furthermore, these young librarians are free from the economic restraints that plagued us at every turn and hence they have more freedom than did we to exhibit their courage and appease their social consciences by wearing them, if not their hearts, on their sleeves. This blessing is not entirely unmixed. Certainly no one would ever want the young to have to heal the scars of a depression, scars which we have found never really completely heal; but a little hunger, just a little hunger, can be of real therapeutic value, a kind of catharsis, from which can emerge a deeper understanding of man and his problems.

Finally, the young activists have been able to articulate their needs and desires with such effectiveness as to arouse honest sympathy in the Establishment. Perhaps this success testifies to their persuasiveness, perhaps it is because the Establishment itself has not forgotten its own youthful struggles, for the dissenters of our day *are* the Establishment of the present. But whatever the reason, certainly youth gained a hearing in Atlantic City that we never did achieve until the passing of time gave us control by default. The meetings of the Council and the membership of the Association are "open," and perhaps that is an accomplishment in which all can take pride.

We of an earlier generation must constantly remind ourselves that just as the young rebels of our day are the Establishment now, so those who today strike at the pillars of society must themselves support the structure tomorrow. This is the way it should be, this is the way the world progresses. Youth must be heard and it must be heeded. "I would be very unhappy," our young friend wrote, "in a profession in which there is no room for growth and improvement." A major responsibility for promoting that growth and improvement must, of necessity, rest upon the shoulders of the young. "Youth is the only wealth," wrote Christopher Morley in *Where the Blue Begins*, "for youth has Time in its purse."

President Dix was entirely right in emphasizing, in his inaugural address, the need for "understanding." We do not need, nor should there be, a "silent majority." A silent majority is the stuff of which totalitarianism is made. A bridge of communication must be built across the generation gap; this is one of the great responsibilities of the library schools. Building bridges of communication across generation gaps is what education is all about. The building of such a bridge will not be easy, it never has been; and, one must add, the older generation must, in large measure, bear the burden of its construction. It is the older generation that possesses the greater share of power, and responsibility resides where the power center is.

But the dissidents, too, must assume their share of the burden. They must act with a sense of responsibility and purpose. They cannot forever indulge themselves in the luxury and self-deception of hedonism. They must not give themselves over to self-pity. They must not robe themselves in the pontifical cloak of Rightness. They must not forget that in those great symbols of the intellectual life, the Medieval universities, especially in Bologna and Paris, the bid for student power came to grief when the aggressive traits of its leaders engendered such abuse and chaos that the oppressive authority had to be taken over by the state, and the university system was set back for generations. As

Jacques Barzun has said, we do not want to return "to 1266 and all that," but there are some disquieting indications that the bid for "student power" has adversely affected governmental support for higher education and might eventually lead to state and political control. Irrational conduct breeds irrational response, and from such confrontations no one profits. The generation gap must be bridged rationally.

Three hundred years before the dawn of the Christian era, Chuang-tsu posed the great question of all communication—"How shall I talk of the sea to the frog," he asked, "if it has never left the pond? How shall I talk of the frost to a bird of the summer land, if it has never left the land of its birth? How shall I talk of life with the sage if he is the prisoner of his own dogma?" Unfortunately, there are prisoners of their own dogma on both sides of the generation gap.

In the early years of his professional career, the present writer, himself one of the dissenting voices, captioned a report for the *Wilson Bulletin*, on the 1936 ALA convention at Richmond, Virginia, with the words of Figaro in Beaumarchais' *Barber of Seville, "Je me presse de rire de tout . . . de peur d'être obligé d'en pleurer."* Today we are still infected with Figaro's cynical pessimism, but we have more hope than we did in the '30s. Even then we saw the menacing shadow of Hitler and the gathering thunderheads of war, and we were attempting to prepare ourselves emotionally for the deluge. Certainly the social problems of today are not insignificant—overpopulation, destruction of the environment, the plight of the cities, racial confrontation, intellectual freedom, war, poverty; we are pressured from every side and we can see no clear solutions. But a quarter of a century of working with students has given us confidence in their capacity to meet these monumental problems head on, and we have not forgotten the "flappers" and the dire predictions about them. Admittedly, the youth of today has a perilous knife-edge to travel, and there are times when they make it very difficult to love them, but we are still very much on the side of youth and we want to stay there. If there is no hope in youth, there is no hope.

So the wheel of fortune turns, ever changing yet ever the same—but never quite the same, either, for it rolls inexorably into a future that we can neither know nor comprehend, a future compounded of menace and promise, of dreams shattered and goals achieved. Yet, with all its folly and all its wisdom, it is the heritage of the young.

# 4

# The Readiness Is All

"Central to the history of the word . . ." wrote Walter Ong, in *The Presence of the Word*, "is a vexing group of phenomena and questions involving the relationship of the word and peace. In some of the perspectives . . . it would appear that the word is an assault or a threatened assault on another person and, to that extent at least, a warlike manifestation." The essential hostility of the word is certainly felt when one attempts to achieve a perspective across the generation gap only to find it shrouded in the mists of polemics, idioms and connotations undefined. But the Rev. Father Ong has also assured us that "the word moves toward peace because the word mediates between person and person. No matter how much it gets caught up in currents of hostility, the word can never be turned into a totally warlike instrument. So long as two people keep talking, despite themselves they are not totally hostile." So we of an older generation must learn to adjust to the invasion of a new, and perhaps even hostile, vocabulary of words and phrases—activism, relevance, involvement, taking a stand, admitting a point of view, fighting along with the community, being committed, working *with* people rather than *for* people, becoming change agents, and being for people on *their* terms, not *our* terms. These are some of the more obvious examples of the language of those who are "with it." William Dix, in his inaugural address as president of the ALA, spoke with some eloquence of the need for "understanding," and indeed this is important, not to say imperative; but lest we lose patience with jargon we should do well to remember that we ourselves did not speak with the tongue of *our* predecessors, and our immediate forebears experienced some difficulty in communicating with us.

Yet, we cannot but flinch at the prodigality with which "demand," both as

Reprinted from the *Bulletin of the Ohio Library Association*, Vol. 40 (April 1970), pp. 4-9.

noun and verb, is used by the new constituency. Demand, indeed, for what and from whom, and by what right? Those of us who, still deep within ourselves, bear the scars of the depression years, will think for a long time before we *demand* anything of anybody. We held with Galsworthy—

> If in a spring night I went by
> And God were standing there,
> What is the prayer that I would cry
> to Him? This is the prayer:
>     O, Lord of Courage grave,
>     O, Master of this night of Spring,
>     Make firm in me a heart too brave
>     To ask Thee anything.

Or was it bravery? Maybe it was only a sense of frustration, an awareness of futility, a whistling to keep up courage. We had to be self-reliant because there was no one else on whom we could rely. We did not enjoy the relative opulence of today's youth, and there were precious few jobs for even the best college graduates in those dark days of economic hardship. We recall hearing William Lyon Phelps, under whom we had studied Browning at Yale, tell the graduates of our Alma Mater, "You have my sympathy, for you are going out into a world that doesn't want you." But whether it was courage or foolhardiness, whatever the rationale, those of us in the library world who, in the 1930s, beat our fists against the pillars of the ALA establishment during the Milam dynasty knew full well that *demand* would, indeed, have been "an assault," or "a threatened assault," on those elect who held the decision-making power, and hence the destiny of the ALA, firmly and relentlessly in their grasp. We could, in those days, never have secured such a hearing on the floor of Council, or at a membership meeting, as was freely granted the New Constituency at Atlantic City and Chicago, in 1969. So, the life span being what it is, our generation became the Establishment by default; and now a young generation snaps at *our* heels, and we do not find it comfortable. The "outs" have always wanted what the "ins" have; stripped of all its patriotic trumpery that was the origin of the American Revolution; and Tory stupidity across the Atlantic probably had as much, if not more, to do with the outcome as did Lexington and Valley Forge. Must change always be forced; must it always leave in its wake the debris of struggle? It seems as though it must, human inertia being what it is.

## BEYOND . . . LANGUAGE . . .

The word is a weapon; we librarians, of all people, should know this. But what lies behind the words of the New Constituency? That is the real question. The task of understanding the young generation is made particularly difficult because, as John W. Aldridge has pointed out in "In the Country of the Young," which appeared in the October and November 1969 issues of *Harper's*, "the kind of communication most favored by the young just happens to be the nonverbal kind, which can neither be described nor objectively evaluated. You can say that you are communicating with someone, and it is impossible to prove whether you are or are not. The whole thing is beyond the power of mere language, and of course it is so clouded by specious religiosity that to question it would be as gross an infringement of the right of worship as asking the devout to demonstrate the efficacy of prayer. It is all a matter of soul speaking to soul." Yet somehow, if we are really to understand the young and are to give youth the sympathy it has a right to expect, we who are their elders must break into this communication chain. The Congress for Change, which met in Washington immediately preceding the Atlantic City conference of the ALA, interrupted its deliberations for the soul music of Natty Bumppo's rock. Unfortunately in this essay we must confine our attention to the recorded word, whatever its limitations and inadequacies.

"We are a society," wrote Loren Eiseley in *The Unexpected Universe*, "bemused in its purpose and yet secretly homesick for a lost world of 'inward tranquility'." The youth of today has, indeed, lost any sense of tranquility. "The thirst for illimitable knowledge," continued the distinguished anthropologist of the University of Pennsylvania, "now conflicts directly with the search for an inward serenity obtainable nowhere upon earth. Knowledge, or at least what the 20th century acclaimed as knowledge, has not led to happiness."

The Social Responsibilities Round Table, the Congress for Change, the Junior Members Round Table, and the librarians for "321.8" are all very like the young activists generally; and all youth is reflecting the malaise that infects a society at the turn of a new decade in an era of *Sturm und Drang*. So it is the responsibility of those of us of an earlier generation who also share these "concerns" to examine, as objectively as we can and as dispassionately as our inherent prejudices will permit, what the young say they stand for, and thus try to accept them "on their own terms." Admittedly they were a noisy group in the Sherman House in Chicago at Midwinter. They confused shouting with dialogue; and though both ALA president Dix and chairman Wagman of the Committee on New Directions for the ALA gave them more than generous opportunity to be heard, they were often rude, impertinent, and particularly unwilling to listen. Yet, beneath all this turmoil we heard the voice of the future, a voice that we will come to know and, somehow, have to learn to understand.

The action of the ALA in establishing the Freedom to Read Foundation, as a legal instrumentality to protect the intellectual freedom of the individual librarian while at the same time insuring the parent association's integrity as a non-profit organization, represents the culmination of attempts which reach as far back as the 1930s to persuade the ALA to assume an active and dynamic role in defending those librarians who have been unjustly discharged from office. But this new mechanism goes far beyond a mere concern with the freedom to read, important though this may be. The scope of the foundation's activities and concerns extends to the protection of those librarians who have been penalized for eccentricities in dress, for expressing as a private citizen unpopular opinions, or for engaging in civil rights activities. This is, indeed, an important step forward and one scarcely dreamed of a generation ago. This new structure was criticized, however—and rather justly, we believe—because it will be dominated by the administrative officers of ALA. But on the other hand, the management of a foundation's portfolio of investments and the proper adjudication of cases that come before the corporation are not responsibilities to be lightly entrusted to the hands of the inexperienced, especially since this new corporation will be, as it must be, closely integrated with the parent association. As a counter action, a group of young dissidents, meeting in Pittsburgh on October 5, 1969, presented plans for the creation of The National Freedom Fund for Librarians, the objectives of which are so broad, so implicit in their assumption that any librarian who is discharged, for whatever reason, is by definition in the right and entitled to financial aid, that the present writer, at least, fails to see how it can possibly avoid financial disaster even if it does not die in the throes of birth. For the same reasons the young activists' attacks at the Chicago meetings upon the attorney for the ALA for alleged conservatism, lack of integrity, and duplicity were unwarranted, unjustified, and completely irresponsible. Nevertheless, they were generously given their hour in court.

## THE CORPORATE STRUCTURE . . .

The task of making the ALA more democratic, of devising electoral and other rules and procedures that will make the association more meaningful and more responsive to the interests of the individual member than it has been in the past, presents a complex of problems that cannot possibly be dealt with adequately in this brief essay. Over the years a series of "Activities Committees" have addressed themselves to this monumental problem, and much that each has done has subsequently been overthrown by its successors, though throughout the continuum there has probably been a net gain for democracy. Almost one-half of the preliminary report of the Committee on New Directions for ALA, and its subcommittees, is devoted to this all-important topic. Here, however, it must be sufficient to say that many of the criticisms voiced both at the Atlantic City conference and at the Chicago Midwinter meeting have justice on their side. Most of the problems evolve out of the numerical growth of the Association and the complexity of professional interests of its members. The corporate structure is far more complex than it needs to be; the bureaucracy on East Huron Street needs thorough renovation; the state associations (chapters) are not adequately represented in the affairs of the association; much too much energy is consumed in keeping the "machinery" running; the Council has grown so large and unwieldy that it cannot "govern," but of necessity delegates much of its authority to the Executive Board; and the rules which the Council adopted in Chicago seem to this writer to contribute to complexity while diminishing democracy. We believe that the terms of office at ALA headquarters should be severely limited; we do not want to live again through the "Milam blood-bath" of the late '40s, for it reflected credit on no one; yet we are fearful that we are heading for just such another "purge." On the other hand, the Washington Office, which demands a very special type of personnel and which has indeed merited all its honors, cannot afford frequent changes in staff. The problems of democracy are indeed difficult. It was Fisher Ames, according to Ralph Waldo Emerson, who likened a democracy to a raft which will "never sink, but then your feet are always in the water."

Professional library education, like education generally, has a multitude of shortcomings for which it must accept responsibility. The young activists are entirely right in their condemnation of the failure of ALA accrediting procedures "in raising the standards of training for librarianship." Yet, they would transfer the authority to accredit library schools to the Association of American Library Schools, and thus give this important responsibility into the very hands of those who so justly merit much of the criticism. At least it is to the credit of the young activists that the proposal has been withdrawn. The real fault lies in the vagueness and generality of the standards themselves and the liberality with which they are applied. We seriously doubt whether the transfer of authority that the young activists suggest would materially improve the results they seek. The present demand for "trained" rather than "educated" librarians to meet existing manpower shortages has resulted in the virtually uncontrolled proliferation of library schools that have inadequate faculties, mediocre resources and little real understanding of what professional education could, and should, be. The streamlining of core curricula and the provision of opportunities for students to enroll in other departments of the university, are much needed reforms that we have long urged. Certainly there is much in the conventional first-year program that could be profitably reduced or even eliminated altogether. Major expansion of interdisciplinary study at the level of the master's degree raises serious problems in time and cost. A two-year program for the first professional degree would be ideal from the standpoint of the student's educational experience, but it would place a severe strain on his already overtaxed bank account. The sixth-year and doctoral program, however, should strongly emphasize study in the substantive fields appropriate to the student's interests, capabilities, and career intentions.

## ... THE PRICE OF EXCELLENCE

We are in complete agreement with the need to include on library school faculties subject specialists who are not librarians, though it is only fair to point out that we ourselves have been severely criticized by the profession for appointment to our own faculty of those who "have never met a library payroll." Happily, this prejudice seems to be on the wane. Inter-institutional student exchanges and transfers are also a laudable idea, but they create serious problems in implementation from the standpoint both of the universities involved and of the student's personal life. An educational program that is fragmented in approach and dispersed over a geographic area can well lead to a smattering of ignorance in an atmosphere of educational chaos. Certainly the curricula of every library school should be under constant review; and there should be a continuing dialogue among faculty, students, and alumni. The more the students and graduates can appreciate the problems of the faculty and the more the latter can come to understand the needs of the former, the better for all concerned, and the greater the possibility of evolving enriched programs of study that are "relevant to today's needs." No one could be more keenly aware of the weakness of our educational system than those who are engaged in it, and constant vigilance translated into remedial action is the price of excellence. Unfortunately, however, there are few "pat" answers and, as John Gardner has so rightly said, "no easy victories."

The "social responsibility" of the librarian has come, in very recent years, to mean, not a reservoir of information available at the will of the patron, or prospective patron, but rather the relationship that librarians and libraries have to non-library problems that impinge upon social welfare and the general good. The latter interpretation is dynamic and activist, while the former is passive, neutralist, and revered by tradition. The conflict is not new, but it has been revived with intensified vigor by the Young Turks. That there are social problems and responsibilities without the library's walls, which are not only monumental but also vital to the welfare, even survival, of mankind, no one can rightly doubt—war, pollution, wastage of natural resources, overpopulation, violence and many others are the proper concerns of the body politic; and it behooves every citizen to make his voice heard about them in the legislative halls. But a professional association dare not dissipate its powers. No resources are unlimited, and if an association does not establish priorities, does not focus its thrusts in ways which relate *directly* to its professional needs, it is certain to suffer.

Therefore, the Activities Committee on New Directions for ALA must draw a sharp line of demarcation between the social responsibilities of the librarian *qua* librarian, and those of the librarian *qua* citizen. Intellectual freedom, the right of every librarian to preserve the integrity of his book collection, the defense of librarians unjustly accused of unprofessional behavior, these are all professional concerns of the librarian *qua* librarian; but overpopulation, wastage of the environment, peace, and crime are the proper concerns of the librarian *qua* citizen and for their advancement or protest the librarian should unite himself with the appropriate action group. Every librarian has the right as a citizen to engage in such action; but only when such conduct impinges upon his professional, or personal, career, only when it jeopardizes his position as a librarian, do such matters become the concern of the ALA. The line between these two areas of social responsibility is not difficult to draw, though it may not be easy to maintain. The *Library Bill of Rights* still provides a solid foundation upon which the social responsibility of the library can be built. We would add to this document only the right of the librarian to conduct himself as a responsible citizen without fear or danger of placing himself in professional jeopardy. But it is not the responsibility of the ALA to make pronouncements, however good or well-intentioned, on those matters which are not profession-ally—and the key word is *professionally*—related to his duties, obligations, and rights.

### ... PROFESSIONAL YOUTH ...

The thoughts of youth are long, long thoughts, as indeed they should be; we would not want them otherwise. But when they reach beyond professional horizons, they may lose their force or even go astray. We do not want youth to dissipate its powers any more than we want the ALA to dilute its professional impact.

Dialogue across the generation gap there must be. "Libraries are predicated on the thesis that dialogue is ever possible," wrote Kathleen Molz in the January 1970 issue of *American Libraries*, "dialogue between past and present, old and young, sophisticate and ingenue, professional and amateur." The library must be true to its heritage in dealing with its own professional youth.

To reject now the needs of the young generation of librarians would be a repudiation of the present writer's own heritage, as well as that of the library itself. But we do wish that the malcontents were a little more objective than they are, more restrained, constructive and focused; less given to excess, generalization, the psychedelic and a disregard of logic, the lessons of history, and the facts. All too often we have been impelled to disapprove of their tactics. But we must never forget that the Young Turks of yesterday are the Establishment of today, and that those who strike at today's pillars of society must support the structure tomorrow; this is as it should be, it is the way the world advances, the only way it can advance. Whatever the cost, youth must be heard and it must be heeded.

One would surely not wish to belong to a profession that was forever static, for change there must, should, and will be. But if change is to be achieved with a minimum of dislocation and unhappiness, and if its benefits are to be brought to the highest possible point of effectiveness, a bridge of understanding must be built across the generation gap. The erection of such a bridge will not be an easy undertaking and, one must add, the burden of its construction must rest primarily with the older generation. It is the older generation that has the greater power, and with that power goes responsibility.

"Have you heard about the man who crossed a parrot with a tiger?" a comedian asked his "straight" man. "No," replied the latter, "but what was the result?" "I don't know," confessed the comedian, "but when it talks you'd better listen." There is both parrot and tiger in the voice of today's youth, and when it talks, we of an older generation had "better listen," for it will speak of change. But youth, too, must remember, as President Kingman Brewster, Jr., reminded a recent freshman class at Yale, that there are no "short-cuts"; and he quoted the words of Robert Maynard Hutchins: "I believe life without theory has come to an end in the United States. A search for principles has begun. We have been absent-minded. We have to think. And the task of revitalizing the American creed and creatively reinterpreting it and making it once more the light and the hope of the world is primarily an intellectual task." To this President Brewster added, "Maybe we had to go through the decade of the short-cuts. But certainly they did not reach, or even touch, the fundamental task. It is still ahead of us. We need a theory that makes sense of our universe, our society, and ourselves. Whatever part of that search is yours, do not forget the magnificence of the challenge." And as President Brewster reminded the Yale freshmen of Hutchins, so we remind *our* generation of Hamlet:

> If it be now, 'tis not to come;
> if it be not to come, it will be now; if it be not now,
> yet it will come; the readiness is all.

# 5

# What Is a Book,
# That a Man May Know It?

Warren S. McCulloch, that distinguished "roving professor" at M.I.T., who stood at the convergence of so many academic disciplines—mathematics, physics, biology, neurophysiology, and the like—and for want of a better term called himself an "experimental epistemologist," says in a biographical note to one of his essays:

> In the fall of 1917, I entered Haverford College with two strings to my bow—facility in Latin and a sure foundation in mathematics. I "honored" in the latter and was seduced by it. That winter Rufus Jones [the distingushed philosopher and historian of the Quaker faith] called me in. "Warren," said he, "what is thee going to be?" And I said, "I don't know." "And what is thee going to do?" And again I said, "I have no idea; but there is one question I would like to answer: What is a number, that a man may know it, and a man, that he may know a number?" He smiled and said, "Friend, thee will be busy as long as thee lives."[1]

I have modified McCulloch's question, not as a forensic trick or rhetorical device, but because it asks the fundamental question lying at the basis of all librarianship. If we could but answer the question: What is a book, that a man know it, and a man, that he may know a book?, the problem of communication, and of librarianship as an integral part of the communication process, would be solved.

If you will regard the library situation as a triangle, of which one side is *books*—and I use books in the generic sense to include all graphic materials—and the second side, *people*, with the base line, *books and people*, thus:

---

Address delivered at the annual dinner of the Cleveland Medical Library Association, Cleveland, Ohio, February 20, 1970, and originally published in *The Bulletin of the Cleveland Medical Library*, Vol. 17 (April 1970), pp. 32-43.

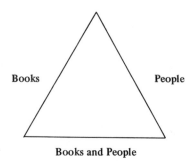

**Books and People**

then it is at this base line that the focus of the librarian's responsibility rests. The librarian is a mediator between man and his graphic records, and the librarian's social role is to maximize the social utility of graphic records for the benefit of mankind. Therefore, the librarian needs to know not only books, as has been said so frequently, but also he must know people and the impact that recorded knowledge has upon human conduct and behavior. Yet, ironically, though this understanding of the relationship between books and people is the very essence of the librarian's task, it is the most mysterious of relationships. We do not know what *really* takes place when reflected light transmitted a message from printed page to eye to brain, and certainly we do not know how knowledge is communicated through a society, a culture.

## WHAT IS A BOOK?

What, then, is a book, that a man may know it? Because people like you and me deal constantly with books, because we take them for granted, we do not often stop to think what a book really is. There have been many attempts to define a book. There are prople who have likened a book to a window—it can provide a view of the outside world; it can give light to the mind; it can ventilate thought; or it may be, like the great Rose Window of Chartres, for aesthetic purposes only. Pierce Butler, who was one of my teachers at the University of Chicago, developed, in a course in bibliography, a definition of a book that, though it was elaborate in its detail, also described a box of breakfast cereal, as he was quick to point out to us.

But of all the definitions of a book that have come to my attention, I like best the one attributed to an 18th-century physicist and writer of aphorisms, Georg Christoph Lichtenberg, who said that a book is a mirror, *"Ein Buch ist ein Spiegel."* A book is a mirror; when a jackass looks into it he will not see St. Paul looking out.[2] I like this definition not merely because it is amusing, but also because it is so very true. We habitually say that a book "says" such-and-such, but of course a book "says" nothing; it is only symbolic markings on paper that have meaning only to the extent that the reader can interpret them. When I look into a book on nuclear physics I do not see Enrico Fermi looking back, but to the nuclear physicist the same book may mean a great deal.

Not only does the content, or meaning, of a book "change" from reader to reader, it "changes" for the same reader over a period of time. I recall that when I was a young man in college and read *King Lear* for the first time, my sympathies were all with the aging king. Goneril and Regan were the incarnation of evil, and Cordelia was the embodiment of all feminine devotion. Today, however, as I read that play, its meaning is entirely changed. I recognize Lear for what he really was—a senile old man, and the two older daughters could scarcely be blamed for not wanting him and his retinue trying to hold on to that which had been given away. Cordelia, on the other hand, I see, not as the frank and honest daughter who paid with her life in defense of truth at any cost, as I had once supposed her to be, but an impertinent little snip. When Lear asked her to say how much she loved him so he could decide whether or not to give her one-third of his kingdom, she replied, in effect, "I love you as much as I'm supposed to, no more, no less." She knew that would set the old man off, and it certainly did. It has been often said that *Lear* does not go well on the stage because the emotions "are too big." Quite the reverse is true; the emotions are petty. I do not mean to imply that *Lear* is not a great play; it is a very great play, and in some ways I think it the greatest play that Shakespeare ever wrote, but it is a study in human ugliness—there's not a lovable character in the whole drama.

We who are compulsive readers tend to forget what a tremendous thing graphic communication is. We read everything. We read what is printed on the cereal box, when we sit down to breakfast, not because we want to know what it says—we know what it says; we read it yesterday morning, and the morning before that. We know that if we send in three box tops and a quarter we'll get a Junior FBI ring and a secret code book—but we have a Pavlovian response to print; if there is something to be read, we read it whether we really want to or not.

"Language," says Susanne Langer, "is, without a doubt, the most monumental and at the same time the most mysterious product of the human mind. Between the clearest animal call of love or warning or anger and a man's least, trivial *word*, there lies a whole day of Creation—or in modern phrase, a whole chapter of evolution."[3] I think she is right, but the linguists will tell you that language is a very imperfect instrument of communication, and I think they are right, too. Leo Rosten has expressed this seeming paradox when he answers his own rhetorical question, "What is a language?"

> It is more than a garment of sounds in which to dress our sensations, or a horn through which to express our ideas. A language is the articulation of a culture, of a certain way of living; and any way of living is jammed with special values and hidden subtleties, assumptions, preferences, implicit judgments.
> Even the 'simplest' tongue of the most primitive people is an intricate web,

woven of words rooted in a distinctive psychological style and philosophical stance. Each of the nearly 3,000 dialects developed by man is a pattern of verbal conventions through which men try to enunciate the swarming sensations of their lives; the life of the skin, the self, the heart, the mind. . . . Through what I can only call the sorcery of words, we try to express the measureless reach of our emotions, our mentation and our imagination.

Is it surprising that so complex a task *is* complex—eloquent, revealing, deceptive, often self-deceiving? For we all carry concepts in an always inadequate basket of words; profound and elusive concepts—about need and desire, intuition and thought, fear, pleasure, amusement, pain; confusion and contempt; ecstasy and horror; the clamorings of hope and the admission of despair; in short, all of the fragile parameters of our convictions about proof, faith, beauty, truth, virtue, sin, glory, guilt.

Language is a miraculous achievement, the greatest single invention of the human race, . . . I have elsewhere pointed out how hard it is for us to realize that a language teaches its users how to think, how to feel, what to see, what to hear. We all assume we are experiencing 'reality' when we are only experiencing life-long conditioning by which our consciousness is bounded.[4]

There is no such thing as perfect communication; there is always a loss. All communication, and especially reading, is active, not passive, and, said Mortimer Adler, "Reading is better or worse according as it is more or less active. And one reader is better than another in proportion as he is capable of a greater range of activity in reading. . . . Strictly speaking there is no absolutely passive reading. It only seems that way in contrast to more active reading. . . . Reading is a complex activity, just as writing is. It consists of a large number of separate acts, all of which must be performed in a good reading."[5] Perhaps the reading of a love letter is the best example we have of the dynamics of communication; the writer puts into it the maximum amount possible of "information," and the reader draws from it all the meaning he or she can. But even a love letter is an open system; there can be, and often is, a substantial hiatus between intent and consequence.

No one really knows the effect of reading, or how reading is related to conduct. Douglas Waples,[6] while at the University of Chicago devoted much thought and effort to the study of what reading does to people, but the best he could do was to identify some of the basic problems and some of the forces implicit in attempting to discover the social effects of reading, and he left behind only unanswered questions. Regrettably, there has never been anyone to carry forward the research he initiated. Only the censors know what reading does to people, while librarians find themselves in the ambivalent position of declaring, without any real evidence at all, that good books will benefit the reader, but "bad" books will not harm anyone. I think there is a paradox here; I find myself unable to believe that we can have it both ways, that we can, so to speak, eat our cake and have it, too. Of course, we know that certain types of reading do influence conduct. We read the instructions that come with a new vacuum cleaner or washing machine, and our behavior toward the operation of that particular device is conditioned by what we read. But I am not, here, talking about that kind of "reading"; indeed, I am not sure that such "reading" is reading at all in the sense I am using it here.

Francis Wayland, in making a donation for the establishment of a public library in the Massachusetts town that bears his family name, complained that the Providence Athenaeum had acquired "books of at least doubtful character, frivolous, and not innocent ... because the young people desired them," and expressed the hope that no such books would find their way in the library he was promoting, for he "would as soon give a child arsenic because he liked it."[7] I, having been over the years both a librarian and something of a student of literature, would like to agree with the good president of Brown University, and believe with him that the reading of "trash" over a protracted period of time will at least injure a reader's sense of taste and style in subtle ways; but I would certainly be hard pressed to *prove* such a thesis. I think that if any of us would attempt in retrospect to identify even one book that had exerted a strong influence upon our behavior and say categorically what the effect was we would be compelled to retreat to the vaguest of generalities in expressing the results of our search. Yet we all know that we are different from that which we would have been had we not been the kind of readers we are. So the question "What is a book that a man may know it?" inevitably leads one into its corollary, "What is a man that he may know a book?"

## WHAT IS A MAN?

The end of all communication, of which reading is, as we have said, one form, is the achievement of like-mindedness. By "like-mindedness," I do not mean agreement, I mean comprehension, understanding of what the other fellow is saying. In the thermodynamic sense, communication is entropic; it is a system undergoing change. Moreover, the system exhibits randomness, disorder, and chaos; in other words, it has "noise." Communication, then, implies a flow of that which is known by the knower to him who is the intended recipient.

Communication begins in an initial inequality of understanding. The communicator (writer) must be superior to the receptor (reader) and the message (book) must convey in comprehensible form the insights that it contains and that, presumably, the receptor lacks. The receptor, then, must be able to overcome, to at least some degree, this inequality. The extent to which equality is approached determines the success of the communication. In short, reading is learning, and man learns only from his betters. Such are the preconditions of learning, but what man is or how he learns is still, in large measure, an unsolved mystery.

Despite the investigations of the neuro-physiologists, our knowledge of how man learns remains at the most elementary behavioristic level. Psychologists have observed the paths of mice in a maze, or the rapidity with which they learn to open a white door behind which there is cheese and reject a black door behind which there is an electric shock, and having done this we make the leap from mouse to man. But I am not at all certain that this is a valid leap, or even that such mousey behavior is really learning. All that such Pavlov-derived experiments would seem to have done is to exhibit the acquisition of information—that is, the generation of adaptive behavior—rather than any real learning. The line of demarcation between the acquisition and learning may be, at its lowest levels, no more than a matter of memory, and a short-term memory at that; but when we speak of learning we speak in terms of the higher cerebral functions confronting the unknown.[8] Despite all our efforts the neuro-physiological process of cognition remain very much a mystery. If we really understood what happens in the human mind when it confronts a library file, the problem of information retrieval would be at least well on the way to solution, if not completely solved.

"The sense, which is the door of the intellect, is affected by individual objects only," wrote Sir Francis Bacon over three centuries ago. "The images of these individuals—that is the impressions received by the sense—are fixed in the memory, and pass into it, in the first instance, entire, as it were, just as they occur. These the human mind proceeds to review and ruminate on; and, thereupon, either simply rehearses them, or makes fanciful images of them, or analyses or classifies them."[9] We know now, of course, that Bacon's psychology was faulty, but at least he performed a service in perceiving that the cognitive process is situated in the brain and is activated through sensory perception.

"The magic loom," Sir Charles Sherrington called the brain, because it weaves patterns of association and relationship.[10] Patterns which are familiar engender a feeling of security, comfort, and pleasure; strange patterns incite discomfort and even fear. We cannot conceive chaos. A table of random numbers can be produced only by machine. We do know, too, that the brain is an elaborate and intricate network through which flow minute electrical currents or impulses; to a point, at least, it resembles a computer. Indeed, John von Neumann, shortly before his death, published a little book in which he elaborated on this analogy between computer and brain,[11] though his thesis has been sharply challenged. The computer's operating principle is linear, it is argued by his critics, whereas the functions of the living brain appear to be non-linear. The firing rate of electrical signals emitted by the sensory end organ corresponds to the stimulus applied to it and in this respect the relationship between input and signal pattern is linear. But by the time the signal, or information bit, reaches the brain through the sensory end organ the signal may be said to fan out and be fragmented so that it is no longer characterized by linearity. Electrical waves flickering through the spaces between the nerve cells are as important to brain function as is the pulse-coded firing of the individual neurons. Thus, the brain cannot be regarded simply as an intricately wired plugboard. Laboratory work at the Brain Research Institute at UCLA, and at a similar institute at the University of Chicago are making impressive headway, as I am sure many of you know far better than I, in unlocking the mysteries of cognition and learning. I need scarcely remind you, however, that there are still vast continents of the brain that are as yet unexplored, and many important questions that are as yet unanswered. The one great obstacle to success in brain research arises from the obvious fact that one cannot examine a living brain in the same way one examines other organs of the body. Someone has said that attempting to study the physiology of the human brain is comparable to smashing a computer with an axe, removing from the wreckage a few handfuls of its tangled components, and from these trying to ascertain how the device works. I am certain that the decades ahead will bring substantial progress in our understanding of cognition. "I think, therefore I am," announced Descartes. If we accept his verdict, we must discover what thought is, if we are to know what a man is that he may know a book.

## INFORMATION STORAGE AND RETRIEVAL

We have all heard a great deal during the past two decades about information storage and retrieval, but it is the retrieval, not the storage, that creates the real problem for the scholar and librarian. New processes of high-reduction miniaturization can go to almost any limit if we are willing to put up with the inconvenience; and even the inconvenience is being reduced along with the text. At the National Cash Register Company, for example, readable linear reduction ratios of 220 to 1 have been achieved through their Photochromic Micro-image (PCMI) technique. Such miniaturization makes possible the photographing of the entire text of the *Bible* on a two-inch square plastic slide. In Germany, the physicist G. Möllenstedt published an electron-microscope picture of his initials, "G.Mo.," which he had written on a metal film with an electronic pencil 80 angstroms wide. Thus it is well within the realm of possibility that with such a pencil 50 to 100 angstroms in diameter one could write letters 300 to 500 angstroms high—i.e., one millionth to two millionths of an inch. A little further work could easily make possible electron-microscope reductions of 200,000 to 1 in each dimension, thus shrinking an ordinary page of print to one square millimeter, the size of the proverbial head of a pin. Richard P. Feynman, a theoretical physicist from the California Institute of Technology, has hypothesized that since organic life is able to store its genetic information at the ultimate molecular level, in the form of long "coded" chains of atoms in the chromosomes, it should be possible to store intellectual information at, or near, the limit of magnification of the electron-microscope.[12] Probably we shall never need such reduction ratios, but there does always seem to be room at the bottom. But what will it profit a man if he has all the books in the Library of Congress in a box on the corner of his desk if he cannot gain access to their intellectual content? I am reminded of a cartoon that appeared in the *New Yorker* some 20 years ago, which showed two little bookwormish men, in a room shelved on all sides with books from floor to ceiling. Books were scattered everywhere, on the floor, on the table, on the chairs, and these two little figures were frantically pawing through them. "What makes me so damn mad," one figure was saying to the other, "is that I *know* the answer is right here in this room!" There could scarcely be a more succinct statement of the problem of information retrieval.

There is no doubt that librarianship faces a crisis whose resolution is still only dimly foreseen. Under the increasing demand for efficient access to recorded knowledge and the exponential growth of that knowledge, conventional library procedures and techniques, admirable as they were for the time they were created, are rapidly breaking down. Yet, somehow this problem must be solved. Derek J. de Solla Price foresees a day when science will drown in, or be suffocated by, the proliferation of its own record, unable to advance because it cannot master the intellectual content of the publications it has already generated.[13]

## THE DYNAMO AND THE LIBRARIAN

I yield to no one in enthusiasm for the computer and the promise that it holds for a new mastery over the intellectual content of libraries. The computer as we know it today is one of man's greatest inventions, perhaps second in importance only to the printing press, and I cannot believe that the library is going to remain untouched by the power of this device. Therefore, I think that the computer is here to stay. But I believe the book is here to stay too, for the book itself is a marvelous instrument for the storage and dissemination of knowledge. We have a long way to go before the computer will replace the book. The computer is linear, whereas the book provides random access. In a very real sense, magnetic tape, like the roll of microfilm, is a reversion to the papyrus or vellum scroll. The codex, with all its limitations, is still very far from being obsolete.

In 1938 Frederick Keppel foresaw the tabulating machine as promising a new era in the analysis of library materials,[14] and in 1945, Vannevar Bush hypothesized the coming of "memex," a personalized machine that would retrieve the intellectual content of recorded knowledge in such a way that the individual scholar could have immediate access to it.[15] After the passing of a quarter of a century, this distinguished former president of the Carnegie Institution of Washington has not foresaken his dream, but he writes: "Will we soon have a personal machine for our use? Unfortunately not. First we will no doubt see the mechanization of our libraries, and this itself will take years. Then we will see the group machine, specialized, used by many. This will be especially valuable in medicine, in order that those who minister to our ills may do so in the light of the broad experience of their fellows. Finally, a long time from now, I fear, will come the personal machine."[16] One does not lightly challenge Vannevar Bush, but I think it entirely possible that the specialized machine may precede such a mechanism for general libraries, for the broad spectrum of materials and needs of the great research library are far more complex and difficult to systematize than the tidy and relatively compact world of the subject specialist. But be that as it may, no one is going to achieve electronically retrieved recorded knowledge in the near future.

The reason for our predicament is simple—we really do not know what it is we want the machine to do. The problem of retrieval is really the problem of the matching of two patterns, the pattern of the organization of the material and the patterned cognition of the user's recourse to it. Since we do not understand the process of cognition, we cannot hypothesize with any degree of accuracy the pattern of recourse to recorded knowledge. In short, we do not know what a book is that a man may know it, nor do we know what a man is that he may know a book. It's as simple as that.

We have tried, without any conspicuous degree of success, to adapt large general-purpose computers to the retrieving of information, on the implicit assumption that information retrieval is somehow like data processing. But every experienced librarian knows that data processing is only a *part*, and a relatively small part, of library service. "The distinctively human goal of learning," wrote Philip Phenix, "is to expand meanings beyond particulars to the larger patterns of understanding. . . . Hence seeing the trees is not appropriate as an ultimate goal of learning."[17] Similarly, one might add that "quick reference"—i.e., data retrieval—is not appropriate as the ultimate goal of the library. The attempt, therefore, to adapt general-purpose computers is an admirable example of what Abraham Kaplan calls "the law of the instrument." Simply stated this "law" holds that man tends to formulate his problems in such a way as to make it seem that the solutions to his problems demand precisely what he already happens to have at hand.[18] To illustrate, if an executive acquires a Xerox machine he immediately concludes that everything that comes from his desk needs to be reproduced in multiple copies for the widest possible dissemination. Kaplan, of course, was applying his "law" to research in the behavioral sciences, but it is relevant to a great variety of human undertakings. The means themselves predetermine what we are to do. "The medium is the message" in more ways than we like to admit. I say that even though I am not "McLuhanitic."

Elting Morison, in a stimulating little book that I would admonish you to look into sometime, presents the thesis that the engineers can do anything, but it is up to the rest of us to tell them what it is we want done. He quotes Thomas Huxley's classic query, "What are we going to do with all these new things?" and implies that Huxley should have asked, "How are we going to reconstruct our social environment so that we can take full advantage of all these new things."[19]

I cannot quite bring myself to share in Morison's faith in the omnipotence of the engineer, but his point is well taken, nonetheless.

The very reason why the engineers have not designed an effective information retrieval device is because we as librarians have not told them what it is we wanted them to do, and we have not told them because we do not know. We do not know because we have never developed a philosophy, a theory, of librarianship itself. I can well remember that in the early 1930s, when I was just breaking into librarianship, I protested loudly that the profession had never developed a philosophy that was uniquely its own. But I was told that such a philosophy would be only "icing on the cake." "A philosophy is all very well," my elders said, in effect, "but it really isn't important." Today, I fear, we are paying the penalty for this neglect of theory. We are confronted by a library world in change and we are not ready for it.

Let me draw an illustration from an entirely different field. You are all, I am sure, familiar with the player-piano, even though such instruments are now relatively rare. These pianos were an early form of the computer, so to speak, their keys being activated by the flow of a column of air, or later an electrical current, according to the spacing of appropriate holes in a wide band of paper tape. In the late 19th century, there were music machines that operated on the same principle; they simulated entire orchestras. Mechanical fingers depressed the strings of a violin across which a mechanical bow was drawn. In these marvelous mechanisms there were horns that blew, drums that beat, and all manner of mechanically activated instruments. What the makers of these machines were doing was emulating the physical movements of the musician in the act of playing.

There is at Central City, Colorado, in the mountains above Denver, a bar, the Gold Coin Saloon, whose owner has a singular facility for reassembling these old music machines; the walls of his establishment are lined with them. I can well remember, on a bright afternoon in early May of 1959, becoming so intrigued with these devices that I was oblivious to the real reason for my entry into the place of refreshment. Indeed, I was again outside in the street before I realized the seriousness of my omission and, I hasten to add, I quickly repaired the unintentional oversight. Such machines dominated the mechanical music field for a time. Few people, in those days, we must remember, ever had an opportunity to hear orchestral music unless they happened to live in one of the large metropolitan centers. Hence, they were dependent either upon piano or organ transcriptions or upon such music machines, if they were ever to experience the ecstasy of Beethoven's "God-like voice."

Then came Thomas Edison. Now I cannot substantiate my interpretation of what he did from any documented source, autobiographical or otherwise, but I think he must have reasoned, either consciously or unconsciously, somewhat after this fashion—music is sound, sound is alternating crests and troughs in air currents, the frequency of which determines the pitch. These air waves beat upon the eardrum, the impulses being thus transferred to the auditory nerves and thence to the brain—I have no intention of explaining to you gentlemen the physiology of hearing. So, Edison must have said to himself something like this, "Let's not make a mechanical musician but a mechanical ear that will simulate hearing rather than playing. Therefore he fastened to the small end of a horn a membrane to which was attached a needle. The needle was placed upon a rotating disk of tinfoil and when Edison shouted "Mary's Little Lamb" into the horn the vibrations activated the membrane, which activated the needle, which in turn cut an oscillating groove into the foil. He then reversed the operation, placed the needle in the groove, the fluctuations of which vibrated the needle and these were transferred to the membrane which activated air currents and the machine squawked "Mary's Little Lamb" back at him. Not exactly high-fidelity, but it is still the basic principle, refined through electronics and the improved composition of the rotating disk, of the modern phonograph.

Edison, therefore, must have begun with an analysis of the problem he was trying to solve, whereas we librarians have been doing nothing more with our general-purpose computers but making mechanical stack-boys, just as the music machines were mechanical musicians. Or, to quote my old friend Robert Fairthorne, we are engaged, not in information retrieval but in document retrieval. But Edison, we must remind ourselves, "had it easy." The process of hearing is open and overt. The process of cognition, by contrast is subtle and largely unknown. What makes our problem so difficult in contrast to his is what Michael Polanyi calls the tacit dimension, by which he means that "we know more than we can tell."[20] Doubtless most of you have been told by your teachers, when you said that you knew the answer to a question but could not explain it, "Nonsense, if you understood it you could explain it." Such a reason is palpably false; if you think it isn't, try to tell someone how you tie your shoe. Of course you can demonstrate the process, but that would be cheating; try to explain it in words. So we know that we use recorded knowledge—we use it every day—but we cannot tell how.

We are still a very long way from the counterpart in librarianship of Edison's phonograph. Despite the great advances in computer technology, it and its programs still have severe limitations. Man's understanding is in a constant state of growth and development under the impact of experience, but the computer cannot grow, it cannot alter itself or its procedures to meet environmental change. Secondly, knowledge and understanding begin with the young child in an intimate association with emotion and feeling, and this association persists throughout life, but these the computer cannot either simulate or experience. Again, the human mental capabilities can serve several motives simultaneously, a capability that is still outside the computer's powers. Yet, let me say again, lest I be accused of being anti-science and a hopeless conservative, that the computer is a very powerful instrument for the solution of certain types of human problems and is growing more powerful with each passing year. I hope the time will never come when a machine replaces the librarian and the book, but there is a computer in your future, make no mistake about that, and it will eventually greatly extend the librarian's capabilities for effective service. So for our purposes this evening, at least, let us think of the computer, not for what it is at the moment—a thing of wires, transistors, and capacitors—but as a symbol of change. Let us think of the computer as Henry Adams thought of the dynamo—as a symbol of force in his thermodynamic analogy of historical evolution. The librarian and the computer exemplify the law of action and reaction between force and force—between mind and nature—the law of progress operating in a young profession that is, we hope, struggling to find itself.[21]

## THE PROBLEM OF SOCIETY

At the beginning of this discourse I observed that the library is a social invention and that its objective is to maximize the utility of graphic records for the benefit of society. Therefore, the librarian must know not only man as an individual but also men in social organization. If we know little about the ways in which the individual acquires and processes knowledge, certainly we know even less about the ways in which a society knows what *it* knows. A society, or a culture, knows both more and less than any of its individual members. Society knows the accumulated content of all the encyclopedias that have ever been written, and no man can know that much. But a man can know the beauty of a sunset or the emotional impact of a Beethoven symphony, and these society cannot experience. How is knowledge generated in a society, and how does it develop and grow? There is not time here to discourse on an area of human inquiry which I have called social epistemology, but I would call it to your attention because it represents an aspect of knowledge that is very vital to the preservation of our way of life. The problems that beset our society today are monumental, they are mountain-high, they reach to the skies, and I am not talking about socialized medicine. Over-population, drug addiction, the emotional problems of youth in revolt, the devastation of our environment, pollution of air and water—and one could go on and on—all pose problems which you, as men of medicine (I will not say "medicine men") must know can be solved only by bringing to bear upon them the total store of wisdom and knowledge that we as a society possess. It has been said by some that man has too much knowledge, so much knowledge that he cannot use it for his benefit. Such an assertion is, of course, utter nonsense. The only cure for "too much" knowledge is more knowledge. Our problem is not that we have too much knowledge, but that we do not have enough knowledge of the right kind. It is no exaggeration to say that on the acquisition and utilization of knowledge rests the future of mankind, and the librarian stands, or should stand, at that very critical point at which knowledge and its utilization converge to drive society forward, in a kind of parallelogram of forces, toward a future that, if it is not flowing with milk and honey, will at least be a better place in which to live than is the present.

The solutions to these problems of knowledge utilization are not going to be easy, and there are no guarantees of success. We do, indeed, have a perilous knife-edge to travel.

"Wohin der Weg?" asked Faust as he set forth on his journey in search of that one perfect moment of supreme happiness, and Mephistopheles replied, "Kein Weg! Ins unbetretene." The way into the future is untrodden; we must find it for ourselves and we will need all the knowledge the librarian can bring us.

Petrarch, the "Morning Star of the Renaissance," the devotee of classical learning, the disciple of Cicero, wrote a delightful little essay entitled *De Vita Solitaria*, in which he states with particular clarity and beauty the position in which I find myself:

> I am only a restless searcher. Though I have always sought the truth, I fear that its hidden retreats, or a certain dullness of mind may have obscured my vision, and in my quest after the thing itself I have often become entangled in mere opinion. Therefore, I have dealt with these matters, not as one who lays down definitions, but as one who tries to study and observe with care. For to define is the prerogative of the wise, and I am neither wise, nor close to wisdom; but in the words of Cicero, only 'a great conjecturer.'[22]

Well, my good friends, a "great conjecturer" is what I have been tonight.

## FOOTNOTES

[1] Warren S. McCulloch, *Embodiments of Mind* (Cambridge: MIT Press, 1965), p. 2.

[2] The original is: "Ein Buch ist ein Spiegel; wenn ein Affe hineinsicht, so kann kein Apostel herausgucken." Georg Christoph Lichtenberg, *Aphorismen, Briefe, Satiren* (Düsseldorf-Köln: Eugen Diederichs Verlag, 1962), p. 48. We have taken the liberty of changing the monkey to a jackass and identifying the Apostle as St. Paul, as it seemed to endow greater authority that way.

[3] Susanne K. Langer, *Philosophy in a New Key* (Cambridge, Mass.: Harvard University Press, 1942), p. 83.

[4] Leo Rosten, "Irony and Insult: the Matchless Ploys of Yiddish," *The University of Chicago Magazine*, Vol. 65 (November-December 1972), p. 8.

[5] Mortimer J. Adler, *How to Read a Book* (New York: Simon and Schuster, 1940), pp. 22-23, 25.

[6] Douglas Waples, Bernard Berelson, and Franklyn R. Bradshaw, *What

*Reading Does to People* (Chicago: University of Chicago Press, 1940).

[7] Letter to Judge Edward Mellen, March 25, 1851. Quoted in Jesse H. Shera, *Foundations of the Public Library* (Chicago: University of Chicago Press, 1949), p. 239.

[8] Some of the more recent and semipopular works on the operation of the brain and the nature of thought are: J. Z. Young, *Doubt and Certainty in Science: A Biologist's Reflections on the Brain* (New York: Oxford University Press, 1960); Dean E. Wooldridge, *The Machinery of the Brain* (New York: McGraw-Hill, 1960) and *Mechanical Man: The Physical Basis of Intellectual Life* (New York: McGraw-Hill, 1968); and Nigel Calder, *The Mind of Man* (New York: Viking, 1970). Reference might also be made to the present writer's *The Foundations of Education for Librarianship* (New York: Wiley, 1972), Chap. I, "Communication and the Individual."

[9] Francis Bacon, *Advancement of Learning*, Book II, Chap. 1. Translations from the Latin vary somewhat.

[10] Sir Charles Sherrington, *Man on His Nature* (Cambridge: Cambridge University Press, 1940), Chapter VII, "The Brain and Its Work."

[11] John von Neumann, *The Computer and the Brain* (New Haven: Yale University Press, 1958).

[12] John R. Platt, *The Step to Man* (New York: Wiley, 1966), pp. 4-5.

[13] Derek J. de Solla Price, *Science Since Babylon* (New Haven: Yale University Press, 1961), pp. 92ff.

[14] Frederick J. Keppel, "Looking Forward; a Fantasy" in Emily Miller Danton, ed., *The Library of Tomorrow* (Chicago: American Library Association, 1939), p. 5.

[15] Vannevar Bush, "As We May Think," *Atlantic Monthly*, Vol. 176 (July 1945), pp. 101-108.

[16] Vannevar Bush, "Memex Revisited" in his *Science Is Not Enough* (New York: Morrow, 1965), p. 100.

[17] Philip H. Phenix, *Realms of Meaning* (New York: McGraw-Hill, 1964), p. 330.

[18] Abraham Kaplan, "The Age of the Symbol," *Library Quarterly*, Vol. 34 (October 1964), p. 303.

[19] Elting Morison, *Men, Machines, and Modern Times* (Cambridge, Mass.: MIT Press, 1966), p. 215.

[20] Michael Polanyi, *The Tacit Dimension* (Garden City, N.Y.: Doubleday, 1966).

[21] Henry Adams, *The Education of Henry Adams* (Boston: Houghton Mifflin, 1927), Chapter XXV, "The Dynamo and the Virgin" (1900).

[22] I am indebted to my colleague, Conrad H. Rawski, for the translation from the Latin.

# 6

# For Whom
# Do We Conserve, or
# What Can You Do With
# a Gutenberg Bible?

What I have to say this evening probably springs from some dark psychological complex, hidden under layer upon layer of deposited experience as a practicing librarian and teacher of librarians, until only a trained psychiatrist could reach the origins that lie hidden below; the search would be like that for Gratiano's wit, scarcely worth the effort. But, if what I have to say be madness, yet there is some method in it, for it is directed toward some of the aberrant forms of the collecting instinct, or perhaps more accurately, mania. We are all pack rats, quite literally book keepers, or, if it sounds more elegant, keepers of books. Most of you are book collectors, bibliophiles, who hoard books for the fun of the chase. Some, like me, are librarians who have dedicated our professional lives to the saving of books so that future scholars can write from them other books to be saved for still other scholars to write still more books until the line, like Banquo's progeny, stretches out to the crack of doom, or, like Tennyson's brook flowing on forever, quite indifferent to the coming and going of men. All too frequently a book, to a bibliophile, is something to be hoarded, to be prized because his fellow collectors and competitors do not own a copy. To a librarian a book is often merely, as Archibald MacLeish has said, "the unit of collection . . . made of print, paper, and protective covering that fulfills its bibliographical destiny by being classified as to subject and catalogued by author and title and properly shelved."[1]

It may be well to set the frame of reference for the discussion this evening with an affirmation of two important axioms. The first is that libraries began in the days of the Sumerians, or of Assur-banipal at Nineveh, or whenever it was, as store-houses. It was for the preservation of the record, the transcript of the culture that libraries came into being; they were the "time-binders" to use the

---

Address delivered to the Caxton Club of Chicago, January 26, 1972. Revised August 1972.

term of the General Semanticists, and they bridged the "generation gap." There has always been a "generation gap," and these places of record where archive and library met were needed to transmit the accumulated record from the old to the young. Libraries were necessary for the education of the priesthoods, for carrying out the business of the state, and for initiation into the professions. Nevertheless, though the conservational function of the library is as old as the institution itself, its meaning has been neglected by many, if not most, librarians. In recent years it has become quite unpopular to refer to the library as a store-house, and the librarian as a pack rat. Such a role is held to be excessively passive, insufficiently dynamic, and not "relevant to today's needs." Such a role has no "outreach," in the contemporary philosophy of librarianship.

Librarians and laymen alike have long ridiculed the Harvard librarian John Langdon Sibley who, according to the oft-told story, happily told a colleague (in some versions the president of Harvard College himself) who had asked after the state of affairs at the library, "All the books are in except two; Agassiz has those and I'm going out to get them now." The anecdote, which may very well not be apocryphal, has been repeatedly used by posterity for its own purposes, usually to discredit the popular image of the librarian as a miser among his treasures or "keeper" who resents any use of his precious volumes, but always omitting the legal background in which Sibley was compelled to operate. Such a reply as he was supposed to have made would have been quite in accord with the statutes of Harvard College of Sibley's day, which required the librarian to see that, on a specified day each year, all books were in the college library, to be inspected by a visiting committee of the Board of Overseers. Sibley, who was the distinguished librarian of Harvard from 1856 to 1877, and who is particularly memorable for the devotion with which he preserved much fugitive material for that posterity which now ridicules him, was a devoted servant of his college and would undoubtedly have followed the rules to the letter. If Louis Agassiz had the books, one can be sure he surrendered them.

The second axiom relates to the strong affinity between private book collectors and libraries. For centuries, patronage of libraries has been a characteristic of men of property, power, and distinction who were themselves avid bibliophiles. Indeed, in the classical world and during the Renaissance, especially, the patronage of a library was a mark of social prestige. Libraries were the Cadillacs, the Rolls Royces, the summer homes at Newport of earlier times. Where would libraries be today without the interest in book preservation of a Petrarch or a Cardinal Mazarin? How great is the debt of the British Museum to Sir Hans Sloane and Robert Bruce Cotton; that of the University of Paris to Robert de Sorbonne; or the college at New Town, Massachusetts, on the banks of the Charles to John Harvard? In more modern times one could point to the book collecting philanthropy of Thomas Jefferson, Huntington, Morgan, Folger; of Astor, Lenox, and Tilden; even this superficial listing reveals the magnitude of the debt.

Science, too, has played its role in giving new tools and processes to assist the librarian "keeper." New photographic processes have provided us with a degree of miniaturization that was undreamed of less than a generation ago. Archival practice has been the recipient of new techniques in lamination, inlays, document storage in inert gases, and glass that filters out harmful ultra-violet rays. Witness the care that has been lavished on the *Declaration of Independence* and the *Constitution* by the National Archives to preserve what is left after some unbelievable, though well-intentioned, bungling during the previous century.[2] As science advances we may anticipate that the techniques of preservation and restoration will be further improved, confronting the librarians with a paper "boom" that threatens to make that of the babies no more than a distant echo. Miniaturization, for example, though it has not achieved the ultimate limit of storing information at the molecular level, can now, by etching with a light pen, produce letters only a few angstroms high. There seems always to be room at the bottom.[3] Science is making it increasingly possible to crowd more and more text into a smaller and smaller space, and to pile it up even higher and deeper more rapidly than we can efficiently retrieve and use it. As our knowledge of natural and synthetic fibers increases, we may expect substantial improvement in the longevity of paper and parchment despite the pollution of the air; in addition, we may have clean air, though that does seem to be in the very distant future. As man's understanding of physics and chemistry grows new processes will doubtless be found that will not only preserve but also restore almost to its original condition the record of the past. In all of these accomplishments, both present and prospective, librarians and archivists can take a justifiable, albeit possibly transitory, pride; but one must also acknowledge that although we seem to be fighting a winning battle against vermin, fire, and flood, we are losing the race to the growing power of preservation and the mass of record which challenges our skill to use. We may yet come to regard the rat as the scholar's best friend, lifting from his stooped shoulders an oppressive burden of documentation. But the elimination, through science, of these destructive "acts of God" and man, is, as Vannevar Bush acknowledges, not enough. It does not answer the nagging question: for whom and to what end do we conserve? Hard on the heels of that question comes its corollary, *what* should we preserve and *what* should we destroy?

The book collector, even the most opulent, is not harrassed by these problems, at least not to the same extent as is the librarian. The bibliophile has only his own idiosyncratic desires to fulfill; he has no clientele whose demands he is supposed to meet. His collecting is usually sharply focused and there is, in his mind at least, a general plan of procedure. Moreover, he is in the game mostly for the love of the chase. There is no board of trustees, no faculty, no irate public snapping at his heels. There is no one to complain of his activities except his wife, and if she becomes intolerable there is always the escape hatch of divorce or homicide. In short, the bibliophile is a relatively free agent, whereas the librarian is hedged about by a variety of constraints which not only must be reconciled and compromised with but also must be weighed in terms of his own philosophy of what his library should be. In such a situation philosophy inevitably suffers, and the librarian permits his library to grow, more or less (and usually more), by fortuitous circumstance.

So the librarian usually seeks the safety that is supposed to reside in numbers, and through quantity seeks, relying on the law of averages, quality: if one buys a great many books, the chance that the right ones are among them will be improved. Thirty years ago, when I was on the staff of the Library of Congress, James B. Childs, who was recognized the world over as the dean of authorities on government documents, once said to me that he couldn't understand "all this fuss over 'book selection,' you just get everything that you can"; and in the realm of official government publications, Childs did. Consciously or unconsciously, every librarian follows this philosophy. Every large metropolitan library, every university library strives to be, if not a little Library of Congress, at least a diminutive Houghton or Beineke; bigger, "better," and with more rare books than its nearest rival. Yet, all librarians pay lip service at least to the fallacy of book collecting for its own sake, and the folly of pride that seems to come from owning a book that few, if any, other libraries have. Perhaps the scholar should be grateful for the omniverous collecting propensity of the librarians, but it is scarcely a guide to efficient procedure. The larger a collection is, the more difficult retrieval becomes and the more expensive it is to organize, administer, and maintain.

Years ago Garrett Hardin parodied the phenomenon of unrestrained library growth in "The Last Canute."[4] In this delightful little piece he tells the story of a philanthropist, a Mr. Babcock, who was alarmed by the increasing size of libraries, and who, therefore, established the New Alexandrine Library Fund, the purpose of which was to make available $20,000,000 to the libraries of Harvard, Columbia, Stanford, and Chicago. The provision was that for each grant of $10, these libraries were required to withdraw and destroy one volume of no fewer than 500 pages. Yale was kept as a control. Only Stanford complied with the terms of the program, and even then not until the amount paid was increased to $20 a volume. The result was that Stanford discarded 17 books. To shorten a very amusing story that every librarian should be compelled to read, the project failed completely, and at the final meeting of the board of trustees of the foundation, on "January 20, 1955," it was reported: that through the efforts of the Harvard Law School, the Supreme Court of the United States had handed down the judgment that, "a personal bequest cannot be made on condition that the beneficiary extirpate part of his person. . . . A university is a legal person. Asking it to destroy part of its library is like asking it to destroy part of its person." Therefore, the Fund was ordered to divide its assets among the four universities. However, $2,000,000 was reserved for the Red Cross, and a hand-lettered copy on parchment of the minutes of the final board meeting was to be given to each of the four libraries, with a gift of $10,000 "to each university for accessioning the document." Whereupon the board adjourned to the apartment of one of its members for "Pilsener and Chateau Wente '47," but not until they had voted to strike from the record an earlier reference to means for propagating termites—"Those termites are our only remaining hope." Hardin's indictment of the librarians is a little harsh, as every librarian knows who has ever been confronted by an irate patron, distressed because a title "essential" to his work was not owned by the library. Yet the fact remains that all too frequently materials are acquired more for prestige than for perusal.

It so happened that the present writer was a graduate student at Yale when the university library acquired its famous Melk-Harkness-Yale copy of the *Gutenberg Bible*, and late one afternoon I was standing by the glass case in which this landmark in the history of printing from movable type was exhibited. It was closing time, and a young woman was removing the two handsome volumes for overnight security in the library vault. Beside me was a young Yale undergraduate whom I did not know, and we both asked the attendant if we might handle these precious books. She readily and graciously agreed. After fondling them for a few moments and admiring their typographic beauty, the undergraduate observed, "What pleases me most is that Harvard doesn't have a copy." What can you do with a *Gutenberg Bible*? Beat Harvard over the head with it, what else? But such triumphs are apt to be short-lived. Not many years passed before Harvard had one of its own. Yale's copy of the first printed edition of the Jewish and Christian Scriptures was, as the librarian of the Benedictine abbey at Melk on the banks of the Danube in southern Austria, briefly described it, "a true jewell," and it had cost Mrs. Edward S. Harkness the sum of $106,000 to be able to present it to Yale as a memorial to Mrs. Steven V. Harkness, who had given Yale its famous Memorial Quadrangle. The cost of the book was a record high in the book market for those days (1926), and one can be sure that Dr. Abraham S. Wolf Rosenbach, who had negotiated the sale at the Anderson Galleries, was also handsomely rewarded for his negotiations. So the war-impoverished monks at Melk were able to keep body and soul together a little longer; the good Dr. Rosenbach added another accomplishment to a long list of successes in the auction room; the Anderson Galleries got their "cut"; Yale had a *Gutenberg Bible*; and Mrs. Harkness has a happy memory. Such satisfactions are scarcely to be deprecated.

I was present also at the formal presentation of the *Bible* to the university, when there were appropriate addresses by Andrew Keogh, then the university librarian, and Chauncey Brewster Tinker, the distinguished authority on James Boswell, who later became the rare-book librarian of the Sterling Library. Professor Tinker quite properly, it seemed to me, raised the philosophical question:

Latent in the minds of all who have come here this afternoon is a question which ought to be faced with courage and which, with a touch of that cynicism which prevails in academic circles, has already been asked with some asperity. Of what use is this book now that we have received it? What can be done with it, except to put it under glass and exhibit it as the most valuable book in our library? . . . Shall we, then, enbalm the book, and lay it away, richly coffined, to sleep in its own dust unto eternity? Why should it ever be disturbed, except by curiosity seekers and our weekend visitors? It has illuminated capital letters and floral decorations on the margins, but even these have been reproduced in facsimile editions of the book. . . . Certain people believe that the library of the future is to consist of autotypes, photostats, and tabloid books to be read with a magnifying glass. . . . I wish I could explain, even to my own satisfaction, why such a library, filled with facsimiles, existing in the midst of a world equipped with all modern conveniences, comforts, and short cuts would be a vapid place. I should be the first to deny the value of photostats, of which I perhaps have made larger use than most, but I cannot deny that they are dull things to work with. They have everything about them but the spark of life. They are like a tailor-made man, authentic and impeccable in every detail, but somehow unconvincing in good company.[5]

Approximately two decades after Mrs. Harkness' gift, Yale acquired an original copy of the *Bay Psalm Book*, at a price double that paid for the Melk *Bible*. Even a distinguished scholar in the history of printing, an authority on water-marks, and a Yale alumnus questioned the wisdom of that purchase. Now I confess to being much more sentimental than most people, even most librarians, over old rare books, and I have derived considerable pleasure from examining my own two facsimile copies of the *Psalms*, and especially those paradoxical lines:

The Lord will come and He will not
Keep silent but speak out.

Yet I cannot but wonder what this inflation signifies for our contemporary sense of values. In 1970 I happened to mention to my friend Verner Clapp that I had been told that Kraus had a copy of the *Gutenberg Bible* that could be purchased for $2,500,000, or perhaps even a little more, whereupon Clapp observed that if he had that kind of money to spend he would purchase the book. When I asked him why, he replied, in words reminiscent of Sir Edmund Hilary, "Because it's there, and there won't be many more available much longer." I agreed and added that I had understood that business was a little slow at the Mainz print shop lately, and that old Johannes was having some problems with his creditor, the goldsmith Fust.

From classical economics we learn that *value* is the ability to satisfy a *want*, and that in a free market, *price* is value expressed in monetary terms. In short, the rare-book market will reflect what the traffic will bear, and the traffic does seem to be bearing more and more; but it is the competition among and between book collectors and librarians that is providing the support.

I have, of course, overstated my case—and deliberately so—in order to make the point that book collecting, both public and private, may be getting dangerously out of control. I am not suggesting that Yale discard its *Gutenberg Bible*, just because it's an old book that nobody much reads any more, or the *Bay Psalm Book* because it isn't used in Battelle Chapel. But I do raise the question of the price we are paying for sentimentality and for the cult of the scarce. To all such questioning I must confess that there are no answers other than to paraphrase *The Song of the Shirt*:

> Oh God, that books should be so dear
> And Scholarship so cheap!

In the early 1920s, when the excitement over the discovery of the tomb of Tutankhamen was at its height, a reporter asked Howard Carter, or perhaps it was Lord Carnarvon himself, if he did not suffer some pangs of remorse or guilt over removing these treasures from the tomb, where the conditions for preservation were almost ideal, and placing them on display in an environment that would most certainly increase their rate of deterioration. His reply stands as something of an answer to Tinker's eloquent but questionable logic. To leave them in the tomb, he responded, where they would be of no value to anyone, would expose them to the depredations of the robber, for a known tomb is always vulnerable to theft. Moreover, once the artifacts were carefully measured, minutely described, and photographed from a variety of angles, it really made little difference to the progress of scholarship whether the originals survived or not. One may charge that this reaction is only rationalization and self-justification, yet it does seem that there is much truth in it. Writing a half century later about the opening of the tomb and the quality of Carter's work, John A. Wilson, formerly director of the Oriental Institute of the University of Chicago, said, "Carter's single-mindedness in demanding that he be allowed to clear the tomb in his own way and at his own pace served notice that Egyptology was a responsible business and not a treasure hunt."[6]

Preservation for preservation's sake, and collecting for its own sake can be, and sometimes are, aberrant forms of librarianship, and often there are many "aberrant librarians" in high places. An illustration is relevant even though it may be "telling tales out of school"—it will not be the first time that I have been guilty of such an indiscretion. Several years ago the chancellor—I believe that was his title—of the University of Texas became, as they say, very "library-minded," but he was plagued by the collector's psychology in believing that the first function of the university librarian is to "mind rare books." So he secured the advisory services of a distinguished librarian on the West Coast, who shall be nameless, who proposed ways in which the rare book collection should be developed. As a result the university spent untold sums of money in the rare book market, while the books sorely needed for the day-to-day work of the scholars and students are, even yet, not to be found in the library stacks. One can see a copy of the first edition of *Hackluyt's Voyages* any time he wants to look at it, but the materials needed for teaching, writing, and research are not there. So serious did the problem become that the students attacked the policy in the pages of the *Daily Texan*, the student newspaper. Here is one form of student protest with which I am in complete agreement. In the auction halls of New York and London, the eyes of Harvard and Yale are upon Texas, for a change, and their gaze is far from being friendly.

What are the charges that can be brought against the collecting mania, other than its diversion of resources that might better be expended elsewhere, such as in fellowships to provide the means for scholars to travel to the appropriate centers where their needs can be fulfilled? There are several. The first can be called "the cult of bibliographic virginity"; a book must show no signs of use. We are all familiar with the bookseller's phrases, "mint condition," or "uncut, as new." Of course if the book is an "association item," marked with the marginalia or other "spoor" of a distinguished personage, the value, and hence the price, is increased substantially. Second, there is the cult of the "point," trivial printing errors that contribute nothing to an understanding of the text, but are valued because they have survived in but a few copies—e.g., the "Breeches" or the "He" and "She" *Bibles*, "the scared codfish," for the sacred codfish in the first printing of Samuel Eliot Morison's *Maritime History of Massachusetts*, or those few copies of the great *Encyclopedia Britannica* that reported in the entry for Peter the Hermit that "he was an emotional revivalist preacher; that his very ass became the object of popular adoration." (I regret that my own copy of "the great *E.B.*" uses the more discreet term "donkey"; the fact that I regret it shows, perhaps, that I myself am not free from the lure of the "point.")

But whether these "points" have any substantive significance or in any other way contribute to the meaning of the text is immaterial to the collector, whose reward may be only the excitement of the chase.

Again, a story may be relevant. I have a very good friend who is a distinguished professor of English literature and a skillful bibliographer, who makes a hobby of collecting books that were given as prizes for scholastic achievement to English schoolboys during the 19th century. These books, which are nothing but trade editions of well-known literary classics and have no intrinsic value in their own right, are especially desirable when their covers bear the coat-of-arms of the school that awarded them. I asked my friend whether he had collected information about the lads who were the recipients of these distinctions, and he acknowledged that he had made a considerable effort to find out what record these promising youths had left behind, what footprints they might have left on the sands of time, but that apparently these young prodigies had done little to bring honor to the old school tie. So my friend has brought together some 400 of these books to form a collection that will probably be deposited at some future date in an academic library, there to be accessioned, cataloged, described, classified, shelved, and preserved for posterity under the proper conditions of temperature and humidity control. Now, tonight, when I "lay me down to sleep," I shall seek Divine forgiveness for this impertinence, for my friend is really a very fine fellow with impeccable credentials as a scholar. Surely every man has the right to collect what he wants and can afford, and probably every collector is a wee bit daft on some subject. I myself, like Stephen Leacock, once began a collection of coins, starting, quite patriotically, with those of my native country, but these were put back into circulation before the collection assumed any great proportions.

It may be instructive to look briefly at a library situation that contrasts sharply with those I have just been describing. My own undergraduate college, Miami University, in the southwestern corner of Ohio, had, when I was a student there, a library of not much more than 100,000 volumes. Even today, at a time when libraries are expanding at an exponential rate, there are probably fewer than 500,000. It could boast of owning no collection that could be characterized as being really rare, with the possible exception of one on the early history of the Ohio River Valley, which the university had received as a bequest. But it had something far more valuable: it had a librarian who not only possessed the gift of scholarship, but who also was an unusually imaginative and astute buyer of books, who kept always in the back of his mind, but never formally expressed, a concept, an ideal, of what the library should be. The name of Edgar Weld King will be quite unknown to most of you, though his father, Henry Churchill King, was president of Oberlin College for 25 years and brought that institution to national greatness. But "Ned" King was, in many respects, what the compleat librarian should be, and few collections of books were so much "the lengthening shadow of a man," as was his. In the library over which he presided for a quarter of a century, there was as little worthless material as I have ever discovered in any assembly of books. Twenty-five years after my graduation, I happened to spend a week at my Alma Mater when I was engaged in writing a paper on bibliographic classification for presentation at a forthcoming conference, and much of the writing of that paper was done in the stacks of the old library. More than ever, I was amazed to discover how efficiently the collection could be used and how much of the material I needed was readily available on the shelves. Virtually all of the materials in philosophy relevant to my work were there, yet the size of the total collection was sufficiently small so that one could find one's way around in it, master it, and in every way manipulate it to meet one's needs. Seen against the backdrop of my years at the Library of Congress, the experience was all the more striking, for at the Congressional Library the sheer bulk of the volumes is itself oppressive and a real handicap to efficient use. Numbers alone do not guarantee security for the scholar; clearly there is an optimum size for a library, but no one knows what it is. Doubtless it is not an absolute but varies from situation to situation. But what those variables are, or how they can be used to discover the optimum, no one knows. Nevertheless, it is clear that the Library of Congress and many other large research libraries have gone beyond, not just the point of diminishing returns, but the point of efficient use.

We have failed to appreciate the meaning of S. R. Ranganathan's Fifth Law, more accurately a precept, of library science—namely, that "A library is a growing organism," by which the distinguished Indian librarian implies that it cannot forever increase in size, and that once it has attained its optimum, it must grow by replacement. Books, like all living things including people, have a right to die. Books, like cells in a living body, become exhausted and must be replaced. The uncontrolled growth of books in a library, like cells in the body, can become cancerous.

> The pride and glory of a public library is not the number of rare books, 16th century editions, or 10th century manuscripts which it contains, but the breadth of the diffusion of books it affords among the people, the number of new readers, the speed with which requests for books are satisfied, the number of books sent to the reader's homes, the number of children it manages to attract to come and read and enjoy the library's facilities.[7]

Thus wrote Lenin after reading the annual report of the New York Public Library for 1911, and a decade later the public library became a major instrument in the Soviet program for the liquidation of illiteracy.

Yet mathematics, which has enabled man to calculate the way to reach the moon, has provided us with no model that will enable us to determine the optimum size of a library for a given situation or a known clientele. At the present time we have nothing but Bradford's law of dispersion, which states that if the journals containing articles on a given subject are ranked in order of the number of contributions relating to articles on a given subject, then successive zones of periodicals containing this number of articles on the subject form a simple geometric series, $1:n, n^2, n^3, n^4. \ldots$ Bradford called the first zone the nucleus of periodicals pertaining to the subject. This law, though it enunciates the behavior of an interesting phenomenon, is of little practical use. It does show, however, that a core of periodicals exists and that these journals can be separated from the top of the ordered list of periodicals dealing with a given subject, and that this core probably represents the most significant sources of information relevant to that subject. Goffman and Morris have shown that the distribution of both circulating periodicals and their users in a medical library seems to obey Bradford's law.[8] Whether the same phenomenon would be exhibited by the serial literature of non-scientific fields or for the use of monographs remains to be shown. But at least the possibility of mathematical expression for the optimum size has been suggested.

But even if we could evolve a valid equation that would demonstrate mathematically, given the appropriate variables, the optimum library size, the question of *what* of the world's total output of books should be preserved would remain unanswered. Preservation of the transcript of the human adventure is, admittedly, the function of the library, and one can not but admire the technology that science has devised to preserve that transcript, even to burying a representative portion of it deep in the earth where it will presumably be safe from all the elements of destruction that man has yet devised. But the nagging question still persists: "Why are we saving it, and what should be saved?" Will there be future generations who may want it, and does anyone care? Policy evolves, or should evolve, from the point where *cognition* (a full awareness of the facts) and *conceptualization* (judgment) meet, harmonize, and interrelate. Yet, in this "book collecting game" in which we are all engaged, we lack both a knowledge of the pertinent facts and the judgment to utilize them effectively in the formulation of policy. Those of us who are responsible for the operation of libraries are beholden to the body politic, to the tax-paying public, or to private philanthropy. As the costs of operating libraries mount, those who hold the purse-strings are increasingly questioning the value of all this preservation. It is easy to accuse the electorate, and the public generally, of anti-intellectualism, and to retreat, licking our wounds in self-pity. Yet the public does have some justification for its attitude. There is little doubt that libraries, along with education at all levels, has wasted too much money in trivia and non-essentials.

For years the world of scholarship thought it a matter of regret and national concern that the Library of Congress had no copy of the *Gutenberg Bible*. Why? No particular reason was given; the mere statement of the fact was its own justification. Then, in the depths of the depression of the 1930s, the distinguished German book collector and apologist for the Nazis, Dr. Otto H.F. Vollbehr, offered to the United States government his collection of incunabula, which included a copy of the *Gutenberg Bible*. Because the Library of Congress had no copy of Gutenberg's famous book, Representative Ross A. Collins, of Mississippi, introduced a bill for the purchase of the collection, and at the hearings on the so-called Collins Bill, the proposed legislation received the enthusiastic support of every book collector and bibliophile in the country. After the bill had been passed and signed by President Roosevelt, someone asked Mr. Collins how, in such times of economic stringency, he could justify to his constituency the expenditure for so much money for a "lot of old books." He replied that he had told the voters of Mississippi that the *Gutenberg Bible* was the original text as dictated to the children of Israel by God Himself. Mr. Collins, I am sorry to report, was defeated in the next election, but his misfortune was probably due more to his support of reduction in the Navy's battle fleet than to his bibliographical activities. These were the days, our older readers will recall, of the famous, or infamous, 5-5-3 ratio, representing the comparative naval strength of England, the United States, and Japan—a ratio that was somewhat altered at

Pearl Harbor on a fateful day in December 1941.

Yet the transcript of the culture must be preserved. We cannot ignore the lessons of history. But today, when taxpayers are looking with increasing skepticism at the rising costs of both education and libraries, neither can afford to invest in frills. We do not suggest, of course, that the preservation of the social transcript is a frill, but we must look critically at our collecting policies at every point, and it may not be easy to tell the uninitiated public why we should keep a lot of "old books." As every librarian knows, the purchase price is not the only cost, and even gifts are not "free." Books must be housed and cared for, and the services and costs are continuing obligations.

Would that there were some "pat answers" to the questions that have been raised here; unfortunately, we have, as yet, no answers—"pat" or otherwise. At least one thing seems certain—book collectors and librarians must learn to work together rather than to compete or work at cross-purposes. You will recall that at one point in John P. Marquand's novel, *The Late George Apley*, Apley shows a guest his particularly fine collection of Chinese bronzes. After they had been admired, Apley observed that he didn't really care much for Chinese bronzes but that the Boston Museum of Fine Arts needed to have its collection enriched, so he was building a collection that would eventually be given to the museum. Here indeed is the true spirit of cooperation, a collaboration that can bring credit and distinction to both collector and librarian.

In recent years we have heard much about the science of "Futurology." Harold Lasswell has been promoting his "social planetarium," which through total sensory experience purports to show man what he and his world will be like five, ten, fifteen . . . years hence. But to the present writer, futurology is not unlike psychoanalysis; we recoil from, or are amused by, many of its absurdities and extremes. Often its practitioners are those most in need of whatever benefits it can confer. Yet both futurologist and psychiatrist may be moving in the right direction, halting and uncertain though their steps may be, always in search of answers to questions about human behavior and conduct.

The storing of unused or unusable recorded knowledge, however magnificently inscribed or bound, is as senseless as the storing of unused money. S. R. Ranganathan has given us as two of his five precepts of librarianship, "Every book its reader" and "Every reader his book," and it is well that every librarian and every book collector remember the wisdom embodied in these dicta. Knowledge for its own sake is not useful knowledge; one may even doubt that it is knowledge at all. The purpose of knowledge is to facilitate adaptive behavior, with the implicit assumption that adaptation will be beneficial to man and to society. If the futurologists are only partly right, we shall have to engage in a great deal of adapting if mankind is to survive. If we are to make the proper and wise choices, if we are to propound the correct alternatives, we must assemble and absorb a vast amount of knowledge, both old and new. Because both librarians and book collectors are custodians of the transcript, the "keepers of the Word," to use Archibald MacLeish's phrase, we like to think and speak of the library as "the memory of society," the social cortex. But the library, like the human brain, is much more than a storehouse. Like the brain it must have a long-term memory, a short-term, and a middle range; it must reject as well as acquire. Librarians cannot go on collecting indefinitely. Some astute wag has observed that he was alarmed by the growth of two things in our society— libraries and cemeteries—and suggested cremation as the solution to both. Indeed, libraries and cemeteries are unique in our society in that both are based on a constantly rising inventory. A number of years ago a distinguished scholar in operations research expressed surprise that the library of the Massachusetts Institute of Technology had not taken an inventory in more than 15 years. I explained that an inventory was very expensive and had been found to be of dubious value. I further explained that when a book was asked for that was neither charged out nor in its place on the shelves a search could be instituted and, when necessary, the missing copy replaced. "But," he exclaimed, "what about the books that are not asked for?" "If no one asks for them," I responded, "who cares whether they are there or not?" He was unconvinced and went away shaking his head in incredulity, "I don't see how a library can operate if it doesn't take an inventory." Well, most of them do operate that way, and they seem to be doing very well, too. The librarian, like Shelley's West Wind, must be both destroyer and preserver. But what do we destroy and what preserve, and for whom? "Ah, there's the rub." We must remember that graphic records and reading represent but a part of the total human experience, only one source of knowledge and information, and for many people, including even the scholar, only a very small part at that. What is preserved is only fragmentary and can be misleading. The exhibition of illuminated medieval manuscripts, for example, has created in the minds of many an assumption that the typical manuscripts of their period were objects of rare beauty. No one knows the effect that rats, mice, fire, and flood have had upon our image of the past. If we judge the future *only* by the recorded experiences of the past, we may discover that the future has gone off and left us. We must build our collections of the past always with an eye to the future. If we insist that the library is the social memory, we would do well to remember that the Red Queen told Alice that it was a great convenience to have a memory that works both ways. Alice replied that she feared her memory did not work in that fashion; she could not remember things before they had happened, to which the Queen responded, "It must be a very poor memory that works only backward." A future of both menace and promise stretches out before us, and if we are to conserve our records for its use we must evolve some notion of what it will be like and what it will want. An awareness of our social responsibilities, a memory that works both ways, a preparedness for that which is to come—these are the foundations of a conservation program, be it for librarians or book collectors.

## FOOTNOTES

[1] Archibald MacLeish, "The Premise of Meaning," *The American Scholar*, Vol. 41 (Summer 1972), p. 357.

[2] Verner Clapp, in a delightful and scholarly paper presented before the 1970 convention of the New York Library Association, has narrated the distressing, though well-meant attempts to preserve, and later restore, both the *Declaration of Independence* and the *U. S. Constitution*. One hopes that his paper will be preserved.

[3] John R. Platt, "Where Will the Books Go?" in his *The Step to Man* (New York: Wiley, 1966), pp. 3-18.

[4] Garrett Hardin, "The Last Canute," *Scientific Monthly*, Vol. 63 (September 1946), pp. 203-208. Reprinted in James V. McConnell, ed., *The Worm Returns* (Englewood Cliffs, N.J.: Prentice-Hall, 1965), pp. 103-13. Hardin's tale is best appreciated when read against the background of Fremont Rider's *The Scholar and the Future of the Research Library* (New York: Hadham Press, 1944). Rider's projections of the growth of the Yale University library caused great alarm and overshadowed his real message, which was to promote Microcards.

[5] Chauncey Brewster Tinker, "The Significance to Yale of the Gutenberg Bible," *Yale Library Gazette*, Vol. 1 (June 1926), pp. 8-9. In the version as originally presented, Tinker used "Arrow-Collar man," but with premonitions of the demise of the Arrow collar. Also, in the oral version he ad-libbed the suggestion that the money spent for the *Bible* might have been used to improve the salaries of librarians.

[6] John A. Wilson, *Thousands of Years: An Archaeologist's Search for Ancient Egypt* (New York: Scribner, 1972), p. 50.

[7] V. I. Lenin, "What Can be Done for Public Education?" *Collected Works*, Vol. 19 (London: Lawrence and Wishart, 1963), p. 277.

[8] William Goffman and Thomas G. Morris, "Bradford's Law and Library Acquisitions," *Nature*, Vol. 226 (June 6, 1970), pp. 922-23.

# 7

# Toward a Theory of Librarianship and Information Science

Libraries are a social invention, originally devised, and for centuries remaining, as repositories of the transcript of their culture. They were essentially archival in character, created to protect the important documents that were necessary for the operation of the state, the transactions of enterprise, and the transmission of religious belief and ritual. They were also centers of scholarship to which learned men could repair to consult the clay tablets, the papyrus and vellum scrolls, and eventually the codices that were needed for the advancement of teaching and inquiry. So far as the surviving record reveals, libraries were first the special responsibility of the state, but the priesthoods and private benefactors soon shared in their development. This multiplicity of functions has characterized the library to the present. They were, then, creatures of the aristocracy and the intellectual elite. It would not be practicable here to trace in any detail the organizational morphology of the library; suffice it to say that the role of the library was broadened from the 18th century on to include a variety of social functions: the support of business and industrial enterprise, of the educational system at all levels, of the popular culture, and of the growing movement for self-education. Horace Mann called the library the "crowning glory of our public schools," and a century later it was, to Alvin Johnson, "the people's university." Thus an instrumentality that was originally the exclusive concern—property, if you will—of the elite, "a nest to hatch scholars," to use John Quincy Adams' phrase, became an agent of democracy, reaching its influence out even to the underprivileged and socially disadvantaged. But always it has been a part of the fabric of society, reflecting the attitudes, values, and goals of the culture that supported it.

---

Presented to the Center for the Study of Democratic Institutions, Santa Barbara, California, November 1, 1972.

## THE PROBLEM OF THE INDIVIDUAL

The sponsorship of the library, then, has throughout history and during varying periods of time been assumed by the nobility, the priesthoods, private benefactors, voluntary associations, business and industrial enterprise, and a variety of governmental agencies represented in the public sector. The library has increased dramatically in size and complexity, has created a body of more or less standardized rules and procedures, has evolved new patterns for its administrative control, and has constantly widened its clientele. However, it has not changed its basic mission, which is to maximize the social utility of graphic records, and it is its special responsibility to operate in that complex association of record and human mind. Yet this relationship, which is at once intellectual, psychological, and physiological, is still only imperfectly understood.

Traditionally librarians have made, either implicitly or explicitly, certain *ad hoc* assumptions about books and men, and the benefits that reading the one brings to the other, but they have not seriously entertained the possibility that, under certain circumstances, and for some individuals, there may be no benefit at all. What is a book that a man may know it, and a man that he may know a book?

There is certainly nothing very esoteric or mysterious about the book as a physical entity; it is familiar to all of us. But the book as an intermediary between communicator and receptor, as a medium that bears the message, a book that can be "known," is only very imperfectly understood. We are all aware that the book as a physical object does not change, but the impact of its intellectual content varies widely from reader to reader and from time to time even with the same reader. *King Lear* when read for the first time by a college student is not the same *King Lear* read by an adult in the years of intellectual maturity. "A book is a mirror;" wrote the 18th-century German physicist and addict of aphorisms, Georg Christoph Lichtenberg, "when a jackass looks into it he cannot expect to see St. Paul looking back." We do know that for a large segment of the population, even in the highly literate Western world, the graphic record is a relatively unimportant source of knowledge. Even for those whose lives are centered about the book, graphic records form only a relatively small part of the total human experience. Harold Lasswell's "social planetarium" is predicated on the use of total sensory perception to achieve insight into what man will be like in the future. Yankee culture has always been ambivalent about the act of reading—on the one hand extolling reading as a "good" in and of itself, while on the other hand decrying "book larnin'." In spite of all our McLuhanesque babblings about the medium and the message, or the scholarly inquiries of Father Ong into the "presence of the word," the effect of the graphic record still eludes us; only your censor "knows."

But when we turn to the second part of our rhetorical question and begin to inquire into the nature of man in relation to the written word, the complexities of the problem increase sharply, for a man is a far more intricate entity than the book. As yet the neurologists, physiologists, and those who have studied the communication process in all its ramifications have been unable to tell us what happens in that mysterious chain of events that takes place from printed page to eye to brain and the behavior that results therefrom. We are concerned here, first with the process of communication itself, and second, with the problem of knowledge. The end of communication is, of course, the achievement of like-mindedness, which is not to be mistaken for *agreement*, but rather *comprehension* of the content of the message. The problem relates to the nature of knowledge itself, of the cognitive process, and of language and its capabilities and limitations in communicating the message. The nature of consciousness and cognition must necessarily be left to the neuro-physiologists and the psychologists. Knowledge may be regarded as that which results in adaptive behavior, but beyond this oversimplified definition, little is known about the nature of knowledge. Language has long been studied by the linguists without their coming to any substantial agreement about its origins or the role played by non-verbal languages. Yet all of these areas of inquiry are fundamental to the work of the librarian. With so many relevant areas yet to be explored, it is small wonder that Waples and Berelson left unanswered the question of "what reading does to people."

## SOCIAL EPISTEMOLOGY

Though the library serves mainly the individual, the ultimate objective is the betterment of society; therefore, the librarian must know not only the cognitive system of the individual, but also the communication network of society. The communication process is a duality of system and message, of that which is transmitted as well as the manner of its transmission. The librarian must view his role in the communication network as being more than a link in a chain, or even a switching-center in a network. He must also concern himself with the knowledge he communicates and the importance of that knowledge to both the individual and to society. Yet the study of the nature of knowledge, and the relationship between that structure as it has developed in contemporary Western civilization and the librarian's tools and resources for intellectual access to it, have received scant attention and no serious exploration.

We are, therefore, here concerned with the need for a new epistemological discipline, a body of knowledge about knowledge itself. The manner in which knowledge has developed and been augmented has long been a subject for study, but the ways in which knowledge is coordinated, integrated, and put to work is, as yet, an almost unrecognized field for investigation. Until recently, epistemology was a branch of speculative philosophy, concerned with *how* we know. The evolution of the science of psychology, however, left epistemology relatively poor in intellectual substance. Today, "scientific epistemology," to use

Eddington's term, has transformed the earlier philosophical and speculative approach into a scientific and largely theoretical study that is concerned with what man can not know—i.e., the limits and constraints of human knowing—but almost always these limits were seen against the background of the intellectual processes of the individual. We have not yet developed an ordered and comprehensive body of knowledge about intellectual differentiation and the integration of knowledge within a complex social organization.

The new discipline that is here envisaged we have called, for want of a better term, social epistemology, or social cognition, which should provide a framework for the investigation of the entire complex problem of the nature of the intellectual process in society—a study of the ways in which society as a whole achieves a perceptive and understanding relationship to its environment. It should lift the study of the intellectual life from that of the scrutiny of the individual to an inquiry into the means by which a society, nation, or culture achieves an understanding of the totality of stimuli that act upon it. The focus of this new discipline should be upon the production, flow, integration, and consumption of all forms of communicated thought throughout the entire social fabric.

If the librarian's bibliographic and information systems are to be structured to conform as closely as possible to man's uses of recorded knowledge, the theoretical foundations of his professional activity must take into account:

• The problem of cognition—how man knows.

• The problem of social cognition—how society knows, and the nature of the socio-psychological system by means of which personal knowledge becomes social knowledge—i.e., the knowledge possessed by a society.

• The history and philosophy of knowledge as they have evolved through time and in a variety of cultures.

• The existing bibliographic mechanisms and systems and the extent to which they are in congruence with the realities of the communication process, the findings of epistemological inquiry, and the substantive content of the body of knowledge itself.

## SOCIAL EPISTEMOLOGY, INFORMATION SCIENCE, AND THE LIBRARY

The socio-epistemological philosophy of librarianship proposed here does not exclude the important contribution that the physical sciences can make to the intellectual arsenal of the librarian. Because a culture, and the subcultures of which it is composed, is a complex social structure brought into being by men who are themselves composites of psychological, biological, and physical phenomena, the physical as well as the social sciences are relevant to the whole problem of social epistemology. If librarianship is to be concerned, as it must be, with the epistemological problem in society, it must also be inter-disciplinary. It must bring to its practitioners the methods of any number of other sciences. The term "library science" is, then, not an obfuscation invented to conceal the flimsy foundations of the scholarship of the field. The real question that librarians must ask themselves is not "Is librarianship a science?" but rather "What kind of science does, or should, librarianship represent?" Few will deny, we believe, that the human use of the graphic records of society is a scientifically based study to which all branches of human knowledge can contribute. Because librarianship is primarily concerned with the utilization of the social transcript by human beings both individually and collectively, it is fundamentally a behavioristic science, but because the methods and findings of the physical and biological sciences are being increasingly applied to the study of human behavior, librarianship must be "scientific" even in the classical use of the term. A librarian, therefore, must be a scientist, not because he may be doling out scientific literature to scientists and will perforce need to communicate intelligibly with the patrons, but because science, in its broadest sense, is the foundation of the librarian's scholarship.

The interdisciplinary focus of systems analysis and operations research has not only direct relevance to the librarian's procedures and technology, but also a symbolic meaning for the epistemological problem; for, as systems analysis directs scrutiny to the interrelations among the component parts of an operating whole, so the mark of social epistemology is that it places its emphasis upon the whole man and the whole society, and all of their ways of thinking, knowing, feeling, acting, and communicating. Science itself is a major social enterprise—carried on by individuals to be sure, but in the present day increasingly by individuals working in concert within the context or environment of educational, research, industrial, and governmental organizations and institutions.

But librarians do not live by the bread of mathematics alone, nor even by the succotash of systems analysis; to say that system is the essence of the science of librarianship states a very narrow and restricted view. The study of social epistemology, which is in reality the study of social cognition, is the proper foundation of a science of librarianship. As a study in its own right it must synthesize and draw upon the work of many disciplines, but it must always focus upon these processes by which society achieves a state of knowing and communicates its knowledge throughout its constituent parts. The librarian's responsibility is the efficient and effective management of the transcript, the graphic record of all that society knows and has recorded about itself and its world. The domain of the library includes what the social organism has learned, its values as well as its facts, its imagery as well as its reality; it is at once historical, contemporary, and anticipatory. Thus, the librarian can carry out his social responsibilities with maximum effectiveness only when he understands the cognitive processes of society and can translate that understanding into service; it is at once derivative, analytic, and synthetic.

Laurence Heilprin has admirably summarized the importance of the epistemological approach to the problems of the librarian, in reviewing an earlier work of the present writer on this subject:

> If the librarian . . . is actually an important service link in optimizing the use of graphic recorded information, then success depends on how much of this process he understands. He must see it all in profile—how we manufacture knowledge, starting with direct sense impressions and including (in science, at least) careful comparison of communicated abstractions. . . . He also will tend to *be* more of a scientist, and in particular will have to understand the way in which what once has been accepted as objective tends with the advance of knowledge to slip back into its prior state of subjectivity. If epistemology encompasses this entire field, including all of communication science, clearly a large expansion is needed in the background of the information scientist. He must at least be aware of the entire process of knowledge, and of the principal constraints on and weak points in its communication. Educators who have to construct courses to guide and instruct the information scientist cannot be less broad than those they are trying to educate. To be a competent teacher in this field will indeed be a challenge. We may conclude that perhaps the main reason why information science has progressed such a short distance as a science is that we do not understand the connections we are groping for here. Lack of knowledge of epistemology is possibly the greatest barrier to improving library and information science.[1]

Heilprin has, to all intents and purposes, made communication science virtually synonymous with information science. It is true that the physical scientists, especially the mathematicians and engineers, have captured the latter and made it their own almost to the exclusion of the librarians, who originally entered the profession largely through the humanities. Heilprin was himself originally a physicist. A reasonable consensus has been reached that information science is an area of research that explores communication phenomena and the properties of communication systems. It draws its substance and techniques from a variety of overlapping disciplines to achieve an understanding of the properties, behavior, and flow of information. It includes systems analysis, environmental aspects of information and communication, information media and language analysis, the organization of information, man-systems relationships, and any other discipline, either established or in the process of development, that might promise to throw light on a particular area of inquiry. By "communication," the information scientist means any kind of knowledge through any medium or environment. But merely to state the definition reveals how very far we are from understanding the nature and behavior of information and the social manifestations of it.

Robert Fairthorne sees in information science "a dangerous tendency to bring in any and every science or technique or phenomenon under the information science heading." He saw in this emerging discipline no "common principles," and one does not create common principles by giving different things the same name. We have no quarrel with the scientist and the engineer—both can make substantial contributions to what we have called social epistemology; but pouring the complex study of social cognition into only the scientific mould denies the obvious fact that man is a social being. He derives information from an infinite array of sources from which he shapes and reshapes his behavior. Nor should the humanities be overlooked, for they, too, have an important role in the cognitive process. It is entirely possible that a scientist can derive as much insight into a problem he is investigating by listening to a symphony as by reading a scientific paper or report. Playing in an amateur quartet may be much more than relaxation for the chemist; it may be an integral part of the creative process. A dream of snakes with their tails in their mouths, rolling like hoops, gave Kekulé the inspiration for the benzine ring. The study of the cognitive process in society can illuminate even the most remote areas of intellectual activity regardless of the methods and techniques that it may borrow from other disciplines.

Already the Russians have subordinated information science to the social sciences. A special committee reporting to the Council for Mutual Economic Assistance has written, "Information Science is a discipline belonging to Social Science which studies the structure and general characteristics of scientific information and also general laws governing all scientific communication processes." But though the Russians have made information science a branch of the social sciences, the focus is still upon *scientific* communication. There would certainly seem to be no valid reason why other substantive areas should not be explored. The information scientist does not, or should not, restrict himself to scientific information.

Our contemporary culture is, of course, deeply rooted in Science, with a capital *S*, and for better or worse it shapes the daily lives of all of us. But recently there has been a growing disillusionment with what the scientists and engineers are doing to society; we are discovering that Science will not solve all the ills by which we are beset, as we so naively once thought it would. Science can be used to destroy as well as to create, and today it is doing both remarkably well. It now seems quite likely that the problems of the "seventies" are much more apt to be in the social, rather than the physical, sciences. Indeed, many of the tasks that confront us will be the correction of social ills that are the heritage of a misuse of Science. Policy at the national, state, and local levels and in all forms of organization, whether in the public or private sectors, derives from the point at which cognition (knowledge of the facts) and conceptualization (judgment) meet and interact. Or, to express the idea with a different analogy, policy results from a parallelogram of two forces—cognition, "telling it like it is"; and conceptualization, the interpretation of those facts in the light of experience, derived from the immediate environment and an understanding of the past.

## THE LIBRARIAN AND THE MACHINE

Perhaps no aspect of librarianship has aroused so much interest, not to say curiosity, in the public mind as mechanized information retrieval; and none has been so unproductive. As early as the late 1930s, Frederick Kepple, then executive director of the Carnegie Corporation of New York, foresaw in the Hollerith tabulating machines the possibility of searching literature when the text was coded in a way appropriate to the machine's capabilities. Hope sprang anew, after World War II, with the development of large-scale general-purpose computers, or "giant brains." One should not say that all attempts to automate indexing, abstracting and literature searching have been a failure, however, for work on the problem is still going forward in many places, and it seems inconceivable that an innovation as inherently powerful as the computer would leave the problem of the library untouched. Nevertheless, the reasons for inconspicuous success up to the present time are numerous. First, the costs of development and the use of such examples as we do have are so great as to be economically impractical. Second, experimentation began with the engineering aspects of the problem; that is, machines were built that were monuments to the engineers' art, but no one knew quite what to do with them when they were built. Technology preceded theory, "software" had been neglected in deference to "hardware," and few understood the linguistic, logical, and organizational problems involved. The result has been that most of the machines have been, not *information* retrieval mechanisms but *document* retrieval devices—electronic stack-boys rather than electronic reference librarians. These machines have emulated the physical behavior of the librarian rather than his intellectual processes. The engineers saw the motions of the librarian as he "fetched and carried," as the early explorers of flight sought to copy the birds. There is as yet no theory of "aero-dynamics" in librarianship.

But to say that the computer has not yet fulfilled its promise as an acceptable instrument for information retrieval does not imply that its coming has been without benefit to the library world. For many library housekeeping operations—fiscal control, circulation records, the preparation of catalogs—the computer has been eminently successful. Moreover, on-line shared-time systems used in conjunction with closed-circuit television have greatly expedited the growth of library networks, such as that of the Ohio College Library Center in Columbus, to the substantial advantage of the participating libraries. Increasingly, libraries are making use of machine-readable tapes produced by other libraries, such as the MARC project at the Library of Congress and comparable services performed by the National Library of Medicine. In such library-related operations as the production of indexes and concordances, the computer has lifted a heavy manual burden of scholarly spade-work. A very limited success has also been achieved in automated abstracting, though its efficiency in this area is yet to be proved. Will these adaptations of the computer become increasingly beneficial as experience is gained? That cataloging and, eventually, reference services in the library will be drastically changed in the not-far-distant future by computer technology has, I am afraid, been an all-too-easy assumption. The god may not be in the machine, after all.

Yet, Archibald MacLeish has pointed out that miraculous as these electronic contraptions are, they have become available

> precisely at a time when the great human need is not for additional information or more rapid information or more universally available information but for the comprehension of the enormous quantities of existing information the scientific and other triumphs of the last several generations have already dumped into our minds. It is not additional 'messages' we need, and least of all additional 'messages' which merely tell us that the medium which communicates the message has changed the world. We *know* the world has changed. . . . What we do not know is how, precisely, it is changing and in what direction and with what consequences to ourselves.[2]

"The application of knowledge to urgent problems," writes Eugene Rostow in a recent issue of the *Yale Alumni Magazine*, presupposes the existence of a body of knowledge that could be applied to their solution. But in many areas, although we have plenty of enthusiasm for the work of applied policy, we have no policy to apply. . . . Our world today is more unstable and more threatening than any universe in which man has had to live, at least since the collapse of the Roman Empire."[3]

Perhaps the greatest contribution that the computer is making to librarianship and may be expected to make in the foreseeable future is not the efficiency that it might be assumed to bring to library operations, but the subtle and intangible way it has of compelling librarians, for the first time, to think analytically and creatively about what they are doing and whether they should be doing it. The computer has given librarians a whole new frame of reference for the methods and techniques which, over the years, they have come unquestioningly to accept as axiomatic. There has been considerable debate in the computer community over whether or not computers can be made which will "think." The debate is a futile one and most of it rests on purely semantic notions. However, there would seem to be a certain reciprocity of relationship between what the applied mathematicians and engineers are doing and the investigations of the cognitive process by the neuro-physiologists and psychologists. As man learns more about the nature of thought he will doubtless be able to fabricate mechanisms that simulate thought, whether they actually "think" or not. And as we learn more about computers we should be able to derive increasingly perceptive insights into the operation of the brain and the central nervous system. To know more than we do now about how man learns—both man as an individual and mankind collectively—is an exciting prospect for both teacher and librarian. But it raises some serious, not to say frightening, problems respecting the possibility of eventual thought control that will make our present concern over censorship pale into insignificance; here would be the ultimate brainwashing. But man is not likely to impose upon himself a moratorium on inquiry; certainly, he has not done so in the past. If we eventually come to understand the process of personal and social cognition, we must also develop an ethic and the necessary controls that will keep it out of the hands of the unscrupulous. We cannot answer Thomas Huxley's question, "What are you going to do with all these new things?" by concerning ourselves only with man's place in nature, as philosophy and science have done in the past, while ignoring man's place in the new environment created by "all these new things." As Elting Morison has pointed out, the rate of change, the uniformity, the repetitiousness of mechanized labor, the mass and tempo of change, all create in the environment conditions that are beyond the human powers of accommodation. The result is a sense of alienation that is intensified by the fact that though the system may have an intellectual and empirical integrity it has no apparent purpose beyond effective operation. Libraries, even highly mechanized and efficiently operated libraries, should not exist to give librarians something to do, though we confess to having seen some libraries that would seem to have no other *raison d'être*. More than ever our society appears to need what libraries have to offer, but what the nature of that need is, and how it should be met, is still unclear.

## THE FLIGHT FROM BIBLIOGRAPHY

"Bibliography bears its investigating torch into all parts of knowledge," wrote Gustave Mouravit, in praising the Burnet system of bibliographic classification when it was at the height of its popularity more than a century ago. Yet almost at the very time that Mouravit was declaring the importance of bibliography to the world of scholarship, and describing the bibliographic problem as being central to the librarian's responsibilities, librarians, inspired by a vision of the library as the great agency of universal education, were turning their backs on their bibliographic heritage. There was nothing inherently wrong, of course, in the librarians' broadening their services and reaching out to "the common man," who then seemed, and still is, the hope of democracy. But when the librarians began to proselyte, they were led to forget that librarianship is fundamentally a bibliographic enterprise regardless of the sophistication of the clientele. We are here, of course, using "bibliography" in its broadest sense, not merely to be confined to the compiling of bibliographies. By the term "bibliographic activity" we would mean to include all those operations, functions, and insights that are required to bring book and user together in an intellectually rewarding experience, and not just putting together, under appropriate headings, a listing of titles. The librarians failed to perceive that one cannot serve the library needs of the "common man," by being a common librarian, any more than a good children's librarian can be a child. To bring books and people together intellectually requires a certain body of knowledge and skills, a certain expertise, which has not been appreciated and for which our present system of education for librarianship has not prepared its students.

The bibliographic enterprise is composed of three constituent elements: *acquisition*, which means knowing what materials to acquire and how to acquire them; *organization*, the arrangement and analysis of the materials so that their intellectual content will be appropriately available; and *service*, which is assistance to the reader. Traditionally these functions have been kept separate on the organization chart of most libraries, each department with its own staff. This practice we believe to have been a mistake, for these elements are not isolates but parts of an integrated whole. Conventionally, we have thought in terms of acquisition librarians, catalogers, and reference librarians, when we should have been thinking of subject specialists who have the competence to unite in themselves the three basic capabilities represented in their subject, or substantive branch of knowledge. A librarian is not just a librarian, he is a librarian of something, a librarian in a specific subject field, and it is, therefore, the librarian's substantive knowledge, rather than the tricks of the librarian's trade, that make him the bibliographer he should be. "What is a book to a librarian?" MacLeish asked the audience assembled for the dedication of the Scott Library at York University in Toronto. "Is it merely the unit of collection, a more or less fungible (as the lawyers put it) object made of paper, print, and protective covering that fulfills its bibliographical destiny by being classified as to subject and cataloged by author and title and properly shelved?"[4] Unfortunately, there are far too many librarians who see bibliography as being no more than such mechanical routines. Just as we would have the computerized information retrieval system be something more than an electronic stack boy, the librarian should be more than a check-girl in a bibliothecal package room. The librarian, to fulfill his destiny, must know the subject field over which he presides, the literature of that field, and must be able to communicate to those who seek his services as one of their peers. To modify the Indian proverb, he must have walked a mile in the patron's moccasins. Yet few librarians have made such a journey.

Libraries have not, as they should have, taken into account subject specialization in the organization of their staffs. To be sure, some of the larger research libraries have used subject bibliographers, where it was forced upon them by linguistic necessity—thus, bibliographers in the Oriental, Middle-Eastern, and Slavic languages are certainly not unknown in large academic libraries where graduate offerings in those areas have made them a necessity. There have also been specialized library facilities to serve particular groups within the university community, of which the industrial and labor relations centers at Chicago, Cornell, Illinois, and elsewhere are good examples. But often the personnel for these specialties are drawn, not from the ranks of the librarians, who receive no adequate preparation for such duties in their professional education, but from the subject field itself. Yet, despite the success of these little principalities within the library empire, librarians have not imaginatively redrawn their general organization charts in terms of subject and bibliographic functions so that acquisition, organization, and service could be subordinate to the subject departmental structure. What would seem to be most needed is a modification of the area study programs in the university curriculum adapted to the departmental structure of the library. Though librarians still pay lip service to bibliography as being central to their profession, it is not reflected either in their professional preparation or in practice.

## THE PATTERN OF THE FUTURE AND ITS MEANING
## FOR THE LIBRARIAN'S PROFESSIONAL EDUCATION

What, then, are the most conspicuous strands that comprise the warp and woof of the library fabric and that are most likely to set the pattern for the future? In the opinion of the present writer, the most important would seem to be the growth of library networks, systems in which the total bibliographic resources of an area or region can be brought to bear at any one point in the whole. For decades librarians have talked about the values of cooperation, and now, at long last, they would appear to be making some progress toward its realization. Libraries can no longer afford the luxury of unrestrained growth, if indeed they ever could; the burden of acquisition must be shared. At a time when the technology of communication is making such impressive advances as it is today, to continue to assemble libraries and information centers in isolation from the other segments of the library community is both economically wasteful and professionally exhausting.

The consolidation of resources represented by the network also makes possible and economically attainable a new type of librarian for which the present writer has long argued—a true bibliographic subject specialist. In the past, such expertise has been denied many libraries because their budgets could not accommodate such highly trained personnel. But once this demand for the specialist materializes and becomes a characteristic of the labor force, the professional education of the librarian will need a thorough, and long overdue, reconstruction. These networks then, should be more than a system of electronic linkages; they should be truly integrated federations of libraries that can be planned without regard to the artificial barriers of political divisions. Such networks can make of the library the great information resource that many of us have long desired, but that in the past has so often escaped our grasp and left dreams unfulfilled.

Closely allied to the emergence of networks is the growing interest among librarians in general systems theory. Admittedly systems concepts have been drawn from a diversity of disciplines, each with its own jargon and emphasis, and it is the nature of organized systems that they present themselves differently to different observers. Yet these theories do provide new and fruitful modes of unification, binding together apparently unrelated areas of discourse or spheres of human activity and thought. To librarianship the value of general systems theory would seem to be this: it makes it possible for the first time to study, and to provide the tools for that study, the library and its operations from an holistic frame of reference; as has so often been true in the past, the library has been fragmented into a cluster of specific operations, often without relation to each other, and lacking the realization that what affects one part may have serious repercussions in others. The value of general systems theory to the librarian is yet to be tested, but certainly it promises a profound revolution in science and other areas of thought, and it now appears that it can give to the librarian insights and comprehension that have long been lacking.

Automation and related technologies, together with the rise of information science, are, in a limited way and despite disappointments and as yet unfulfilled promises, already making some significant contributions to the library's operations, especially those repetitive tasks that are mechanical rather than intellectual.[5] Other and far-reaching developments may be expected to follow during the coming generation, but perhaps most important of all they signify a shift from the humanities, which for so many centuries dominated librarianship, to the physical, biological, and social sciences. The humanities still hold an important place in the librarian's arsenal of capabilities, but we are beginning to get a much more balanced intellectual attack upon library problems than has previously existed.

But we must not let our enthusiasms for electronic gadgetry obscure the basic fact that, at least to the present time, it has done no more than substitute one technology for another. We are only doing by mechanical means that which we have always done. A computer-produced catalog is no different in its underlying principles from the conventional card catalog with which we are all familiar. We should not decry the benefits that a new technology can bring, but neither should we assume that it represents a fundamental change in the theory of the library art.

Stimulated perhaps by growing unemployment in other academic and professional areas of intellectual endeavor, recruits to librarianship are increasingly bringing with them advanced study in the academic disciplines; librarianship should profit from this "invasion." This situation recapitulates in large measure that of the depression of the 1930s, when librarianship was greatly strengthened by the addition to its ranks of young scholars, well trained in a substantive field, who turned to librarianship to escape the economic stringency besetting their original career choices. But librarianship, too, is already feeling the pinch of depression, so how long the present situation will continue is problematical. For the moment, at least, the library world should be the beneficiary of the "ill wind" of others.

Finally, in this brief catalog of current trends in librarianship, there is the growing awareness that the library, especially the public library, does have an obligation to be relevant to today's social needs, to use the jargon of the young activists, and to extend its services to the disadvantaged, the deprived, and the rejected minorities. We are concerned when the librarian tries to play social worker, but certainly he, or she, should cooperate with the social worker in bringing the power of the recorded word to bear upon the serious social problems plaguing our communities. Actually, though the clientele may be markedly different from the past, the nature of the librarian's task may not be so drastically changed. As John Gardner has said in *The Recovery of Confidence*,

> Young idealists who profess utter emancipation from the past pour out torrents of words about the values they wish to live by, and lo, they turn out to be, for the most part, updated versions of very old values. True, the values have been ignored, traduced, lied about, manipulated, and falsified. But that only says that they need rescuing.[6]

To change an agency created by and for the scholarship of an elite to one that serves the informational needs of the masses will present some problems, but the transformation is not impossible, and the survival of democracy may depend, in part, on just such a change.

Even this brief listing of the more conspicuous changes that are now taking place in librarianship should be sufficient to emphasize the need for a complete renovation of the librarian's professional education. Despite the progress that has been made in the training of the librarian since the end of World War II, and there have been impressive gains, the overwhelming reaction of the present writer, after a quarter of a century of library school teaching and administration, is a great lack of enthusiasm for it. This is probably a terrible confession for me to make, especially after having just published a 500-page book on the subject, but it is not easy to react otherwise and retain one's intellectual integrity. It is difficult to escape the conclusion that library education represents what is, perhaps, least important in the librarian's professional equipment, and that what makes a good librarian good is his mastery and understanding of the substantive knowledge represented by the materials over which he presides. The library should be the "crowning glory" of our educational system, and not, as the sixth president of the United States said, merely "a nest in which to hatch scholars." The needs of the scholar are certainly not to be minimized, but the library should also be a place to which the good citizen can turn to make himself a better, more enlightened, citizen. Therefore, the first need of the librarian is a good general or liberal education. For if there is any profession whose practitioners should "see life steady and see it whole," it is certainly librarianship. The conclusion would seem to be so obvious as to make argument unnecessary; yet one of the great problems confronting the library school today is the number of students who come to its doors lacking just such secondary and undergraduate preparation.

Beyond general education there is subject specialization in a respectable academic discipline, which should be pursued by the student to at least the level of the master's degree, and preferably beyond. The library recruit should bring to the library school a thorough education in the literature of his chosen field, the structure of that literature, its "land mark" contributions, its schools of thought, its problems, and the advances toward their solution. Thus equipped, he should be able to communicate with and even anticipate the needs of the scholar, while not damaging his capacity to present to the intelligent layman, or the layman with little formal education, the relevance of that field to the needs of the citizen. With such a background, the student should be ready to pursue his professional training, which should emphasize the bibliographic aspects of his specialty, administrative and management theory, and communication theory and information science as they all relate to library functions and practices. There will be those, of course, who will argue that such a program will be so expensive that it will place the librarian economically beyond the reach of the small to medium-sized communities. But a doctor in a small town does not need to know less medicine than his colleague in the city. Moreover, the growth of library systems should bring these human resources within the budgetary limits of the smaller urban centers. The question is not, can we afford such librarians as are here envisaged, but can we afford not to have them? The farmer is as important a part of the democratic system as the city dweller, and he has as much of a right to the best library resources as his brother on Fifth Avenue. Realistically, of course, the opportunities possessed by the two can never be completely equal, but certainly the differential does not need to be as great as it is today. In the language of the marketplace, librarianship has not "sold itself" to the community in the way it should; on the other hand, let us face it, it has not had too much to sell.

In the past the education of the librarian has, by implication at least, been predicated on the possibility of attaining an encyclopedic mastery of all knowledge. But that objective was never quite possible to realize, and attempts to achieve it end in either pedantry or dilettantism. A truly educated man is not one who knows "everything," but one who is constantly learning. In urging that the librarian prepare himself to qualify as a subject specialist, we are not suggesting that he be what is often described as a "narrow specialist." He who is narrowly expert is often only broadly ignorant, and his broad ignorance will make him an inadequate specialist. What gives depth and meaning to specialized knowledge is the general education upon which it is based and from which it is intellectually derived.

Perhaps the librarians should have concerned themselves with the way the encyclopedists organized knowledge; perhaps they should have regarded, as did Diderot and d'Alembert, knowledge as a unified whole, a system of interrelated sub-systems, rather than as pigeon-holed and ticketed into the neat little compartments of the Dewey Decimal system. Librarians have paid dearly for their failure to study the classification and organization of knowledge, for they thereby lost a perspective, a sense of unity of purpose, that they badly needed. Again, systems theory has relevance, for knowledge itself is an integrated system brought together through the organizing capacity of the human intellect. A library is not, or should not be, a multi-volume almanac or book of facts.

A word, and for present purposes no more than that, should be added about research in librarianship, whose state distresses many of us even more than that of library education itself, since so much time and effort are being wasted on matters that are trivial. The most important single fact about research in librarianship (in its epistemological relationships) is that much of it cannot be done by librarians. The librarian's scholarship is derivative. It must wait upon the results of inquiry in such fields as linguistics, anthropology, the social and physical sciences generally, physiology, medicine, systems analysis, communication theory, the science (if there be one) of administration and management, education, learning theory, and a host of other disciplines. Many of these branches of knowledge have given librarians tools with which they can cultivate their own fields of inquiry, but the librarians must either learn to use these unfamiliar tools or call upon the assistance of those skilled in their use. Librarians must stop toying with these tools in the pretense that they are pushing back the frontiers of knowledge. A continuing dialogue between the librarians and the appropriate scholars in relevant fields there must be, but it must not stop with the exchange of words. The librarian who desires to engage in honest research must become so knowledgeable about the fields related to his inquiries that he can select from them and apply them to his own research in valid and fruitful ways. Form, method, and technique, much less imitation, are not the essence of inquiry. One does not produce valid research by playing the sedulous ape to the methodists in their white aprons, in the hope that form will yield substance.

## THE BURDEN OF THE LIBRARY

There are, for the human mind, but two sources, broadly speaking, of knowledge, wisdom, and truth—experience and record, typified in our culture by the laboratory and the library. The purist will argue, of course, and quite rightly, that both are experience (one direct and the other vicarious), but it will not serve our purpose here to debate semantics. The point is that the library as the main repository for record is a major source of vicarious experience. Yet few agencies in our society, including the educational system, have suffered such neglect and are so confused about what they are supposed to do. The founding fathers of the Republic were right in insisting that the success of a democracy depends upon an enlightened electorate, and that man must learn to act so that it can truthfully be said that "the voice of the people is the voice of God." Yet today the problems of our nation have become so complex that rational action, even for the most enlightened, becomes almost an impossibility.

Underlying all our problems, in this writer's view, is that of uncontrolled population growth; to it almost all our other ills can be traced. Even with the remedies now available it seems entirely possible that the will to use them may be coming too late, especially in those parts of the world in which remedial measures are most needed. The Rev. Thomas Malthus may be proved right after all: it may be that population, even in Western Europe and on the American continent, increases more rapidly than the means of subsistence. But probably uppermost in the minds of the majority is the folly of the brutal and absurd war in Vietman, which has not only shamefully wasted our physical and human resources, both ours and theirs, but also, even worse, has eroded our national character to a point unequalled since the moral decay of the Athenians that followed the Peloponnesian war, from which Athens never recovered. Hard upon the heels of these catastrophes come such concerns as the destruction of the environment; the rising tide of crime; the increase in drug traffic and addiction; the problem of race relations in all its subtlety and ugliness; inflation; and, for our country particularly, the international monetary situation. But there are other social problems that are much less conspicuous than those just mentioned: the increasing mobility of our population, which destroys man's roots in the soil and makes all life seem transitory and merely a series of episodes; the loosening of ties that once bound family and friends so securely; an economy so heavily dependent on the automobile that all else must be sacrificed to it; the problem of readjustment to automation, the profitable use of leisure time resulting therefrom, and the need for retraining personnel for service, rather than productive occupations that are directed toward the making of "things" (in the library the proper use of automation has frequently drained away resources that might better have been invested in the acquisition of materials or the improvement of the bibliographic competence of the staff); distrust of all governmental institutions together with the apathetic acceptance of corruption as a part of "politics"; the wresting of power from Congress by the Executive which seems to suggest a potential for dictatorship greater than this writer has ever seen; the growth of censorship and the restrictions being imposed by government on the news media; the artificial stimulation of "wants" beyond the economic ability of many to fulfill, which is the curse that uncontrolled salesmanship has placed upon us; and the decay of standards of moral conduct, which is by no means confined to the young. The list is impressive and bewildering; small wonder that youth is in revolt.

We would not, of course, maintain that the library has the key to unlock the solutions to all of these problems, but certainly its resources, when properly used, can provide badly needed insights into the character of the problems, the solutions that have been attempted in the past, and possible alternative courses of action. But a book that is never read, no matter how potentially valuable, is worthless. The library cannot force its services upon an unwilling or unprepared body politic. It must depend upon the school to create an intellectual climate in which youth and adult will voluntarily seek the benefits that the library can provide, and the schools are not doing so. If the end of education is to develop the capacity to propound alternatives, then the educational system in its entirety—meaning the school, the library, and the agencies of adult education—must work together to create an enlightened electorate capable of rational choice. Yet not in the memory of this writer has the public been so sheep-like, and has democracy so trembled on the brink of disaster. We would not "cry havoc" or surrender to despair, but we have never forgotten from our undergraduate years, a sentence with which that distinguished sociologist, E. A. Ross, concluded one of the chapters of his introductory text in sociology: "Humanity," he wrote, "has a perilous knife-edge to travel, and humanity may fail." These words were written, mark you, just after we had concluded a war of which it was said that "we stood at Armageddon and we battled for the Lord," and that in so doing the world had been made "safe for democracy." Yet little more than a decade later an unknown Austrian house-painter would "let slip the dogs of war," and after that Korea and Vietnam and terror of the bomb—all from a country that boasts that it has the finest public library system in the world.

## FOOTNOTES

[1] Edward B. Montgomery, ed., *The Foundations of Access to Knowledge; A Symposium* (Syracuse, N.Y.: Syracuse University Press, 1968), pp. 26-27.

[2] Archibald MacLeish, *Champion of a Cause* (Chicago: American Library Association, 1971), p. 246.

[3] Eugene V. Rostow, "In Defense of the Ivory Tower," *Yale Alumni Magazine*, Vol. 35 (June 1972), pp. 4, 6.

[4] Archibald MacLeish, "The Premise of Meaning," *American Scholar*, Vol. 41 (Summer 1972), p. 357.

[5] Nevertheless, despite the promise of the computer, even for repetitive tasks, it is only fair to report that in at least one situation replacement of the computer by human beings has proved profitable. The *Wall Street Journal* for February 15, 1972, announced that at the California Commission for Teacher Preparation and Licensing, elimination of the computer in favor of human skills enabled the agency to reduce its staff from 240 to 106 and pare the time for processing credentials from 95 days to 10. As one agency official expressed it, "The computer was a good worker, but it just couldn't compete with people."

[6] Quoted in the *Christian Science Monitor*, June 29, 1972.

# 8

# Apologia pro Vita Nostra

Man tends to rise, according to the Peter Principle, "to the level of his incompetence," but librarians seem to sink—at least, so it has always appeared. They have an innate sense of inferiority about what they do that beclouds their professional identity. Doctors understand that their mission is to cure people of disease, lawyers know that their business is the law, and teachers do not question their responsibility to instruct the young. Librarians, by contrast, are never sure what they are supposed to do, or so it seems to us on the south side of those vast inland seas known as the Great Lakes. Hence the *apologia* of our title has a kind of *double entendre*. The doctor struggled upward from witchcraft and sorcery. The chemist required centuries to free himself from alchemy. Science emerged from magic. But librarianship began as the highest form of scholarship—the man of all learning, the polyhistor, searching the writings of the past for their meaning. So it was with the scholar-librarians of the Ancient World, the monastic recluses of the Middle Ages, the learned men of the Renaissance, and on into the rise of science and the revolution in thought that was the Enlightenment. So it also was in the Eastern Empire when Constantinople was the seat of learning and the preserver of Graeco-Roman culture. Over the centuries the role of the librarian was clear: he was, when not himself a productive scholar, the staff on which the scholar leaned most heavily; he knew the scholar's needs and he knew his books. His library was for the intellectual elite and he was of the elite himself. He did not worry about his social position or his professional status. In short, he knew who he was. He was the grammarian Euphorion, brought to Antioch by Antiochus the Great to be librarian of the royal library. He was Richard de Bury planning an ambitious library for Oxford

Reprinted from the *IPLO Quarterly* (Institute of Professional Librarians of Ontario), Vol. 14 (July 1972), pp. 7-19.

University. He was Gabriel Naudé scouring the book marts of Europe for Cardinal Mazarin. He was the historian Beluze building a library for the French minister, Colbert. He was Joseph Green Cogswell exploring the book resources of both Europe and America for John Jacob Astor. Yes, he was even William Smith Shaw, stuffing the pockets of his greatcoat with books as he moved among his Bostonian friends, exclaiming, "Sir, the Athenaeum must have this," so have it he must, and have it he will, and have it he does.

Then, toward the close of the 19th century, librarianship turned a corner into a new and different world. No one has as yet been able convincingly to explain what happened, why the library altered its course and became centrifugal rather than centripetal. There were probably many reasons for the change—the proliferation of print, which may have robbed librarianship of some of its intellectual glamor; the rise of democracy and universal education, which tended to discredit the older view of the library as the property of the elite; the growth of libraries themselves, which forced institutionalization upon them; or the decay of the scholarly tradition in all aspects of 20th-century life. But whatever the reason, or reasons, librarians forsook their earlier bibliographic orientation and became administrators, managers, and social missionaries seeking to spread the gospel of enlightenment to the masses.

To be sure, the proud scholarly tradition lingered on. There were still such names as William Frederick Poole, John Shaw Billings, Joseph Sabin, Wilberforce Eams, Charles Evans, J. Christian Bay, and Lawrence C. Wroth, but the ranks were growing thin.

Now, it is not our intention to suggest that these changes were bad; indeed, they were wholly admirable. The role of the library in supporting universal public education and in elevating the level of popular culture cannot justly be criticized. Moreover, many libraries had suffered seriously from bad, or at least weak, administrative practices. Scholarship and administrative competence do not go hand-in-hand. Many of the most scholarly librarians were very poor administrators. But the new librarianship did exert some unfortunate side-effects, to borrow the jargon of medicine. The change left many librarians confused as to their true role. It directed their professional activities, especially their professional associations, away from scholarship and toward promotional efforts. The occupational fortunes of librarians began to overshadow all other considerations. Some unhealthy, if not unholy, alliances began to be formed between librarians and the book trade or the manufacturers of library equipment. The professional associations became special interest groups, and the change wrought real havoc to the programs of library schools. In short, the change brought to librarianship a kind of modified trade-unionism.

So far have the librarians drifted away from their traditional bibliographic role that Archibald MacLeish, in dedicating the new library at York University in Toronto, could ask, not entirely rhetorically:

> . . . what is a book in a collection?—a book in a library?—to a librarian? Is it merely the unit of collection, a more or less fungible (as the lawyers put it) object made of paper, print and protective covering that fulfills its bibliographical destiny by being classified as to subject and being cataloged by author and title and properly shelved? Or is it something very different? Is it still a book? Is it, indeed, something more than a book, being a book selected to compose with other books in a library? But, if so, what has it become?[1]

This distinguished poet and former Librarian of Congress sees the librarian as being much more than a hewer of wood or drawer of water at the beck and call of the patron. The questions he has raised are certainly not new, though he has given voice to them only recently; they have troubled librarians for more than half a century. So librarians, grown quite conscious of the tarnish that has besmirched their once bright shields, turned to professionalism to remove the stain, rather than asking, as they might have done, what it was that had polluted their intellectual environment.

Librarianship, the argument ran, has been an acknowledged and honorable profession ever since King Assurbanipal founded the royal library at Nineveh. We are librarians, therefore we are professionals and what we do is, by definition, professional too; and page after page of polemic has been written to clinch the point. Librarians ransacked their own libraries in search of a reliable definition of a profession and, having found it, said, "See how neatly librarianship fits the terms." But agreement was not universal; there were those, mainly non-librarians, who declared that "The Emperor has no clothes," and that the terms of the definition were not met by what most librarians of today actually do.[2] Sterile as the debate has become, one more review can be justified on the grounds that it does shed some light on the librarians' attempt to understand themselves; to discover their own identity; to ascertain what is unique to librarianship and makes it what it is, differentiating it from all other forms of human activity.

What, then, is a professional person? The linguist, or lexicographer, would doubtless point out that the adjective derives from the verb *to profess*, and the professional, like the professor, is one who subscribes to a belief, a creed, or a body of knowledge, especially a body of theoretical knowledge. Over the years, however, the term has been expanded to include a cluster of characteristics, or precepts, that have been used to identify a particular human activity as being professional. Most of those who have written on the subject in recent years have, either directly or indirectly, adopted the classical definition of the term set forth by Abraham Flexner when, in 1915, he wrote of social work as a profession.[3] For present purposes, however, Justice Louis D. Brandeis' definition is adequate. A profession is, he says:

> . . . an occupation requiring extensive preliminary intellectual training pursued primarily for others and not merely oneself, and accepting as a measure of achievement one's contribution to society rather than financial reward.[4]

For centuries only law, medicine, theology, and teaching possessed credentials sufficient to qualify them as professions; but, because great prestige was attached to and implicit in the term, other activities began vigorously to seek its sanctions. Words 'wear out,' or lose their significance often with astonishing rapidity, and so it has been with *profession*. Today, there are few occupations who do not think of themselves as professions. When the present writer was young, an automobile tire repairman set himself up as a 'tireologist,' and the *Oxford English Dictionary* cites a use of the term in which a baker was referred to as being in "the muffin profession." Even the time-honored criterion that the professional works for public service rather than financial reward has lost its meaning in the usage of *professional* as opposed to *amateur*.

Such linguistic deterioration, then, seems to make meaningless the long debate over whether librarianship is a profession, but the *identity* of the librarian *qua* librarian is not to be taken lightly. Nor are librarians alone in this renewed search for identity; other professions are experiencing the same reappraisal of their activities *vis-à-vis* their role in society.[5] Let us, therefore, give up this foolish chase after the elusive will-o'-the-wisp of professionalism. Despite its deterioration and the stamp of social approval that it no longer brings, there is about it something of the quality of the hedonic paradox. The pursuit of professionalism, like the search for pleasure or happiness as the chief end of life, is not to be found in and of itself, but is the result of selfless devotion to service to others. Let us not make of ourselves the Epicureans, so to speak, of the intellectual life. Rather, let us address ourselves to the important question of the identity of the librarian as a librarian and the meaning of that role in and to society.

If the lessons of history mean anything at all, it would seem axiomatic that the primary concern of the librarian is with graphic records, with the transcript of the culture, with bibliography in its broadest sense. *Biblioteki Froneos Medeontes*—libraries are the guardians of knowledge—was the motto chosen for *Beta Phi Mu* when that honor library fraternity was founded; but by "guardian" the founding fathers did not mean that the contents of the library were to be preserved for only those clerks, as Naudé has said, with clean hands. The fact that history has shown libraries to have always been for the intellectually elite does not mean that the library is to remain forever closed to those from the ghetto or the slum who might wish to seek its benefits. The fact that the library has been, and the present writer hopes will remain, a place for reading, for thought, for serious contemplation, probably means that a relatively small proportion of the population will come to its doors, cerebral activity never having been popular with the majority. Sidney Ditzion wrote of the public library as the "arsenal of a democratic culture," but he did not mean that it was to be surrounded by fortifications that only the most intrepid and determined could penetrate. The library cannot divorce itself from the life that flows about its pillared entrance. But neither can it follow every meandering path that trails across the map of the human adventure or it will surely lose its way.

Today librarianship, along with most other occupations, is being pressured to become "relevant"; to stand against war, against despoiling of the environment, against poverty, crime, censorship, and prejudice. But which of these is the proper responsibility of the librarian as librarian and which the concern of the librarian as a good citizen? The two roles are easily confused. The answers are not to be found in some vague concept of professionalism, but in a clear understanding of what librarianship is and what the librarian's social responsibilities are. Libraries do not exist to give librarians something to do, yet we all know that librarians do make purposes of practices, and do create mechanisms—card catalogs, classification schemes, vertical files—that threaten to turn a justifiable means into the ultimate justification of an end.

In the middle and later years of the 19th century, those laymen who were urging the establishment of public libraries assumed that it was a right and proper obligation of a democracy to maintain collections of books, books of lasting value, to which anyone could have recourse if he so wished. But it never occurred to them that it might be a concern of government if the people did not wish to expose themselves to these assembled writings. Doubtless they assumed that a supply of such books would create its own demand, and young men would forsake the grog-shop for the library and young women would be saved, as one writer expressed it, "from those depths of degradation to which only a woman can fall." Whatever the response of the public, the obligation of government ended when it provided the *means* for "self-improvement," the means by which the citizen could improve his lot. Not many generations were to pass, however, until government, and the public which gave it power, began to realize that increasing population and industrialization were making the maintenance of a democracy a very complicated undertaking indeed—especially when it was being threatened by the simpler and more direct affirmations of the dictatorship. Self-government of a people, especially when those people number into the millions, are spread over a large geographic area, and possess many ethnic and cultural heritages and economic interests, raises problems that have not yet been solved; but they are problems for which, somehow, a solution must be found if the democracy is to survive. No one need be surprised, therefore, if questions are raised about the capacity of a people to govern themselves, or the amount of freedom a democratic society can tolerate without disastrous consequences. In raising such questions one is, of course, not challenging the value of a democracy or its superiority over other forms of government, but merely asking how can a democracy best be made to work? And, in our opinion, despite the fact that the basic assumptions of democracy are being attacked in many parts of the world, democracy must work.

If a democracy assumes the responsibility of supporting libraries, then the library has a positive obligation to contribute to the advancement of democracy. We would not suggest that the library become, therefore, an instrument of propaganda; that lesson was sadly learned with the U.S. Information Centers. We are merely saying that, despite the historic role of the library, it is today insufficient for the library simply to wait for the inquisitive to come to its doors, or to give its services to pedants or incipient pedants who will only swell the verbal tide. We believe that the affirmative and urgent obligation of the library is not unlike that of the university—to mediate between books and those who need them, to the end of improving the lot of the individual and of society. There was more wisdom in Carlyle's famous observation than is generally recognized, and its meaning might be even more clear if it were reversed to say that the true library of these days is a university. We would be the last to deny the recreational and pleasurable values of reading—we have partaken of those delights too often ourself to be unaware of them. But we insist that the primary responsibility of the library is educational—to stimulate the intellect, to broaden the reader's experience, and challenge him into new avenues of creativity. In a very real sense the library is the laboratory of the mind. If the task of the librarian, then, is to bring graphic records and people together in a meaningful relationship, what must the librarian be? Hugo Blotius, the 16th-century librarian of the Hofbibliothek in Vienna, said that the librarian should be "learned in languages, diligent, and quiet," and that "if not of noble blood he should be given a title to enhance the dignity of his office." In 1780, Cotton des Houssayes told the general assembly of the Sorbonne that when he reflected on the qualities needed by the librarian he found them to be so numerous and "in such character of perfection," that he could not trust himself to enumerate them, let alone "trace their true picture." Yet he did say (be it noted, in Latin), "Your librarian should be, above all, a learned and profound theologian, but to this qualification, which I shall call fundamental, should be united vast literary acquisitions, an exact and precise knowledge of all the arts and sciences, great facility of expression, and lastly, that exquisite politeness which conciliates the affection of his visitors while his merit secures their esteem." From Sir Thomas Bodley we learn that a librarian, in addition to being a man of learning, should not be "encumbered with marriage nor with a benefice of cure," but "a personable scholar and qualified, if it may be, with a gentlemanlike speech and carriage . . . able to interteine comers in aswel of other nations as our owne, with meete discourses for the place."[6]

   To the modern mind such descriptions of the attributes of the ideal librarian sound more like *Euphues* than *The Organization Man*, but at least they do emphasize the librarian as scholar. The librarian, if he is to perform his duties wisely, must understand that he is more than a custodian, a "keeper"; and that books, like his patrons, have an intellectual as well as a physical life. The true librarian is probably to be found somewhere between the extremes of John Lyly and William H. Whyte; and where one places him tells more about one's attitude toward librarianship than it does about the professionalism of the librarian. Graphic records are, of course, physical objects which must be arranged, properly labeled, and described so that they can be retrieved on demand. But the librarian who is no more than a check-boy in the parcel room of culture has no responsibilities other than to be precise, orderly, pleasant, and patient. He serves only when he stands and waits. At a time when books were scarce and their care was a special concern of the scholar, the view of the librarian as a keeper of *physical* objects was to be expected, and indeed necessary. Thus, in 1649, John Dury, deputy keeper of the King's medals and library, wrote of the duties of the librarian:

> For if Librarie-Keepers did understand themselves in the nature of their work, and would make themselves, as they ought to bee useful in their places in a publick wie; they ought to become agents for the advancement of universal learning . . . the end of that Imploiment, in my conception, is to keep the publick stock of Learning, which is in Books and MSS, to increas it, and to propose it to others the waie which may bee most useful unto all. His work then is to bee a Factor and Trader for helps to learning, and a Treasurer to keep them, and a Dispenser to applie them to use or to see them well used, or at least not abused.[7]

But the keeper of books as *intellectual* objects has quite different responsibilities, responsibilities only marginally suggested by Dury. The librarian who is concerned with books as intellectual objects is, as MacLeish has said, "the keeper of the Word," and the keeper of the Word must be its partisan and advocate. The Word, the Idea, is never preserved by keeping it in storage. The book as the Word, as Idea, as intellectual object, is in and of the mind and can be preserved only by preserving the mind's perception of it. The intellectual book, unlike the physical book, is not only a heritage from the past to which the future has a right, but a construct of the mind which exists only in that continuing and ever-present Now. It is the intellectual book, not the physical book, that defines the mission of the library and makes it the force that society has the right to expect it to be. It is in the librarian as keeper of the intellectual book, and only by necessity of the physical book, that his professional identity is to be sought. Ralph Beals made much the same point, though more metaphorically, when he likened the librarian to an anthologist, a weaver of garlands.

> Without detracting from the claims of librarianship to be a science or discounting the contributions already made to the science of librarianship, which I myself think very great, I should like to suggest that the librarian, like the anthologist, is also an artist . . . The museologist, the anthologist, and the librarian take as their *metier* not color, line, and words but the finished product of painter, poet, scholar and novelist, working with these larger, more intricate media to express intentions of their own.
> In the larger, scholarly libraries, the librarian, like the editors of the *Patrologia*,

or the *Monuments Germaniae Historica*, sets himself the high task of representing many subjects that crowd the limits of his spacious canvas, and his particular delight is in the minuteness and accuracy of his rendering.[8]

He goes on to say that the special librarian works a smaller canvas, concentrating on comprehensiveness and "forging all together as the links of a perfect chain." The public librarian cannot evade the responsibility "of portraying the full range of our civilization in all its pulsing human aspects." One can argue that Beals has mixed his metaphors a bit, but he does make clear that it is the mission of the librarian, in whatever kind of library he is employed, to communicate "the good, the true, and the beautiful in whatever terms may prove perceptible to those with eyes to see and ears to hear."

Ortega y Gasset has adopted a position that will not be popular with the legions in defense of intellectual freedom, but it will elicit a sympathetic response from all librarians who feel themselves threatened by inundation from the paper flood. The librarian, he says, must "tame the book," for there are, according to him, too many books, too many worthless books which must be eliminated, and people read too much. "The condition of reading without much effort, or even without any effort, the innumerable ideas contained in books and periodicals have accustomed the common man to do no thinking on his own account; and he does not think over what he has read, the only method of making it truly his own." Therefore, the librarian of the future must direct his readers, especially his non-specialist readers, "through the *selva selvaggia* of books. He will be the doctor and the hygienist of reading." Thus Ortega y Gasset concludes, "To my mind the mission of the librarian ought to be, not as it is today the simple administration of the things called books, but the adjustment, the setting to rights, of that vital function which is the book."[9]

Let us grant, then, that the librarian has a choice between being a keeper of books as physical objects and a keeper of books as products of the intellect, the transcript of the human adventure; we submit, without discrediting the obvious need for the custody of physical objects, that the highest calling of the librarian, the mission that raises his activities above the level of the mundane, is to be a keeper of the intellectual record, a keeper of the Word. This choice must be made by each librarian for himself; but if he chooses the latter, where does he look for his professional identity, for an *apologia pro vita sua*?

He is not likely to find it in library school; library schools are little given to things of the intellect, being, as they are, mostly concerned with housekeeping, management, administration, and short-cuts to the tricks of the librarian's craft.

Certainly he will not find it in the professional societies with which he may affiliate, for they are composed of people like himself, to whom the society's affairs are always secondary to a primary concern, which is the job. Moreover, as the society grows in size, the spatial differences among its component groups tends to increase and diverge until the common bonds of understanding that originally brought the group together into a voluntary association weaken, fragment, and even dissolve. Most professional associations, if they are not unabashed pressure groups, are offerings on the golden altar of economic fortune to elicit the favor of the rich and the good, and to atone for our professional sins—like the sacrificial goat.

He will not find it by trying to fit his activities into the clichés of a vague professionalism, tested by the artificial procedures of licensure, registration, certification, and accreditation. Nor will he find it among his working associates who, if they are concerned at all about the problem of their social rationale, are as lost as he. Finally, he will not find it in the literature of librarianship, for that literarure mainly reflects the *malaise* that infects the field.

No, the librarian will not find his professional identity externally. He must look within himself to discover: first, what is to be a librarian; second, what it means to be the kind of librarian he is; and finally, what kind of librarian he, and nobody else, is. Whether he will be an administrator of books as physical objects or a Keeper of the Word is a decision that only he can make, a decision that can be made by him and him alone.

Never was the Word more important than it is today. The profound and troubled alteration of our time affects the role of the librarian in very significant and fundamental ways. The quiet cloister that was the little Carnegie Library of our childhood is today an anachronism. The librarian can no longer think of his profession in negative and custodial terms. At a time when the freedom of the individual and the right to privacy are being tested on every hand; at a time when anti-intellectualism is popular as never before and works of great artists are being desecrated; at a time when race prejudice is "good politics"; at a time when mankind itself is threatened with extinction by the technological refinements of war, the destruction of the environment, and the menace of unrestrained population growth; the librarian must speak out affirmatively in defense of the Word and in preservation of the integrity of his book collections. "Light, light in floods," wrote Victor Hugo in *Les Miserables*, "no bat resists the dawn." Three decades earlier the dying Goethe had cried, *"Licht! mehr Licht!"* Never has the librarian as keeper of the Word had such a responsibility nor such a challenge.

In 1940, shortly after Archibald MacLeish had accepted the post of Librarian of Congress, and the skies over Washington were already darkening with the "locks of the approaching storm" against democratic institutions, he asked himself:

> If democratic government now admits an affirmative interest in the education of the citizen what then is the present obligation of the libraries democratic governments support? . . . And if they have become people's universities, what are their obligations to the people? Can they continue to feel that they have satisfied their obligations to the people if they wait for such readers as may care to come?

Can they continue to feel that they have satisfied their obligations to the people if they offer every facility to scholars who will make, from the books in their collections, other books to be added to other collections?

For himself, he answered:

> I do not believe that libraries, any more than any other institution created by men, can be set above change; that librarianship, like every other human activity, must be continuously reinvented if it is to live; and that none, or so it seems to me, is under heavier responsibilities to the present than those whose profession is to conserve the past.[10]

The librarian can win back his once proud tradition only when he recognizes himself as an educator in the broadest sense; only as an educator can he find justification for his professional life. The librarian as keeper of the Word, as custodian of the record of the human spirit, must, above all, be an educated man, where being an educated man means being not one who is omniscient but one who is constantly learning. To conserve the record of the past while still remaining responsive to change is the peculiar mission of the librarian, for the librarian stands at the junction where past and future meet in the ever-present now. This mandate is not as paradoxical as it might seem, for past and future have much in common and the latter cannot dissociate itself from the former. John Gardner, in a quite different context, has admirably expressed the relationship in *The Recovery of Confidence*:

> Young people who profess utter emancipation from the past pour out torrents of words about the values they wish to live by, and in, yet they turn out to be, for the most part, up-dated values of very old values. True, the values have been ignored, lied about, manipulated, and falsified. But that only says that they need rescuing.[11]

The task of the librarian, then, is to rescue the past for the enlightenment of the present, to preserve the past not for its own sake or for the curiosity of the antiquarian, but for the meaning that it has for today and tomorrow.

The library, like the university, should be not only a house of intellect but also a joyous place, for the pursuit of learning is a joyous chase. In your stewardship of the records of the human spirit, and in the affirmation that is the communication of their wisdom to others, you should find that joy.

## FOOTNOTES

[1] Archibald MacLeish, "The Premise of Meaning," *The American Scholar*, Vol. 41 (Summer 1972), p. 357.

[2] See, for example, William J. Goode, "The Librarian: From Occupation to Profession?" *Library Quarterly*, Vol. 31 (1961), pp. 306-18, and Mary Lee Bundy and Paul Wasserman, "Professionalism Reconsidered," *College and*

*Research Libraries*, Vol. 29 (January 1968), pp. 8ff.

[3] Abraham Flexner, "Is Social Work a Profession?" *School and Society*, Vol. 1 (1915), pp. 901-11. *See also* H. H. Vollmer and D. L. Mills, *Professionalization* (Englewood Cliffs, N.J.: Prentice-Hall, 1966), pp. 34-43.

[4] Quoted by Deborah Shapley, "Professional Societies: Identity Crisis Threatens on Bread and Butter Issues," *Science*, Vol. 176 (May 19, 1972), p. 778.

[5] *Ibid.*

[6] From Archibald MacLeish, "Of the Librarian's Profession," *Atlantic Monthly*, Vol. 165 (June 1940), p. 786.

[7] Quoted *ibid.*, p. 788.

[8] Ralph A. Beals, "The Librarian as Anthologist," *D. C. Libraries*, Vol. 12 (January 1941), p. 19.

[9] Jose Ortega y Gasset, "The Mission of the Librarian," *Antioch Review*, Vol. 21 (Summer 1961), p. 154.

[10] Archibald MacLeish, "The Obligation of the Librarian in a Democracy," *D. C. Libraries*, Vol. 11 (January 1940), p. 18.

[11] Quoted in *The Christian Science Monitor*, June 29, 1972.

# II.

# Of Library History

# 9

# The Literature of
# American Library History

## I. JOSIAH QUINCY AND THE HISTORY OF THE
## BOSTON ATHENAEUM

In the autumn of 1847 Josiah Quincy (1772-1864), at the age of 75, retired to the seclusion of his private library, lighted his study lamp, and set himself to the task of writing the history of the Boston Athenaeum.[1] Behind him lay a period of service in the Congress of the United States, five terms of militant reform as Boston's "great mayor," and 16 tumultuous years of vigorous liberalism as president of Harvard University, not to mention an ancestry that could be traced back to Edmund Quincy, who migrated to America in 1633. Nor was this role of historian a new one to Josiah Quincy. In 1840 appeared his two-volume history of Harvard, which, Samuel Eliot Morison says, "lasted almost a century as the standard history" of that university.[2] Also, in 1846, he had simultaneously begun work on the life and journals of his uncle, Major Samuel Shaw,[3] and his municipal history of Boston.[4] That his interest in books and libraries was considerably above the average is evident from the size of his own private collection, his participation in the establishment of the Athenaeum, and his active campaigning for a fireproof building for the Harvard library, which resulted in the use of the Christopher Gore bequest for the erection of Gore Hall.[5]

On April 27, 1847, the cornerstone of the Athenaeum's new Beacon Street "edifice" was laid, and for the ceremonies Quincy prepared a retrospective sketch of the library. Thus was brought to focus the need, subsequently expressed by a number of the proprietors, for a detailed history of the Athenaeum. Says Quincy:

Expansion of an article originally published in *The Library Quarterly*, Vol. 15 (January 1945), pp. 1-23. Published by the University of Chicago Press.

> Although aware that the materials for the task were, some of them, difficult to be obtained, my relation to the founders of the Athenaeum, and to the institution itself, induced me to comply with their request.[6]

Work was interrupted in 1850 by the death of his wife, but his son adds:

> My father soon sought relief from the presence of this great grief which study and occupation could afford. He busied himself with finishing his History of the Boston Athenaeum, which had been delayed, as he says himself, by circumstances for which he was not responsible.[7]

The book came from the press in 1851 and was "very well received," says Edmund, "by the proprietors of the Athenaeum and the general public."[8] Such were the circumstances surrounding the composition of what may be categorically declared the first formal history of an American library.[9] Doubtless mere priority would not justify further consideration of the book, but additional importance attaches to it because, as a piece of historical writing, it so completely reflects the contemporary influences attendant upon its inception; its subject treatment is typical of library historiography for the three-quarters of a century that were to follow.

That the proprietors of the Athenaeum felt the need for a history of their library is not surprising, for the decades between 1830 and 1850 were an era of unprecedented interest in the American past. It was the period of Jared Sparks' greatest activity; George Bancroft was making American history popular to a degree previously unequaled; Parkman, Prescott, and Motley were emphasizing the dramatic element in history; and that "spectre of the Athenaeum," Richard Hildreth, was striving to present

> the founders of our American nation unbedaubed with patriotic rouge, wrapped up in no fine-spun cloaks of excuses and apology, without stilts, buskins, tinsel, or bedizzenment, in their own proper persons, often rude, hard, narrow, superstitious, and mistaken, but always earnest, downright, manly, and sincere.[10]

The reasons for this sudden and widespread popular concern with the past are likely to be found in the number of influences inherent in the life of that time. American nationality was definitely on the march, and from this growing enthusiasm there arose a natural and spontaneous desire to inform the world concerning the United States and the events that resulted in the new freedom. Furthermore, the occurrences surrounding the Revolution had receded sufficiently to permit a proper historical perspective, while most of the participants in these events had died, leaving the record of their lives open and available to the scholar. On the economic side American capital had grown sufficiently to support historical research and to contribute to the establishment of libraries within whose walls the scholar might obtain many of the materials he desired. International contacts, too, were becoming more important through the efforts of Ticknor, Everett, and Emerson. Good publishing media, such as the *North American Review*, were available to the young and ambitious scholar. Finally, there was the stimulus of an increasingly eager reading public.[11] Quincy's *History of the Boston Athenaeum* was conditioned by all these tendencies, and to the student of library historiography it is therefore of more than passing interest. The expression of an age, it merits a consideration of its three outstanding characteristics.

Its most obvious quality as historical writing is, of course, its factual and narrative character. Quincy writes in the Preface:

> My chief object has been, by abstracting and condensing, to enable the Athenaeum to narrate its own history; which would thus be unexceptionable in form, and more satisfactory in effect.[12]

One cannot decry this procedure. Quincy's essential preoccupation with the event *per se*, divorced from any causal factors that might give to the event a wider meaning, was typical of historical writing in general before Darwin and Huxley opened new vistas for historical exploration and gave the historian new tools with which to work.

The second quality of the book is its essential didacticism. Quincy was not merely preserving a record of events surrounding the inception and growth of the Athenaeum; he was definitely attempting to present a picture of the Athenaeum that would be an inspiration and hence promote continual financial support. He concludes the *History* with these words:

> Nor can the writer of this History refrain, on this occasion, from expressing, in behalf of his departed friends and contemporaries, the delight they would have felt, if, looking through the long vista of nearly fifty years, they could have seen a result thus exceeding their fondest and brightest literary and patriotic visions;—if the little band of enthusiastic scholars, when casting together, from their scanty means, a few volumes to form a collection of "periodical publications", could have beheld in the distance these small seeds expanded into a library of more than *fifty thousand* volumes . . . the hearts of each and all of them would have been filled with a joy and exultation, which those alone can understand and realize, who, like them, combine, as an active principle of their lives, a love of literature with a love of country.[13]

Further, Edmund Quincy, in speaking of the book and his father's labors upon it, adds:

> This work was very well received by the proprietors of the Athenaeum and the general public; and, besides recording the services and characters of several excellent and accomplished men whose memories were fading out of the minds of this generation, it brought the importance of maintaining such an institution distinctly to the attention of the community.[14]

The degree to which this purpose was achieved is again attested by the son:

> . . . and it were not, perhaps, too much to claim for him that . . . his History materially helped to revive the public interest in the Athenaeum, and to promote the movement which soon afterwards placed it on its present [1867] enlarged and permanent foundation.[15]

Josiah Quincy's object was, then, twofold: first, by commemorating the acts of the Athenaeum's founders, to deepen popular consciousness of the growing American heritage and, second, to impress upon a younger generation the importance and value of the Athenaeum as a cultural asset and, in so doing, to make more certain its future support. In this, too, his work was part and parcel of the stream of contemporary historical writing Prescott and Motley were writing history that showed the triumph of Protestantism over Catholicism, Weems attempted to teach the youth moral virtue as exemplified in the life of our first president; and Bancroft, by his spiritual exultation over the achievements of God, democracy, and progress in American history, was striving to combat a sensitiveness to European criticism that sprang from the realization that those republican institutions of which America should be so proud were on trial before the world. So, too, was Quincy an exemplar of that intense loyalty to American potentialities which de Tocqueville called *le patriotisme irritable*.

Finally, Quincy's *History* is nostalgic in tone—a quality closely related to its didacticism and originating from the personal elements inherent in its composition. That the author was an old man, between the ages of 75 and 80, at the time of the book's writing has already been mentioned. As a member of Congress he had violently opposed Jefferson's embargo, had been an advocate of New England secession, and had generally represented a conservative point of view. Truly a Colonial Whig, born after his time, he was, as Lowell picturesquely phrased it, "an old Roman of the elder virtuous days . . . an example of stalwart and antiquated Federalism."[16] In 1853 he was to assume a leading part in defeating George Ticknor's proposal to merge the Athenaeum with the Boston Public Library then being formed.[17] Moreover, in writing of the Athenaeum, he was writing about his friends.

> All of them were my contemporaries, and, with the exception of Gardiner, Emerson, and Kirkland, my juniors. With most of them my intercourse had been intimate; and I could not but regret that so little is known of them by a generation now enjoying the benefits of an institution which had its origin in their love of letters and their patriotic spirit.[18]

As he wrote in the Preface to the *History*, so also in his journal he says:

> I am well repaid for all the difficulties and trouble attending it [the composition of the Athenaeum history] by the satisfaction I feel at having been instrumental in preserving the memory and services of some of my early friends, and by having done justice, though feebly, to their merits.[19]

Small wonder, too, that William Smith Shaw, the first librarian of the Athenaeum, struggling against poor health, obsessed with the idea of that library, and with pockets bulging with books, is seen as essentially a romantic figure, of whom Quincy wrote in the Preface:

> With William Smith Shaw, who is better entitled than any other individual to the name of Founder of the Athenaeum, my intimacy, through his whole life, was

strict and confidential. I was a constant witness of the energy, zeal, and devotedness with which he watched over it in its embryo state, and knew his fond anticipations concerning its future greatness and usefulness.[20]

In addition to this basic emotion, already strongly intrenched in Quincy's spirit, there was the event of his wife's death in the midst of his work on the *History*. Her death terminated a married life of 53 years, thus severing another link with the past and intensifying Quincy's personal identification with the Athenaeum— "the strong hold which an institution of this character takes upon the affections."[21]

From the evidence presented by Quincy's *History* one may conclude that the writing of the history of libraries may be as deeply rooted in contemporary life as the establishment and development of the libraries themselves. Does the writing of library history reflect the writing of history in general? Is American library historiography as integral a part of the contemporary social pattern as are the libraries of which it treats? Should the writing of library history take into account the fact that libraries are a manifestation of the social and economic environment, shaped by and not insulated from the action of contemporary life? Assuming these questions to be answered in the affirmative, what direction should the future writing of library history take? These are the questions that the present discussion attempts to answer.

## II. THE COMPILATIONS OF JEWETT AND RHEES

For the 50 or 60 years that followed the publication of Quincy's *History*, the stream of historical writing about libraries was little more than a trickle. Both in quantity and in quality it is unimpressive. But in 1851 and in 1859, respectively, there appeared two volumes which, though neither consciously nor dominantly historical in intent, contain data that are of considerable importance to the historian and that therefore merit consideration in a survey such as this. In the former year Charles C. Jewett, then librarian of the Smithsonian Institution, published his *Notices of Public Libraries in the United States*,[22] followed in 1859 by William J. Rhees' *Manual of Public Libraries*.[23]

Jewett's main objective was to present a statistical survey of public library resources in the United States as of the middle of the year 1849, and, he adds, "I have endeavored to collect such historical, statistical, and descriptive notices as would be of general interest; together with such special details as would be beneficial to those who are engaged in the organization and care of similar establishments."[24]

It should be noted that Jewett was not the first to survey library resources in this country. In 1724 the Bishop of London sent a circular letter to all parish churches in Maryland asking certain questions regarding the church facilities. Among these questions he asked: "Have you a parochial library? If you have, are the books preserved, and kept in good condition? Have you any particular rules and orders for the preserving of them? Are these rules and orders duly observed?" Over 20 parishes responded.[25]

Between the years 1799 and 1818, Benjamin Trumbull, then collecting materials for his history of Connecticut from 1630 to 1764, wrote to an important individual, usually one or more of the ministers, in practically every Connecticut town. In these letters he posed 10 questions concerning the historical development of the town, its date of settlement, its church history, its municipal growth and expansion, its schools, its industries, and even the history of its Indians. As the final question he wrote: "What libraries are there in the town? When instituted, and of what number of volumes do they consist?"[26] Trumbull used the answers to the library question for the writing of only a summary statement at the end of his *History*, but the material on libraries established before 1801 has been summarized in tabular form by R. Malcolm Sills and Eleanor Stuart Upton of the Yale Library staff.[27] Following a similar method, Horace Mann, when secretary to the Board of Education of Massachusetts, sent, in 1839, an inquiry addressed to "school committees and other intelligent men" residing in every town of the Commonwealth. Because "it would be highly useful and interesting to know what means exist, either for cultivating or gratifying habits of reading among the young; and also, to what extent persons of a more advanced age avail themselves of the researches and attainments of other minds, through the medium of regular courses of lectures, on literary or scientific subjects," he took "the liberty to propose" 11 questions concerning libraries, lyceums, and institutes in every community.[28] In 1845 a survey of American libraries was made by Hermann Ludewig of Dresden.[29] In 1849 Henry Barnard published a list of the "public" libraries of Rhode Island.[30] Many yearbooks, almanacs, etc., published summary statistical tables of libraries, but most of these are drawn from the basic sources mentioned above. Important as these surveys are—and their value as source material for the historian is certainly not to be doubted—they have been excluded from the present consideration because they are not actually the writing of library history. Except for their information on the dates of establishment, they were contemporary, not historical, accounts; and, though they are historical material today, they were not such at the time of their writing.

Rhees' *Manual* was originally planned as a continuation of the Jewett compilation and, indeed, draws to some extent from that report.

> When ... the work was presented to the Secretary of the Institution [i.e., the Smithsonian Institution, of which Rhees was the chief clerk], he found it so extended with the matter not within the original design, that he did not think himself authorized to adopt it as a Smithsonian report on *libraries*. The work is therefore published by the compiler in the belief that the additional matter, while swelling the cost beyond the appropriation which was made for it by the Institution, will greatly increase its value, and render it more acceptable to the public.[31]

Rhees' purpose, too, had a certain element of didacticism. He adds:

> It is hoped, however, that the facts presented will be considered valuable and instructive, and will not only serve to throw new light on our advancement as a people; but will tend to produce greater interest in those powerful means of mental and moral improvement, – our Public Libraries.[32]

In both volumes the historical material is all too brief for the complete satisfaction of the historian; always factual and never interpretive, it is grist for the historian's mill rather than true historical writing itself. Yet, as compendia of existing knowledge of library development, they represent an early and important attempt to record with a considerable degree of accuracy the significant facts surrounding the growth of libraries over the country.

## III.  EDWARD EDWARDS

In the year of Rhees' *Manual* there appeared in England a two-volume work with the title *Memoirs of Libraries*,[33] by Edward Edwards, sometime supernumerary of the British Museum, afterward its historian, and later the first librarian of the Manchester Free Library.[34] The treatise in general is, of course, concerned primarily with the situation in Great Britain, but considerable space is devoted to foreign countries, and in this the United States is granted a not inconspicuous share. He divides American libraries into five major groups according to type—collegiate libraries, proprietary and subscription libraries, congressional and state libraries, town libraries, and school-district libraries—and adds a chapter on the Smithsonian Institution.[35] Richard Garnett, in his sketch of Edwards appearing in the *Dictionary of National Biography*, credits him with being an able and conscientious historian, but Edwards' work on American libraries is certainly of little real value to the student on this side of the Atlantic. Throughout he leans very heavily on Jewett's *Notices*, adding only occasional material from a few other obvious sources and contributing nothing that the student of American library history would not find elsewhere in more complete form.[36]

Ten years later Edwards brought forth another volume on the history of libraries—his *Free Town Libraries*, appearing in 1869.[37] Again the material is predominantly British, but the section dealing with the United States, though limited in scope, marks a distinct advance over the earlier work. Edwards begins his discussion with the bequest, in 1700, of the private library of Rev. John Sharp to the city of New York, for the foundation of a public library, and the eventual conversion of that collection into a proprietary library. He then turns to the Loganian Library of Philadelphia and its consolidation with Franklin's Library Company. Collegiate and school libraries, the use of the school collections as parish and township libraries, and, finally, the reversion in recent years to municipal responsibility for library support, all receive some attention. Nor did Edwards forget the emerging library movement in the hinterland beyond the Alleghenies, for he particularly stressed the situation in Ohio and Indiana, drawing his material largely from Rhees' *Manual*. In the main, however, his attention is focused upon the Boston Public Library and the Astor Library of New York, the histories of both these institutions being presented in considerable detail.

Edwards' main sources were Jewett and Rhees, together with such published reports of individual libraries as were available to him. Today his work is not important to the historian of the library movement, but at the time of its appearance it probably represented a useful compilation of existing knowledge. At least, his was an early attempt to see American library history in terms of the whole and as a definite cultural movement, and he may very well have left the contemporary reader with something akin to a real feeling for the larger aspects implicit in the growth of American libraries.

## IV.  THE REPORT OF 1876

The historical approach was inherent in the editorial plan for the justly famous *Report* of 1876.[38] The Preface to it says, in part:

> After considerable study of the subject and consultation and correspondence with eminent librarians, the following plan was adopted: To present, first, the history of public libraries in the United States; second, to show their present condition and extent; third, to discuss the various questions of library economy and management; and fourth, to present as complete statistical information of all classes of public libraries as practicable.[39]

The editors further add that it was deemed advisable to treat the historical material generally, and by type of library, rather than to emulate Jewett and Rhees by giving historical accounts of each individual institution.

Horace E. Scudder was selected to prepare the initial chapter on "Public Libraries a Hundred Years Ago." Scudder begins by pointing out the relationship between the public library and public education, and the necessity that the development of the former wait upon the extension of the latter. He further suggests that the growth of the library may be regarded as a kind of index to the state of public opinion on the subject of culture. Thus, for a brief period, the modern reader anticipates a real attempt to link the library movement with coeval social phenomena, only to be disappointed when Scudder soon drops back into the accepted pattern of presenting library history as a mere skeletal sequence—a chronicling of events surrounding the formation of individual collections.

Yet Scudder's survey is the most extensive and most nearly complete of any up to that time, and its weaknesses are the same as those of the other contributors who wrote about the libraries of theology, law, the government, prisons, and all the rest. Much less concerned than he with the historical approach, they quickly gloss over institutional antecedents and pass on to a consideration of the condition of the libraries at the time of writing. Minute scrutiny of the deficiencies of the individual parts of the 1876 *Report* renders disparagement easy, but viewed in the large, as a well-rounded whole, there can be no doubt that the compilation represents a landmark in the writing of library history. Certainly it was much more extensive in scope and pretentious in plan than anything attempted up to the time of its projection. That it achieved a certain degree of success in presenting to the reader a picture of the expansion of the library movement into many phases of contemporary life cannot be denied.

Neither before nor since has American librarianship produced so nearly complete a survey of the state of professional knowledge. Much of what is written today with all the freshness and enthusiasm of novelty may be found in the essays of this compilation. A monument to the greatness of American library pioneers, within these 1,100 pages are combined both historical writing as such and the *materia historica* of the future investigator. After three-quarters of a century the practicing librarian can still read it with profit, and the historian of American librarianship dare not ignore it.

## V.  JUSTIN WINSOR

Of the three historians who, between 1850 and 1900, were writing about libraries—Quincy, Scudder, and Winsor—doubtless the reputation of the last is most secure. A true historian in his own right, as well as the only one of the three who was a practicing librarian, Justin Winsor's main contributions to American library historiography are a series of four essays published in the *Literary World* in 1879, a chapter on libraries in his *Memorial History of Boston* (1881), and an address at the dedication (1894) of a new library building for Northwestern University.[40] In addition, his *Narrative and Critical History of America*[41] contains scattered references to the development of libraries. By way of evaluation, suffice it to say that his contributions follow the pattern established by his predecessors and that he places particular emphasis upon the growth of the Boston Public Library and the influence of Vattemare. Teggart, writing in the *Literary Journal* in 1897, says: "Professor Justin Winsor seems to have been one who, at a time, had dreams of being the historian of American libraries."[42] But the present writer is unable to find any other evidence that Winsor even gave such a "dream" serious consideration.[43] Rather, it is surprising that, being a librarian of prominence and influence, first at the Boston Public Library and later at Harvard, as well as an historian of acknowledged reputation, he did not combine the two interests and write more extensively of library history. The reasons for such neglect are probably to be found in the absence of sufficient historical perspective on American libraries at the time Winsor was doing most of his work—a limitation that he as a professional historian would quickly recognize—and a preoccupation with a multitude of other activities that he may have considered more worthy of his effort.

Finally it is relevant to recall that Winsor is today remembered by historians not so much for his historical writings or interpretations as for the great mass of source materials he unearthed.[44] Channing quite rightly said of him that he "made the scientific study of American history possible by making available the rich mines of material."[45]

## VI. WILLIAM I. FLETCHER

Less than 20 years after the publication of the 1876 *Report*, William I. Fletcher, then librarian of Amherst College, began his initial chapter of his *Public Libraries in America* with these sentences:

> The public library of today, like other social institutions, is the result of a long evolution. In one sense a creation of the nineteenth century, not to say of its latter half, in another and truer sense it is but a normal development from its predecessors.[46]

On the next page he asks rhetorically:

> But when did the public library movement begin? . . . Apparently it waited for that child of the Reformation, whose ominous name is Revolution, to turn the key which should open libraries to the people. For surely the spirit of the Revolution, in its sanest manifestation, moved BENJAMIN FRANKLIN and other men of his kind in their thinking and acting on political and social subjects; and probably with FRANKLIN, more than any other, originated the impetus to this movement.

Fletcher maintains, and quite rightly, that it was the subscription libraries that were the true progenitors of the modern public library, and he continues:

> It is quite common to look upon the later movement by which libraries came to be supported by public funds derived from taxation as marking the beginnings of the public library. In one sense this view is correct; but when it is noted how naturally and inevitably the public library of FRANKLIN'S institution has grown into the more recent form, it is easy to perceive that in the establishment of these subscription libraries, the public-library movement really began. From the first these institutions were for the benefit, not of the few, but of the many. In most cases the fees were so small that they were supposed not to deter any from joining the association.[47]

He sees the public library as an outgrowth of the spread of popular education and as closely allied to the lyceum lecture system.

> Not much was said in those days about socialism, but it was really a long step in the direction of true socialism when the public library was added to the public school as a State function. It was a recognition of the claims of the masses for all that the body politic can do to enlighten and elevate them,—a recognition, in fact, of that solidarity in the body politic by virtue of which, if one member suffer, all the members suffer with it.[48]

One would scarcely acclaim this as a Marxist interpretation of the origin of the public library movement, but it was a decided innovation. Here for the first time was a real attempt to view the library historically as a social agency, conditioned by and emanating from its social milieu.[49] He pictures the appearance and spread of public libraries not in atomistic terms of specially created and independent units but as causally related and integrated social phenomena. Fletcher has, indeed, come to a sociological interpretation without actually developing his ideas. His was an entirely new concept of library origins—embryonic, to be sure, yet nevertheless a real preliminary attempt to examine past events in the light of social causation. It had not been done before; it was not to be undertaken again for nearly 40 years.

## VII.  OTHER NINETEENTH-CENTURY MATERIALS

The 19th century cannot be dismissed without passing reference to the ninth *Report* of the Massachusetts Public Library Commission.[50] Published in 1899, it followed the Jewett-Rhees tradition though limited to Massachusetts, presenting alphabetically by towns the history and current status of their several libraries. The *Report* differs from its predecessors, however, mainly by its inclusion of *all* known public and quasi-public libraries, whether extant at the time of compilation or not, whereas the Smithsonian reports were predominantly concerned with operating institutions.

Nor would this section of the survey be complete without at least casual mention of the histories of libraries in local history compilations, which were particularly important in the New England area. These were prepared by scores of individuals of widely varying degrees of historical competence, but, in general, prior to the 20th century and before the entrance of commercial exploitation into the local history field, their contents are factually reliable and not unimportant.[51] The material on libraries contained therein varies tremendously in length and detail from mere passing reference to such extensive treatment as that of Samuel Swett Green for Worcester, Massachusetts.[52] Their great merit so far as the historian of library development is concerned lies in the fact that their authors were themselves often active in library promotion in the towns about which they were writing and not infrequently could speak from firsthand knowledge of the events set forth. Though the approach is generally from the point of view of the antiquarian, these bulky volumes are a well-stocked hunting ground for the library historian in search of factual information available in no other printed form.

## VIII.  THE EARLY YEARS OF THE TWENTIETH CENTURY

The same tendencies apparent in the 19th century continued through the first three decades of the 20th. If there was any change, it found expression in a slight lessening of interest in historical compilations and general surveys of library expansion and an increasing impulse to write factual histories of individual institutions. Some of the latter were "occasional" history, strongly motivated by a desire to celebrate anniversaries, centennials, or other commemorative events.[53] Since the main characteristics of the writing in this period are essentially identical with those of the preceding century, there is little of value to be derived from a detailed discussion of the specific works. It will suffice here to point out a few of the more important productions.

Before the century began, George C. Mason had issued his *Annals of the Redwood Library and Athenaeum*, which, decades later, is still the definitive account of that important association.[54] In 1900 James F. Brennan wrote of the Peterborough Town Library,[55] and four years later appeared William Dawson Johnston's *History of the Library of Congress*,[56] of which only the first volume, covering the years 1800 to 1864, was ever published. Regrettably, an adequate history of our national library, especially for the post-Civil War period, still remains to be written.[57] For the present, we must be content with David C. Mearns' delightfully written and historically accurate, but all too brief, *The Story Up to Now*, which first appeared in the *Annual Report of the Librarian of Congress* for 1946, and was subsequently published under separate cover.[58] Mearns is a trained historian with a gifted literary style, and his years of experience in the Library of Congress gave him an unusual perspective of the growth of that institution.

In 1908 Keep's *History of the New York Society Library*, with its important preliminary chapter on the history of libraries in Colonial New York, was published by the De Vinne Press.[59] In 1911 appeared Horace G. Wadlin's history of the Boston Public Library,[60] and it was followed in 1923 by Lydenberg's substantial volume on the New York Public Library.[61] Philadelphia, too, received its share of attention with Lewis' account of the Apprentices' Library (1924)[62] and Gray's book about Franklin's Library Company (1936).[63] Certain areas, as well as individual institutions, were being examined historically. Typical of this interest in regional library history were: *Legislative History of Township Libraries in Michigan* (1902);[64] George Watson Cole (1927) and Frank L. Tolman (1937) on library development in New York State;[65] Part I, "Libraries," of Stephen B. Weeks' "Libraries and Literature in North Carolina in the Eighteenth Century" (1895);[66] and studies of the Reverend Thomas Bray's establishment of parish libraries in the colonies along the Atlantic Coast.[67] During this same period a few sporadic biographies and memoirs of librarians were also published. In 1913 appeared the reminiscences of Samuel Swett Green. The title, *The Public Library Movement*, is deceptive, for it is scarcely more than a chronological presentation of library events during the life of the author.[68] As Green was an active participant in the formation, in 1876, of the American Library Association, and at its first convention read a paper on the "Personal Relations between Librarians and Readers,"[69] such a compilation could have been highly useful. The book is disappointing, however, in its failure to contribute much of value to the historian's store of basic data.

In 1924 the American Library Association inaugurated, with the publication of Lydenberg's *John Shaw Billings*, a series of biographical sketches of American library pioneers, of which to date, seven titles have appeared.[70] This series is too limited in scope and treatment to be very satisfactory as historical data. The need is great for a number of scholarly monographs that will really interpret the lives of American library pioneers, but for the present these sketches are, for the men involved, the best that the profession can offer.[71]

Other biographies of varying length have appeared from time to time, but none of these has been definitive.[72] Frank Kingdon's narration of the life of John Cotton Dana is in the tradition of the "American Library Pioneers" series.[73] Grosvenor Dawe's biography of Melvil Dewey is an incredibly sentimental performance that beggars description.[74] The perspective on Dewey and his work is now sufficiently great to make possible a sane appraisal of his contribution to American librarianship. Perhaps only the psychologist is adequately equipped to study the origins of that excessive devotion to Dewey which, during the early years of the present century, so hampered the growth of a true professionalism in library affairs.

As to general histories of the library movement, the years between 1900 and 1930 were as sterile and unproductive as the preceding century. Herbert B. Adams occasionally included historical material in his *Public Libraries and Popular Education*,[75] but his treatment is slight. In view of his work as a professional historian, his indifference to the historical relationships between the public library and movements for popular education is surprising. Ainsworth Rand Spofford presented a brief survey of library history in his *A Book for All Readers* (1900).[76] In the 1910 and subsequent editions Arthur E. Bostwick prefaced his *American Public Library* with an historical section,[77] and the American Library Association included two pamphlets on library history, both by Bolton of the Athenaeum, in its series of manuals on library economy.[78] But none of these even pretends to be an important contribution to the literature of the field.

One should not dismiss the writing of library history during this period without at least passing mention of a projected work that never reached completion. During the early years of the century an antiquarian, James Terry of Terryville, Connecticut, began the collection of materials for a study of early library development in the 13 original states. To this end he brought together, through correspondence and travel, a considerable collection of library records and notes, including the minutes of meetings of library proprietors, catalogs of books, and constitutions of library societies—all of which, after his death, were deposited in the American Antiquarian Society of Worcester. His data are most nearly complete for the New England states, especially Connecticut. He knew of the Trumbull manuscripts at Yale and took much information from them.

Viewed from the standpoint of sound historical research, his methods were not always the best, and yet he assembled a quantity of information that the historian should not overlook.[79]

Such was the writing of library history during the decades between the work of Josiah Quincy and the beginning of the 1930s. Throughout the later years the scope of library history writing became broader but not much deeper. It was impressive neither in quantity nor quality. On occasion it is doubtful whether it should be called "history," for the writing of true history involves synthesis—evaluation and interpretation of relationships—not just a chronological recital of isolated facts. Factual, and factual only, this writing certainly was, and as such it can hardly be classified into any "historical school." Because its main object was to record the remote event, it contained little analysis or interpretation. This recitation of historic facts revealed a continuing picture of library expansion and development, and there was a didactic impulse, probably quite unconscious, to contrast the library poverty of an earlier day with the relative prosperity of a later time.

At the turn of the century and after, American librarianship entered its professional adolescence. Extremely conscious of its own youth, awkwardness, and rapid growth, it was, nevertheless, quite proud of its approaching maturity—proud, too, to have cast aside the remnants of its infancy. As librarians began to feel this new satisfaction in their professional accomplishments, the urge to point with pride to the contrast between the struggles of the pioneers and the permanence of contemporary achievement became irresistible. Such contrasts did not discredit the work of the founding fathers but emphasized anew the solidity of the structure they had built. Historical narrative, therefore, could give meaning to the efforts of the librarians and, in a sense, become an apologia for their labors. When they viewed in retrospect the progress they had made, they could see themselves as a part of the heritage of a growing nation and identify themselves with the strengthening intellectual fiber of American culture.

But there were influences other than this self-justification that were helping to determine the character of the library historiography during this period. Inherent in the rapid growth and immaturity of the profession was an absence of historical perspective, which denied objectivity. Librarians were themselves insufficiently removed temporally from the events of which they wrote to be able to see them steadily and see them whole. The very expansion of the profession and the constant demands for technical improvement precluded concern with a receding past. The old scholarly librarian of the 19th century was passing from the scene, and in his place came administrators and organizers, and others like them, who were acutely aware of the needs of the present but generally indifferent to the links with the past. A new age of preoccupation with the techniques and economics of the profession had begun, and there was little time for reflecting on or investigating origins.

Neglect of the librarian by the professional historian is equally explainable, for new forces were making themselves felt in American historiography, and historians were busy with a reconsideration of older values. With the passing of the 19th century came the new history, bringing reaction against the intellectual sterility of laissez faire and bankrupt conservatism. The influence of von Ranke and his insistence upon the narration of past events as they actually happened—*wie es eigentlich gewesen*—had waned. For it was substituted the philosophy of another German, Lamprecht, who, as he toured America, was preaching a concept of history in terms of conflict between the individual psyche and the social psyche and the importance of the *Zeitgeist* to historical interpretation. There was a growing distrust of the "cold historic fact." The facts of history began to assume a relative position as individual entities in a larger whole. They came, as Carl Becker said, "in the end to seem something solid, something substantial like physical matter, something possessing definite shape and clear, persistent outline—like bricks and scantlings; so that we can easily picture the historian as he stumbles about in the past, stubbing his toe on the hard facts if he doesn't watch out."[80]

The fact was seen as a symbol, a simple statement, a generalization composed of a myriad of simpler facts and itself a part of a larger generalization inseparable from the wider facts or generalizations which it symbolized. The impact of an increasing body of scientific knowledge and the groundwork of Darwin and Huxley was still present, but it was an influence of a different sort. Gone was the romantic faith in the scientific concept of a causal and necessary evolution of history, and in its place was a new humanitarianism and a new optimism born of scientific achievement; a new belief in the possibility of progress rooted in the renaissance of science and education. There was an increasingly Marxist emphasis on the historical importance of the masses. Finally, there was the pragmatic motif of James and Dewey, introducing tolerance into historical writing. Refuting animism, the pragmatist found himself asserting either the inherent interdependence of the several aspects of history, and hence the invalidity of their isolation, or the conviction that though all aspects are interwoven, ultimately they are expressions of but one—the economic.[81] In the wake of these new currents came the need to reexamine American history. Turner analyzed the influence of the frontier and Beard the economic interests represented by those who favored the adoption of the Constitution; Ulrich B. Phillips, a disciple of Dunning and Turner, applied the thesis of the latter to a reconsideration of the South; and slightly later came such historical series as the Yale "Chronicles of America," and the unfinished "History of American Life," edited by Schlesinger and Fox.[82] The new historians were laying a foundation of sound scholarship upon which, as will be shown later, an objective consideration of library origins might rest; but in this reappraisal itself the library was neglected.

## IX. THE NEW LIBRARY HISTORY

Then, in 1931, there appeared, in the pages of the first volume of the *Library Quarterly*, a harbinger of a new phase in library historiography—Arnold Borden's brief but provocative essay on "The Sociological Beginnings of the Library Movement in America."[83] Borden, who, as a student at Harvard, was doubtless influenced by current social theory, sought to turn the findings of these new investigations upon the library as a type of social phenomenon. He held the rapid growth of libraries between 1850 and 1890 to have been the result of three major forces: first, the promotional work of the federal government as exemplified by the activities of the Smithsonian Institution and the Bureau of Education; second, the nourishing influence of philanthropy; and, third, and most significant of all, the power of an expanding democracy. For Borden the library was, above all else, a result of the growing demand during the 19th century for popular education, of the rising economic status of the working classes, of the shortened working day and a resultant increase in leisure, with universal manhood suffrage as the crystallizing force. In short, he was taking up the democratic theme where Fletcher, to whom he refers, had left it almost 40 years before. Borden did not develop his theories to any considerable extent; his paper was little more than a prefatory note. Reconsidered a decade later, his thesis sounded almost platitudinous—so far did thought about library origins advance in that time. The present writer is not, however, able to forget the impact on his own thinking of Borden's concluding paragraph:

> Students of library history, therefore, must not look upon the library as an isolated phenomenon or as something which has been struck off the brains of individuals in moments of philanthropic zeal. The universal emergence of the library as a public institution between 1850 and 1890 suggests the presence of common causes working to a common end. From the point of view of history as well as from that of contemporary conditions the library needs to be studied in the light of sociology, economics, and other branches of human knowledge.[84]

The exact extent of Borden's influence is difficult to determine. Certainly the multitude of references to his essay in subsequent writing testifies that at least it was widely read. But in the final analysis his article would seem to be indicative rather than influential. Borden's piece was the first indication that thinking about library history had begun to recapitulate the thinking about history in general. The new concepts of the social philosophers were beginning to percolate downward into the librarians' own little cosmos. Intensified by the encroachment of the economic depression of the 1930s, the influence of social forces upon the library became more and more pronounced. The accelerated rate of library expansion that characterized the years following the close of World War I began slowly to decline; librarians were of necessity growing increasingly aware of the importance of social theory and their relation to it. As income began to shrink and curtailment of services became imperative, librarians were compelled to look upon their institution as being inherently related to the welfare of the supporting social fabric. Even before Ballard and Martin proclaimed the library to be a social institution,[85] the concept had begun to take shape in professional thinking, and Borden was the first to give it a historical interpretation.

In the following year Borden again published in the *Quarterly* a historical study, limited this time to a consideration of 17th-century American libraries. But he did not follow the high ideals he had previously proposed. He set forth the incidents surrounding the formation of the Harvard College library, described the Keayne bequest of a "publick" library to Boston, and examined the private libraries of the Mathers and William Brewster—all of which he found predominantly theological—as well as the more cavalier collections in the tidewater South. Yet the entirety of these collections meant to him, as to his predecessors, merely a manifestation "of the proud cultural traditions that hovered in the background of all the colonists."[86] He expressed surprise over the discovery that "a community necessarily preoccupied with blazing paths through the American jungle can account for itself so well in the matter of books,"[87] forgetting that the Mathers and Brewsters, far from being concerned with the opening of the West, were precursors of a Tory aristocracy that almost a century later threatened to divide a struggling nation. Thus Borden fell a victim to those very faults which previously he had deplored in others, and discovered, as Teggart says of Winsor, that "it is easier to write the history of libraries in pre-library days."[88]

In 1933 appeared Pierce Butler's *Introduction to Library Science*, which included a chapter on "The Historical Problem."[89] Butler, as a student of James Harvey Robinson and other leaders in the history field, was well trained in the new historical methods that were receiving much attention during the early years of the century. These he has applied to a consideration of the historical problem as it relates to the library. He attempts to get beyond the platitude of the existence of the book as a physical artifact that is possible only in a civilized society, to the recognition that every major change in the social ideal has produced an alteration in the constitution of the library. In the expansion of the library movement in America he discerns a motivation that derives from the rise of capitalism and the identification of social privilege with economic status, a "sentimental Victorian liberalism idealizing itself as Lady Bountiful," an "emotional response in the hearts of the American people," and a variety of personal factors constantly obtruding themselves in the causal train of historical development. Butler holds that a knowledge of library history has practical value for the librarian, since the librarian's interpretation of his official duties is in a great measure dependent upon his conceptions of the interrelationships of historical phenomena: "Librarianship, as we know it, can be fully apprehended only through an understanding of its historic origins."[90] Again, "it is obvious that the librarian's practice will be determined in part by his historical understanding,"[91] and "unless the librarian has a clear historical consciousness ... he is quite certain at times to serve his community badly."[92] Thus has Butler thrown about his philosophical interpretation of library history a cloak of utilitarianism that may at times obscure the central problem. By implication, at least, his insistence upon the practical applications of historical knowledge has subordinated history to the operational objectives of library administration.

Douglas Waples, in his guide for investigators of library problems, finds the scope and benefits of historical criticism potentially the most comprehensive of any of the research procedures he describes.[93] Centering his discussion on five publications, selected with reference to the historical method as applied to research in librarianship,[94] he shows them to be typical of as many kinds of historical study related to libraries:

> (1) comprehensive criticisms of different historical phases of the library as an institution; (2) studies of particular elements of the library ... to identify institutional trends; (3) analyses of present library policies and objectives in terms of the policies conspicuous in earlier stages of library development; (4) evaluations of library policy based on distinctions between policies shaped by contingent or accidental social influences and policies responding to perennial influences; and (5) studies of 'the history of the problem' which are logically prerequisite to research in any field.[95]

Such were the doctrinal bases of the new history of librarianship. The remaining task is to consider their expression in contemporary writings about the library as an historical phenomenon.

The case for philanthropic benevolence as the great motivating force in library development is stoutly championed by James H. Wellard.[96] Looking at American public library growth by the reflected light of conditions in England, he sees it not as a mass of democratic movement from "below" inspired by the desires of the "common man," but as an imposition from "above" by a wealthy and paternalistic minority who knew what was best for the people and gave it to them despite popular apathy:

> If the data of the historical introduction and our interpretation of them are correct, it was not definite, articulated 'social forces' which brought the public library into being so much as the efforts of progressive and philanthropic citizens who foresaw the need of such an institution before the people themselves did. . . . 'The voting strength of the people,' for instance, is not apparent in the establishment of British public libraries; to the contrary, the electorate as a whole seemed comparatively indifferent.[97]

The influence of the Carnegie endowments was used to clinch the argument. But Wellard neglects to point out that the library movement had its roots deep in the first half of the 19th century and even many years earlier. Libraries were spreading rapidly over America long before 1900, whereas, as Learned has shown, Carnegie grants for library buildings numbered but 14 prior to 1898, as contrasted to over 1,600 library buildings erected with Carnegie funds subsequent to that date.[98] In other words, Wellard, who was generalizing from only the English pattern, failed to realize that philanthropic bequests did not create a need for libraries; they merely helped to alleviate a demand that already existed.

A quite different aspect of the problem has been presented by Sidney Ditzion,[99] who sees the library as at least partially the result of increasing urbanization, the need of laborers for technical and recreational reading, and the desire of the mill-owner to increase, by education, the skill of the foreign-born worker. All such forces implicit in an expanding industrial society Ditzion sees tapped by those interested in gaining extensive support for popular education and public libraries through rationalistic and emotional appeals that pictured the library as the savior of youth, a competitor of the grogshop, a potent enemy of crime.[100] The growth of the library is seen essentially as resulting from a fundamental democratic need of contemporary society crystallized into reality by the opportunism of public leaders. Within its self-imposed limits the study is carefully developed and well documented. That it fails to present a complete picture the author himself would be the first to admit. To link the library with the extension of the educational system is certainly valid, for, though the growth of libraries necessarily lagged behind the establishment of schools, the two were undeniably related. The only objection that might be raised is that the study describes a relationship rather than explains a motivation. In a sense, it begs the question; the problem is made more difficult because it is less selective. In short, instead of attempting to discover the social forces that created the library, the study makes it necessary to determine the forces that brought both the school and the library into being. Nevertheless, Ditzion's studies are the first important attempts to arrive at a real understanding of a few elements of library origins.

At this same time there appeared certain other writings which, if not directly in the current of the new history, were at least influenced by it and hence deserve mention here. Houlette reconsidered the work of the Reverend Thomas Bray and the parish libraries established through his influence, in an essay that draws heavily from standard treatments of the subject.[101] Hazel A. Johnson reviewed the life and professional contributions of John Cotton Dana, appending an extensive and much-needed bibliography of his writings, prepared with the cooperation of Beatrice Winser.[102] Thomas E. Keys examined the collections of Colonial private libraries and found those in New England to be predominantly theological, those in the central Atlantic area indicative of a more democratic spirit in their owners, and those in the Colonial South more cavalier.[103] His conclusions, though they reflect the popular view that regional differences in reading habits were important, are based on quite incomparable data. Because he has contrasted the libraries of New England divines with secular collections in other parts of the Atlantic coastal area, his theories cannot be taken seriously.[104]

Louis Shores' doctoral dissertation, published in 1935 under the title *Origins of the American College Library, 1638-1800*,[105] is essentially, as far as library historiography is concerned, a hybrid form. The first portion of the book is a sketchy factual summary of the early history of each of the nine college libraries along the Atlantic seaboard,[106] considered in a manner reminiscent of the older history. But the remainder, and by far the greater portion, of the volume attempts to relate the development of the college library to the development of the curriculum, the objectives, and the administrative policies of the college itself. The book's weaknesses lie in its numerous errors of fact, its reliance upon sources of doubtful authenticity, and its failure to synthesize its array of material and to come to grips with the basic problem.[107] Historically, the development of the college library rested squarely upon the development of the college; the one was dependent upon the other in the exact degree to which education was book-centered.

Other contributions to library history may be briefly noted. Joseph T. Wheeler, in his doctoral dissertation on "Literary Culture in Colonial Maryland, 1700-1776"[108] has much of importance to say about the early libraries, especially the circulating libraries, of that colony. Frank K. Walter considered the early Sunday-school libraries in a brief paper that throws much light on these neglected collections.[109] Monaghan and Lowenthal make interesting and important use of the circulation records of the New York Society Library in developing their presentation of social life and culture in New York City in 1789.[110] Herbert Ross Brown, in his account of the sentimental novel in America, shows the circulating library to be a most important agent for the distribution of popular fiction,[111] and George C. Raddin analyzes the offerings of Caritat's Circulating Library in his *An Early New York Library of Fiction*.[112] One of the best presentations of library development in relation to the cultural and economic life of a single community appears in Harriet S. Tapley's *Salem Imprints, 1768-1825*,[113] where the early libraries of Salem, Massachusetts, are studied in some detail, with emphasis on their evolution from the cultural environment. Finally, it appears that those interested in the historical emergence of the library in this country are becoming interested in the sources for historical research in the library field. Nathaniel Stewart's "Sources for the Study of American College Library History, 1800-1876,"[114] devotes far too much attention to only secondary sources[115] but nevertheless is indicative of a growing desire of those writing about library history to evaluate the accuracy of their data.

The fullest expression of the new tendencies in the writing of library history is to be found in two studies. One is the opening chapter of Carleton B. Joeckel's *Government of the American Public Library*[116] and the other Gwladys Spencer's dissertation on the origins of the Chicago Public Library.[117] Joeckel's primary concern is, of course, with the rise and development of governmental relationships and administrative functions, but these are so inextricably intertwined with other factors that to consider a part necessarily involves some attention to the whole. The opening sentences of the book are most significant:

> Perhaps more than any other function of local government, the free public library of today is intimately linked by tradition, by custom, and even by law, with its historic backgrounds. Without a preliminary view of the institutions which preceded it and out of which it developed by a slow evolutionary process, and without sympathetic appreciation of the stages through which it has progressed as a part of the governmental structure, it is difficult to understand clearly the forms library organization has assumed today.[118]

Obviously, Joeckel has segregated only certain threads from the complex fabric of library history, and he would be the first to admit that his is not a comprehensive treatment. Nevertheless, the threads which he selected are of major importance in determining the pattern of library development, and his examination of the governmental warp and woof clarifies for the historian the intricacies of the entire design. Furthermore, this chapter unmistakably designates the path that the writing of library history must follow if it is to achieve its fullest significance.

The principles suggested by Joeckel have been given complete expression by Miss Spencer's study, which, despite its title, is really a history of library development in Illinois. Like Joeckel, under whose direction the study was in part prepared, she has emphasized the library's contingency upon trends in local government and public administration, but she has also considered other influences congenial to library establishment. In the pages of her work there appeared, for the first time, a balanced presentation of the many social forces that contributed to public library formation. Miss Spencer not only brought to light many facts which had hitherto been unknown but by her method demonstrated the value of relating progress to contemporary social phenomena.

The first half of this century closed with the publication of two particularly significant studies. The first to be completed, though not the first to appear in print, was the present writer's *Foundations of the Public Library*, which sought to identify the economic and social forces that contributed to the evolution of the public library and its antecedents, much in the manner suggested by Arnold Borden.[119] In addition to the social setting, the work emphasized the rise in New England, during the Colonial period and the period of the Republic, of the social library and the circulating library, with particular attention to their organizational structure, their governmental relationships, and the characteristics of their book collections as they changed from 1629 to 1855. Sidney Ditzion's *Arsenals of a Democratic Culture* began essentially where the present writer's work had stopped, but covered a wider canvas by including the Middle Atlantic states as well as New England.[120] Ditzion's study, which is unusually well documented, stressed many of the same influences that he had portrayed in his earlier writings cited above, and owed much to the influence of Merle Curti. Both studies had begun as doctoral dissertations and represented a long period of reflective inquiry that stretched over some 10 to 15 years. Thus, the works of Spencer, Ditzion, and Shera set the pattern for a comprehensive history of the American library movement, though at this writing such a generalized treatment has not yet appeared.

## X.  FROM MID-CENTURY TO THE PRESENT

Alfred Hessel's *Geschichte der Bibliotheken* had, for some years, been a standard short history of the libraries of the world. In 1943 Reuben Peiss completed his translation of the first eight chapters. The work, as the translator says in his preface, emphasized "the development of the library as an institution within the framework of general cultural trends."[121] Such praise may be somewhat over-generous, but it is a good short history, although it neglects the history of the library in America. Because the original terminated its narrative with the First World War and the translation was published in 1950, Peiss added a ninth chapter, which updated the original and devoted considerable attention to libraries on this side of the Atlantic. Unfortunately, this account is not particularly good; it attempts to cover too much in too limited a space, and its emphasis is not always well proportioned.

C. Seymour Thompson's huge manuscript on the history of the American public library represented years of patient effort but it was not accepted for publication until 1952, when the newly established Scarecrow Press issued in photo-offset a very condensed version.[122] The work, although it is the result of diligent digging, is superficial, and is essentially a reversion to the old anecdotal history, untouched by the new currents of social thought that had animated Spencer, Ditzion, and the school they represented.

When Oliver Garceau prepared his study of the public library in the political process for the *Public Library Inquiry*, he prefaced it with a chapter on "The Foundations of Library Government," which treated such facets of library history as 17th-century religious and humanistic learning, the 18th-century social setting, the influence of the Enlightenment, the social library, the beginnings of the public library, early library government, the social setting and characteristics of later library development, and the rise of the professional librarian.[123] The preparation of this chapter was largely the work of a trained historian and a member of Garceau's research staff for the *Inquiry*, C. Dewitt Hardy. Hardy had been recruited from the departments of history and government at the University of Maine. Hardy's work, by his own acknowledgment, leans heavily upon Shera's study of the beginnings of the public library movement in New England.

Albert Predeek, when he was librarian of the Technische Hochschule in Berlin-Charlottenburg, had travelled widely in England and the United States, had known many distinguished librarians in those countries, and was thoroughly familiar with librarianship in both nations. As a consequence of his experience, he was invited to prepare the section on history of libraries in England and the United States from the Renaissance to the beginning of the Second World War, for the third volume of the monumental *Milkau-Leyh Handbuch der Biblio-thekswissenschaft*. Because the text was in German, and rather difficult German at that, Predeek's treatment of American library history was unknown to most American librarians until 1947, when it was translated by Lawrence S. Thompson and published by the American Library Association.[124] In his introduction the translator admits that the book "does not pretend to be the final word on the subject," and adds that "a few changes have been made by the translator in the text and notes."[125] Unfortunately, he did not make enough changes; at least in the American section, inaccuracies abound, and probably few historians of the American library scene will give the book more than scant attention.[126] Though not strictly library history, one should mention the appearance, in 1950, of John Lawler's account of the origins and development of the H. W. Wilson Company.[127] The work is unique in that it is the sole representative in library history of the historical treatment of a commercial enterprise, a genre of historical writing that has recently become quite popular as a branch of economic history.

In the mid-20th century the interest in library history rose strikingly, stimulated perhaps by the lengthening perspective on the profession, and supported by a growing nationalism following World War II and the rise of the United States to a position of preeminence in international affairs. In 1947 the Library History Round Table was formed under the auspices of the ALA, sparked by Louis Shores and Wayne Shirley, and in January 1966 the *Journal of Library History* began publication, with Shores as its editor. The meetings of the Round Table have been popular from the start, and the journal, which has expanded its scope to include the philosophy of librarianship, enjoys a healthy circulation. Aspects of library history have always been popular with library school students as subjects for their master's essays, and the inauguration of doctoral programs by a number of library schools reflects the same enthusiasm in doctoral dissertations. While the master's essays tend to be an uninspiring lot, they may help to salvage some records that might otherwise be lost. Michael Harris has performed a useful service in bringing much of this material together in his *Guide to Research in American Library History*.[128]

The present writer has for long argued the desirability of a new approach to library history—the history of *librarianship* as differentiated from the conventional history of libraries, a history that would inquire into the origins and evolution of the particular library services or functions. To date, however, only two major inquiries of this kind have appeared. The first was Kenneth Brough's *Scholar's Workshop*, the purpose of which was to trace the conceptions of library service as exemplified in the histories of Harvard, Yale, Columbia, and the University of Chicago. Thus, he sought, as he writes in the preface, to answer such questions as:

> What opinions have existed concerning the importance of the library in the university?
>
> How have the functions of the university library been defined?
>
> What differentiation of service has been considered desirable for the several classes of the clientele of the library: professors, graduate students, undergraduates, and the non-university public?
>
> What thoughts have arisen about the nature and extent of the materials which the library should collect?
>
> What ideas have emerged concerning the accessibility of books?
>
> What conceptions have evolved with relation to the kind and amount of aid to be given to readers?
>
> How has the role of the librarian changed?[129]

In style and manner of presentation the book left something to be desired, but it was "a good college try," and as a pioneering effort in a new direction it merits considerable praise.

A much more successful effort than Brough's, perhaps because of its sharper focus, was Samuel Rothstein's *The Development of Reference Services*. "There is clearly room and need," the author has written in his introduction, "for a series of evaluative studies of the development of American library services which could eventually be put together to form the desired definitive history of American librarianship," and it is his hope that his book will make a contribution toward that end. Therefore he has set out to "furnish the historical background for one of the continuing problems of American librarianship—the provision of reference service in research libraries."[130] Unhappily, Rothstein's dream of a major synthesis of the development of library services and functions is still unrealized, but he has made an excellent beginning with his unusually well-documented study.

To return to the more conventional forms of library history, during the past two decades there have appeared two major histories of individual libraries that set the standard for this genre. Both were written by trained historians rather than librarians, and both have great literary merit as well as historical competence. Both, too, were written in celebration of the centennials of their respective libraries, a rather unusual thing, since such occasional history is frequently not the best. The first is Walter Muir Whitehill's account of the Boston Public Library, published in 1956,[131] and the second, Clarence H. Cramer's *Open Shelves and Open Minds*, which narrates the first hundred years of the Cleveland Public Library.[132] Admittedly, both Whitehill and Cramer had excellent material with which to weave their tapestries, rich in the picturesque and replete with strong personalities. But these advantages should not detract from the accomplishments of the authors, whose works highlight the mediocrity of far too much library history.

A third major history that might be ranked with Whitehill and Cramer is Phyllis Dain's *The New York Public Library: A History of Its Founding and Early Years.*[133] The volume is the first in a projected series covering the complete history of the N.Y.P.L., and covers the merger of the Astor and Lenox Libraries with the Tilden Trust to form the present monumental institution at Fifth Avenue and 42nd Street. The author had two goals in mind: "to complement and to some extent supersede" Lydenberg's earlier study, and to set the development of the library "against the history of New York City and its library conditions." The first goal has been admirably achieved; whereas Lydenberg concentrated on descriptions of the individual reference and circulating libraries that formed the merger, Dain is primarily concerned with the process of merger itself, its economic, political and personal complications. But she fails in her second objective, to relate the founding of the library to the larger social setting. In short, Dain does not provide an integrated social history of a large metropolitan library; nevertheless, as a well-documented study of the men and policies that shaped the New York Public Library from the early 1890s to 1913, the book is an important contribution to American library history.

The biography of librarians is still popular with doctoral candidates in library schools, but most such studies still remain in the archives of the schools that granted the degrees. Two creditable works have appeared in print, however, and in their scope and depth they surpass the *Pioneers* series of a generation ago. Edward G. Holley's *Charles Evans*[134] and William Landram Williamson's *William Frederick Poole*[135] were both doctoral dissertations, and both reflect the intellectual discipline that one has the right to expect from candidates for the degree. The latter is substantially a shortened form of the original manuscript, and this writer believes it to be the better of the two books. Moreover, Poole had greater influence in the library profession than Evans, and Williamson has woven into his account much valuable material about the early years of the ALA, Poole's contemporaries, and library development generally during the last decades of the 19th century. But there may be some bias in this judgment, since Williamson began the study under my direction, a pleasant association that was necessarily interrupted when I left Chicago for Cleveland. Personal preferences aside, both are admirable examples of excellence in scholarly biography.

A third biography, which deserves to be ranked with the two preceding ones, but which differs from them in several important ways, is Maurice Tauber's biography of Louis Round Wilson.[136] Unlike the others, it was not written for an academic degree; rather, it represents an act of homage and devotion. The author was selected by the subject as his official biographer and the two worked closely in the preparation of the manuscript. Thus, Tauber had available to him a substantial amount of material, reminiscences, and unrecorded anecdotes that would be denied to future historians. For this advantage, of course, he paid a price with respect to perspective and a degree of objectivity. Nonetheless, his work will probably stand as the definitive statement about Wilson.

To complete this review there remain to be considered a group of historical writings that do not fit precisely into any of the categories set forth in the preceding pages. In a substantial volume of over 500 pages, Thomas Spencer Harding has recorded the origins and development of the college literary societies during the 19th century, the character of their libraries, and the role they played in the history of the college library itself.[137] The author has shown that the influence of these literary society libraries in the history of the academic library is far greater than anyone had suspected; indeed, this influence represents a rather striking parallel with that of the early social library in the stimulation of the public library movement, illustrating, once again, the importance of the voluntary association in library history.

The influence of Andrew Carnegie's philanthropy upon library development had never been studied in depth until George S. Bobinski published his *Carnegie Libraries*.[138] This volume, a happy blending of sound scholarship and good writing, treats in comprehensive detail the history of Carnegie's philanthropy, the means by which grants for Carnegie buildings were obtained, the architecture of those structures, reaction to the donations, libraries that never materialized, the impact of the Johnson report and the end of the Carnegie giving, how the Carnegie libraries fared, and the impact of Carnegie influence upon public library development in the United States.

Except for a few widely scattered articles written during the 1930s and 1940s, no attempt was made to set forth the history of library education until 1952, when Robert D. Leigh published his survey of library education for Alice Bryan's *The Public Librarian*, one of the volumes of the *Public Library Inquiry*.[139] Up to that time the best account had been Louis Round Wilson's paper in the Chicago conference of 1948.[140] By the time the paper was presented Wilson had long been retired from the deanship of the Graduate Library School of the University of Chicago, and had lived through, and personally participated in, many of the developments he narrates. It still remains one of the best sources on the history of library education, especially with regard to the role of the ALA and its Board of Education for Librarianship, the creation of which had followed the publication of the Williamson Report. Ray Trautman's history of the School of Library Service at Columbia is a relatively brief study, considering that the library school has the longest history of any in the United States, but it is a good source book for the early records of both Albany and Columbia.[141] After such a long period of neglect of library education, 1961 brought two books on the subject, both of which narrate the history of library education to 1923 and the publication of the Williamson Report. Sarah Vann's *Training for Librarianship Before 1923*,[142] had begun as a doctoral dissertation. Carl White's *Origins of the American Library School* was written near the end of an active career as teacher and dean.[143] These books are of two quite different types, each with its own virtues, and together they make a good team which I have found useful in my own studies of library education.

## XI. CONCLUSION

The original version of this paper, which appeared in 1945, concluded with a plea to view the history of the American library movement as the result of a complex system of social forces.

> The relation between the library as the product of its culture and the social milieu in which it exists is polydimensional and reciprocal. It has no objective existence but reacts to and is reacted upon by its environment. Hence, one must ever be careful to avoid the easy fallacies of oversimplification and one-sided causation. Doubtless the threads of causality that converge at any given time to create a specific social phenomenon stretch back through the historical continuum to the primordial time, and any definite 'origin' must always be relative to its antecedents. . . .

Such insistence on the sociological origins of librarianship is scarcely necessary today. Library history has matured during the past three decades. Yet the fact remains that many of the questions raised in the 1945 paper are still not adequately answered: What were the influences that brought the library into being? How deeply was the library rooted in a conscious need? Did the library result from a spontaneous enthusiasm of the populace, or did it come from the untiring efforts of a few? Who were those forgotten men and women who were responsible for the demand for free library service, and what were their motives in so doing? To what extent did the idea of the public library become incorporated with the *mores* so that it grew to be a hallmark of municipal progress? What was the part played by philanthropy? Was philanthropy the *deus ex machina* that saved the library during its formative period, or was it no more than an ornamental superstructure imposed upon an agency the permanence of which had already been assured? To what extent does the library signalize the spread of socialization as an assumption by the body politic of a function in which private enterprise and voluntary association has failed? Was the library a cause or an effect of social change? How was it related to the spread of popular education? Of all the social phenomena by which the library is surrounded, which were related to it, and which were not? As Berr and Febrve express it, how can one differentiate accurately among "contingency," "necessity," and "logic" in library causality? To this long list other questions can now be added: When does a culture, or a sub-culture, reach a point at which library or bibliographic service becomes necessary to it? How and why did the several functions of the library emerge? Why did librarianship forsake scholarship for popularity and mass culture? What was behind the librarians' constant search for professional identity? One could go on and on. Certainly we have not yet achieved a true historical synthesis of the library's past, and we dearly need to.

One source of historical knowledge that has been sadly neglected, to our great loss, is that of oral history. While assiduously collecting the oral history of others, librarians have neglected their own. Already it is too late to record many of the great voices of librarianship who could speak unrestrainedly of their past, and further delay will erode this source of library history even more. Such records must be carefully gathered, and properly safeguarded, with the same regard for legal niceties which accompany any personalized memoirs, but we must not suffer more losses in this area than we can help. Even as this is being written we must recall that Verner Clapp, one of our richest sources of historical knowledge about librarianship in general and the Library of Congress in particular, has passed from the scene. *"Rien ne manque à sa gloire, il manquait à la nôtre,"* the Académie Française ordered inscribed on a bust of Molière, belatedly recognizing his genius a century after his death. The oral history of librarianship and libraries must not be allowed to suffer any more such unrecorded losses as occurred with the death of Verner Clapp.

A defense of library history is scarcely needed.[144] Though the past cannot provide all the answers to the problems of the present and the future, it is only the past we have, and as such it is our sole resource for an understanding of who and what we as librarians are. Only history can give us the key to our professional self-knowledge.[145]

## FOOTNOTES

[1] Biographical data are from Edmund Quincy, *Life of Josiah Quincy of Massachusetts*, 5th ed. (Boston, Fields, Osgood & Co.. 1869), and James Walker, "Memoir of Josiah Quincy," *Proceedings of the Massachusetts Historical Society*, IX (1866-67), pp. 83-156.

[2] Biographical sketch of Josiah Quincy in the *Dictionary of American Biography*, IX, 310. It was Morison's own tercentennial history of Harvard that rendered Quincy's *History* obsolete.

[3] *The Journals of Major Samuel Shaw, the First American Consul at Canton, with a Life of the Author* (Boston: W. Crosby & H.P. Nichols, 1847).

[4] *A Municipal History of the Town and City of Boston* (Boston: C.C. Little & J. Brown, 1852).

[5] "Report on the Condition of the Library," *Seventh Annual Report of the President of Harvard University* (1833), pp. 4-6. *See also* Quincy's *Considerations Relative to the Library of Harvard University, Respectfully Submitted to the Legislature of Massachusetts* (Cambridge: C. Folsom, 1833).

[6] *The History of the Boston Athenaeum, with Biographical Notices of Its Deceased Founders* (Cambridge: Metcalf & Co., 1851), p. iii.

[7] Edmund Quincy, *Life of Josiah Quincy*, p. 500.

[8] *Ibid.*

[9] This, of course, ignores fugitive materials such as W. Smith, "Notes for a History of the Library Company of Philadelphia," *Waldie's Portfolio* (Philadelphia, September 26, 1835), p. 100, as well as brief and sketchy historical notices appearing in the periodical press and frequently prefixed to the early printed catalogs of individual libraries.

[10] *The History of the United States of America*, rev. ed. (New York: Harper & Bros., 1871), I, vii. The great popularity of history at this time is evident from the fact that Weem's *Life of Washington* reached some 70 editions, and by 1875 the early volumes of Bancroft's work had appeared in 20 editions. *See* Michael Kraus, *A History of American History* (New York: Farrar & Rinehart, Inc., 1937), Chaps. V-VIII; Vernon L. Parrington, *Main Currents in American Thought* (New York: Harcourt, Brace & Co., 1930), II, 437ff; and Van Wyck Brooks, *The Flowering of New England* (New York: E.P. Dutton & Co., 1936), Chap. VI. This American enthusiasm for American history was, of course, one manifestation of a larger movement which in Europe brought about the publication of important nationalist histories resulting largely from the atmosphere created by the revolutions of 1830. Bismark is said to have thought that the German professors of history were surpassed only by the Prussian army in doing most to create the new Germany under the hegemony of Prussia.

[11] Frank Luther Mott, *A History of American Magazines, 1741-1850* (New York: D. Appleton & Co., 1930), Part III, "The Period of Expansion: 1825-1850," pp. 339-528.

[12] *History of the Boston Athenaeum*, p. v.

[13] *Ibid.*, pp. 239-41.

[14] Edmund Quincy, *Life of Josiah Quincy*, p. 500.

[15] *Ibid.*, p. 501.

[16] Quoted in Parrington, *Main Currents*, II, 279.

[17] Josiah Quincy, *An Appeal in Behalf of the Boston Athenaeum, Addressed to the Proprietors* (Boston: J. Wilson & Son, 1853).

[18] *History of the Boston Athenaeum*, pp. iii-iv.

[19] Quoted in Edmund Quincy, *Life of Josiah Quincy*, p. 500.

[20] *History of the Boston Athenaeum*, p. iv.

[21] *Ibid.*, p. v. The tenacity of this hold and the degree to which Quincy esteemed the original plans of the founders of the Athenaeum are apparent from his vigorous opposition to the movement to convert the Athenaeum into a public library for the city of Boston. So vigorous was Quincy's leadership that the plans set forth in the spring of 1853, by Ticknor and his liberal followers, to make the Athenaeum really public were defeated in a vote of the Athenaeum proprietors that has become historic in the annals of that library. Quincy's *History* should be read in the light of this defense. *See* Josiah Quincy, *An Appeal in Behalf of the Boston Athenaeum*, and Edmund Quincy, *Life of Josiah Quincy*, p. 501.

[22]Washington: Smithsonian Institution, 1851.

[23]*Manual of Public Libraries, Institutions, and Societies in the United States and British Provinces of North America* (Philadelphia: J.B. Lippincott & Co., 1859; reprinted: Urbana, Graduate Library School, University of Illinois, 1967).

[24]*Ibid.*, p. 4.

[25]The results of this survey are to be found in William S. Perry, *Historical Collections Relating to the American Colonial Church: Vol. IV, Maryland* (New York: AMS Press, 1970), pp. 190-232.

[26]The answers to these questions are preserved in their original letter form in two large scrapbooks now the property of Yale University, and for the opportunity to make use of this important source material the present writer is deeply indebted to Bernard Knollenberg, librarian, and Anne S. Pratt, reference librarian, of that university.

[27]"The 'Trumbull Manuscript Collections' and Early Connecticut Libraries," in *Papers in Honor of Andrew Keogh, Librarian of Yale University, by the Staff of the Library, 30 June 1938* (New Haven: Privately printed, 1938), pp. 325-42. Stills and Upton supplemented the Trumbull data with information gleaned from other sources in their attempt to present a truly definitive list of Connecticut libraries prior to 1801. The replies to Trumbull's questions vary, of course, in detail and accuracy; but, taken as a whole, this collection is the most important single source on early libraries in this country. Since Connecticut was among the first of the colonies to have a wide social library development, the collection's importance for general library history transcends state boundaries.

[28]A summary, by counties, of the results of this questionnaire was included in Mann's third annual report, published in the *Common School Journal*, II (1840), 122-28. As far as the present writer knows, the replies to Mann's letters have not been preserved.

[29]"Bibliographie und Bibliotheken in den Vereinigten Staaten von Nord-Amerika," *Serapeum: Zeitschrift für Bibliothekswissenschaft, Handschriftenkunde, und ältere Litterature*, VI (1845), 209-24; VII (1846), 113-23, 129-72, 178-92, 204-206.

[30]*Report and Documents Relating to the Public Schools of Rhode Island, 1848* (Providence: Published by order of the General Assembly, 1849), pp. 425-28.

[31]Rhees, *Manual of Public Libraries*, p. v. A portion of the report was published as an 80-page pamphlet by the Institution.

[32]*Ibid.*

[33]*Memoirs of Libraries: Including a Handbook of Library Economy* (London: Trübner & Co., 1859). As a matter of fact, this work appeared while Rhees' *Manual* was in the process of publication, and parts of his sections dealing with library practice are drawn from it. *See* Rhees' Preface, p. vi.

[34] The standard biography of Edwards is Thomas Greenwood, *Edward Edwards, the Chief Pioneer of Municipal Public Libraries* (London: Scott, Greenwood & Co., 1902). *See also* Oskar Thyregod, *Die Kulturfunktion der Bibliothek* (Haag: Nijhoff, 1936), pp. 101-103.

[35] Edwards, *Memoirs of Libraries*, II, 163-243.

[36] As evidence of the superficiality of Edwards' treatment, witness his discussion of the Boston Athenaeum, which he has drawn from Jewett's sketch without even taking the trouble to go back to Quincy's *History*, published almost a decade before Edwards' work appeared. It is also to be noted that even Garnett's praise is not unqualified, as he points out that much of the statistical data collected by Edwards is not reliable.

[37] *Free Town Libraries, Their Formation, Management, and History, in Britain, France, Germany, and America, Together with Brief Notices of Book Collectors and of the Respective Places of Deposit of Their Surviving Collections* (London: Trübner & Co., 1869). *See* especially Book III, "Free Town Libraries in America," p. 269-343.

[38] United States Bureau of Education, *Public Libraries in the United States of America, Their History, Condition, and Management: Special Report* (Washington: Government Printing Office, 1876).

[39] *Ibid.*, p. xiii.

[40] "The Beginnings of Our Public Library System," *Literary World*, X (1879), 121-22; "M. Vattemare and the Public Library System," *ibid.*, pp. 185-86; "The Results of Vattemare's Library Scheme," *ibid.*, pp. 281-82; "The Library Movement Thirty Years Ago," *ibid.*, pp. 330-31; "Libraries in Boston," in his *Memorial History of Boston, Including Suffolk County, Massachusetts, 1630-1880* (Boston: James R. Osgood & Co., 1880-81), IV, 279-94; and "The Development of the Library: Address at the Dedication of the Orrington Lunt Library, Northwestern University, Evanston, Ill.," *Library Journal*, XIX (1894), 370-75. *See also* his semi-historical article, "The Boston Public Library," *Scribner's Monthly* [later *Century Magazine*], III (1871-72), 150-56.

[41] Boston: Houghton, Mifflin & Co., 1884-89. For library material *see* the Index under "Americana." Winsor also has some claim to consideration by virtue of his collection of statistics of libraries in America and Europe, which he published in the 17th annual report of the Boston Public Library (1869).

[42] Frederick J. Teggart, "On the Literature of Library History," *Library Journal*, XXII (1897), C38.

[43] Teggart, himself a librarian at Leland Stanford University, might possibly have obtained such a conception direct from Winsor. Biographical material on Winsor is astonishingly scarce for a figure so prominent. The best sources are Edward Channing, "Justin Winsor," *American Historical Review*, III (1897-98), 197-202; Horace E. Scudder, "Memorial of Justin Winsor, LL.D.," *Proceedings of the Massachusetts Historical Society*, XII (2d ser., 1899), 457-82;

the biographical sketch by James Truslow Adams in the *Dictionary of American Biography*; and William F. Yust, *A Bibliography of Justin Winsor* (Cambridge: Harvard University Library, 1902).

[44] Kraus, *A History of American History*, p. 579.

[45] Channing, "Justin Winsor," p. 198.

[46] Boston: Robert Bros., 1894, p. 9.

[47] *Ibid.*, p. 11.

[48] *Ibid.*, p. 14. *See also* William I. Fletcher, "The Proprietary Library in Relation to the Public Library Movement," *Library Journal*, XXXI (1906), C268-72.

[49] This does not mean that Fletcher was the first to consider the library as a social agency or even to apply the specific term "social institution" to it. Josiah P. Quincy, grandson of the historian of the Athenaeum, had referred to the library as a "social institution" in 1876, in his *The Protection of Majorities* (Boston: Roberts Bros., 1876), p. 105. In the same year he again referred to it as "the one secular institution which encourages self-development as an aim" ("Free Libraries," in the *Report* of 1876, p. 390). Fletcher's contribution rests on the fact that he was first to see the historical emergence of the library as a sociological phenomenon.

[50] *Ninth Report of the Public Library Commission of Massachusetts, 1899*, Public Document No. 44 (Boston: Wright & Potter Printing Co., 1899).

[51] By "local" histories are meant both town and county histories; though as far as the libraries are concerned they all really reduce to town histories, since most of the county histories, though prefaced by a certain amount of information relating to the county as a whole, are largely collections of the histories of the individual towns.

[52] "Public Libraries [in Worcester]," in D. Hamilton Hurd, comp., *History of Worcester County, Massachusetts* (Philadelphia: J.W. Lewis & Co., 1889), II, 1491-1509.

[53] Good examples of this are *The Athenaeum Centenary: The Influence and History of the Boston Athenaeum from 1807 to 1907, with a Record of its Officers and Benefactors, and a Complete List of Proprietors* (Boston: Boston Athenaeum, 1907), and *One Hundred and Seventy-Fifth Anniversary of the Incorporation of the Redwood Library* (Newport, R.I.: Redwood Library, 1922).

[54] Newport, R.I.: Redwood Library, 1891.

[55] "Peterborough Town Library: The Pioneer Public Library," *Granite Monthly*, XXVIII (1900), 281-91. A further account appeared at the centennial celebration in 1933 with George Abbot Morison's address before the New Hampshire Library Association (*The Centenary of the Establishment of Public Libraries and the Forty-Fourth Annual Meeting of the New Hampshire Library Association, Held in the Unitarian Church and Parish House, Peterborough, New Hampshire, August 22-24, 1933*, pp. 5-27).

[56] Washington: Government Printing Office, 1904.

[57] Lucy Salamanca's journalistic account of the Library of Congress is at best only an unreliable and superficial treatment. Though she does not mention Johnston, Miss Salamanca leans heavily upon his work for the material in the first half of her book, *Fortress of Freedom: The Story of the Library of Congress* (Philadelphia: J.B. Lippincott Co., 1942).

[58] David C. Mearns, *The Story up to Now* (Washington, D.C.: The Library of Congress, 1947).

[59] Austin B. Keep, *History of the New York Society Library, with an Introductory Chapter on Libraries in Colonial New York, 1698-1776* (New York: De Vinne Press for the Trustees, 1908).

[60] *The Public Library of the City of Boston: A History* (Boston: Trustees of the Public Library, 1911).

[61] Harry Miller Lydenberg, *History of the New York Public Library: Astor, Lenox, and Tilden Foundations* (New York: New York Public Library, 1923).

[62] John F. Lewis, *History of the Apprentices' Library of Philadelphia, 1820-1920, the Oldest Free Circulating Library in America* (Philadelphia, 1924).

[63] Austin K. Gray, *Benjamin Franklin's Library: A Short Account of the Library Company of Philadelphia* (New York: Macmillan Co., 1937). This was first published in 1936 under the misleading and inaccurate title, "The First American Library."

[64] L. M. Miller, comp., *Legislative History of Township Libraries in the State of Michigan from 1835 to 1901* (Lansing: R. Smith Publishing Co. for the Board of Library Commissioners, 1902).

[65] Cole, *Early Library Development in New York State (1800 to 1900)* (New York: New York Public Library, 1927); Tolan, "Libraries and Lyceums," in Alexander D. Flick, ed., *History of the State of New York* (New York: Columbia University Press, 1937), IX, 47-91.

[66] In *Annual Report of the American Historical Association for the Year 1895* (Washington: Government Printing Office, 1896), pp. 171-224.

[67] Bernard C. Steiner, "Rev. Thomas Bray and His American Libraries," *American Historical Review*, II (1896-97), 59-75; William D. Houlette, "Parish Libraries and the Work of the Reverend Thomas Bray," *Library Quarterly*, IV (1934), 588-609 (leans heavily on Steiner); Bernard Steiner, ed., *Rev. Thomas Bray: His Life and Selected Works Relating to Maryland* (Baltimore: Maryland Historical Society, 1901). Another Southern library receiving historical attention was the Charlestown Library Society. *See* "Original Rules and Members of the Charlestown Library Society," *South Carolina Historical and Genealogical Magazine*, XXIII (1922), 163-70.

[68] *The Public Library Movement in the United States, 1853-1893* (Boston: Boston Book Co., 1913).

[69] *Ibid.*, p. 19.

⁷⁰Harry Miller Lydenberg, *John Shaw Billings, Creator of the National Medical Library and Its Catalogue, First Director of the New York Public Library* (1924); Robert Kendall Shaw, *Samuel Swett Green* (1926); William Parker Cutter, *Charles Ammi Cutter* (1931); Linda A. Eastman, *Portrait of a Librarian: William Howard Brett* (1940); Chalmers Hadley, *John Cotton Dana* (1943); Fremont Rider, *Melvil Dewey* (1944); Joseph A. Borome, *Charles Coffin Jewett* (1951). There was also published a collection of brief biographies: *Pioneering Leaders in Librarianship*, ed. by Emily Miller Danton (Chicago: American Library Association, 1953). Reference should also be made to Josephine Adams Rathbone, "Pioneers of the Library Profession," *Wilson Library Bulletin*, Vol. 23 (June 1949), 775-79.

⁷¹The standard biography of Billings is Fielding H. Garrison, *John Shaw Billings: A Memoir* (New York: G.P. Putnam's Sons, 1915).

⁷²Harry Miller Lydenberg, "A Forgotten Trail Blazer [Joseph Green Cogswell]," in William Warner Bishop and Andrew Keogh, eds., *Essays Offered to Herbert Putnam by His Colleagues and Friends on His Thirtieth Anniversary as Librarian of Congress, 5 April, 1929* (New Haven: Yale University Press, 1929), pp. 302-14; Carl B. Roden, "The Boston Years of Dr. W. F. Poole," *ibid.*, pp. 388-94; F. J. Teggart, "An Early Champion of Free Libraries [Jesse Torry]," *Library Journal*, XXIII (1898), 617-18; William A. Slade, "As It Was in the Beginning [Ainsworth Rand Spofford]," *Public Libraries*, XXIX (1924), 293-26.

⁷³*John Cotton Dana: A Life* (Newark, N.J.: Public Library and Museum, 1940).

⁷⁴*Melvil Dewey: Seer, Inspirer, Doer, 1851-1931* (Lake Placid, N.Y.: Lake Placid Club, 1932).

⁷⁵"Home Education Bulletins," No. 31 (Albany: University of the State of New York, 1900).

⁷⁶New York: G.P. Putnam's Sons, 1900, pp. 295-320.

⁷⁷4th ed. rev.; New York: D. Appleton & Co., 1929, Chap. II, "Library Growth and Development in the United States," pp. 5-19.

⁷⁸Charles K. Bolton, *American Library History* (1919) and *Proprietary and Subscription Libraries* (1917). Bolton had previously written of early social and circulating libraries in two excellent short treatments for the Colonial Society of Massachusetts: "Social Libraries in Boston," *Publications of the Colonial Society of Massachusetts*, XII (1908-9), 332-38, and "Circulating Libraries in Boston, 1765-1865," *ibid.*, XI (1906-7), 196-207. The treatment of circulating libraries is particularly good.

⁷⁹There is some evidence that Terry planned to include the history of libraries in states other than the original 13 and may even have thought in terms of a history of libraries for the entire country. Probably the best part of his collection is that which includes the early records, minutes, catalogs, and charge books of the individual libraries.

[80] Unpublished address before the American Historical Association at Rochester, N.Y., in December 1926, quoted extensively by Harry Elmer Barnes in his *A History of Historical Writing* (Norman: University of Oklahoma Press, 1937), p. 267.

[81] *See* Charles A. Beard, *An Economic Interpretation of the Constitution of the United States* (New York: Macmillan Co., 1941), Chap. I, "Historical Interpretation in the United States."

[82] *See* the Foreword in Arthur M. Schlesinger, *New Viewpoints in American History* (New York: Macmillan Co., 1922). A criticism of this type of historical writing is to be found in Allan Nevins, *The Gateway to History* (Boston: D.C. Heath & Co., 1938), p. 271.

[83] *Library Quarterly*, I (1931), 278-82.

[84] *Ibid.*, p. 282.

[85] Lloyd Vernor Ballard, *Social Institutions* (New York: D. Appleton-Century Co., 1936), Chap. XII, "The Public Library"; Lowell Martin, "The American Public Library as a Social Institution," *Library Quarterly*, VII (1937), 546-63.

[86] Arnold K. Borden, "Seventeenth-Century American Libraries," *Library Quarterly*, II (1932), 147.

[87] *Ibid.*

[88] Teggart, "An Early Champion of Free Libraries."

[89] Chicago: University of Chicago Press, 1933, Chap. IV.

[90] *Ibid.*, p. 81.

[91] *Ibid.*, pp. 89-90.

[92] *Ibid.*, p. 101.

[93] *Investigating Library Problems* (Chicago: University of Chicago Press, 1939), Chap. VI, "Historical Criticism."

[94] The five titles are: Henri Berr and Lucien Febrve, "History," *Encyclopedia of the Social Sciences*, VII, 357-68; Nevins, *Gateway to History*, Chap. IV, "One Mighty Torrent," Chap. VII, "Pilate on Evidence," and Chap. VIII, "Problems in History"; Butler, *Introduction to Library Science*, Chap. IV; Martin, "The American Public Library as a Social Institution"; and Carter V. Good, A. S. Barr, and Douglas E. Scates, *The Methodology of Educational Research* (New York: D. Appleton-Century Co., 1936), Chap. VI.

[95] Waples, *Investigating Library Problems*, p. 46.

[96] *Book Selection: Its Principles and Practice* (London: Grafton & Co., 1937), Chap. IV, "Trends in the American Public Library Movement during the Nineteenth Century," pp. 47-58; Chap. V, "Summary and Interpretation of the Historical Findings," pp. 59-68.

[97] *Ibid.*, p. 60. Reference should also be made to Wellard's later book, *The Public Library Comes of Age* (London: Grafton & Co., 1940), Part I: "The Public Library as a Social Force" and Part II: "The Sociology of the Public Library."

[98]William S. Learned, *The American Public Library and the Diffusion of Knowledge* (New York: Harcourt, Brace & Co., 1924), p. 71 and table following p. 72.

[99]"The Public Library Movement in the United States as It Was Influenced by the Needs of the Wage-Earner, 1850-1900" (unpublished A.M. thesis, College of the City of New York, 1938); "Social Reform, Education, and the Library, 1850-1900," *Library Quarterly*, IX (1939), 156-84.

[100]"Mechanics' and Mercantile Libraries," *Library Quarterly*, X (1940), 192-219; "The District-School Library, 1835-55," *ibid.*, 545-77; "The Social Ideals of a Library Pioneer: Josephus Nelson Larned, 1836-1913," *ibid.*, XIII (1943), 113-31.

[101]"Parish Libraries and the Work of the Reverend Thomas Bray."

[102]"Joseph Cotton Dana," *Library Quarterly*, VII (1937), 50-98.

[103]"The Colonial Library and the Development of Sectional Differences in the American Colonies," *Library Quarterly*, VIII (1938), 373-90.

[104]Economic and social differentials were more important in determining reading habits than geographic location. After the Mather period the reading tastes of New Englanders were strikingly like those in other parts of the country. The present writer has further considered the Keys theory in his review of Brown's *Sentimental Novel in America*, *Library Quarterly*, XII (1942), 133-36.

[105]George Peabody College for Teachers Contributions to Education, No. 134 (New York: Barnes & Noble, 1935).

[106]The colleges included are Harvard, William and Mary, Yale, Princeton, Columbia, Pennsylvania, Brown, Rutgers, and Dartmouth.

[107]"Apparently to Mr. Shores a library of five thousand volumes is just a library of five thousand volumes; the titles and contents of the volumes, or how or by whom they were used, are matters of secondary importance" (review by Samuel Eliot Morison in *New England Quarterly*, VIII [1935], 430-31).

[108]Unpublished Ph.D. dissertation, Brown University, 1938.

[109]"A Poor but Respectable Relation—the Sunday-school Library," *Library Quarterly*, XII (1942), 731-39.

[110]Frank Monaghan and Marvin Lowenthal, *This Was New York: The Nation's Capital in 1789* (Garden City, N.Y.: Doubleday, Doran & Co., 1943), pp. 147-67.

[111]*The Sentimental Novel in America, 1789-1860* (Durham, N.C.: Duke University Press, 1940), Chap. I and *passim.*

[112]New York: H.W. Wilson Co., 1940.

[113]Salem, Mass.: Essex Institute, 1927, Chap. VIII, "Libraries." For the sake of completeness one should also mention Ruth S. Granniss, "American Book Collecting and the Growth of Libraries," in Hellmut Lehmann-Haupt, Ruth S. Granniss, and Lawrence C. Wroth, *The Book in America* (New York: R.R. Bowker Co., 1939), pp. 295-384; and Carl L. Cannon, *American Book*

*Collectors and Collecting from Colonial Times to the Present* (New York: H.W. Wilson Co., 1941). But both of these are essentially reversions to the earlier methods of writing library history.

[114] *Library Quarterly*, XIII (1943), 227-31.

[115] Not until almost the end of the article does he mention the all-important records and documents of the colleges themselves: "Finally, records and documents of individual colleges constitute a rich source. Minutes of the faculty library, where they are not confidential, may be used to great advantage" (*ibid.*, p. 229).

[116] Chicago: University of Chicago Press, 1935.

[117] *The Chicago Public Library: Origins and Backgrounds* (Chicago: University of Chicago Press, 1943).

[118] Joeckel, *Government of the American Public Library*, p. 1.

[119] Jesse H. Shera, *Foundations of the Public Library: The Origins of the Public Library Movement in New England, 1629-1855* (Chicago: University of Chicago Press, 1948).

[120] *Arsenals of a Democratic Culture: A Study of the American Public Library Movement in New England and the Middle States, 1830-1900* (Chicago: American Library Association, 1947).

[121] Alfred Hessel, *A History of Libraries*, trans. with supplementary material by Reuben Peiss (Washington, D.C.: Scarecrow Press, 1950), p. iii.

[122] *Evolution of the American Public Library, 1653-1876* (Washington, D.C.: Scarecrow Press, 1952).

[123] *The Public Library in the Political Process* (New York: Columbia University Press, 1949), pp. 3-52.

[124] Albert Predeek, *A History of Libraries in Great Britain and North America*, trans. by Lawrence S. Thompson (Chicago: American Library Association, 1947).

[125] *Ibld.*, pp. v-vi.

[126] *See* review by J. H. Shera in *Library Quarterly*, Vol. 18 (July 1948), 225-28.

[127] *The H. W. Wilson Company* (Minneapolis: University of Minnesota Press, 1950).

[128] Metuchen, N.J.: Scarecrow Press, 1968.

[129] *Scholar's Workshop: Evolving Conceptions of Library Service* (Urbana, Ill.: University of Illinois Press, 1953), p. xii.

[130] *The Development of Reference Services through Academic Traditions, Public Library Practice, and Special Librarianship*, ACRL Monograph, No. 14 (Chicago: Association of College and Research Libraries, 1955), p. 1.

[131] *Boston Public Library: A Centennial History* (Cambridge, Mass.: Harvard University Press, 1956).

[132]*Open Shelves and Open Minds: A History of the Cleveland Public Library* (Cleveland: Case Western Reserve University Press, 1972).

[133]New York: The New York Public Library, 1972.

[134]*Charles Evans, American Bibliographer* (Urbana, Ill.: University of Illinois Press, 1963).

[135]*William Frederick Poole and the Modern Library Movement* (New York: Columbia University Press, 1963).

[136]*Louis Round Wilson: Librarian and Administrator* (New York: Columbia University Press, 1967).

[137]*College Literary Societies: Their Contribution to Higher Education in the United States, 1815-1876* (New York: Pageant Press, 1971).

[138]*Carnegie Libraries: Their History and Impact on American Library Development* (Chicago: American Library Association, 1969).

[139]"The Education of Librarians," in Alice I. Bryan, *The Public Librarian* (New York: Columbia University Press, 1952), pp. 299-428.

[140]"Historical Development of Education for Librarianship in the United States," in Bernard Berelson, ed., *Education for Librarianship* (Chicago: American Library Association, 1949), pp. 22-37.

[141]*A History of the School of Library Service, Columbia University* (New York: Columbia University Press, 1954).

[142]Chicago: American Library Association, 1961. One should also call attention to Miss Vann's *The Williamson Reports: A Study* (Metuchen, N.J.: Scarecrow Press, 1971), which appeared as a companion volume to the publication of the two Williamson Reports of which the earlier, and suppressed, version had not previously been available in print.

[143]New York: Scarecrow Press, 1961.

[144]Jesse H. Shera, "On the Value of Library History," *Library Quarterly*, Vol. 22 (July 1952), 240-51.

[145]*See* R. G. Collingwood, *The Idea of History* (Oxford: The Clarendon Press, 1946), p. 10.

# 10

# The Beginnings of Systematic Bibliography in America, 1642-1799[1]

As the American colonists began to establish themselves, to conquer a strange and hostile environment, and to transform the eastern boundaries of the wilderness into productive farms and thriving urban communities, a culture, at first traditionally European but later more characteristically native, began to take shape. One of the manifestations of this incipient culture was the urge to assemble collections of books, both private and quasi-public, that would expand intellectual horizons and stimulate and support an indigenous scholarship. In the beginning Europe, and especially England, was the major source of book supply, but local presses were soon established and it was not so very long until domestic publishers began to compete with the trans-Atlantic market. How, then, did those charged with the responsibility of assembling library collections inform themselves concerning contemporary book production? Where could they turn for information about and listings of the most desirable titles? In short, what was the structure of the bibliographic system that supported and made possible the formation of libraries in America from, roughly, 1630 to the beginning of the 19th century? No essay as brief as this can present definitive answers to such questions until more extensive research has provided the requisite information, but at least the major problems can be stated, some basic procedures advanced, and, perhaps, some progress made toward a real understanding of the beginnings of systematic bibliography in early America.

By the time the Massachusetts Bay Company had secured its claims in the New World, systematic bibliography had achieved a very substantial degree of maturity across the Atlantic. In fact, only two years after Columbus first set foot on American soil Johann Tritheim published at Basle his *Liber de*

Originally published in Frederick R. Goff, ed., *Essays Honoring Lawrence C. Wroth* (Portland, Maine: Anthoensen Press, 1951), pp. 263-78.

*scriptoribus ecclesiasticis*, to be followed a year later (1495) by his *Catalogus illustrium virorum Germaniae*, and thus became known as "the Father of Bibliography." Tritheim's work was succeeded by other compilations of ecclesiastical writings, by alphabetical catalogs of prohibited books, and, most important, by subject bibliographies in medicine and law. Thus bibliography in Europe continued to develop until, by the middle of the 16th century, Conrad Gesner was able to assemble the first universal bibliography, listing some 15,000 titles by approximately 3,000 authors in a work that was elaborately and painstakingly classified and that was provided with an author and subject index to the whole. During the 17th century the center of bibliographic activity shifted from Germany to France and Italy, where it remained until well toward the close of the 18th century, after which England began to produce the best bibliographic work.

In America the first faltering step in the direction of bibliographic listing may be seen in the lists of theses issued by Harvard College and first printed by the Cambridge Press beginning in 1642 and continued at irregular intervals until at least the close of the 17th century.[2] These lists, entitled severally, *Theses philologicas*, *Theses philosophicas*, and later, *Theses technologicae*, were modelled after those issued by the universities of Oxford, Cambridge, and Edinburgh, and were broadsides issued at the time of the college commencement. Here was set forth in print the titles of the theses that the candidates for degrees had been prepared to support during their courses of academic training. In later years, as the lists grew in length, they were roughly arranged under such broad subject headings as *Logicae*, *Grammaticae*, *Rhetoricae*, *Mathematicae*, *Physicae*, and *Ethicae*. They were, of course, not bibliographies in the sense of being listings of published treatises, but at least they were an attempt to inform the public of the activities and interests of a pioneer world of scholarship.

According to Evans, and so far as the present writer knows, no new evidence has been discovered to invalidate the statement: the first true bibliography to be issued in Colonial America was a quarto catalog of 16 pages listing *The Library of the Late Reverend and Learned Mr. Samuel Lee*, the whole of which was "exposed . . . for sale" by Duncan Campbell, at whose instigation the catalog was printed at Boston by Benjamin Harris in the year 1693 (*Evans* 645). Two years later, Michael Perry printed, probably in Boston, Cotton Mather's *Piscator Evangelicus, or the Life of Mr. Thomas Hooker, the Renowned Pastor of Hartford Church, and Pillar of Connecticut-Colony, in New England* (*Evans* 727), a duodecimo of 45 pages which contained at the end a listing of 34 titles of Cotton Mather's publications. This would appear to be the first bio-bibliography to make its appearance in the Colonies.

American contributions to subject bibliography during the 17th century, then, are hardly to be described as impressive. Obviously the few scattered libraries, most of them private collections, were compelled to look to England

and the Continent not only for the major portion of their book stocks, but for practically all of their bibliographic assistance in book selection.

The first years of the 18th century showed little improvement, such catalogs as have survived being entirely listings for auction sales. The first of these was issued in Boston in 1717, and was an 80-page catalog of the library of Rev. Ebenezer Pemberton. It still remains the earliest example of a surviving auction list (*Evans* 1921; *McKay* 5). Five other such auction catalogs appeared before 1720, but it was not until 1723 that the first catalog of a "public library" was printed in America. This was the *Catalogus librorum Bibliothecae Collegii Harvardini*, a quarto of 106 pages, printed in Boston by B. Green, and compiled by Joshua Gee (*Evans* 2432, 2641). The first supplement was issued a year later, and a second appeared in 1735. Today, one would scarcely call the library of Harvard College a "public" institution, but its collections were available to those outside the immediate student body and faculty, and it was probably as nearly public as any contemporary collection, except possibly those books in the Boston Town House that were acquired from the bequest of Captain Keane, and other donations. Thus the college had been in existence for almost a century before the holdings of its library were generally made known.

The 1720s brought two other bibliographic contributions that merit attention here. A second example of bio-bibliography, a catalog of the writings of the Rev. Samuel Willard, appeared as an appendage to his *Compleat Body of Divinity*, printed in Boston by Green and Kneeland in 1726 (*Evans* 2828). In the same year Cotton Mather included in his *Manuductio ad Ministerium; Directions for a Candidate of the Ministry* (Boston, Thomas Hancock, 1726) "A Catalogue of Books for a Young Student's Library" (*Evans* 2772) which is, so far as the present writer knows, the first selective bibliography issued as a book-selection aid to appear in the Colonies. That the list was regarded as being of some value may be assumed from the fact that John Ryland expanded it for his edition of Mather's work, published in London in 1781.

Thus, by the time that Benjamin Franklin put forward his project for the establishment of the Philadelphia Library Company, generally considered as the beginning of the movement for the founding of social libraries in America, the best that this country could offer as bibliographic aids for the formation of such collections were a few scattered booksellers' catalogs, mostly listing the contents of private libraries, one printed catalog of the Harvard College Library, two brief bio-bibliographies of New England divines, and one selected list of titles recommended to students of theology. Since Franklin brought together in his company a group composed mainly of artisans and small tradesmen, it seems hardly likely that he found any of these bibliographies particularly useful. It is known, of course, that the first books were English imports, so one may assume that he, like many of his later countrymen, placed his faith in the English book market and such assistance as it could provide. In fact, the two printed catalogs of the Philadelphia Library Company, for 1733 and 1735 (*Evans* 3714 and 3950), and a catalog of the Boston bookseller T. Cox (*Evans* 3765) are the only surviving bibliographic compilations produced in the decade of the 30s. The Cox item, though it is arranged neither alphabetically nor by subject, merits some special mention inasmuch as it lists 856 titles and qualifies as the first true American bookseller's catalog.

In New London, Connecticut, in 1743 appeared a small pamphlet (of 31 pages) by Samuel Johnson, entitled *An Introduction to the Study of Philosophy, Exhibiting a General View of all the Arts and Sciences, for the use of Pupils. With a Catalogue of some of the Most Valuable Authors Necessary to be Read in Order to Instruct them in a Thorough Knowledge of Each of them. By a Gentleman Educated at Yale-College* (*Evans* 5220). This, like Cotton Mather's list of 1726, is a selective bibliography primarily for the use of students. Again, toward the close of the decade, in 1747, William Stith appended to his *History of the First Discovery and Settlement of Virginia*, printed at Williamsburg (*Evans* 6071), a catalog of charters or letters patent which were "still extant in our publick offices in the Capitol, or in other authentic papers and records," which stands as perhaps the first attempt on this side of the Atlantic to systematize public documents. These same 10 years also brought the first catalog of the library of Yale College, New London, 1743 (*Evans* 5320), which displayed its holdings in a classified arrangement with the location symbol for each title; Benjamin Franklin's 16-page catalog of "choice and valuable books," enumerating 445 titles, printed in Philadelphia in 1744 (*Evans* 5396); and the 1741 catalog of the Philadelphia Library Company, with its supplement of 1746 (*Evans* 4787; 5853). Systematic bibliography was not progressing rapidly, but it was progressing, and just at the time that the first social libraries were being formed in Philadelphia, Durham, Saybrook, Lebanon, Pomfret, and Newport. Slowly and steadily bibliographic activity was gathering strength.

From this time to the eve of the Revolutionary War the volume of catalog publication steadily increased, and of this a substantial proportion was issued by booksellers, either as auction catalogs or as listings of their regular book stocks. From 1750 to 1775 some 35 booksellers' and auction catalogs are known to have been issued, exclusive of a large number of "ghosts" listed by both Evans and McKay from information derived from advertisements in the local press. The social libraries, too, began to publish catalogs of their holdings—The Library Company of Philadelphia issued catalogs in 1757, 1764, 1770, and 1775 (*Evans* 8006; 9794; 11820; 14392); the Union Library Company of the same city published its first catalog in 1754 and a revision 11 years later (*Evans* 7295; 10139); and catalogs came from the Burlington, New Jersey, Library Company in 1758 (*Evans* 8096), the first catalog to give the place and date of publication; the New York Society Library in the same year (*Evans* 8217); the Loganian Library of Philadelphia in 1760 (*Evans* 8715); the United Library of Saybrook,

Lime, and Guilford about 1760; the Redwood Library at Newport, Rhode Island, in 1764 (*Evans* 9764); the Juliana Library Company of Lancaster, Pennsylvania, in 1765 and 1766 (*Evans* 10034; 10350); the Providence, Rhode Island, Library Company in 1768 (*Evans* 11051); and the Charleston, South Carolina, Library Society in 1770 (*Evans* 11596). Among the colleges, Yale revised its catalog in 1755 (*Evans* 7598), Princeton printed its first in 1760 (*Evans* 8683), and Harvard published a selected list in 1773 (*Evans* 12805). This proliferation of catalogs of all kinds is paralleled by the spread of social libraries which were, during the same period, becoming firmly established in the colonial culture.

None of these catalogs was conspicuously important as an example of the bibliographer's craft, being usually poorly organized, lacking in bibliographic detail, and in other ways generally crude. A few, however, should be mentioned here as examples of the limited advances that were being made. John Mein's catalog of 1766 arranges 1,741 numbered items in broad subject groupings and is, as Brigham says, the largest bookseller's catalog issued up to that time. The catalog of Cox and Berry (Boston, 1772) included only 1,475 titles, but Brigham characterizes it as "an intelligent catalogue." The authors are arranged alphabetically, though the work concludes with a six-part subject arrangement— Law, Medicine, French Books, Old Folios and Quartos, School Books, and "Little Books for Children." Though Robert Bell did not arrange the titles in his catalog, issued from Philadelphia in 1773, in any kind of order, except to group them according to size, his was the first to quote prices. Finally, attention should be called to John Ash's *Grammatical Institutes*, 7th ed., printed in New York by Hugh Gaine, in 1774 (*Evans* 13123), which contained "A Collection of Books Proper for Young Gentlemen and Ladies, to Shorten the Path to Knowledge."

The turbulence of the Revolution and its immediate aftermath were not encouraging to bibliographic activity, though the decline in catalog production is not as sharp as one might expect. Bell, of Philadelphia, seems to have continued his catalogs without regard to economic and political disturbances. Both Evans and McKay, especially the latter, list a large number of auction "catalogues" during these years, but doubtless most of them, if they existed at all, were only manuscript inventories. Nevertheless, 14 booksellers' and auction catalogs give evidence of having been published from 1781 to 1790, though of this number almost half (14) bear the imprint date of the single year 1790. Also, during this period publishers began the practice of including lists of their wares at the end of their publications. The first to do this would seem to have been Thomas Dobson of Philadelphia, who in 1790 appended a list of books "printed for and sold by" him to his edition of George Campbell's *Dissertation on Miracles* (*Evans* 22387). In 1787 Isaiah Thomas published his first catalog (*Evans* 20745) which, though it was arranged by subject (within which the titles were arrayed in no order), was not the particularly good example of bibliographic work that one might have expected from one so interested in the art of printing and the conservation of books. At this time by far the most progressive of the booksellers with respect to bibliographic techniques was Samuel Campbell of New York, whose catalog of 1787 (*Evans* 20260) prefaces its 1007 numbered titles with a carefully developed subject index. But it was in his catalog of 1789 that he made the biggest forward step yet taken in the improvement of bibliographic procedures. This 58-page catalog, listing over 1,500 numbered titles, is not only arranged by subject, but is the first bookseller's catalog in this country to give for each entry the place and date of publication. This catalog was later excelled by that issued from his shop in 1794, but it is sufficient to establish him as perhaps the most important of American pioneer bookseller-bibliographers. Also one should mention Claudius P. Raguet's catalog, devoted exclusively to French books, which was issued in Philadelphia in 1790 and which is the first surviving example of such a compilation issued in America during the 18th century.

The impact of the war was also felt by the social and academic libraries which curtailed sharply their publication of catalogs. Nevertheless, a broadside displaying two columns of titles came from the Foster, Rhode Island, "town library" in 1781 (*Evans* 19410) and the Union Library Society of Wethersfield, Connecticut, issued a 19-page listing of its holdings in 1784 (*Evans* 18882). Similar catalogs came from Franklin, Massachusetts, perhaps in 1786[3]; from the Union Library Company of Hartborough, Pennsylvania, in 1788 (*Evans* 21138); from the New York Society Library and the Philadelphia Library Company, both in 1789 (*Evans* 22018 and 22066); and from Harvard College in 1790 (*Evans* 22559). The 1789 catalog of the Library Company of Philadelphia is of particular interest in that its classification is based on Francis Bacon's divisions of knowledge according to the human faculties of Memory, Reason, and Imagination. One might legitimately suppose that such an arrangement was suggested either directly or indirectly by the work of Thomas Jefferson who, in 1783, had organized the catalog of his library in a similar fashion. Also, like the catalog of Samuel Campbell of the same year, the entries in the Philadelphia listing indicated place and date of publication.

The concluding decade of the 18th century brought a tremendous expansion in catalog production, especially booksellers' catalogs, just as it brought to the social library a new era of unprecedented growth. Over 80 booksellers' catalogs were issued during the decade of 1790-1799, whereas only 56 such titles had been published up to that time. Except for the catalogs of colleges, other forms also showed an important, though less spectacular, increase. Of all of these, space permits the selection of only a few for special comment. As suggested above, Samuel Campbell's catalog of 1794 (*Evans* 26728) is a true bibliographic landmark, and even today it remains a useful list for historians and others interested in the book resources of the early Republic.

Thus, the compiler wrote in a brief prefatory statement:

> The various impositions to which the public are often subjected, in purchasing incorrect or spurious editions, has induced S.C. to print after the name of each book, the place where, and the time when printed, that purchasers may at one view observe that the books in this collection are in general the best editions, and many of them scarce and valuable.

Quite obviously Mr. Campbell believed that the volume of publication was sufficiently great that the simple listings of his contemporaries were insufficient to meet the need for more adequate bibliographic organization. The care with which the list was prepared also suggests that it was not his intention that it should be examined and tossed aside, but that it should be kept for future reference. The pamphlet begins with a fairly detailed index of subjects, which has the appearance of a table of contents. Of the 1,664 titles, arranged by subject, 408, or approximately one-fourth, are American imprints. This catalog represents, as Evans has said, "a distinct advance from the practice in general use up to that time, which had concerned itself more with the title and size of a volume than with its authorship, date, or place of printing."

Three other booksellers' catalogs are likewise of special interest. Moreau de Saint Méry issued in Philadelphia in 1795 a catalog (*Evans* 29107) having, in addition to the customary English list, four pages of Latin titles, five pages devoted to Italian, German, and Dutch, and 31 pages of French items, the most extensive French list yet issued in America. The catalog of John West, printed in Boston in 1797 (*Evans* 33205) was the first to be devoted exclusively to American imprints, and listed approximately 650 entries. But it is Caritat's *Feast of Reason and the Flow of Soul* (*Evans* 36279) that Brigham considers the most important bookseller's catalog of 18th-century America, though he, quite properly, laments the omission of such bibliographical information as the place and date of publication. This 215-page compilation, which was intended to serve both as a sale catalog and as a presentation of the holdings of the compiler's circulating library, was the largest and most extensive yet published, including almost 2,700 titles. The compilation is divided into three parts: Arts, Sciences, etc.; Poetry and Dramatics; Romances, Novels, Adventures, etc. In this last category almost 1,000 items are listed, and for the first time the authorship of the fiction is given. Annotations indicating the value of the work are often included, but this New York bookseller was not the first to annotate his entries, as Rice & Company of Philadelphia, about 1791, appended to many of their titles long descriptive notes or quotations from reviews. With the work of Campbell and Caritat, however, American book-trade bibliography was beginning to show some degree of maturity.

During the 1790s, two "special library" catalogs appeared that are pioneer examples of their type. In 1790 the medical library of the Pennsylvania Hospital in Philadelphia published a catalog and supplement, totalling 78 pages, of the books in its collections (*Evans* 27510). Six years later the newly founded Massachusetts Historical Society made public the holdings in its library in a catalog of 40 pages printed by S. Hall of Boston. Thus medicine and history, as one might have guessed from their importance in 18th-century American life, were the first disciplines to have available special bibliographies devoted to their respective fields.

Of even greater interest to the student of the growth of library book collections was the bibliography published in 1793 by Thaddeus Mason Harris, then librarian of Harvard College, under the title *Selected Catalogue of Some of the Most Esteemed Publications in the English Language Proper to Form a Social Library* (*Evans* 25587). Since this little pamphlet and its relation to the growth of social libraries has been dealt with more fully elsewhere by the present writer,[4] suffice it here to emphasize its importance as the first American guide to a book selection program for "public" libraries, and to point out that, departing from the customary practice of arranging its titles in broad subject categories, it was classified according to Bacon's organization of knowledge, as modified by d'Alembert. Harris, like Campbell, recognized the growing bibliographic problems raised by the proliferation of printed materials, which had "become so exceedingly numerous as to require uninterrupted attention, through more than the longevity of an antediluvian to peruse them all." Also, law was included with medicine and history as a discipline needing bibliographic attention when, in Richmond, Virginia, in 1796, was published a four-page folio extract from a letter from Thomas Jefferson to George Wythe, in which the third president of the United States presented a list characterized by Evans as a "carefully prepared bibliographical statement of Early Virginia laws ... an indispensible guide to the student and collector in this field of research" (*Evans* 30637).

The limitations of space prevent any more detailed consideration of the many bibliographies mentioned in the preceding pages. All of them have substantial antiquarian interest, and no small value as documentary evidence for a study of the sociological development of systematic bibliography. That bibliographic activity along the Eastern seaboard was slowly increasing in volume and importance up to the close of the 18th century is apparent from Table I. Admittedly these statistics are modest, since they are limited to titles actually known to have existed; but even were they swollen by the inclusion of all the alleged catalogs enumerated by Evans and McKay, it seems unlikely that the general configuration would be seriously altered. The degree to which bibliographic activity paralleled that of social library establishment during the same period is evident from even a cursory comparison of Table I with Table II. One would certainly not be so bold as to say that either was a direct consequence of the other. Both, rather, were manifestations of the growing importance of printed records in the cultural pattern that was then emerging.

## TABLE I

### Book Catalogs Published in America,
### by Date of Publication, 1731-1799*

|  | 1731-1740 | 1741-1750 | 1751-1760 | 1761-1770 | 1771-1780 | 1781-1790 | 1791-1799 | Total |
|---|---|---|---|---|---|---|---|---|
| Booksellers' and Auction Catalogs | 1 | 1 | 10 | 14 | 14 | 30 | 68 | 138 |
| Social Library Catalogs | 2 | 2 | 5 | 9 | 2 | 6 | 31 | 57 |
| Circulating Library Catalogs | – | – | – | 3 | – | 5 | 6 | 14 |
| College Library Catalogs | – | 1 | 1 | – | 1 | 1 | 2 | 6 |
| "Special Library" Catalogs | – | – | – | – | – | – | 2 | 2 |
| Total | 3 | 4 | 16 | 26 | 17 | 42 | 109 | 217 |

*Examples before 1731 are so scattered that their tabular presentation seems impracticable.

*Main Sources for Table 1.*

Charles Evans, *American Bibliography* (Chicago: Blakely Press, 1903-1934).
George L. McKay, *American Book Auction Catalogues*, 1713-1934 (New York: New York Public Library, 1937).
John Eliot Alden, *Rhode Island Imprints*, 1727-1800 (New York: R.R. Bowker, 1949).
Harriet S. Tapley, *Salem Imprints*, 1768-1825 (Salem: Essex Institute, 1927).
A. Rachel Minick, *A History of Printing in Maryland*, 1791-1800 (Baltimore: Enoch Pratt Free Library, 1949).
Clarence S. Brigham, *American Booksellers' Catalogues*, 1734-1800. *See* Goff, *Essays*, pp. 31-68.
Other library catalogs held by American Antiquarian Society, unpublished list supplied by C. S. Brigham.

## TABLE II

### Social Libraries Established in New England,
### by Date of Founding, 1731-1800

|  | 1731-1740 | 1741-1750 | 1751-1760 | 1761-1770 | 1771-1780 | 1781-1790 | 1791-1800 | Total |
|---|---|---|---|---|---|---|---|---|
| Number of Libraries | 4 | 6 | 6 | 13 | 22 | 59 | 266 | 376 |

The production of print, the assembly of libraries, and the need for bibliographic organization, all bore a relationship to each other, and any alteration in one of these three elements was invariably and eventually reflected in the other two. All of them were responsive to cultural and social forces whose nature has not yet been fully explored by bibliographic scholarship, but a knowledge of these forces is, nevertheless, essential to a real understanding of the place of the book and the library in American society.

In presenting Table III, the author is quite well aware that he is treading on potentially dangerous and very controversial ground. Yet the hazard seemed justified by the light which such a chronological enumeration throws upon the emergence of the several types of bibliographic services and the sequence of their development. At least it is suggestive of the manner in which bibliography began and the interests and needs that were paramount in its incipient growth.

## TABLE III

### Chronological Listing of Innovations in
### American Bibliographic Development

| Date | Innovation | Title of Work | Evans Number |
|---|---|---|---|
| 1642 | First listing of academic theses | Harvard College. *Theses* . . . | 9 |
| 1693 | First "true" bibliography | Catalog of Library of Rev. Samuel Lee. Boston | 645 |
| 1695 | First bio-bibliography | Cotton Mather. *Piscator Evangelicus* . . . Boston(?) | 727 |
| 1717 | Earliest surviving auction catalog | Catalog of books of Rev. Ebenezer Pemberton. Boston | 1921 |
| 1723 | First college library catalog | Harvard College. *Catalogus librorum* . . . Boston | 2432 |
| 1726 | First "book selection" aid | Cotton Mather. *Catalogue of books for student's library.* Boston | 2772 |
| 1733 | First social library catalog | Philadelphia Library Co. *Catalogue.* Philadelphia | 3714 |
| 1734(?) | First bookseller's "stock" catalog | T. Cox. *Catalogue.* Boston | 3765 |
| 1743 | First catalog with location symbols | Yale College. *Catalogue.* New London | 5320 |

**TABLE III (cont'd.)**

| Date | Innovation | Title of Work | Evans Number |
|------|-----------|---------------|--------------|
| 1747 | First documents listing | William Stith's List of Characters in his *History* . . . Williamsburg | 6071 |
| 1758 | First catalog to give place and date of publication | Burlington Library Co. *Catalogue.* Philadelphia | 8096 |
| 1765 | First circulating library catalog | John Mein's *Catalogue.* Boston | 10069 |
| 1766 | First catalog to emphasize "books of entertainment," i.e. novels | John Mein's *Catalogue.* Boston | _____ |
| 1773 | First catalog to indicate price | Robert Bell's *Catalogue.* Philadelphia | _____ |
| 1787 | First catalog with extensive subject index | Samuel Campbell's *Catalogue.* New York | 20260 |
| 1789 | First bookseller's catalog to give place and date of publication | Samuel Campbell's *Catalogue.* New York | _____ |
| 1790 | First bookseller's list to appear as supplement to published title | George Campbell's *Dissertation on Miracles* . . . Philadelphia (Thomas Dobson's list at end) | 22387 |
| 1790 | First "special library" catalog | Pennsylvania Hospital. *Catalogue.* Philadelphia | 22795 |
| 1790 | First catalog devoted to foreign titles | Claudius Raguet's *Catalogue of French Books.* Philadelphia | _____ |
| ca.1791 | First catalog with extensive annotated entries | Rice & Co. *Catalogue.* Philadelphia | _____ |
| 1793 | First book selection aid for "public," i.e., social, libraries | T.M. Harris' *Selected Catalogue* . . . Boston | 25587 |
| 1796 | First historical society library catalog | Massachusetts Historical ciety. *Catalogue.* Boston | 30770 |
| 1797 | First catalog devoted exclusively to American imprints | John West's *Catalogue.* Boston | 33205 |
| 1799 | First catalog to indicate authorship of novels | H. Caritat's *Catalogue.* New York | 35279 |

From what has been said in the foregoing, then, and from a thoughtful examination of these simple statistical tabulations, perhaps a few tentative conclusions can be advanced. The first and most obvious conclusion is that booksellers' and auction catalogs represented the great bulk of American bibliographic production during the 18th century, and that similar compilations of the holdings of academic and other libraries increased with relative slowness. Bibliography, then, was being promoted most vigorously by that group which needed it most, and to whose financial interests it was most vital. Second, despite the preëminence of commercialism, a wide variety of interests was represented by bibliographic activity of divers sorts, even during the early years. Similarly, differing kinds of bibliographic information were set forth to serve different purposes; for example, Samuel Campbell's inclusion of place and date of publication in his listings was far more useful and important to libraries, both academic and "public," than to individual purchasers of his wares. Third, American bibliography did not begin where European bibliography left off, but started afresh, hammering out its own techniques and procedures as best it could. Fourth, America did parallel Europe, however, in the early importance of medical and legal bibliographic activity. The compilation of laws themselves appeared very early indeed, the first being those of the Massachusetts Bay Colony, compiled by Richard Bellingham (*Evans* 28) and issued in 1649, but these were excluded from the present investigation since, though they represent a systematic presentation of one type of information, they are not, in the strict sense, bibliography. Fifth, bibliography began as a purely personal and individual undertaking; even when the sponsoring agency was a group or a corporate body the work was individual. Not until book resources increased greatly in volume and bibliographic procedures attained a relatively high degree of maturity and refinement did cooperative activity emerge. Sixth, the growth and development of bibliography parallels the increase and expansion of book production, bookselling, and library promotion.

In conclusion, one should restate the exploratory character of the above presentation. Four important steps yet remain to be taken before definitive conclusions can be advanced. Further checking of bibliographic sources and the holdings of important libraries must be continued; existing catalogs must be more fully examined as to the extent of their listings, the objectives they were supposed to meet, and the character of their bibliographic techniques; the lives and writings of those known to have been concerned in bibliography need careful study; and finally the great mass of as yet unexplored journal literature must be searched for bibliographic contributions that would not have been listed in the sources here consulted. This last might prove to be a very rewarding operation indeed and might well completely alter certain of the conclusions here hypothesized. But at least some progress has been made if it is now possible to see more clearly the path which future investigation must follow and those stones along the margin that yet remain unturned.

## FOOTNOTES

[1] The author wishes to acknowledge his particular indebtedness to Clarence S. Brigham, Director of the American Antiquarian Society, who not only made freely available, in advance of publication in the present symposium, the manuscript of his bibliography of booksellers' catalogs; but in addition, at some personal inconvenience, checked the holdings of the American Antiquarian Society for other types of book catalogs so that the tabulations herein presented might be as nearly accurate as possible.

[2] *See* Charles Evans, *American Bibliography* (Chicago: Blakely Press, 1903-1934), items 9; 12; 22; 41; 59; 92; 102; 108; 123; 140; 148; 638.

[3] So dated by Blake in his *History of Franklin*, but Brigham points out that the copy in the American Antiquarian Society lists several books dating from the 1790s and 1801-1807. This catalog is now generally considered to have been printed in 1812.

[4] Jesse H. Shera, *Foundations of the Public Library* (Chicago: University of Chicago Press, 1949), pp. 110-14.

# 11

# On the Value of Library History

"Librarianship, as we know it, can be fully apprehended only through an understanding of its historic origins. . . . It is obvious that the librarian's practice will be determined in part by his historical understanding. . . . Unless the librarian has a clear historical consciousness . . . he is quite certain at times to serve his community badly."[1] Thus wrote Pierce Butler almost two decades before the Public Library Inquiry sought to assess the American public library through the application of the most approved techniques of sociological analysis. At first blush, Butler's insistence on the importance of historical awareness for an understanding of the role of the library in modern society might seem to be a little more than an impassioned outcry of a spirit in protest against an age that has rejected the values of history—against a world which has come increasingly to believe that it, like Lot's wife, would suffer disaster if it were to pause, even briefly, for a retrospective glance. It is indeed true that Butler was contradicting the popular trend when he so emphatically enunciated his belief that librarianship could not fulfill its highest social destiny if librarians remained ignorant of the historical development of the library as a social agency. In the early 1930s American librarianship was striving, as it still is today, for professional respectability. There was a growing faith that librarianship had, or could be given, an intellectual content, and that content was sought in an ever-growing corpus of principles and techniques for the manipulation, operation, and administration of library materials. This was the day of glory for the technicians in their white aprons, and everywhere attention was concentrated on process rather than on function.

In opposition to this excessive preoccupation with the techniques of library operations, Pierce Butler wrote his *Introduction to Library Science*. In this credo

Reprinted with permission from *The Library Quarterly*, Vol. 22 (July 1952), pp. 240-51. Published by the University of Chicago Press.

not only did he set forth a philosophic frame of reference within which librarianship could be seen as an integral part of the contemporary culture, but he argued strongly for a recognition of history as basic to an understanding of the library in relation to its coeval culture. Not only did he reveal that a knowledge of history is essential to the librarian's complete intellectual equipment, but he showed history itself to be the logical starting point for almost every inquiry into the nature and function of the library as a social agency.

This struggle to win for history a recognition of its importance as a constituent element in the emerging scholarship of library research has not yet been won; it has, in fact, lost ground with the increasing tendency to adopt, for research in librarianship, the methods of investigation of the other social sciences. As librarians have rushed to apply the form, if not the substance, of social science research to library problems, means have often been mistaken for ends, techniques have been employed without thought of their appropriateness, results have been hastily interpreted, and the historical method has been all but trampled underfoot.

The purpose of the present essay is, therefore, threefold: 1) to examine again the contribution which history can make to an understanding of the role of the library in society; 2) to identify and isolate, if possible, the reasons for the decline in the importance of history as an aid to the better understanding of the library as a social agency; and 3) to indicate the future course that research in library history should take, if it is to justify the time and effort spent in its pursuit.

## THE SOCIAL VALUE OF HISTORY

Before one can make a case for the justification of library history as an essential part of the intellectual content of librarianship, one must first attempt to determine the social utility of history itself. The writing of history is one of the oldest major forms of human literary activity, if not the oldest. This very fact of survival for so many centuries is in itself eloquent testimony of its social importance. Yet it is only within the last century or two that scholars have begun seriously to speculate about the specific values that history has to offer. Not content with the easy assumption that history, like virtue, is its own reward, many scholars have devoted countless hours to the reexamination of history, in the hope of extracting from it an apologia, an adequate justification, an answer to the question, "What is history for?"

In the final analysis, all arguments in support of the social utility of history derive from the analogy between the memory of the individual and history as the collective memory of the group. An awareness of one's past is, for the individual, an essential part of the reasoning, or thinking, process. John Dewey, indeed, held that "thinking is a reconstructive movement of actual contents of experience in relation to each other."[2] Admittedly, societies lack the capacity of the individual for the automatic recall of past experience, and, in the absence of an organic memory that can store experiences and reproduce them when needed, the society must create its own group memory. Thus, the habit of recording in some graphic form the accounts of past experience appears even among primitive societies. As this utilitarian history was developed and refined, it gave rise to a new kind of creative narration, in which concern with accuracy was united with the pleasure of knowing the past and retelling it for the benefit of others. "The general verdict of our Western civilization," writes Crane Brinton, "has been that a knowledge of history is at the very least a kind of extension of individual experience, and therefore of value to the human intelligence that makes use of experience. And certainly the kind of knowledge we have called cumulative—natural science—is committed to the view that valid generalizations must depend on wide experience, including what is commonly called history."[3]

But the purpose of history is more than recall. Memory is not enough. The simple narration of past events is insufficient unless it is supplemented with an active understanding that can draw from this reconstruction of the past a synthesis, a series of generalizations, that not only will give the past a living reality but will make of it a medium for the better understanding of the present. Without such interpretation, history degenerates to an empty antiquarianism pursued for its own sake. The late R. G. Collingwood supplied possibly the clearest explanation of the true purpose of history, when he wrote:

> *What is history for?* ... My answer is that history is 'for' human self-knowledge. It is generally thought to be of importance to man that he should know himself: where knowing himself means knowing ... his nature as man. ... Knowing yourself means knowing what you can do; and since nobody knows what he can do until he tries, the only clue to what man can do is what man has done. The value of history, then, is that it teaches us what man has done and thus what man is.[4]

Thus he derives his complete definition of history as

> ... a science, or an answering of questions; concerned with human actions in the past; pursued by interpretation of evidence; for the sake of human self-knowledge.[5]

History, then, is a social science in the broadest sense, and the methods it employs are identical with the methods of the social scientists insofar as they can be practicably applied to the available historical data. The use of social science techniques in historical research is limited only by the peculiarities that inhere in the data of history itself.

But Clio is no mere stepchild of the social scientist; she is, in fact, a social scientist in her own right. The increasing attention which historians are directing toward the growth of institutional history—the history of business corporations, for example—the history of economic phenomena, and the historic impact of urbanization all testify to the historian's use of generalizations contributed by the other social sciences. The historian, in turn, contributes to the social sciences a check on such sociological generalizations. As Gottschalk has pointed out, the historian can serve the other social scientists in three ways: 1) by discovering historical cases that will illustrate and support social science generalizations, 2) by discovering cases that will contradict such generalizations, and 3) by applying social science generalizations to historical trends or series of similar or related historical events to test the validity of the former.[6] Hence "finding contraditions in and exceptions to social science generalizations is one of the ways the historian can best contribute to an understanding of society."[7] Not only, then, does the historian provide the other social sciences with data derived from his investigations, but his work supplies a check on the validity of their concepts. The social scientist who rejects as inconsequential the findings of history is as unscientific as the historian who pretends to write about past social phenomena or social behavior without knowing the findings of the social scientists in relevant fields.

## THE SOCIAL UTILITY OF LIBRARY HISTORY

The writing of library history in the United States began, as was inevitable, with the long, tedious, and often uninspiring narration of the events, personalities, and circumstances surrounding the formation, growth, and development of individual institutions. These largely antiquarian biographies of libraries and librarians were an essential prerequisite to generalizations concerning the emergence of the library as an institutional form. Roughly three-quarters of a century was devoted to this kind of minute exploration of library history, years which brought forth such notable works as Quincy's *The Boston Athenaeum*, Mason's *The Redwood Library*, Johnston's *The Library of Congress*, Wadlin's *The Boston Public Library*, Lydenberg's *The New York Public Library*, and a host of less ambitious works. Biographies of librarians were less numerous and, on the whole, less successful; but here one might well mention Garrison's *John Shaw Billings*, Kingdon's *John Cotton Dana*, and the half-dozen useful little volumes in the "American Library Pioneers" series.

By the 1930s there had accumulated a sufficient body of these historical data to enable a few individuals to discern the broad general outlines of the emergence and development of the library as a social institution, to relate it to its contemporary social milieu, and to identify, in a general way, the forces that brought the library to its present state of development and shaped its institutional form. Thus Arnold Borden's speculations on the sociological beginnings of the American public library as a social institution were carried forward in the more comprehensive investigations of Ditzion's *Arsenals of a Democratic Culture* and the writer's *Foundations of the Public Library*. At the same time, the antiquarian approach was not entirely abandoned, and factual studies of individual libraries continued to be produced, many of them limited to unpublished theses sponsored by and carried out in the several library schools. Research in library history is, of course, far from exhaustive (it can, in fact, never really attain completion), but the available syntheses show the major lines of development that characterized the growth of the American public library and reveal it as a part of the process of the institutionalization that is characteristic of our culture. One may, therefore, appropriately inquire into the value of these investigations and their true bearing on the practice of librarianship.

What is the real value of library history? Perhaps such a question can best be answered by describing certain situations in which a disregard of library history has resulted in confused thinking and much misdirected effort, consequences which eventually are professionally disastrous and socially regrettable.

## THE ADULT EDUCATION MOVEMENT OF THE 1930s

A quarter of a century ago librarians, inspired by the plans of the American Library Association for an "expanded program" of activities and eagerly seeking a promising cause with which they might ally themselves, seized with missionary ardor upon the newly invented term, "adult education." Though the phrase was new, the idea was at least as old as Benjamin Franklin's *Junto*. The social libraries of the 18th and 19th centuries were voluntary associations of adults eagerly seeking "self-improvement." But the mortality rate of these organizations was high, in spite of the initial enthusiasm of their founders. The 19th century brought with it the lyceum movement, the mechanics' institutes, the literary societies, the associations for the education of the merchants' clerks, and the Chautauqua movement.

In 1925 William Jennings Bryan died in Chattanooga, Tennessee, within the very shadow of the unhappy Scopes affair, and with him went the Chautauqua movement, to which he had contributed so much of his vitality. By this time, too, the old Chautauqua Literary and Scientific Circle was, for many people, little more than a childhood memory; *Acres of Diamonds* had become almost legendary; and even the parent-institution, "simmering in the tepid lakeside sun," would hardly have been recognized by its founders, Vincent and Miller. Already the motion picture, the automobile, and even the radio were making the village get-together less and less important in American community life.

The death of the traveling Chautauquas in the last magnificent gesture of the Jubilee Year may have accentuated the rapidly changing pattern of American culture, but it did not mean that the popular urge for "self-education" had disappeared. If the brown tents of the Chautauqua had been stored away for good, their place was soon to be taken by the American Association for Adult Education and its forums, discussion groups, adult education councils, and directed reading programs.

All the aberrant manifestations of the urge for the intellectual growth of the adult directly or indirectly stimulated a temporary interest in the growth of library book collections. Many of the movements actively included libraries and library promotion as important segments of their operating programs. But even at a time when the public library was itself expanding rapidly in both number and size of collections, every attempt to associate the library movement with that of adult education met with conspicuous lack of success. Virtually every library that owed its existence to the initiative of the lyceums, the Chautauquas, or the library circles died with the demise of the movement itself.

Yet this eagerness of librarians to ally themselves with a social movement so obviously less stable than their own reappeared with renewed vigor in the 1930s. In this recrudescence of the cultural urge the librarians were, as they had been in an earlier day, the willing, eager, and often misguided disciples. Everywhere librarians began the establishment of readers' advisory services, the formation of forums and discussion groups, the promotion or encouragement of adult education councils, the preparation of selected reading lists for "adult beginners." The American Library Association sponsored "Reading with a Purpose," and all turned to the "A Cube E" for hope, guidance, and inspiration. In scarcely more than a decade, the tumult reached its highest pitch when Alvin Johnson published his *The Public Library—a People's University.* Extremists even went so far as to argue that, if libraries were to play their proper part in adult education, they themselves would have to publish books especially suited to its needs.[8]

No one reflected that the very arguments advanced by Johnson, which then seemed so convincing, were almost identical with those employed a century earlier by Henry Barnard, Horace Mann, and others seeking to promote an incipient public library movement. No one turned back the pages of history to discover that for decades such arguments had fallen on ears that were almost totally deaf to such appeals. No one recalled that every attempt to associate the library with universal "self-improvement" had been conspicuously unsuccessful. No one reflected that attempts to associate libraries with Franklin's *Junto,* the lyceum movement, the self-help associations of mechanics' apprentices and mercantile clerks, the Sunday-school movement, and the literary and scientific reading circles had all failed to achieve permanence. The fact that the library has none of the attributes of "a people's university" bothered no one. In short, there was a universal unawareness of the fact that this entire program was a serious distortion of the historic role of the library in society.

Today the adult education movement, if not dead, is certainly suffering a lamentable malaise; but the popular faith in the self-education of the adult still persists, and, if there has been disillusionment concerning the efficacy of "reading with a purpose" and the generosity of Andrew Carnegie, faith has found restoration in the "American heritage" and the benevolence of Henry Ford.

## THE PUBLIC LIBRARY INQUIRY

When Robert D. Leigh and his associated experts in the social science disciplines began their "appraisal in sociological, cultural, and human terms of the extent to which the [public] librarians are achieving their objectives" and set out to assess "the public library's actual and potential contribution to American society,"[9] they unquestioningly accepted the time-honored assumption that "the major objectives of the American public library are ... education, information, aesthetic appreciation, research, and recreation,"[10] and it was within this frame of reference that the Inquiry staff conducted its investigation. This was in itself a wholly unscientific procedure, but the Inquiry did not stop here. It made further assumptions which Mr. Leigh has stated as follows:

> From their official statements of purpose, it is evident that public librarians conceive of themselves as performing an educational task. The library, however, may also be thought of as a constituent part of public (or mass) communication: the machinery by which words, sounds, and images flow from points of origin through an impersonal medium to hosts of unseen readers and audiences. . . . And the public library's services to its patrons are in direct, though often unacknowledged, competition with the commercial media. One clue, then, to the discovery of the public library's most appropriate role in contemporary society is to see it against the background of the whole enterprise of public communication.[11]

Following this line of reasoning, Campbell and Metzner surveyed, for the Inquiry, the use made of the public library by the adult population in 80 selected communities. Their conclusion was that the public library is "failing to a considerable extent as an agency of mass communication and enlightenment."[12] It is their opinion that "the library suffers from being a quiet voice in an increasingly clamorous world" and "there is reason to believe that through broader services and a more active information program this fraction of the population (which it now serves) could be considerably increased."[13]

Mr. Leigh and his staff of social scientists must have taken some passing notice of the history of the American public library. In fact, Oliver Garceau devotes the opening chapter of his *The Public Library in the Political Process* to a historical consideration of "The Foundations of Library Government." But they could not have read this history with much care or thoughtfulness. Even a cursory examination of the history of the American public library would have made unmistakably clear that the public library never has been, and probably never was really intended to be, an instrument of mass communication. The public library, as we know it today, came about through the efforts of small and highly literate groups of professional men—scholars, lawyers, ministers, and educators—who sorely needed books for the performance of their daily tasks and who, through their efforts, convinced their respective communities of the social utility of supporting a public library. Even George Ticknor, who argued more emphatically than most for the public library as an agency of popular culture, helped fill the shelves of the new Boston Public Library with titles that more properly belonged in the study of the man of letters.

If one learns anything at all from library history, it is certainly that the public library has never evinced any of the attributes of a mass-communication agency. It has never had a "captive audience"—not even an "elite" captive audience. Similarly, the librarian has never been a "manipulator" who seeks to win the agreement of as large a part of his captive audience as possible to his particular aims. Furthermore, in the library the initiative has always come from the library patron, never from the librarian. The librarian has never been able to bend his patron to his purpose as has the radio commentator or the newspaper columnist. Thus, any attempt to study the public library as a segment of the existing system of mass communication ignores history, and the Public Library Inquiry, in so doing, may have committed a costly and disastrous blunder.

The fallacies of the 1930s and 1940s were reborn in the late 1960s and the early years of the 1970s, in the demand, coming mostly from the young, that the library be a "change agent," an instrument whereby the socially disadvantaged, the unhappy dwellers in the ghetto, could be lifted from their social and economic misfortunes into a world of middle class respectability. The fact that, since the days of ancient Egypt, the library had been an elitist institution seemed to have been either forgotten or ignored. The argument was far from new, though; to the young activists it was not only new but also "revolutionary." The library as a social instrumentality can, of course, change; what man has made man can also remake. But those who do the remaking should be aware that what they are attempting has not been successfully done before, and that in the process of transformation the library will receive a devastating wrench from the traditional moorings to which it has been tethered for centuries. The pains of rebirth (to change the metaphor), if indeed there should be a rebirth and not a miscarriage, will at best be severe. No one will deny that the disadvantaged need, and should have, all the help they can get. But librarians do not know, and have made little if any attempt to find out, whether the library is qualified to provide the kind of assistance needed to accomplish this new task.

To be sure, during the early decades of the present century some of our great public libraries did much to "Americanize" the immigrant; but this immigrant presented quite a different problem. The immigrant was not culturally deprived; he brought with him a rich tradition that the socially disadvantaged of today do not possess. In short, he was ripe for what the public library had to offer, as were his children. He had endured poverty in his homeland and he had probably escaped from a socially hostile milieu, but he believed in himself, and he knew that "the Melting Pot" was a land of opportunity only if he would make it such by his own efforts. He had determination and a sense of purpose, and he told his children, in effect, "Go to the public library. Read good books, and make yourself an American of which you can be proud." He was of the elect; he needed what the public library had to offer; and he built a nation.

## THE PROBLEM OF DEFINITION

The misconceptions that underlie both the adult education movement and the Public Library Inquiry derive from the same fallacious definition of the "educational" function of the library. The concept of the library as an educational agency is a direct transfer to librarianship of the 19th-century Enlightenment and the belief in the idea of progress and the perfectibility of man. Through the influence of 19th-century educational leaders, this dogma of human perfectibility was transformed into a general conviction that intellectual improvement—i.e., the education of the young—was a universal social responsibility; and thus began the ever-expanding movement for free, tax-supported public schools.

But this new urge for universal education was met by two opposing forces. The first came with the realization that men are not created intellectually equal and that there are great masses of the population incapable of assimilating the traditional classical scholarship, which in previous centuries had been restricted to the few who could profit from such rigid mental discipline. Hence, popular education was expanded, through such instruments as the Morrill Act, to include training in the agricultural and industrial technologies, partly because the basic acceptance of popular education was thereby extended and partly because there was in our increasingly technological culture a growing need for people trained in these skills.

The second counteracting force came with the discovery that our cultural pattern was not similar but dual—that, in addition to the Greco-Roman culture that had up to this time dominated popular education, there was an independent folk culture, which was not derivative but which had its roots in the hearts, minds, and experiences of the masses of the people.

These opposing forces, then, brought schism to the educational world, but the librarians continued to cling tenaciously to the traditional 19th-century concept of education as an attempt to impose upon the public the traditions of classical scholarship and to translate popular culture into "elite" terms. Thus, many librarians view their institutions as bulwarks against an encroaching flood of cultural mediocrity and seek to explain away their failure to "educate" the masses. This unrealistic infatuation of the librarian with his educational responsibilities arises in part from a desire to share in the prestige that the professional educator has long enjoyed in American culture, but it is in large measure the result of the deterioration of the definition of education itself. During the last few decades the term "education" has been so broadly and loosely applied that it has now very nearly lost all meaning. Today almost every human experience has been described at one time or another as being "educational," and even the advertiser who discourses at length on the deleterious effects of certain tobaccos upon the membranes of the "T-Zone" has come to think of himself as a missionary of popular enlightenment.

Such absurdities force a return to the original definition of "education," as derived from the Latin *educere*, "to lead forth." The educator, then, is a leader, one who conducts the student from a world that is familiar to a land that, at least for the student, is unexplored. The librarian, by the very nature of the responsibilities which he has assumed, cannot function effectively as such a leader. Only in a few isolated instances has personal contact between patron and librarian made possible the student-teacher relationship; yet from just such exceptions has grown a whole myth concerning the "educational" role of the librarian in society. So long as the social responsibility of the librarian remains the collecting, organizing, servicing, and administering of the graphic records of civilization and the encouragement of their most effective utilization, he cannot be an educator in the proper sense. To superimpose upon his established functions these irrelevant tasks will certainly confuse his objectives, if it does not actually destroy the true purpose for which the library was created.

This does not imply that the librarian must resign himself to a passive role in society, that he must continue to be "a quiet voice in an increasingly clamorous world." To be sure, the world would doubtless profit from an increase of vocal restraint. The librarian is at complete liberty to promote his services with all the intensity and drive that he deems desirable; but if his vigor is misdirected, it can result only in frustration and eventual failure. Nor does this argument suggest that a social agency cannot attempt to change, even drastically, its function in society; but the proponents of such alteration must be aware that the course which they are proposing is counter to the historical trend and may well involve grave risks. To reason that, because educators and librarians both make use of books and ideas, librarians are therefore educators is equivalent to saying that Old Dutch Cleanser is a food merely because it is usually kept in the kitchen and used by the cook.

## REASONS FOR THE NEGLECT OF HISTORY

Though one may grant that an understanding of the past is of major importance to those engaged in the social sciences, either as practical workers or as scholars, it still remains true that the uses and limitations of historical study have long been debated. As Crane Brinton points out, "there have always been individuals to whom the study of history seems unprofitable, even vicious, a limitation on the possibilities of soaring that the human spirit not dragged down by history might have."[14] There are a number of reasons for this growing lack of interest in history that is so strikingly characteristic of the historian's colleagues in the other social sciences, even though the popular appeal of history still remains relatively strong.

With the maturation of the social sciences as a recognized field of scholarship has come the development of a whole new constellation of techniques for the isolation, analysis, and investigation of social phenomena. In past centuries man turned to history alone, as today he turns to the entirety of the social sciences, for an understanding of man's social behavior. Then history was the only key to an understanding of man as man. But today history no longer provides the sole textbook for the study of human social, psychological, economic, and political behavior. With the evolution of specialized techniques in each of these branches of social science, there has arisen not only a diminution of the prestige of the historian but a concurrent distrust of his methods. Thus social scientists generally have come to consider history, if not actually a sterile and fruitless field of investigation, at least an academic adornment to be pursued only for its own sake, with little or no thought to practical utility. In short, they would challenge Collingwood's defense of history that "the only clue to what man can do is what man has done" and that the "value of history, then, is that it teaches us what man has done and thus what man is." That the social scientists, in following this line of argument, are pursuing a dangerous path has been suggested in the illustrations above.

The second argument that has been so successfully used against the historian arises from the belief that an increasingly complex pattern of social behavior denies the predictive value of history. If there have been those who have clung to the belief that history does not repeat itself, it is only because they subscribe to the popular adage that even a donkey will not stumble over the same stone twice. In this the social scientists have been strongly supported by the historians themselves, who have been eternally timid in defending the predictive value of their craft even when they must have known that a donkey will stumble over the same stone not only twice but many times. The Bourbons never learn. The great powers of the world relentlessly precipitate wars, fight them, win and lose them, and then go about the business of fomenting future conflicts with policies and practices almost identical with those that brought on earlier international strife. The cynical aphorism that "man learns nothing from history except that he learns nothing from history" is too often true. But man does sometimes learn something from history—though not so much as he should—and the real question is: Does his wisdom increase with sufficient rapidity to avoid catastrophe?

But the third and basic reason for the decline of history may be charged directly to the historians themselves. When Leopold von Ranke first enunciated his conviction that the task of the historian was to re-create the past "wie es eigentlich gewesen ist," he inaugurated a new era of scholarly accuracy in historical writing. At the same time he shackled historians for generations to come to a blind devotion to the fact *per se*, and from this bondage the historians have even yet been unable to free themselves. The result has been that synthesis and interpretation have been forsaken in the mad scramble to reexamine all history in the light of the new Rankean methodology. Thus has arisen a widespread belief that the true historian busies himself with the minutiae of historical detail, having little or no regard for the significance of the factual remains that he is able to uncover.

Such a criticism does not imply that the Germanic influence in historical scholarship is to be disparaged. The historical documents which von Ranke found stood in need of just such searching criticism and analysis as his methods could give, and the school of historical writing which he found merits all the credit given to it. No history can rise above the level of the accuracy in factual detail upon which it rests. But historians have often forgotten that syntheses and interpretations are also *facts* and that their truth to reality is often more important than the lesser values of their constituent elements. Truth itself is absolute, not relative, but the *importance* of truth can display an infinite degree of variation. Robert Maynard Hutchins has said:

> Philistines will ask, what is truth? And all truths cannot be equally important. It is true that a finite whole is greater than any of its parts. It is also true, in the common-sense use of the word, that the New Haven telephone book is smaller than that of Chicago. The first truth is infinitely more fertile and significant than the second. . . . Real unity can be achieved only by a hierarchy of truths which shows us which are fundamental and which are subsidiary, which significant and which not.[15]

Similarly, the question of whether or not General Custer disobeyed the orders of General Terry and of which man was more responsible for the disastrous massacre of the Seventh Cavalry at the battle of the Little Big Horn is less important than the whole fact of governmental stupidity in dealing with the problems of the American Indians. Yet an excessive amount of historical scholarship has been channeled into establishing the truth or falsity of the insignificant trifles, and, for all its good intentions and lofty motives, it has in many ways rendered history a real disservice.

## THE REORIENTATION OF RESEARCH
## IN LIBRARY HISTORY

If the writing of library history is to realize its fullest possibilities, it must be subjected to a drastic reorientation that will bring it into conformity with an underlying philosophy respecting the social function of the library itself. During the last two decades the earlier writing of library history has been severely criticized because of an excessive preoccupation with antiquarian detail and a provincial point of view. This charge that the authors of library history saw the library as an isolated and independent agency existing in a social vacuum was a thoroughly justified and wholesome criticism, and it prompted some useful exploratory thinking about the relation of the library to its coeval social milieu. But it did not go far enough. Even those writers who tried to present the library in sociological terms confined themselves to its institutional structure and form. They described, with a reasonable degree of success, *how* the public library assumed its present institutional pattern, but they did not question the current underlying assumptions about the function of the library in society, and hence they failed to explain *why* it came to be the kind of public agency it now is.

This complete failure of library history to come to grips with the problems of interpreting the social context from which the library arose may be explained in another way. "Man," says Pierce Butler, "is 'a thinker . . . a tool-user, and a social being,' and therefore his culture is trichotomous—'an organic integration of a scholarship, a physical equipment, and a social organization.' "[16]

Valid library history, then, can be written only when the library is regarded in relation to this tripartite division of culture, a phenomenon that has physical being, that is formed in response to social determinants, and that finds its justification as a segment of the totality of the intellectual processes of society. The library is an agency of the entirety of the culture; more specifically, it is one portion of the system of graphic communication through which that culture operates, and its historic origins are to be sought in an understanding of the production, flow, and consumption of graphic communication through all parts of the social pattern.

One may properly conclude, therefore, that the historical emergence and development of the library as an agency of this process of graphic communication must be viewed in a framework of effective investigation into the whole complex problem of the trichotomous culture, a study of those processes by which society *as a whole* seeks to achieve a perceptive or understanding relation to the *total* environment—the physical, the social, and the intellectual.

So long as the process of communication was personal, direct, and immediate, the problem of transmission was a simple and local matter. But as it became possible to extend the communication processes to ever greater dimensions through space and time, as the pattern of culture became increasingly complex, and as the informational needs of society became more divergent and even conflicting, an understanding of the historical development of the several aspects of culture becomes mandatory. Although the ultimate aim of such a study is effectively to order our communication processes to the end of greater benefit to society, it cannot proceed toward any valid conclusions without first answering such questions as: What have been the respective roles of the "personal carrier" and of the graphic record in the communication process? How did the main stream of graphic communication grow to its present flood proportions? What tributaries fed its turbulent waters, and how and to what extent did it irrigate the surrounding wastelands of human ignorance? What is the real contribution of libraries to this enrichment of the culture? What can be known of the past that will promote the exploitation of truth and the avoidance of error? What hope is there for the future ordering of graphic communication for the benefit of mankind? Even the mere listing of such questions reveals the depth to which their answers must be rooted in an understanding of the past.

The limitations of the present discussion preclude the possibility of describing in detail a research program in the history of librarianship and bibliographic organization that would contribute to the answering of such questions. But a few topics for investigation may be suggested that should exemplify the kind of historical inquiry which the writer has in mind.

It would seem to be a truism that the history of the library is related to the history of book production itself and that the two should be investigated in relation to each other. Yet we do not know what state of complexity a literature must achieve before society demands libraries of varying degrees of structural intricacy or subject specialization. The profession already possesses a series of histories of individual "special" libraries in medicine, business, industry, commerce, and the like; but all these, placed end to end, do not present a useful history of the special library movement in this country. No history of special libraries has yet been written that will answer such questions as the following:

1. What kinds of special libraries appeared first?

2. What was the structure of the business or industry at the time the special libraries for that particular enterprise developed?

3. What was the "structure" of the literature of that particular field—i.e., was it largely contained in books, in periodicals, or in special reports?

4. What were the basic informational needs of the enterprise, and what kinds of publications were essential to the meeting of these needs?

5. What was the maturity of the bibliographic organization for the particular field to be investigated; were its materials well organized bibliographically, or were there few bibliographies, guides, and indexing or abstracting services?

6. In all these respects, how does one field compare with another or one period with another in the demands that it makes for library and bibliographic resources?

Such an intensive analysis, not only for the special library but for the public library, the large research library, and the other bibliographic services that have been stimulated by our increasingly complex system of graphic communication, would contribute substantially to our understanding of the place of the library in our society.

Without such a "clear historical consciousness," is the librarian likely "at times to serve his community badly"? Indeed, without such an understanding, he is in constant danger of not serving his community at all. The degree of his success will be determined largely by the extent to which practical considerations are founded upon historic truth. To paraphrase the words of a German writer on archeology, library history is the concern of every librarian, for history is not an esoteric or special branch of knowledge but a synthesis of life itself.

When we busy ourselves with library history, librarianship as a whole becomes our subject. History is not an occasional or partial affair, "but a constant balancing on the point of intersection where past and future meet."[17]

## FOOTNOTES

[1] Pierce Butler, *An Introduction to Library Science* (Chicago: University of Chicago Press, 1933), pp. 81, 89-90, 101.

[2] John Dewey, *Essays in Experimental Logic* (Chicago: University of Chicago Press, 1916), p. 176.

[3] Crane Brinton, *Ideas and Men* (New York: Prentice-Hall, 1950), p. 19.

[4] R. G. Collingwood, *The Idea of History* (Oxford: Clarendon Press, 1946), p. 10.

[5] *Ibid.*, pp. 10-11.

[6] Louis Gottschalk, *Understanding History* (New York: Alfred A. Knopf, 1950), p. 252.

[7] *Ibid.*, p. 253.

[8] James Truslow Adams, *Frontiers of American Culture* (New York: Charles Scribner's Sons, 1944), p. 230.

[9] Robert D. Leigh, *The Public Library in the United States* (New York: Columbia University Press, 1950), p. 3.

[10] American Library Association, Committee on Post-war Planning, *A National Plan for Public Library Service*, (Chicago: American Library Association, 1948), p. 107, summarizing from the committee's *Post-war Standards for Public Libraries* (Chicago: American Library Association, 1943), pp. 19-24.

[11] Leigh, *Public Library*, 25-26.

[12] So interpreted by William S. Gray, "Summary of Reading Investigations, July 1, 1949 to June 30, 1950," *Journal of Educational Research*, XLIV (February 1951), 403.

[13] Angus Campbell and Charles A. Metzner, *Public Use of the Library and Other Sources of Information* (Ann Arbor: Institute for Social Research, University of Michigan, 1950), p. 45.

[14] Brinton, *Ideas and Men*, p. 19.

[15] Robert Maynard Hutchins, *The Higher Learning in America* (New Haven: Yale University Press, 1936), p. 95.

[16] Pierce Butler, "Librarianship as a Profession," *Library Quarterly*, XXI (October 1951), 240.

[17] C. W. Ceram [pseud.], *Gods, Graves, and Scholars* (New York: Alfred A. Knopf, 1952), p. 20.

# 12

# The Library as
# an Agency of
# Social Communication

The act of communicating is, by definition, the transmission of a message from a communicator to a receptor. The message may be a simple signal or an extensive body of oral or recorded symbolic or pictorial representations. Communication can take place within an individual organism, between two individuals, or among the members of an aggregate, but always there is a mutually intelligible 'language' as well as a carrier or medium; and while there may be multiple receptors, in any given instance there can be only one transmitter. Just as in the biological organism there is a neural communication system, so in organized societies there is a social communication network. While the agencies that are a part of this network are easily recognized and their functions easily identified, the fundamental nature of the communication process within society is only imperfectly understood. Students of society know lamentably little about the ways in which knowledge and information are communicated within a culture, even a primitive culture. For that matter, psychologists and specialists in the operation of the human nervous system know precious little about the communication of information within the individual. Analogies have been drawn with the electronic circuitry of the computer just as the communication of information within a society has been likened to the spread of epidemics in a population.

A society is, of course, an aggregate of individuals held together by a complex of cultural and institutional bonds. A society can scarcely know what is not known by any of its members, though the sum of that knowledge may induce in the actions of the group behavior patterns that differ markedly from those of the individuals that compose it. The study of the ways in which a society achieves an understanding relationship with its environment is what

Originally published in the *Journal of Documentation*, Vol. 21 (December 1965), pp. 241-43.

Margaret Egan called 'social epistemology,' and it is fundamental to a theory of librarianship.

Graphic records are both an extension of and a check upon the accuracy of the human mind. They are, in the terminology of the semanticist, 'time binders,' which span the temporal and spatial disturbances of our three-dimensional world. The document is an extension of the human powers of communication, and the library is a means for extending the life-span of the document. Like all other social agencies, it has arisen from, and is shaped and reshaped according to, social necessity. Thus, as graphic records came into being in response to the need of society for a medium that would communicate messages essential to the operation of the social structure, to religious doctrine or ritual, or to any other activity in which the members of the society might engage, so there arose the demand for an agency to control such of those records as needed, for any reason whatever, to be preserved. From the very beginning, libraries have always been an integral part of the 'business' of operating a society, hence a legitimate collective concern.[1] As the culture matured and became more sophisticated, its dependence upon graphic records increased, and changes in the culture were reflected in the librarian's responsibilities.

The librarians of the great collection at Alexandria were much more than mere keepers of the papyrus rolls. They were scholars who studied the texts in their care, participated in the educational and religious activities of their society, and in a variety of ways were an influential force in the total communication system. The Medieval libraries and the libraries of the Renaissance did not basically alter these original functions, but they directed them into different channels, again according to their respective social milieus. The invention of printing and the rise of scientific enquiry broadened and increased the importance of the librarian's role. Not only did books become more plentiful than they had been during the centuries before Gutenberg, but also the libraries in which they were housed were in a very real sense the laboratories of the scientists. From the 17th century to the beginning of modern times, the scientist had only the most meagre of apparatus with which to conduct his investigations. He found it necessary, therefore, to turn to the writings of his predecessors as the most important single source of the knowledge that he needed.

The invention of printing released the bonds that had so firmly restricted knowledge to the privileged few, and made possible, during the 19th century, the realization of the American dream of universal education. The emergence of local library societies in the towns of New England and elsewhere along the Atlantic Coast, the growth of the public library, and the rise of academic libraries were tributaries that fed the rich stream of social communication and that gave strength to the democratic movement in the formative decades of the United States.

The complex communication system that operates today in the Western world depends upon many instrumentalities, of which the library is but one. One need not dwell upon the impact that the telegraph, the telephone, the radio and television, not to mention the newspaper and the periodical, have made upon the communication patterns of our society. Each of these has had its effect upon the role of the library. With them has come a new urge on the part of the librarian to assume a vigorously active role in communication. Librarians no longer are content to accumulate materials in anticipation of use, but seek to engage actively in bringing their resources to the attention of those who need them. The growing importance of all types of graphic records to the successful operation of contemporary society, conditioned as it is by and to science and technology, has forced the librarian to search for and adopt new methods and techniques for making recorded information available not only to scholars but also to business, industry, and government. Effective use of the library has been demanded by the educational system, for elementary and secondary schools as well as institutions of higher learning. In recent years the introduction of automation into a variety of learning and teaching activities has provided the librarian with potentially powerful tools for increasing his effectiveness as a communicator, though the capabilities of these developments have not yet been fully realized.

Over the centuries library techniques and procedures have evolved only slowly and pragmatically, in response to assumed needs and patterned upon *ad hoc* methods. Only rarely have librarians thought seriously of their libraries as social agencies; as Douglas Foskett has said, they have failed to give "serious consideration to the role of libraries (not merely public libraries) in a society, and how the professional community as a whole can best serve society as a whole."[2] This is very true, but it may not be entirely the librarians' fault if they have nothing to draw on for their practice but unvalidated assumptions—not to say guesses—about the ways in which individuals and societies acquire knowledge and the networks by which knowledge is disseminated. What happens within that psycho-physiological process that takes place when a human mind confronts a library store or the bibliographic tools that are intended to be the key to it? How does the knowledge that the individual assimilates become a part of the collective intelligence of a culture? How is social behavior influenced by the knowledge that society absorbs? These are the basic problems that confront the librarian and should guide his professional practice. Obviously, librarians cannot seek unaided the answers to such questions; they must enlist the help of many specialists in many disciplines. Furthermore, they can, and must, apply the work of others to their own *Weltanschauung*. In the largest sense, the proper study of librarianship is man.

## FOOTNOTES

[1] Parenthetically, one should mention that over the centuries libraries have served as symbols of social position, and that their possession or endowment has long been a mark of status. Such recognition of the library is in itself evidence of the value that society places upon it, even though the prestige the library could confer upon its donor had no more to do with its effectiveness as an agency of communication than does the possession today of an expensive automobile relate to the motor car as a means of transportation.

[2] Foskett, D. J., *Science, Humanism, and Libraries* (New York: Hafner, 1964), p. 239.

# III.

# The Reference Function of the Library

# 13

# Foundations of a
# Theory of Reference Service

In accepting your very flattering invitation to deliver two lectures, the one on "Foundations of a Theory of Reference Service," and the other on "The Changing Role of the Reference Librarian," at your conference on *The Three Rs—Reference, Research, and Regionalism*, I realize that I have rather impaled myself on the horns of a dilemma. It is not easy to discuss a theory of reference service without considering the role of the reference librarian, for "theory" and "role" are inevitably interrelated and neither can properly be considered without reference to the other. In short, I am in somewhat the position of a public lecturer who, upon being invited to address a ladies' club, submitted five possible topics. The ladies were so impressed with his offerings that they invited him to present the entire series; in itself an innocent enough request, but for the fact that all five topics were the same speech. Nevertheless, I shall endeavor to escape between the horns of the beast by which I am threatened.

Before we begin to think specifically about the foundations of a theory of reference service, we must first think about the foundations of a theory of librarianship itself, for reference work is part of the larger whole—the totality of the librarian's function—and any operation must be seen in the light of its professional setting. One should not discuss any one particular library activity in the abstract. Librarianship, I fear, has suffered too long from neglect of the holistic perspective.

## THE FUNCTION OF THE LIBRARY

What is the function of the library in society? I believe we will all agree that

---

Revision of an address delivered before the Reference Round Table of the Texas Library Association, March 25, 1966, and subsequently published in *Reference, Research, and Regionalism*, supplement to the *Texas Library Journal*, 1966, pp. 13-20.

it is to maximize the social utility of graphic records for the benefit of the individual, and through the individual the improvement of society. Robert A. Fairthorne, the distinguished British information scientist, has expressed this point of view admirably, albeit somewhat paradoxically, when he says that the business of the librarian is ignorance—the ignorance, that is, of his patron. Thus he has written:

> ... ignorance makes the librarians' task possible, for the librarians' task is to help the reader to find out what people have to say; not to expound to the reader what has been said, as a substitute for the author; not to make use of what has been said, as a substitute for the reader; not to tell the reader what he ought to read, as a substitute for God.

Therefore, Fairthorne concludes that the librarian

> must be knowledgeable about discourse, not what the discourse may be about, if anything. He must therefore know who writes about what, what he has written, where and when, how to get hold of it, the sort of people who read it, what they think about it, what sort of words and language are used.[1]

What Fairthorne is saying, then, is that bibliography, in the larger sense, is the business of the librarian, and that bibliography is still, as it always has been, central to librarianship. I would like you to think of the library system in terms of a triangle, of which one side is *acquisition*, one *organization*, and the third, *interpretation*, or service.

FIG. 1.

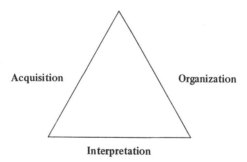

Acquisition     Organization

Interpretation

Acquisition means knowing what to acquire and where to acquire it. Organization encompasses the techniques and methods for making available the intellectual content of that which has been acquired. Interpretation implies the strategies by means of which the wanted intellectual content is delivered to the user. The interdependence of all these is obvious; one cannot operate effectively without the other two. It is, of course, in interpretation that the work of the reference librarian has its being and comes to a focus; here is to be found the act of mediation, the true social role of the library. In reference work we are, then, performing those operations that lie at the very heart and soul of the library as a social instrumentality. Now, of course, if I were addressing a group of catalogers, I would doubtless say that *they* represented the library's heart, and they would doubtless nod their heads in approval. If I were addressing a meeting of acquisition librarians, I would point out that the first function of the library is to build a book collection and that a library is not a library if it does not have a collection of books. Actually I would not be hypocritical in making any of these statements. A library is a tripartite unity of interrelated activities; it is not just a collection of books—not even of classified and cataloged books. "Books are for use," wrote S. R. Ranganathan, in his Five Laws of Library Science, and he amplified that assertion by declaring that every reader should have his book and every book its reader. But, however effective the librarian's technology may be, not every reader can find the book he wants, or that minute part of the book that he needs, which is why we have reference librarians. They are the true mediators between man and graphic records; they are the ones who give the library its social role. Probably very few reference librarians have spent much time thinking about the theoretical aspects of what they do, but they know very well how they do it. They are engaged in a very special kind of discourse the nature of which I shall discuss in more detail in my remarks at the general session this evening.

## THE LEVELS OF REFERENCE WORK

Reference work, as I shall try to explain this evening, has grown without design; rather, it seems to have arisen from fortuitous circumstance, probably because in the early history of the library bibliographic mechanisms were so inadequate that the user needed help to gain access to the library's resources. Indeed, a sociologist friend of mine once argued that modern techniques of bibliographic enterprise were ruining librarians, that the reader should be perfectly capable of finding things for himself. But we can assume, I think, that the origins of reference work as we know it today began with a rather casual assistance to the reader in finding what he wanted. From such casual beginnings it developed into what we might call an on-the-spot answer to the user's inquiry, a sort of hit-and-run procedure.

From such casual, off-the-cuff beginnings reference work developed on three levels, all of which are practiced today. The first, of course, is little more than helping the patron find a particular book whose author or title he knows, sometimes accurately but more frequently erroneously: he wants a book by Samuel Eliot Morison, but has been spelling Samuel's honored surname with two *r*'s. Such service is dull, routine, and certainly not in the least challenging, but it is important and it can pay very big dividends in reader satisfaction. It can give the patron the impression that the reference librarian is a very knowledgeable person. After all, great oaks really do grow from little acorns. The frustrated user's little problem seems very large to him, and who are we to pass judgment on its magnitude?

The second level is the hit-and-run dimension that I mentioned above. To most librarians, I would assume, this represents the essence of the librarian's reference activity; certainly it is the basis of most reference courses in library schools. It is the reason why students' noses are rubbed raw in *Winchell* or *Shores*, or whatever guide to reference sources may be popular at the time. Such activities on the part of the reference librarian should certainly not be regarded with disdain, but I have long been unable to suppress the uncomfortable feeling that these activities have dominated for too long the reference courses in library education programs. If Custer was defeated at The Little Big Horn, where is the Big Big Horn? What about "The Charge of the Heavy Brigade?" Where can I find a picture of the Church of England? You, I am sure, know them all well. Too well? Perhaps.

Finally, there is the level toward which I believe and hope that reference work is tending more and more—the truly professional level of the literature search necessitated by the increasingly complex questions that confront our society. Demand for such service will surely increase as society's problems grow in complexity; and if the library does not assume its proper role in meeting this demand, it will lose its support to other, and perhaps entirely new, agencies. The important question is, have we qualified ourselves to meet such a demand, and if not, can we do so?

There are two functions or two ways of looking at reference work—either of which has its own particular virtues and own particular place in the library system. One is an education function, helping the reader to help himself—not getting the answer for him but showing him how the library operates and what sources it has to which he might turn. This is particularly relevant for reference work in the school or academic library system.

With the development of the specialized libraries and librarians serving research teams, industries, businesses, executives, etc., this educational role of the reference librarian diminishes. Such patrons don't want to learn; they want information and it is up to the librarian to get it. When I was a research assistant and bibliographer for a foundation studying population problems, the director said to me: "I don't care what you do with your time as long as you get for me what I want when I want it." I was his computer; he programmed me and it was up to me to produce the "print out."

I think this kind of reference work is definitely on the increase, for two reasons: first, because the volume of material has become so great—Jack Dalton last night referred to the knowledge explosion. I have always rather been at odds with that point of view. I don't see it so much a knowledge explosion—it's a *paper* explosion. We live in a paper economy. Paper makes us go. If we didn't have paper, where would we be? More and more these symbolic representations of things on paper are coming to replace the things themselves. When I was a boy growing up, and even before that dim and distant past, people judged position, status, wealth in terms of *things*. You owned a house, you owned so many acres of land, you owned this or that. Now, of course, you own some of these things, but mostly you own pieces of paper, pieces of paper that come out of Wall Street. The value of these pieces of paper has more relation to other pieces of paper on Wall Street than to the actual thing they represent. How many times have you bought stock in something simply because it was a good product. The stock never went any place, even though the product was good. Sometimes you have bought pieces of paper representing stock in companies that were making products of dubious quality, at least in your opinion—yet the market value of the stock continued to rise. Thus do symbols have a reality all their own; not infrequently, these values are seemingly unrelated to the physical realities for which they stand.

## THE PROBLEM OF UNDERSTANDING

In a very real sense representations are the reference librarian's business. Representations are, of course, the vehicles of communication. The user's needs and the librarian's response must be expressed in symbols. Yet these symbols can be barriers to understanding, too, as we all know. These symbols have no fixed or permanent identity of their own; they have only that meaning which is given to them by the user, and our power to communicate successfully depends entirely upon a consensus, a grneral acceptance, of the particular meaning attached to any particular symbol. Moreover, we do not understand how these symbols are processed by the human brain. In short, we do not understand cognition, learning, or the ways in which they influence behavior. The whole profession of librarianship is predicated on the assumption that knowledge can be communicated; we know from past experience that it can be and is, but we do not understand in any real sense how such communication is accomplished. The reference librarian does not know how she does what she does, but she does it anyway, like the bee who flies without understanding the laws of aerodynamics.

We do not even understand how the individual—in this case, the reference librarian—communicates with himself. I would wager that few reference librarians can explain in any precise way their methods of search, or how their decisions are made. Certainly, with this audience I need not belabor the mystery of serendipity; we have all experienced it, and made very good use of it, too.

## ORGANIZATION AND RECOURSE

So we do our work as best we can, retrieving information as best we know how. We ignore the complexities that haunt us when we are aware of them, simply because we lack the knowledge to do otherwise. In effect, and whether we know it or not—and this is relevant to the cataloger, the classifier, the organizer, as well as to the reference librarian—we are matching two patterns:

the pattern of the organization of material (the classification schemes, the indexes, the bibliographies, the abstracting services) with the pattern of the user, the pattern of recourse to the library store—the library collection—the total sum of the resources the library has. The closer one can bring these two patterns to coincidence, the closer one is going to come to satisfying the user.

In the past and still to a large extent in the present, we have only been able to make *ad hoc* assumptions about the pattern of organization in terms of patterns of use. The cataloger sits at his desk and says, "I have this book on economic conditions in Germany since the Second World War. Under what headings would a person who might want to use this book look?" The answer would be, "Obviously a user would look under 'Germany—Econ. condit.—1945'," or whatever date you might want to put on it. Having done this, the cataloger has gone about as far as he can go. At last we have standard lists of headings, standard dictionaries of terminology with which we hope the user will familiarize himself. He has first to put himself more or less back in the position of the cataloger. In effect he has to say, "Now I want this material. Where would a cataloger put it?" Sometimes it's a bit hard to figure out, especially if he doesn't know how the brain of the cataloger works, and few people do, including the catalogers.

The person who compiles a bibliography is much better in this respect and in a much stronger position strategically than the cagaloger. The cataloger works from the book to the subject to the user. The user, unless he is looking for a particular book, begins with the subject. The cataloger and the user, you see, approach the problem from completely opposite points of view. I suppose it's rather remarkable and a tribute to the effectiveness of our cataloging operation that they meet as frequently as they do.

We all know that a catalog at best (and this, of course, is where the reference librarian comes in) brings out only a relatively small portion of the library's resources. I think it was Grace O. Kelley's study back in the '30s that showed that cataloging brought out only about 30 percent of the total resources of the library on any given subject. This varied somewhat from subject to subject, but there is always material in encyclopedias, periodicals, and handbooks which is not analyzed in the catalog. The reference librarian has to build a bridge among all the tools of the library, using the handbooks, encyclopedias, the bibliographies and so on to bridge these gaps. Basically, the catalog is the key to the library store. It records what the library actually has. The reference librarian, I think, historically came into being because of the gap between the key to library resources and the resources themselves. In other words, the key was only an imperfect key, unlocking only certain doors; there were a lot of other doors around that the key wouldn't fit. So in a sense, the reference librarian, the keeper of the keys, has all these other resources to investigate. Again, you see, the reference librarian stands at a very crucial point where the resources of the library and the clues to these resources come together at the crossroads—the reference librarian's desk.

This is the real act of mediation that we have been talking about: bringing together people and recorded knowledge in a fruitful relationship.

This whole relationship is extremely complex. I am not going to talk about that this morning because I have to have something for tonight. I am not going to talk about the role of computers because I am going to talk about that tonight. Let me say one thing—I will have to repeat it tonight—the computer, the work of the computer, is helping us, I think, to understand this complex relationship because, as we build computers, we learn more about thought processes—there are some similarities between computers and brains.

As we work with computers and learn how they operate and how they can be improved, we learn more about the brain by analogy. As we work with the brain and learn more about the whole process of cognition, we are more able to build computers that can simulate thought or seem to simulate thought. We are out in the wide, blue yonder now and I don't want to say any more about that, but I did want to point out that I think the reference librarian can be immeasurably helped by computers—not just as machines to improve access to the intellectual content of the library, but also to help in understanding the thought processes that one goes through or should go through in working with the patron.

## MEASUREMENT FOR EFFECTIVENESS

Despite all of our talk about reference work, I think the thing that astonished me was that we have been doing this now for at least 50 years or so in one way or another—yet have never developed any real theory or standard of measurement for our effectiveness. How effective is a reference librarian? Well, in many respects, they are pretty effective.

My old teacher and later colleague Pierce Butler of the University of Chicago used to say, "What is all this talk about learning about reference tools and where stuff is in the library? I just go into the big reading room in the Harper Library and stand there and look helpless. Miss Ver Nooy comes and gets me what I want." Well, I am sure there is a lot of truth in this. Certainly reference librarians have been badgering away as best they can and are getting surprisingly good results. I have always marveled at what a really imaginative, intelligent, skilled reference librarian can do with nothing more than the unabridged dictionary, the *Encyclopedia Britannica*, *Shakespeare*, the *Bible* and the *World Almanac*. When you give her those, there isn't much she can't do with them, one way or the other—learning to pull out of these resources, imaginatively, the kind of information that will take care of a tremendous proportion of the inquiries that come to the librarian. I don't want to put the reference librarian in a strait jacket. I would hate to hear an administrator say he thought that these books were all a reference librarian needed to work with.

We have, however, become extremely skillful in doing something without knowing why we are doing it or even, in large measure, how we are doing it. We are like Molière's bourgeois gentleman, who had been speaking in prose all his life and didn't realize it. We have been doing these operations, complex as they are, as I will try to show tonight, without really knowing how extremely complex this reference process is. We have grown up with it.

## THE NEED FOR MECHANISMS

With the pressure of the explosion of the recorded word the problem of securing access to needed information is no longer simple. We are forced to look critically at what we are doing because the old techniques simply don't work. A good reference librarian, however excellent she may be, cannot possibly carry in her head all the things she needs to know. No one can. We must devise some kind of mechanism—computer or computer-like device if you will—that will help us. But do not be led astray, the mechanism does not have to be a machine in the strict sense.

One of the first inventions of this sort was Poole's *Index to Periodical Literature*. I think we have now worked so long with periodicals that we don't realize what tremendous impact the rise of the periodical made on librarianship. Life was pretty simple when there were nothing but monographic books on a particular subject, and they were classified according to subject. When the periodical became prevalent in the scientific field, it was far more important than the monograph; information is first reported in the periodical. The periodical is a terrible hodge-podge. Even when it relates to one particular twig on one particular branch of a scientific discipline, it is still a conglomerate. This upset the whole library picture and made a tremendous impact on it.

We are more and more being compelled to invent mechanisms to ease the burden of the reference librarian. We must think increasingly in terms of the reference process and what it involves.

## THE EVALUATION OF SERVICE

Despite our lack of knowledge (I don't want to say "ignorance" because we're not really ignorant—but we certainly have enormous gaps about what reference work really is psychologically), we have never developed any real standards for evaluation. Here, I think, is a job that is fundamental if we are going to talk about foundations or a theory of reference work. We must not only learn what reference work *is* and what it involves, but also how we measure its effectiveness. How do we know when reference service is *good*?

I suppose no reference librarian is ever really satisfied with what she is doing. She thinks "There must be some other place I should have looked or some other aspect I should have considered." That's sort of a vague and general evaluation. Mostly, we depend on reader satisfaction. If the reader went away happy, then we were happy. If he was unhappy, then, of course, that rubbed off on us and we worked some more until we finally made him happy or convinced him this was all we could get, all that was available, and that was the end of it. While it's the best measure we have at the present time, it's a pretty shaky way to do our job. Because the reader thinks he is satisfied, everyone is happy—but should he be satisfied? He got what he thought he wanted, but did he really get what he needed? We will talk more about this tonight when we talk about process.

We have no real valid measurement of effectiveness and I must frankly admit I don't know how we will develop it, but I think we must. This whole question is economic. Again, reference librarians are going to have to spend some time on it because they have a professional obligation, a duty to do so.

How much time should we spend on any one question? What is a reference question "worth"? I remember talking years ago when I was still in Chicago to one of the members of the staff at the Public Administration Clearing House about this problem of measuring the value of library service. How do you measure this? How much will we suffer economically in pure dollars and cents if we don't have any library service? I pointed to these as particularly difficult things to measure, and he said, in effect, "The librarian has it easy. How do you measure the value of a fire department or police department? How much of the house would have burned down, how much would the economic loss be if we didn't have a fire department? Or how much crime would we have if we didn't have a police department?" How do you measure this? It is extremely difficult but I do think we can do more than we have done in trying to evaluate library service of all kinds.

Librarians, you know, are such dedicated souls. We will spend hours on something that really isn't worth that much effort, that much expenditure. Dedication becomes absorbed into our professional psychic. We have an economic problem, and I don't think it is a diminution of the reference librarian's role to say that we ought to put a period to some of these things. I believe we ought to say "This is far enough, and beyond this it is not our professional responsibility to go." There is a point somewhere along the line of search at which we must stop.

The other aspect of reference work that involves economics is the relation of reference work to the other operations of the library, which may be a little more directly measurable. If you save money in the Catalog Department, you may spend more in the Reference Department. Or if you go all out for cataloging, maybe you save time for the reference librarians—you have to evaluate these relationships.

When I was head of the Technical Services of the University of Chicago, the catalogers in my domain (and I, too, to a large extent) were always trying to simplify cataloging: "We don't need all this bibliographic detail." Who were the ones who were complaining about our attitude? It was the reference librarians. "Oh, but we have to have that detail. We do need it." It is certainly true that the more information there is on the cataloging card, the more it will help the reference librarians. Choices do have to be made. Operations do have to be looked at critically. All this information may be valuable at some time, but what is the probability that anybody is going to use it?

## ESTIMATED USE OF BOOKS

I think librarians have not worked with probabilities as much as they should. They have always worked on the assumption that everything they acquire is going to be useful. Yet when closed stack collections are examined, there will be dozens of books whose cards indicate that nobody has ever used them at all (no one has ever taken them out). Particularly in the large research libraries, there are huge quantities of material that are either not used or used very little. That doesn't mean that the acquisition librarians or the bibliographers were doing a bad job. I think a research library *should* buy material that is going to be used seldom. This is becoming a very tough problem and I don't think anybody has the answer to it.

But catalogers and reference librarians, too, proceed on the assumption that every book is going to be used like every other book, and that therefore it needs the same kind of treatment. I recall that Ralph Beals once observed, as we were checking the stacks of the University of Chicago library for material that could be sent to storage, "You know, the heaviest user of our library is the bindery"; and he was very right.

If one would chart a curve as indicated in Figure 2, with the vertical axis representing volume of use and the horizontal axis numbers of titles, it would indicate that a limited number of books are heavily used while a very large number are used little or not at all.

FIG. 2.

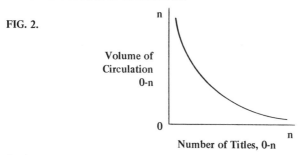

Such a curve is, of course, only a crude approximation, but perhaps it illustrates my point.

## CONCLUSION

We must take probabilities into account, simply because libraries are so growing in size that we can't do anything else. This enormous increase is a result of a paper explosion. We are going to have to develop economic foundations of library operations, to view the library as a system and develop networks.

I am sure I have raised more questions here than I have answered. I knew I was going to do that, simply because I don't have the answers. None of us has the answers. But if I have stimulated your thinking a bit, if I have brought you to a point where you might look at some of these things a little differently from the way you did, if I have you pondering about what your problems really are—maybe the hour won't have been wasted after all.

## FOOTNOTES

[1] Robert A. Fairthorne, "The Symmetries of Ignorance," in Conrad H. Rawski, ed., *Toward a Theory of Librarianship* (Metuchen, N.J.: Scarecrow Press, 1973), p. 263.

**14**

# The Challenging Role of
# the Reference Librarian

Texas Friends: It is a great pleasure to be with you this evening; in fact, all this week. As I have often said, I'm a kind of Texan myself. In 1890 or 1900, my favorite uncle (God rest his soul) bought a quarter section of Texas land in Pecos County not very far from Fort Stockton. He always thought there would be oil on that land, but we never got enough oil out of it to lubricate our lawnmower. There wasn't any water on it either. There was nothing but stone and we had all the stones in Ohio that we needed. He willed the property to me and I thought that the least I could do in memory of my uncle was to pay taxes on it for a while. So I paid taxes on it in the Depression until I got a little tired of that. Finally I just quit paying taxes, and when I was a graduate student at the University of Chicago in 1938, I received a telegram from the Sheriff of Pecos County. Heaven knows how he found out I was in Chicago, but the Fort Stockton Public Library must have a good reference librarian. At any rate, this telegram from the Sheriff said that if I didn't pay the delinquent taxes on this land, he was going to sell it at a sheriff's sale. Well, my first impulse was to wire back, "Go ahead and sell it, Buster"; but then I thought why should I pour more money into this property? Why should I spend money to tell him to do what he was going to do anyway? So I just dropped the telegram into the wastebasket, and such was the end of my career as a Texan.

I must confess that I was a little concerned when I got off the plane at Austin because I expected to be met by the Sheriff of Pecos County. The Texas Rangers always get their man, you know. But much to my relief I was greeted by

Revision of an address delivered at the Second General Session of the Annual Conference of the Texas Library Association, Austin, Texas, March 25, 1966, and subsequently published in *Reference, Research, and Regionalism*, supplement to the *Texas Library Journal*, 1966, pp. 21-34.

three charming young women. After this speech the Sheriff may show up yet; I don't feel to secure even now.

I am in a little bit of a predicament tonight because I spoke to the reference librarians this morning, and I am somewhat afraid that I am in the situation tonight of having two speech titles and only one speech—but we will do the best we can. Now, let's get to the business at hand.

## REFERENCE SERVICE DEVELOPMENT

Reference work, as we know it today, is of singularly and, to me at least, surprisingly recent origin. Of course, I suppose librarians have been helping readers in one way or another ever since the days of the Alexandrian Library; perhaps even Assurbanipal may have had some of his favorite concubines help users to find the clay tablets they wanted to read. But be that as it may, the 1853 conference of librarians, held in New York City, made no mention whatever of reference work or readers' services, and it was not until the famous first conference of the ALA in 1876 that that great library pioneer with the incredible name of Samuel Swett Green, who was librarian of the Worcester Free Public Library, talked about aid to readers.[1] Otis Robinson, of the University of Rochester, picked up Green's ideas, which were also in harmony with the library philosophy of Justin Winsor of Harvard, and from then on they very slowly and quite deliberately evolved, like Topsy, into modern reference service. Reference work was tied in, at first, with the educational function of the library—you can see that Harvard was early with this point of view—tied in with the idea of promoting "culture." So, in its early stages there was a kind of union of what today we call reference work and readers' advisement services.

I think we can identify two reasons for the development of reference service as we know it today. First, there was a growing professionalism among librarians. Professionalism had its first major push with the 1876 conference which the American Library Association formed and, of course, Melvil Dewey introduced this concept of a new librarianship at Columbia and later at Albany. Reference service was also promoted, at least in part, by the changing patterns of scholarship, an influence, of course, which relates primarily to the academic situation.

Research as we know it today, particularly as it is taught in graduate schools, is Teutonic in origin. It goes back to the German seminars and that great migration of American literary figures and other scholars to Germany in the 1840s and 1850s and even earlier, and the introduction of the German seminar at Johns Hopkins and later throughout the academic world. This movement, because of the changing pattern of scholarship, has had a great deal to do with the development of reader services on this side of the Atlantic. Reader service, then, began as a vague, generalized, not particularly planned, aid to readers; it evolved, although no one ever really defined what reference work is, into a kind of spot information service—a "hit-and-run" technique. Reference service fulfilled its purpose most fully for the individual working in a field with which he wasn't familiar—a biologist, for example, who needed some sociological information, or a humanist wanting to know something about biology. A specialist working in his specialty has always said, "I don't need the reference librarian. I know more about my particular subject than he does." And, of course, in a sense he is right.

## REFERENCE SPECIALISTS

Now we are again in a period of transition and change. We are moving from this spot-check, hit-and-run technique (although this will always play a part in the reference field) to a more serious attack upon reference problems. The "generalized" reference librarian, the image that most of us have when we say "reference librarian," is giving way to subject specialists attached to libraries. These may be bibliographers, for want of a better term. They specialize in certain areas of knowledge, at least in the three major branches—the sciences, the humanities, and the social sciences—in which they have equipped themselves not only through graduate study in librarianship, but also through graduate study in a subject field. In some instances, I must confess, although I am talking against myself as a library school dean, perhaps the graduate study in the subject field is the more important of the two. But I won't press that position too hard. The important point is that we are moving in the direction of a corps of specialists who give quite sophisticated reference assistance, not only to the general reader, or to the reader working in an area unfamiliar to him, but most important of all to the specialist himself. Such bibliographic reference experts can meet the specialist on his own terms.

## INFORMATION CENTER SYSTEMS

The next logical step (and now, of course, as we move into the future your guess is as good as mine) is the development of information center systems. You have all heard about information centers from non-librarians. As some of my good friends say, and I think rightly, "What *is* a library but an information center?" But the information center as I conceive of it focuses on a certain area of subject knowledge, which may be quite minute. The next progression from these highly specialized information centers is toward a network of related centers across the country. The Library of Congress, as you all know, is already playing with this idea, as is the National Library of Medicine. I surmise that the National Library of Agriculture will follow suit. It has, in fact, to a certain extent actually done this through the Agricultural Extension Service and the County Agent program. These are all trends that I think will increase in importance in the future.

Why will they be more important? I think almost inevitably it is because of the tremendous proliferation of paper. It is easy to say "knowledge," and there has been a proliferation of knowledge. Certainly since the Second World War, knowledge has pushed ahead at tremendous rates. Even worse for the librarian, however, there has been a tremendous proliferation of *paper*. I called it in my remarks this morning "the paper explosion." It is not really a knowledge explosion. This explosion is causing a tremendous problem because all these papers have degrees of value. A lot of them are pure junk; a lot are repetitious; and down at the bottom there is a kernel of good hard important material. But good hard important material for whom and for what purpose? I think we are going to have to move in the direction of information center networks staffed by experts who can evaluate what they collect. There will probably always be a place for the reference librarian as we know him today, with his hit-and-run technique, his spot information. But I think a great deal is going to develop in the next 15 or 20 years relating to information center networks. I am convinced that the information center, with its highly skilled subject-oriented staff, is in our future.

We have never really defined what reference work is, but I think that it is more or less implicit from what I have been saying. Reference work runs the whole gamut from the vague notion of "helping readers" to the very esoteric, very abstract, very highly specialized information service. We have never really settled in our own minds what reference work is, but I don't know really, in this particular situation at least, that it makes very much difference whether we have defined the term or not. The main point, of course, is that we have library materials and we want somebody to use them—to use them in a way that will benefit him and benefit society. What you call the individual who does the work, or how you define his particular role is not too important.

## THE INTRODUCTION OF AUTOMATION

Another element in this changing pattern of reference service is the introduction of automation. I want to talk about that a little because automation, an extremely slippery subject to deal with, is subject to much misinterpretation. Like any innovation that comes over the horizon, it is always greeted in one of two ways: either people say it is no good at all, or they think it is going to be the savior of whatever it is supposed to save—librarianship, in this case. Both extremes are wrong. Automation has a place in the library, and to me it seems inconceivable that a force that has the power of automation and that is developing as rapidly as automation is will leave the library untouched. I can't believe the library will be overlooked by the machine. On the other hand, we must admit that many of the attempts, up to the present time, to supply automative techniques to the library operations have not been conspicuously successful.

I attended a conference—Jack Dalton referred to it last night—sponsored by Woods Hole, Massachusetts, last summer, called the Intrex Conference. Intrex is an acronym for information transfer equipment. Information is not retrieved any more, it is transferred. This conference brought together two very disparate groups of people. There were the computer boys, on the one hand—dyed-in-the-wool computer hardware fellows—and there were the librarians. For the first week or two they had a devil of a time communicating. I am not sure they ever did really communicate. Nevertheless, for better or worse, something beneficial did come out of the encounter. I think that for the first time the librarians began to see, albeit in a somewhat confused and ill-defined fashion, the possibilities inherent in the mechanized handling of information, and the fact that it *does* have tremendous possibilities for librarianship. On the other hand, the engineers, the computer boys, began to learn more about librarianship than they had ever known before. To me the most helpful, the most encouraging thing I heard during the period that I was there, was one computer man's comment, "There is a helluva lot more to this damn library business than I ever realized." This is so very true. Engineers tend to think of information retrieval as simple data processing, as though all the reference librarian does is just hunt out data, go to a handbook and find the atomic weight of silver, or something simple like that. Well, of course, I don't need to tell reference librarians that, while this is an important part of what they do, it is by no means all of what they do. Life isn't that simple. You don't just plug into a computer and say, "I want this particular piece of information," then wait for the machine to spew it out. It is silly to go to a computer and program it to find the date of George Washington's birth, when one can go the *Dictionary of American Biography*, or one of many other sources, and find it.

I didn't see the library exhibits of the Seattle World's Fair or the New York World's Fair, but from what I have heard I think both of them were unfortunate in their planning. One of my faculty was at Seattle where, as you know, they programmed a certain section of the index to the Great Books *Syntopican.* You were given a series of questions from which you picked out a question such as what did Plato say about love, or something of the sort, whereupon they pushed the computer button and you got the citation. They went through all of this rigamarole, my good friend and colleague said, while there was the *Syntopican* sitting right on the shelf where anyone could open it up and get the answer. Not only that, but he would get a lot more information than came out of the computer. The New York story came from another member of my faculty who went to the New York World's Fair. There, you will remember, visitors were given a series of questions or topics from which to make a choice. The topic was plugged into the computer and the computer did a print-out of a bibliography. My associates said to the little girl who was in charge that day, "Wouldn't it be easier to have a stack of mimeographed bibliographies and let people pick them up for themselves?" And she replied, "Oh, yes, it would, but it wouldn't be nearly so dramatic!"

## THE POTENTIAL OF AUTOMATION

It is unfortunate that we have misused computers—prostituted them, if you will—for tasks for which they are not efficient or even competent. Now that I have talked against the computer boys, let me say a little about the positive side of their point of view. It is true that computers have enormous capabilities, fantastic capabilities when you come right down to it. When you hear a good computer man talk, even when he is talking reasonably, conservatively, and rationally, it is evident that the potential of these mechanisms is really tremendous and is getting more tremendous every day. But in spite of the future promise of these giant brains—and I am convinced that they have promise— perhaps one of the greatest assets which they bring is that they are as they are. Because they are man-made mechanisms, they force the librarian for the first time to analyze seriously what he is really doing. That is, if for no other reason, the librarian will have to analyze his operations to combat the arguments and exaggerated claims of the computer boys. Thus the machine has a kind of irritational value, which is good. The reason the computers have not achieved the success that some of their most ardent proponents have insisted they have, or could have, is that we, as librarians, have not been able to help the computer designers and manufacturers understand what it is we really want, and what it is we really do. There is a relation between the exaggerated claims of the engineers and their ignorance of what librarianship is. I don't necessarily damn the librarians for this ignorance of the engineers, because we are doing a lot of things that we don't quite understand and that nobody else understands either.

We are dealing with a very subtle relationship between the human mind and the printed page. Although we all exercise this relationship every day, every hour, and almost every waking minute of every day, we still don't know what goes on in this cognitive process. How do we know what we know? What is the cognitive process? The answer is to be found in knowledge about knowledge itself. How do we know about knowledge? How do we learn? Thus we are brought squarely back to epistemological foundations, and by applying it to the whole social structure I have adopted a term that some of my friends delight in throwing at me, "social epistemology"—knowledge of the ways in which knowledge is disseminated throughout a society. How does society learn? We know only the most simple elements of learning; but we don't even know how a child learns to speak. There are several theories about how a child learns to talk, but nobody knows how the child achieves speech. There are no really primitive languages for us to study. The best research now seems to suggest that speech arises from the babbling instinct. Babies babble and when they see their elders talking they babble in imitation, until finally they begin to make intelligible sounds or signals. But nobody understands the language process.

Human beings are human beings by virtue of their ability to speak to one another. Though animals can, and do, communicate by means of signals, some of which are audible, "man was not man until he spoke." Indeed many anthropologists predicate the existence of culture on the presence of a communication system. "We live in a sea of words," wrote the editors of *Harper's*, connoting love, hate, joy, hope, the past, present, and future. Words define and bind individuals, cultures, nations. Without speech, there would be no politics and hence no society; no moral purpose and no civilization. Speech, to be sure, has a price. It may corrupt thought, make evil, incite revolution. The power to voice an authoritative conclusion is the power to govern. Thus, rulers suppress words they consider seditious; freedom of speech is rare in history."[2] "Silence," wrote George Bernard Shaw, "is the perfect expression of scorn." There are even linguistic philosophers who hold that language was devised for purposes of deception, for lying; but one may hope that it is not so utilized by reference librarians, even though a life of strict and unwavering adherence to the truth would be at least a very unhappy life, if, indeed, not an impossibility. At best, it would probably be a very short life. We all lie, and excuse ourselves with the attributes of "little," and "white."

There is no such thing, of course, as perfect communication. But I think the computer and the development of automation is forcing us, and will continue to force us—and I think it is extremely good that it is forcing us—to analyze many human activities, including those of the librarian.

## APPLICATIONS OF AUTOMATION

One of the best examples of the engineer's misunderstanding of the library search process is the Eastman Kodak Minicard. This machine, I suppose, not many of you have even seen. It utilized little strips of microfilm, little pieces of microfilm about the size of a special delivery postage stamp, or maybe a trifle larger. One-third of it was used for a code or pattern of black and white dots, which could be arranged in a great variety of patterns. The other portion of the film was given over to the text of the document. These bits of film were spindled on long sticks. Questions were expressed in terms of the code, and the machine would search these little pieces of microfilm; whenever a match of the pattern was achieved, a relevant document was identified and an enlargement of the text on the microfilm was automatically made. This text was usually an abstract. The device was a magnificent piece of engineering. I have never in my life seen an optical system that compared with it. Those minute black and white dots, and the speed with which they could be "read" and shot through the system, the lens train, the triggering of the photo-electric cell in a strobescope arrangement—all were almost beyond belief in their perfection. What happened? Nothing, because nobody knew what to do with the thing once it was made. There was no system to apply to it. So Eastman Kodak, after spending about $6-million of Air Force money, originally your money and mine, gave the whole thing up. And there the prototype sits, as I have said in another connection, like a Cadillac rusting in the midst of the Amazon forest because it can't go any place.

We have got to think our procedures and processes through. Let me take an illustration that shows this in a completely different field. For millenia man has wanted to fly as the birds do. Quite understandably, he began by imitating the physical motions of birds—using his arms and legs as wings. But it was not until he became aware of the laws of aerodynamics that he ceased his flapping and was able, for a few brief moments at least to lift himself from the ground in heavier-than-air craft. Up to that time only the balloon had been successful. But whereas thousands of years spanned the distance between the notions of Daedalus and Icarus and those of the Wright brothers, only two to three decades separated the experiments at Kitty Hawk from the engineering of Robert Goddard and Wernher Von Braun. There are two lessons in this illustration, so far as the librarian is concerned: first is the tremendous acceleration, during the past three-quarters of a century, in scientific and technological advance; and second, and more important for our immediate purpose, is the lesson that man does not achieve technological advances in automation by emulating the physical motions of the librarian as he goes about his business of bibliographic or reference search. We cannot achieve automated information retrieval without understanding the psychological principles involved. A mechanical robot, even a highly sophisticated electronic robot, is not an adequate substitute for the reference librarian—in fact, it is not a substitute at all.

So much of what automation has been doing in librarianship up to the present time (and I suppose our errors are very human, as man always seems to have to blunder at first) has not reproduced with these computers what the brain does in processing and retrieving information. We have been making, in effect, mechanical stack-boys. This is exactly what Minicard was. The stacks, of course, were all on little pieces of film, but it searched the films just as a boy would search the stacks for a book for which he had the call number. In the case of Minicard, the pattern of black and white dots was the call number. Most of our automation has been this sort of mechanization; it has not really been intellectually based. So, if we are going to make any progress, we must begin by examining the library process, and especially the area that conerns us tonight, the reference process. When men invented the automobile they didn't put an internal combustion engine on legs. They didn't make a mechanical horse. Oh, perhaps there were those who made such a horse just to see if they could do it, but nobody, even the inventors, ever took the idea very seriously. Yet we are, in effect, at the present time, pretty much in the stage of making mechanical horses to pull the library load.

## THE REFERENCE SYSTEM

Now, let's move from this plea for analysis of the reference system to an examination of the reference system itself. I have made, with the very good offices of Mrs. Boyvey, a couple of transparencies. (I just wanted to show you that I was up to date on all the new audiovisual media.) We begin (Fig. 1), of course, with a need. There must be some kind of need, a felt need. You remember a couple of years ago librarians were all talking about "felt needs." There is always a need of some sort; reference work begins with an awareness of ignorance. And if there is a need, there must be an inquirer. This is the second element in the process. He has, in one way or another, a vague awareness of the need, and he verbalizes that need in the form of a question, and we move to our third element in the diagram, the interrogation, which is a verbalized form of the patron's need—the inquirer's need. Now, I don't have to tell the reference librarians that inquirers are very inept at verbalizing their needs. Every librarian has had the experience of trying to dig out of the patron what it is he really wants. I am sure that all of you could fill the evening with accounts of experiences with inarticulate patrons.

But we move on from the inquiry to the librarian, who must interpret the inquiry not only in terms that he can understand, but also in terms of the mechanism he employs for retrieval. First, there is the search strategy that he will use, because the search strategy depends on how he interprets the question and the search mechanism. He sees the whole situation in terms of an environmental relationship, so the search strategy must derive from his interpretation of the entire situation. Again we see this process, a basic one of communication between questioner and librarian, and the strategy must be interpreted in terms of communication between librarian and system including the mechanism he is using.

Now, I am using the term "mechanism" in a very generic sense. I don't necessarily mean a computer or any mechanical device. A card catalog, a reference book, and an index are all mechanisms in one way or another. They are agents, or instrumentalities, if you will, in the sense in which I am using the term. So the librarian must interpret the question in terms of the mechanism he uses to gain access to the next element, the library store. Of course, the pattern of organization of mechanisms used, whether it be subject headings in the *Reader's Guide*, or class numbers of books on the shelf, must somehow be brought into alignment with the organization of the question. And once he gets to the store, there is finally the end result of retrieval, or output. As you can see, there are many ways to go astray in this process. But basically, it all goes back to two problems: one is the linguistic problem—the problem of communication, the problem of achieving understanding between the user, or borrower, or inquirer, and the librarian and his interpretation of what the borrower wants, or what he thinks he wants, or what the librarian thinks he should want. Here lies the first

FIG. 1.

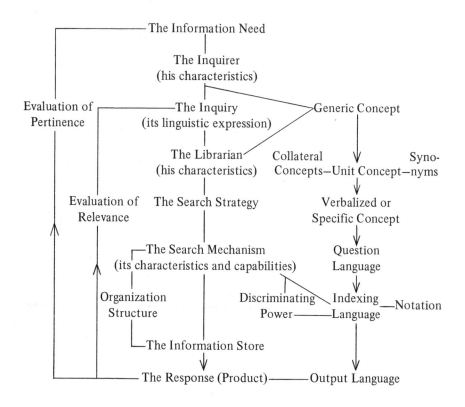

big pitfall. The second pitfall, of course, is the interpretation by the librarian of the organizational pattern, and the capabilities of the mechanism used in the search. The first problem is linguistically based—the problems with synonyms, correlates, relational aspects, and so on. The second problem relates to the discriminating power of the search mechanism. To translate that fancy language into library terminology, it relates to the breadth of the subject headings, or tags, the minuteness of the classification, and the depth of subject analysis. In terms of the computer, of course, it is the capacity of the machine to store and the depth of the program it employs. How fine a differentiation can you get or how fine do you want to get? Sometimes you may want to move in your search for the specifiċ back to the more general or down the hierarchy from general to specific; it is all a part of the discriminating power of the system. I think you can see that we have here no simple data processing problem.

On the other side of the diagram, I have indicated the problem of relevance and pertinence. Here again we encounter the fancy language that I think may be indigenous to Western Reserve. We have used pertinence to refer to the true success of the search, the degree to which the output is appropriate to the *NEED*. The *need* at the very top of the diagram and the output at the bottom. We must always ask, "How pertinent is this; does the one really relate to the other?" Relevance, on the other hand (it is necessary to make these distinctions when you are talking about the reference situation) is the relation between the *question* and the output. That is, it is perfectly possible to have a fine reference system that for every *question* retrieves 100 percent of the related material, but the material may be not pertinent because the question does not reflect the actual *need*. So one has to distinguish between these two characteristics of the reference system.

An enormous amount of work needs to be done in interpreting the total environment of the reference situation. We have been playing with some of this at Western Reserve. For example, we have a mathematician who has been working on ways of expressing by mathematical equation the prediction of pertinence, and the chances of predicting and achieving pertinent information from a particular situation given certain variables. I am not sure that I understand what he is doing, but the Air Force is terribly impressed, and that is just fine with me. So, you see, we are talking here about an extremely intricate situation which has a lot of variables in it.

Most of all, I would call to your attention the line of communication that runs from the inquirer to the librarian and thence to the search strategy, which defines the environment in which the reference librarian operates. Now, the dyed-in-the-wool computer boys say this can be completely automated, like the old Sterling chewing gum when I was a boy—"untouched by human hands." The inquirer can have, as they say, a dialogue with the computer through the use of a console. One types out the question and if it isn't sufficiently precise the computer tells him so. Thus, the dialogue progresses until the problem is defined. I have been told that this dialogue can be completely automated. Maybe it can, I don't know. Of course, why anybody would want to have a dialogue with a computer instead of a pretty reference librarian I can't understand, but there is no accounting for taste. But anyway, they say this process can be completely automated.

Now, in a kind of curious sense, you see, this is a throwback, a reversion, to the days of our old friend Samuel S. Green and his predecessors, because they believed that the library was organized in such a way that anybody could use it without the intervention of the librarian. But Green and Justin Winsor and their colleagues thought that there must be professionals to give the reader assistance. Thus, history, in a sense, has come full circle. We are looking now—at least, some people are looking—at a time when again we don't need reference librarians. Well, I am not so certain that the day of the reference librarian is passing, and moreover I don't think that day should pass. I think the reference librarian, or the subject specialist at least, will be with us for a long, long time. As one of my friends said: "The human being is still a damn good computer, and it has the great advantage that it can be produced by unskilled labor."

Figure 1 provides the foundation for the next two, and these two may make the first one easier to understand. I hope that these diagrams, in the light of what I have been saying, are relatively clear, if not entirely self-explanatory.

## THE NEW LIBRARIANSHIP

Well, where do we end up in all of this? I think we are moving forward into a new era of librarianship. Some very significant changes in the pattern of librarianship, and reference librarianship in particular, are going to come about. These changes, of course, raise a problem for those of us in library education. What does one teach youngsters about this new librarianship? Any professional school, library or otherwise, must educate its students for the future because it is in the future that they will be practicing their profession. But what do you do when you don't know what the future will be like? I think all we can do, really, is to try to develop in our students a flexibility of mind and an attitude of open-minded inquiry, a hospitality to innovation, a willingness not to take anything for granted and not to be conservative, but to look hard at everything and judge it on its own terms as best one can—not be frightened of it because it is new or different. I have sometimes used the analogy that a library school dean and faculty are in the position of an engineer who is trying to remodel his locomotive while the train is going down the track. You must not educate a student so far ahead of the profession that he can't do anything when he gets out into the working world. You must strike a balance between the present and the future.

FIG. 2.

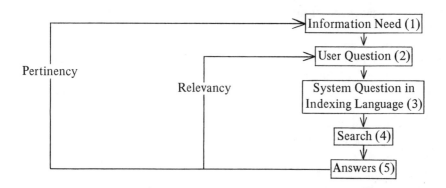

From Alan M. Rees, "Semantic Factors, Role Indicators, *et alia*–Seven Years of Information Retrieval Research at Western Reserve University" *Aslib Proceedings*, Vol. 15 (December 1963), p. 359.

FIG. 3.  OPERATIONAL STRUCTURE OF THE REFERENCE PROCESS

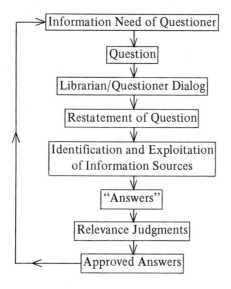

Diagram courtesy of Alan M. Rees.

## CONCLUSION

I think we are moving toward a tremendously exciting time. I wish I were 40 years younger than I am, and a whole lot smarter. Particularly a whole lot smarter. If I were smarter maybe I could put up with what time I have left. There are some tremendously exciting things coming over the library horizon, and they are not all coming out of librarianship. I don't think they need to. But I do think we librarians must be alert to them. We must interpret them in terms of our own operations, our own objectives, our own function. I have said that the librarian's role is to maximize the social utilization of graphic records for the benefit of mankind. Of course we will make mistakes. There will be blind alleys that we will explore. There will be all kinds of argument and polemics. There will be vested interests that will be threatened. But these things do eventually shake down, and I think the profession is going to be the richer for it.

If you forget everything else that I have said tonight, and you probably will, I hope you will remember one thing. I emphasized this point this morning and I am coming back to it tonight. Librarianship is a system composed of a series of interrelated subsystems. The reference librarian, the cataloger, the order librarian, and the rest of the staff do not work in a vacuum. Their responsibilities are not little discrete units. They form a unity. I have long held that the world of knowledge is a unity, and librarianship is unitary, too. I have long been a strong advocate of the concept of the universality of knowledge; that knowledge is not a continuum of isolated facts, bits of information, or even disciplinary areas. These are all interrelated. The poets for a very long time have been aware of the essential unity of nature and of life, and I might do well to call Shelly as my witness. You will recall that he once wrote:

> The Fountains mingle with the River
>   And the Rivers with the Ocean,
> The winds of Heaven mix forever
>   With a sweet emotion;
> Nothing in the world is single;
>   All things by a law divine
> In one spirit meet and mingle.
>   Why not I with thine? —

Shelly, of course, was speaking of love, and probably that last line is neither relevant nor pertinent to a talk on reference work. Still, I'm not so sure; I have known some reference librarians who could do with a little love in their lives.

But it would be more to our purpose this evening to quote the words of another poet, one who has himself been a librarian. Thus spoke Archibald MacLeish at the dedication of the Countway Library of Medicine in Boston:

> The mere existence of a library collection, as distinguished from a warehouse full of printed pages, presupposes the intellectual coherence of the materials collected. Books can be brought together according to an organization, a classification of

one kind or another, only if what they *contain* composes an organization—composes, that is to say, a whole of which no part is foreign to any other part. All, it must be assumed, have come from the human mind and all are therefore parts of human knowledge, and human knowledge, by hypothesis, is one—one because the human mind can hold it.

When the hypothesis breaks down, when human knowledge is no longer one because the human mind can no longer hold it, when there are parts—essential parts—of human knowledge which are not knowable at all to the vast majority of human minds, the library is in trouble. It can no longer perform its function of making the knowable known at the time and place where it is needed. . . . There is no such thing as knowledge by itself but only knowledge to the knower, and the knower is never anything but man, man in his old condition as man, man with his wonder on him. . . . Because the library recognizes . . . that the god is in the question, not the answer. . . . Because the library recognizes, as the university recognizes, that it is only when the answer is responsive to the question, when the science has been mastered by the man, that civilization is possible.[3]

Of course we have it on the authority of John Milton, that "They also serve who only stand and wait," but few of the reference librarian's patrons would appreciate such questionable consolation. It were far better that it be said of the reference librarian as Matthew Arnold said of Sophocles, that he "saw life steady and saw it whole."

## FOOTNOTES

[1] At the historic conference of librarians held at Philadelphia in 1876, Mr. Green presented a paper in which he argued for "The Desirableness of Establishing Personal Intercourse and Relations Between Librarians and Readers in Popular Libraries." A shorter title was used when the article was published in the first volume of the *Library Journal*, Vol. 1 (1876), pp.74-81.

[2] "A Perilous Policy," *Harper's*, Vol. 246 (March 1973), p. 55.

[3] Archibald MacLeish, "The Knower and the Known," in his *A Continuing Journey* (Boston: Houghton Mifflin, 1967), p. 247-49.

# 15

# "Viewpoint Shift" in Reference Work

The teaching profession has long been puzzled by a particular psychological phenomenon that manifests itself as a shifting standard in the marking of examination papers. Beginning with a pre-determined set of criteria the instructor soon finds that, influenced by the quality of the answers given by the students in response to a particular group of questions, unconsciously he has raised or lowered his original standard and at the end is measuring the achievements of his pupils on a totally different basis. Thus the results of the examination are about as valid as the measurements of an engineer would be had he performed his calculations with the aid of an elastic slide rule. Such a predicament does not necessarily reflect unfavorably upon the ability of the teacher; rather, it is a more or less inevitable result of the responses set up in any active mind when influenced by a varying series of stimuli.

Essentially the same reaction is to be observed in the mental processes of the reference librarian, though here it reveals itself as a definite, yet frequently unconscious, shift in viewpoint. Assuming categorically a situation wherein an investigator is engaged in the collection of materials relative to a given dominant generalization, the supporting evidence for which, as will be explained later, is not specific factual data, and that it is discovered that such is not available in the particular form originally desired; it will accordingly be found that the investigator's entire outlook toward the problem is colored by and shifted in the direction of the materials that are available, and at the end he may find himself at a point quite remote from that established as his objective at the beginning. Assuming further that the investigator in the above is a reference librarian in search of materials for a research worker, or "client," the problem is further complicated by the introduction of an additional element: the mental processes

Reprinted with permission from *Special Libraries* 25 (no. 10): p. 235-237 (Nov. 1934).

and reactions of the research worker for whom these sources are being assembled, and who, in turn, may react quite differently to the available data. Thus, the problem that immediately arises is the prevention of this divergence of viewpoint, and the constant focus on the objectives of the reference librarian and his client.

For purposes of clarification let us analyze a specific example. Suppose a reference librarian is to prepare a bibliography dealing with the social influences of the Industrial Revolution upon a given population. In this connection it may be particularly advantageous to obtain any biographical material which presents the mental reactions of the individual to the growth of industrialization, either in England or America. Singularly enough, the literature of social and industrial history is largely destitute of anything touching these important influences. Even the ubiquitous "Grandmother Brown" seemed utterly oblivious to the revolutionary social changes that went on during her "hundred years." Thus the search being but ill productive, the mind of the librarian turns inadvertently toward the lines of development suggested by De Tocqueville, who comes the nearest to giving that which is sought, but whose emphasis is upon the political aspects rather than the economic and industrial. Or, again, the more obvious sources of Hawthorne or Thoreau and their respective revolts against the new industrialism may hold the attention. Further complications arise when the research worker, for whose use the bibliography is being prepared, brings to the problem a totally different set of mental reactions, and may, perhaps, become involved in the social philosophies of Carlyle and Ruskin, or perhaps in the biographical writings of labor leaders such as Gompers, Debs, or Mitchell. So the trail ends—far from the original goal.

This hypothetical illustration has been sketched in the broadest general outlines, and with a corresponding overemphasis upon the element of digression. In actual practice the whole process is far more subtle.

Superficially, the problem seems to resolve itself into one of slovenly thinking on the part of the librarian, and this would be undoubtedly true if we were here concerned with specific factual information. There would be little to excuse one for digression when searching for the per capita wealth of the British Isles, or the rice exports from China in a given decade. To go astray on reference questions such as these would most certainly savor of the naive ambitious young librarian who, when asked for a copy of one of Molière's plays, and finding no copy available, brings forth a different one in the hope that it "may do just as well." Nor are we here concerned with the struggles of an immature mind laboring to master the intricacies of reference work. We are not dealing with either incompetency or dilettanteism.

Reduced to its most elemental form, "viewpoint shift" arises from the overt facts that active mature minds attack the same problem from different angles, react dissimilarly to identical stimuli, and arrive, therefore, at divergent conclusions. All of which may produce a thoroughly unsatisfactory relation between the librarian and his patron, and, far more serious from the standpoint of our present concern, may work to destroy that close harmony of collaboration which it is so essential to establish between the special librarian and his particular clientele.

There are, then, as we have seen, several factors contributing to the increment of "viewpoint shift," all of which are more or less inherent in many specific situations. Above all, the condition arises only when the type of material desired is not available, or at least is considered to be unavailable by the individuals concerned. Again the situation develops not with reference to concrete factual data, but rather with regard to abstract generalizations and broad theories where specific quantities are much less conspicuous and lines of demarcation less distinctly drawn. Fundamental, too, is the psychological aspect of the inquiring mind of the librarian attempting unconsciously to adapt itself to the substitute materials that are available, obviously akin to which is the innate desire to "find something," the refusal to admit defeat, the antipathy to returning to the client empty-handed. Finally, the whole is further complicated by the reactions of the client himself.

It is useless to attack the problem by any one of its several horns. Librarians cannot control the types of questions that are placed before them, nor the amount of material that is available. Even their mental processes are not always guided by their own volitions, and certainly they can not be held responsible for the psychological reactions of those for whom they work. All of these elements are indigenous; while any solution of the problem must take them into account, they cannot themselves be used in a remedial capacity.

Obviously, the first essential is a thorough mental grasp of all the factors of the job in hand. Establishing complete clarity and understanding at the beginning will not only do much to prevent later "viewpoint shift"; it will also save future embarrassment. Yet despite the overt importance of this single element, how frequently one hears, at the end of a fruitless search, the librarian's half plaintive, half apologetic exclamation, "Oh, then this isn't what you wanted? I guess I didn't understand."

Also of assistance in preventing this deviation from the essential task to be performed is a frequent mental review of the problem in question. For not only is it a valid psychological principle that frequency of recall is one of the major aids to memory, but it further gives the worker a panoramic survey of the situation and enables him to fit into their relative places the materials that he has been able to find.

More important than either of these, however, and here the special librarian is at a distinct advantage because he serves a more or less fixed clientele, is the development between librarian and patron of a thorough understanding of each other's point of view. Here the collaboration cannot be too close, for insofar as the librarian sees the problem through the eyes of him whom he serves, by so much will his usefulness and efficiency be increased. That in such matters the special librarian must know his particular field thoroughly is so palpably true as to need no exposition. But the really successful special librarian must know much more than the mere literature of his subject; he must know the minds of his patrons, understand their peculiar mental reactions, develop sympathetic and parallel mental associations. To the public librarian, encountering scores of patrons daily, this is a difficult if not impossible task, but to the special librarian working intensively with a limited group day after day it is thoroughly feasible.

By this it is not meant that a tangential excursion from the particular point in hand is not beneficial; it may as a matter of fact do much to clarify the whole, so long as such deviations are subordinated to the central idea. Certainly in the preceding paragraph it was not the intention to imply that one should cultivate the viewpoint of one's patrons as a policy of sheer diplomacy. The kowtow is degrading both to master and slave, and the librarian who subordinates his own personality and convictions to those of his client is indeed a lost soul. But the growth of a healthy relationship and collaborative spirit between the two, when based on a common bond of mutual respect and integrity, will do much to simplify major difficulties in reference work and to obviate that all too frequently iterated criticism on the part of the patron that the librarian has "completely missed the point."

# IV.

# Documentation

# 16

# Special Librarianship
# and Documentation

For half a century special librarianship and documentation have coexisted as separate, even disparate, manifestations of general library practice. At times their paths have crossed and recrossed, run parallel, or diverged sharply, yet every attempt to describe or define their relation to each other or to identify their place in the parent discipline of librarianship itself has been conspicuously unsuccessful. In large measure this failure to comprehend the essential unity of documentation and special librarianship as the focus of more general library objectives may be explained in terms of historic development, of nationality of origin, or of excessive restriction in the definition of function.

Admittedly, there have been many who have maintained that documentation was no more than a European term for a form of librarianship that on this side of the Atlantic has been called special librarianship. There have been a few, like Ernest A. Savage,[1] who have stoutly insisted that the future of the general public library lies in intensive subject specialization and departmentalization. But the great majority of practicing librarians have not as yet grasped the true meaning and importance of this holistic point of view.

Specialization of library collections began at a surprisingly early date. The social libraries that spread so rapidly throughout the eastern half of the United States during the 18th century and the early decades of the 19th, and that were the first manifestations of a public library movement in America, had not long been in existence before a degree of specialization of function began to emerge. Certainly among the first to appear were those of the historical societies, the theological libraries, the legal collections for the use of the early bar associations and legislative bodies, and the agricultural libraries supported mainly by local agricultural organizations. But perhaps the nearest parallel of the modern special

Originally published in *Library Trends*, Vol. 1 (October 1952), pp. 189-99.

library is to be found in the mechanics' and apprentices' libraries and the mercantile libraries that were so prevalent in the industrial and commercial urban centers during the 1830s and the 1940s. Even Benjamin Franklin's *Junto* and its descendant, the Philadelphia Library Company, began with the pragmatic need of the young artisans for materials that would improve their technical efficiency. The special library is deeply rooted in American library history.

Furthermore, there is ample evidence that the early advocates of the modern public library regarded bibliography, or more precisely, bibliographic organization, as the central problem of general librarianship even though they did not specifically state that the public library of the future should become a nucleus of integrated specializations. Men of the stature of Edward Everett and George Ticknor, especially the former, though they paid lip service to an assumed demand for "popular" reading materials, clearly envisaged the incipient Boston Public Library as an instrument that would serve the bibliographic needs of contemporary scholarship.[2]

The Reverend John B. Wight,[3] in urging library legislation, argued before the Massachusetts General Court that one of the primary objectives of the bibliographic resources and services of public libraries was to increase the efficiency of farmers, mechanics, merchants, manufacturers, physicians, teachers, lawyers, and the other professional classes. Charles Coffin Jewett, the first American to lay the groundwork for a great national union library catalog, wanted to make of the newly founded Smithsonian Institution a great national bibliographic and documentation center;[4] and under his leadership the general problems of bibliography and bibliographic organization received a major share of the attention of those present at the first conference of American librarians.[5] With like earnestness, William F. Poole believed that one of the major tasks of the professional librarian was to develop an adequate subject index to periodical publications; and again, largely through his leadership, when the American Library Association was founded in 1876 the deliberations of the group were predominantly concerned with bibliographic operations.[6]

But by the close of the 19th century American librarianship had largely turned away from this original emphasis on the more effective bibliographic organization of its resources and had begun to think of the library as being almost exclusively an agency for popular education. This diversion, though unfortunate in its effect upon the future of American librarianship as a profession, was perhaps a natural consequence of the growing belief that in universal education was to be found the key to social progress. But however meritorious the objective, it had the disastrous effect of diverting librarianship from its proper concern with the analysis and organization of recorded knowledge, and instead directed most of its energies into activities which were alien to its institutional nature and could not be effectively translated into successful library operation. This diversion not only weakened the profession of librarianship by splitting it into two opposing factions. It also created a barrier between the two factions that, even to this day, has prevented a common bond of understanding and a unanimity of action, with the result that it is almost impossible for librarians to think clearly about the functions of the library in contemporary society.

At the very time that librarians were beginning to be lured by the will-of-the-wisp of "self-improvement," or "adult education," into the marsh-lands of popular culture, important events were taking place on the continent of Europe. In 1892 Paul Otlet and Henri La Fontaine, both of whom were engaged in assembling documentary materials in the social sciences, laid the foundation in Brussels for the International Institute of Bibliography (now the International Federation for Documentation), with its world bibliography and bibliographic center.[7] Quite naturally they turned to the librarians for their techniques; they adopted, but extensively modified and expanded, the Dewey Decimal System of library classification to create their own Universal Decimal System; they adopted the standard library card for their bibliographic operations; and they turned to the catalogs of the great libraries of the world for the nucleus of their world bibliography.

Apart from these techniques, however, their point of view, their philosophy, had almost nothing in common with the practicing and professionally conscious librarians on this side of the Atlantic. In a real sense the work of these two men and their associates was a reversion to an earlier philosophy of librarianship, but because, in practice, it differed so markedly from the current vogue it came to be known as "documentation." This "new" discipline of documentation enlisted considerable support in England and on the continent, but for almost half a century American librarians remained largely oblivious to it.

Even in America, during these years, there was some dissension in the library ranks. Early in the 20th century John Cotton Dana, librarian of the Newark Public Library, and a group of like-minded associates, became aware that there was a large group of potential library patrons, mainly among the commercial and industrial interests in society, whose "special" library needs were being neglected. The immediate result of this awareness was the creation of departments in certain of the larger public library systems to specialize in service to this particular clientele; and in 1909 the Special Libraries Association was formed. It was not Dana's intent that this should be a schism from the ranks of the American Library Association. At the Mackinac Island Conference of the ALA in 1910 he made a last desperate attempt to secure the incorporation of the Special Libraries Association into the older organization; but his efforts resulted only in keen personal disappointment and he was compelled to report: "My suggestions to the Executive Board in this line were as definitely ignored by the Board as have been many other suggestions from me. That there is a very active library organization, affiliated but not a definite part of the American

Library Association is a fact which is not due to me but to shortcomings elsewhere."[8] He saw the rise of the special library as an almost inevitable consequence of the fact that the "library idea" had been "more or less academic, monastic, classic" while "the rapid development of special libraries managed by experts . . . is simply an outward manifestation that the man of affairs has come to realize that printed things form the most useful and most important tools of his business, no matter what that business may be."[9] The character of the special interests the new association was intended to serve is best indicated by the seven committees designed to coordinate and promote activities among libraries in the fields of agriculture, commercial associations, insurance, legislative and municipal reference organizations, public utilities, sociology, and technology.[10]

For over 30 years the Special Libraries Association represented the nearest American approach to that kind of library activity and point of view which in Europe had received widespread recognition as documentation, though the elements of documentation are closely discernible in the growth of subject departments in a few of the largest public libraries, and in many of the activities and policies of university libraries. In 1937, American librarians first officially recognized documentation as an important bibliographic discipline by organizing the American Documentation Institute. This organization originated from the activities in documentation that had been carried forward by Science Service, dating from 1926 (especially the work done by Science Service under grants from the Chemical Foundation) and from the Bibliofilm Services organized in 1935 at the Library of the U.S. Department of Agriculture.[11,12] This new institute, which was affiliated with the International Federation for Documentation, was designed as an assembly of representatives from leading scientific and scholarly societies, councils, and institutions, both public and private.

It is important to note that in the beginning documentation was very narrowly interpreted by the founding group as being restricted almost entirely to the promotion of new methods of photographic reproduction; and it is significant that almost immediately it began to publish, with the aid of the American Library Association, *The Journal of Documentary Reproduction*, which survived through 1942. This excessive emphasis upon photographic techniques, especially as they relate to the production and use of microfilm, is still strong among American documentalists. But with the revival of interest in the Institute that followed the Second World War, the term began to be much more broadly interpreted and more nearly approximated its use in Europe. The reorganization of the American Documentation Institute, now in progress, to make it a true society of documentalists, should further broaden its scope and expand its activities.

In addition to these three major lines of development presented by general librarianship, special librarianship, and documentation, there have been overlapping and tangential activities. At the present time the Special Libraries Association maintains a national Committee on Documentation. The Committee on Bibliography of the American Library Association has, of recent years, been largely concerned with problems of bibliography and documentation. The American Chemical Society has become extremely active in promoting improvements in the bibliographic organization of the literature of chemistry. The American Standards Association has just recently begun to reexamine the problems of improving bibliographic standards. Finally, even the library schools, which for some time have recognized the growing need for personnel trained to meet the problems of special librarianship, are in a few instances beginning to associate with such preparation some attention to the closely related techniques and procedures of documentation.

From this review one may conclude that bibliographic organization is an historical unity comprising as its major constituents general librarianship, special librarianship, and documentation. One may further conclude that special librarianship and documentation have a common root, and that their divergence has been largely an historical accident, the results of which were intensified by differences in terminology rather than in kind. Finally, recent history suggests that the present chaotic and uncoordinated proliferation of these related activities will increase rather than diminish unless a persistent and determined effort is made toward reunification. Yet, if the same status quo is allowed to persist, the profession of librarianship will not only lose control of its very substance, but it will deteriorate into a simple custodial operation.

Despite the fact that the practice of special librarianship and documentation is not new, neither term has as yet been adequately defined. Broadly interpreted, the special library is any collection of library materials assembled to meet the needs of a particular group of users. Thus in a general sense, the historical, medical, legal, or theological library is a *special* library. One might even go so far as to maintain that academic, school, or children's libraries could be included in this same general category. But a definition so inclusive contributes little to any real understanding of the nature of the special library and its relation to documentation. John Cotton Dana, in his presidential address before the first convention of the Special Libraries Association characterized the special library as "the library of a modern man of affairs."[13] But he quickly admits to the inadequacy of such a definition and hastens forward to a discussion of the special library in terms of library service to business and industry. This concept, later expanded to include a wide variety of private and public enterprises, has remained today substantially unchanged.

Attempts to define documentation have been no more successful. The most recent, that of Briet,[14] holds that the materials of documentation are all indication, concrete or symbolistic, preserved or transcribed, with the purpose of representing, of reconstituting, or of proving either a physical or intellectual phenomenon. But this definition suffers from the fault of being materialistic rather than functional. In a sense it avoids the question by defining documentation in terms of the materials with which documentalists do their work. By contrast, Mortimer Taube has defined documentation in operational terms as "the complex of activities required in the communication of specialized information including the preparation, reproduction, collection, analysis, organization and dissemination of graphic."[15]

Also appropriate to the present discussion would seem to be the definition of Egan and Shera,[16,17] who made documentation a part of their inclusive concept, bibliographic organization. They defined bibliographic organization as being concerned with "the channeling of graphic records to *all* users for *all* purposes, and at *all* levels (of use) in such a way as to maximize the social utilization of recorded human experience."[17] By contrast, documentation, as they have described it, is limited to the world of scholarship, and the objective of documentation is to bring together all the scholarly activities in which graphic records are used and all the intermediary services which transmit this recorded material from the scholar-as-producer to the scholar-as-consumer.

But Egan and Shera do not interpret scholarship in the narrow academic sense, nor do they see the work of the scholar as being confined to pure research. Rather they are following Pierce Butler,[18] who defines scholarship as the total intellectual output of a culture; and they insist that the literature of scholarship is as much concerned with the technological, administrative, and operational activities of society as it is with the investigatory or research accomplishments. Thus one may accurately apply to documentation the time-honored slogan of the Special Libraries Association—"Putting Knowledge to Work."

Special librarianship developed because of the inability of traditional library techniques to meet the increasingly complex informational needs of business and industry. Similarly, documentation was the outgrowth of the desire of a small group of men to destroy the national barriers to the flow of scientific information, and it received a new vitality when World War II brought into existence a need for greater and more efficient access to information than traditional library methods were able to give. Though both special librarianship and documentation, in practice, respond to a wide variety of dissimilar demands, they find a common basic unity in their objective—to facilitate the flow of recorded information to appropriate segments of a complete culture.

The similarities in special librarianship and documentation may be emphasized by a discussion of the operational characteristics of documentation and their application to the work of the special library as well as to the documentation center. Documentation is generally considered to comprise four major activities: acquisition, organization, dissemination, and preparation and publication.

*Acquisition.* The problem of acquisition is so familiar to all aspects of librarianship, in whatever form, that any discussion of it here would seem to be unnecessary. Techniques may differ from agency to agency in accordance with the nature of the material and the needs of the clientele, but the underlying principles are essentially the same. Suffice it here to point out that the special library and the documentation center are both heavily dependent upon a variety of highly specialized bibliographic tools for effective acquisition; but they, too, have a very great stake in the improvement of national and international enumerative and subject bibliographic services. Such great bibliographic monuments are the very foundation of any effective system of special bibliographic services.

*Organization.* Organization is composed of three elements: a) identification, b) arrangement, and c) analysis. Again the parallel with traditional library practice is evident. Identification is largely synonymous with descriptive cataloging, though it should be pointed out that special librarians and documentalists often employ simplified descriptive techniques; however, the procedures are based on, or derived from, accepted library rules. One should emphasize here, too, the frequent similarity between special library and documentation procedures and the techniques customarily employed by the archivist, particularly his techniques for the calendaring of documents, or his preparation of general descriptive summaries for the identification of large blocks of closely related materials.

Arrangement, of course, includes classification, a method of subject arrangement in which both special libraries and documentation centers have done a considerable amount of effective pioneering. Practice here has generally followed one of three patterns: a) the expansion or elaboration of existing library schematisms, such as Dewey, the Universal Decimal Classification, or that of the Library of Congress; b) the use of a familiar notation employed by one of these three schemes but applied to a completely different array of terms; and c) schematisms with a philosophical orientation completely different from those traditional to librarianship.

The third subdivision, analysis, might well include classification, since it, too, is an instrument to facilitate subject access. But analysis is usually understood to be restricted to those operations in which the subject content of the material is extracted or separated from the material itself and hence is freed from the arrangement of physical units. Analysis, then, includes such operations as subject cataloging, indexing, abstracting, annotating, and the preparation of special subject bibliographies for particular purposes. In all of this, one should emphasize that special librarianship and documentation do not differ from traditional librarianship in kind but in degree and intensity of analysis. Many public libraries do some indexing and even abstracting on their own initiative, usually with reference to materials of particular local interest; and many college and university libraries, especially in their subject departments, prepare special bibliographies and lists. But the special librarians and the documentalists have, in general, carried on these operations more extensively and incorporated them more intimately into their basic procedures.

*Dissemination.* No special librarian needs to be reminded of the importance of the routing of recent acquisitions to the appropriate members of his clientele. But dissemination involves more than mere routing. It can, and often does, involve the free distribution, or even the actual sale, of materials deposited in the special library or documentation center. The dissemination of book lists, special bibliographies, and the like is familiar enough even to the librarian of the small or medium-sized public library. The dissemination of "primary" material is less common, though even here the *Bulletin of the New York Public Library*, the *Yale University Library Gazette*, the Boston Public Library's *More Books*, and the *Harvard Library Bulletin* frequently reproduce rare and valuable materials from their own collections.

Dissemination, however, also includes "control," which concerns limiting access to certain types of materials to those authorized to use them. The problems raised by "security regulations" were all too familiar to all librarians who were in any way associated with the operations of the information services of the United States government during World War II, and this was especially true for the librarians and documentalists of the intelligence agencies. But this barrier to the free flow of information, which is as ancient as the guild system itself, is being increasingly fostered by competition in commerce and industry. This is particularly true for information about patentable or potentially patentable processes, or other varieties of confidential data. Censorship has been traditionally repugnant to librarians, and the profession has opposed it on many occasions, but this is censorship "in reverse." For censorship purports to protect the public from *error*, whereas security is, in effect, a restraint upon *truth*. But in the latter case the social consequences may be far more serious, and the dangers cannot long be ignored by special librarians and documentalists.

*Preparation and publication.* The concept of the special library as an agency for the composition, preparation, and publication of *primary* materials is probably the least familiar to the librarian. Yet there are a number of large special research libraries that have initiated programs of this sort. The New York Public Library has not limited its publications entirely to bibliographic compilations. The publication of source materials, often in its annual reports, has given to the world of scholarship some conspicuously successful examples of this kind of publication. The preparation of special reports for distribution within the parent organization is not uncommon among special libraries. Certainly there is no good reason why such publication should not be more fully exploited by the special librarian and documentalist, and in many respects the special library or documentation center is particularly well equipped to serve as the logical agent for the preparation and publication of materials drawn from or based upon the wealth of their resources.

In one sense every library may be regarded as a "special" library by virtue of its adaptation to the particular needs and requirements of its patrons. Historically both documentation and special librarianship are rooted in the parent discipline of general librarianship. But general librarianship can hardly be said ever to have existed in a pure state, for specialization of library function was implicit from the beginning. When any group establishes a library, it is motivated by a particular purpose or objective, and the library which it forms will reflect that purpose or objective iñ its collection and service. As it has been said, "Special librarianship is the documentation of an idea." That idea may be as broad or as narrow as the human mind can conceive, it may be spiritual, it may be humanistic, it may be educational, it may be scientific, sociological, or technological, but whatever its nature and scope the library will be "special" to that purpose.

## FOOTNOTES

[1] E. A. Savage, *Special Librarianship in General Libraries, and Other Papers* (London: Grafton, 1939), pp. 24-50.

[2] J. H. Shera, *Foundations of the Public Library* (Chicago: University of Chicago Press, 1949), Chaps. 6-7.

[3] J. B. Wight, "A Lecture on Public Libraries Delivered in Boston in the Hall of the House of Representatives, 1854." MS in possession of the Wight family.

[4] J. A. Borome, *Charles Coffin Jewett* (Chicago: American Library Association, 1951), Chaps. 4-8.

[5] G. B. Utley, *The Librarians' Conference of 1853* (Chicago: American Library Association, 1951).

[6] *Library Journal*, Vol. 1, 1876.

[7] S. C. Bradford, *Documentation* (London: Crosby Lockwood, 1948), Chap. 8.

[8] J. C. Dana, as quoted in C. Hadley, *John Cotton Dana, a Sketch* (Chicago: American Library Association, 1943), pp. 88-89.

[9] *Ibid.*, p. 88.

[10] "The Constitution of the Special Libraries Association," *Special Libraries*, 1 (January 1910), 8.

[11] "Report of the President of American Documentation Institute, January 27, 1938," *Journal of Documentary Reproduction*, Vol. 1 (Winter 1938), 33-36.

[12] V. D. Tate, "Introducing American Documentation," *American Documentation*, Vol. 1 (January 1950), 3-7.

¹³J. C. Dana, "The President's Opening Remarks," *Special Libraries*, Vol. 1 (January 1910), 4-5.

¹⁴Suzanne Briet, *Qu'est-ce que la Documentation?* (Paris: Editions Documentaires Industrielles et Techniques, 1951), p. 7.

¹⁵M. Taube, Editorial, *American Documentation*, Vol. 3 (January 1952), ii.

¹⁶Margaret E. Egan and J. H. Shera, "Prolegomena to Bibliographic Control," *Journal of Cataloging and Classification*, Vol. 5 (Winter 1949), 17-19.

¹⁷J. H. Shera, "Documentation; Its Scope and Limitations," *Library Quarterly*, Vol. 21 (January 1951), 13-26.

¹⁸P. Butler, *Scholarship and Civilization* (Chicago: Graduate Library School, University of Chicago, 1944).

# 17

# Research and Developments in Documentation

He who undertakes the task of describing research in librarianship soon finds himself in a position not entirely dissimilar to that of the German scholar who began his two-volume treatise on "The Snakes of Ireland," with the assertion "Strictly speaking, there are no snakes in Ireland." To the often-repeated charge that there is very little research in librarianship the field of documentation is scarcely immune.

"Research" is, of course, a slippery word, and all that masquerades under that title is not properly so. As here defined, research is that form of human activity whereby answers are sought, with as great an approximation of truth and accuracy as human knowledge makes possible, to basic or fundamental questions concerning the phenomena of the universe. Research is not concerned with the trivial and unimportant; it is much more than mere fact-finding; it is pursued by means of the application of certain accepted methods or procedures which, in the light of experience, seem most likely to produce truthful results. Its end is the advancement of human understanding.

The building of a new machine or the designing of a new system is not research; it is invention or development, though it may be based upon the findings of research. The ascertaining of a well-known fact—i.e., the atomic weight of silver—is not research but "reference work," though the fact revealed may, at one time, have been the product of research. The promulgation of a questionnaire and the tabulation of the answer are not research, though they may occupy valid places in the research process. Research is usually thought of in terms of analysis, though synthesis may also play a vital role in the research process. Therefore, to be identified as such, research is to be known by the materials it works upon, the methods it employs, and the ends it seeks. It is

Published originally in *Library Trends*, Vol. 6, No. 2 (October 1957), pp. 187-206.

governed only by the principles of integrity and objectivity, and it rejects all authority except that of valid evidence. Properly used, it lies at the very foundation of all knowledge and understanding; prostituted, it becomes only a sacred cow that gives no milk.

The third element in the title of the present essay, "documentation," refers to that form of bibliographic organization, or librarianship if you will, that is concerned with the systematic mobilization of the total graphic resources of society for improving the scholarship of the culture. Stated somewhat more precisely, documentation may be defined as that aspect of librarianship which is concerned with the organization and dissemination of graphic records for their most efficient use within and among groups of specialists, to the end that they will receive, in as effective a manner as possible, the data and other information that they require for the prosecution of their work. In this ancient catalysis between man and the written word the documentalist and the librarian are specialists, each in his own right, in the communication of recorded information. The investigator, or research worker, and the documentalist are both engaged in activities directed toward the advance of human knowledge, the one concerned with extending the boundaries of knowledge and the other with making that knowledge more socially useful. They are natural partners in a team dedicated to the advancement of human understanding.[1] In a world in which progress is so heavily dependent upon the effective use of recorded information, why has so little attention been directed toward those forms of research that will increase man's understanding of the ways in which knowledge grows and is utilized and the methods by which the process of utilization may be augmented and improved? The past record of research in documentation and librarianship is not one to inspire confidence in an early solution to the many vexing problems which must be solved before the swelling flood of graphic records is effectively harnessed.

This essay describes trends in current research in documentation through an analysis of research in progress. During the past year, two surveys of research and development in the field of documentation have been conducted. One was the work of Mrs. Helen L. Brownson and Miss Madeline M. Berry of the Office of Scientific Information of the National Science Foundation; the other was prepared by the Committee on Research and Development of the American Documentation Institute, under the direction of the committee chairman, Saul Herner of Herner, Meyer & Co., Washington, D.C. To both of these surveys the present writer is heavily indebted, though to their data he has made some additions of his own. (The National Science Foundation survey was prepared for internal use and has not been published. The report of the A.D.I. Committee, which makes extensive use of the N.S.F. study, is scheduled for publication in *American Documentation*, and it is the hope of the Herner Committee that its survey will be continued on an annual basis.)

Probably no survey of research in progress is ever entirely complete; there is always at least one significant project that lies quietly hidden only to arise wraith-like from its self-inflicted obscurity to haunt the compiler at the most embarrassing moment. Nevertheless, sufficient care has been expended on this listing to make it a reasonably reliable source for identifying the general contours of current research and development in documentation.

The present roster lists 76 studies in progress, or just completed, as of the end of the first quarter of the present calendar year. In addition to the data compiled by Mrs. Brownson and Miss Berry of the National Science Foundation, inquiries requesting information on studies in progress were sent to 60 scientific, technical, and professional societies; to deans or directors of approximately 50 library schools; to the editors of an equal number of library and documentation journals; and to 24 industrial firms known to be actively interested in the field. The tabulation indicates that, numerically, the burden of research and development in documentation is being carried on largely at the library schools and at industrial and business organizations. The figure for the library schools is, however, very deceptive inasmuch as there is a heavy concentration of work in a limited number of institutions.

Only nine projects are listed as being directly under government auspices, but this figure, too, must be judiciously interpreted, because many of the other projects being carried forward by both profit and non-profit organizations are subsidized by substantial grants from the federal government. It would seem to be conservative to say that probably more than 75 percent of the work in this field is government supported; in terms of dollars invested, the proportion might well be even higher. It is interesting that only one public library has listed a project, yet in many of the larger metropolitan libraries the opportunities to study and make use of documentation techniques are manifold. This lack of interest on the part of "traditional librarianship," in the new potentialities inherent in documentation may explain why practicing librarians seem to be contributing little to the development of this field.

TABLE I

Research in Documentation by
Type of Sponsoring Organization

| Type of Organization | Number of Projects |
|---|---|
| Library Schools | 26 |
| Business and Industrial Organizations | 23 |
| Universities and Other Non-Profit Organizations | 16 |
| United States Government | 9 |
| Private Individuals | 2 |
| Total | 76 |

The survey included, in accordance with predetermined policy, those "projects involving research, development, or testing in eight aspects of documentation—organization, processing, production, dissemination, storage, retrieval, equipment, and use and user needs."[2] The final listing has been categorized by the Committee into eight classes which, in general, conform to the above areas, but which are not entirely mutually exclusive or discrete.

TABLE II

Classification of Research Projects
by Subject Groups

| Subject | Number of Projects |
|---|---|
| Use of Information and User Requirements | 17 |
| Indexing, Cataloging, and Classification | 14 |
| Coding for Mechanized Searching Systems | 13 |
| Equipment for Information Storage, Retrieval and Reproduction | 12 |
| Theory | 8 |
| Mechanical Translation | 6 |
| Production and Dissemination of Published Information | 5 |
| Education and Training for Documentalists | 1 |
| Total | 76 |

Perhaps the most striking characteristic of the data in Table II is the relatively even frequency distribution of subjects throughout the major portion of the range. The very sharp drop-off in studies of theory is to be anticipated because of the relative difficulty in obtaining financial support for such investigations. Here is a lesson that should be heeded by those charged with responsibility for supporting research in documentation. Though the study of the use and user requirements constitutes the largest single category, it is still relatively small in comparison with the amount of attention being given to the design and construction of systems and related problems and techniques for making information available. This would seem to suggest that, like other librarians, documentalists have been quite willing to hypothesize use and to construct systems and devise techniques based on such hypotheses without objective knowledge of the ends to be met.

Perhaps, however, the most startling development revealed by these statistics, to one who has been associated with the documentation field for almost 30 years, is the shift in emphasis. Twenty years ago such a report as this would have portrayed great interest in methods of photographic reproduction, especially microphotography, and allied techniques. This is certainly no longer true, so far as the professional documentalists and librarians are concerned.

Today the major burden of research and development in the areas of photographic reproduction have been largely assumed by the commercial manufacturers and their own professional organization, the National Microfilm Association. The Microphotographic Laboratory was established in the late 1930s at the University of Chicago by a grant from the Carnegie Corporation, to explore, through an active research program, the potentialities inherent in microfilm and allied techniques, but it has long since abrogated its original mandate and become little more than a service agency for the sale of film. The same is true for the laboratory, established under a similar grant, at Massachusetts Institute of Technology. Thus, the time when documentation was equated with microphotographic reproduction has yielded to a new period in which the emphasis is on systems for information retrieval. Thus, too, did the original *Journal of Documentary Reproduction* reemerge after World War II as *American Documentation*, with a considerably broadened scope.

No one would pretend, least of all the editor, that *American Documentation* accurately reflects the state of research among American documentalists. Nevertheless, an analysis of its contents over the past seven years gives some clue to the general pattern of interests in the field from which research activity and projects originate.

As Table III indicates, the dominant position of contributions dealing with the production and dissemination of recorded information is to be interpreted largely in terms of the early emphasis on microphotographic techniques. In more recent years there has been increasing attention given to indexing and other information retrieval systems, and to the coding of material for use in such systems. Articles on equipment, mechanisms, and machines are, perhaps, fewer in number than one might expect. Over the years there has been a steady, but modest, concern with theory, although much of it might better be characterized as "theorizing," since conclusions are based more upon speculation, opinion, or conjecture than upon any really fundamental research. Finally, the attention being paid to studies of use and use requirements is disappointingly small. Yet the vexing question still persists: How can effective systems be devised without a solid understanding of the uses to which they are to be put? Despite its position in the table, mechanical translation is arousing considerable interest among documentalists, but there are media other than *American Documentation*, and better suited to the needs of the field, for the publication of work in this area. Finally, in view of the great demand for documentalists at the present time, it is regrettable that more attention is not being paid to the study of their professional education and training.

The charge that a journal inevitably reflects the interests, enthusiasms, and biases of its editor is unquestionably valid, and *American Documentation* has had to endure to fewer than three in its eight short years of life (V. D. Tate, 1950-51; Mortimer Taube, 1952; and the present writer from 1953). Neverthe-

**TABLE III**

**Distribution of Articles in American Documentation, by Subject, 1950-1957**

| Subject | 1950 | 1951 | 1952 | 1953 | 1954 | 1955 | 1956 | 1957* | Total |
|---|---|---|---|---|---|---|---|---|---|
| Production and Dissemination of Published Information (Including Editing)** | 16 | 22 | 2 | 5 | 4 | 2 | 8 | 2 | 61 |
| Indexing, Cataloging, Classification, and Abstracting | 1 | 3 | 7 | 3 | 11 | 5 | 7 | 6 | 43 |
| General Surveys, Descriptions, and Bibliographies | 6 | 4 | 2 | — | 4 | 9 | 3 | 4 | 32 |
| Coding for Mechanized Searching Systems | 2 | 2 | 1 | 2 | 4 | 6 | 5 | 5 | 27 |
| Theory | 2 | 2 | 3 | 1 | 3 | 2 | 3 | 4 | 20 |
| Equipment for Information Storage, and Retrieval | — | 1 | 1 | 3 | 2 | 3 | 1 | 1 | 12 |
| Use of Information and Use Requirements | — | — | 1 | 2 | — | — | 2 | — | 5 |
| Education and Training | — | — | — | 1 | — | — | — | — | 2 |
| Mechanical Translation | — | 1 | — | — | — | — | — | — | 1 |
| Total | | | | | | | | | 203 |

*Includes only issues for January, April, and July.

**Prior to the beginning of 1952 this item was almost entirely confined to problems in the production of microfilming and microfilming techniques; after that date there appeared relatively little on microfilming, with considerably more attention to problems in dissemination, security, editing, etc.

**TABLE IV**

Distribution of Articles in the Journal of Documentation, by Subject, 1945-1956

| Subject | 1945 | 1946 | 1947 | 1948 | 1949 | 1950 | 1951 | 1952 | 1953 | 1954 | 1955 | 1956 | Total |
|---|---|---|---|---|---|---|---|---|---|---|---|---|---|
| General Surveys, Descriptions, and Bibliographies | 12 | 5 | 14 | 6 | 6 | 8 | 7 | 3 | 4 | 4 | 3 | 3 | 75 |
| Indexing, Cataloging, Classification, and Abstracting | 2 | 7 | 3 | 4 | — | 6 | 4 | 3 | 3 | 5 | 5 | 5 | 47 |
| Production and Dissemination of Published Information | 7 | 2 | 1 | 3 | 3 | — | 2 | 1 | 1 | — | — | — | 20 |
| Planning of Documentation Centers, Libraries, etc.* | — | 5 | — | 1 | — | — | — | — | — | — | — | — | 6 |
| Theory | 1 | — | — | — | — | — | 1 | 1 | — | 1 | — | 2 | 6 |
| Coding for Mechanized Searching Systems | 1 | — | — | — | — | — | — | 1 | 2 | — | — | 1 | 5 |
| Education and Training | — | — | 1 | — | — | — | — | — | — | — | 1 | — | 2 |
| Equipment for Information Storage Retrieval | — | — | 1 | — | — | — | — | — | — | — | 1 | — | 2 |
| Mechanical Translation | — | — | — | — | — | 1 | — | — | — | — | — | — | 1 |
| Use of Information and Use Requirements | — | — | — | — | — | — | 1 | — | — | — | — | — | 1 |
| Preservation of Materials* | — | — | — | — | — | — | — | — | 1 | — | — | — | 1 |
| Total | | | | | | | | | | | | | 166 |

*Category does not appear in Table III.

less, if one were to superimpose upon the pattern of contributions published in this journal a profile of the subject distribution of papers presented at the annual meetings of the American Documentation Institute, there would probably be no very significant variation. When documentalists meet they discuss, in general, the same topics that they write about.

Table IV presents a comparable tabulation of subject distribution for the British *Journal of Documentation*, which evinces some striking contrasts to its American counterpart. British concern with problems of classification stands out in marked contrast to the relative neglect of this fascinating subject by their cousins on this side of the Atlantic. The British have also published a greater proportion of articles describing documentation installations, surveys of the several aspects of the documentation field, and subject bibliographies. On the other hand, American documentalists have emphasized the design of systems, with particular emphasis on coding and the construction of codes for specific purposes. Both have seriously neglected basic theory, studies of use, and the professional education of documentalists. Research, as defined at the beginning of this discussion, is poorly represented in both tables. Americans, perhaps because of their insatiable appetite for gadgets and mechanisms, have emphasized, much more strongly than the British, the techniques of documentary reproduction, especially microfilm and micro-opaques. The typical American documentalist, too, has almost an aversion for traditional methods, whereas in England, published materials treat some aspects of traditional librarianship as properly belonging in the province of the documentalist. This may, in part, be explained by the fact that in the United States the Special Libraries Association and the American Documentation Institute are separate and distinct organizations, in Great Britain the two are united in a common organization, Aslib, which sponsors the *Journal of Documentation*. Even the point of view of the archivist has infiltrated the documentation field in England, and there is some consideration, in the pages of the *Journal of Documentation*, of the problems of document preservation and repair. It may well be that the documentalist and the archivist have much more in common than is generally realized, at least among Americans.

Finally, and distressingly, both groups know that to describe is far safer and easier than to analyze, measure, and evaluate, and that speculation is more intriguing than the slow tedious drudgery of research.

From the sources mentioned in the preceding pages, the following roster of current research and development projects in documentation has been prepared. It represents, insofar as is possible, the situation as of April 1, 1957. The descriptions are given as presented by the respective authors.

*Coding for Mechanical Searching Systems*

• A study of means for organizing the subject content of patents to make them amenable to machine searching. (D. C. Andrews and B. E. Lanham, and Associates, U.S. Patent Office)

• The development of tailor-made classification, indexing, and coding systems for manual and machine storage and retrieval of information. (S. Herner and R. S. Meyer, Herner, Meyer & Co., Washington, D.C.)

• The development of a mechanical searching code by means of an analysis of a significant sample of the collection being organized, the collection of concepts into related classes, and preparation of a thesaurus-like index to the documents. (H. P. Luhn, Engineering Laboratories, International Business Machines Corporation, Endicott, N.Y.)

• The study of structural relationships between the ideas in documents in large collections, with a view toward making indexing codes more amenable to mechanical searching devices. (Calvin Mooers, Zator Co., Cambridge, Mass.)

• Coding system for the mechanical storage and retrieval of information on chemical compounds. (A. Opler and T. R. Norton, Dow Chemical Co., Midland, Mich.)

• The development of a general searching system embodying completely automated conversion of the language of a reference to its syntactic-topological equivalent, and retrieval by high-speed, large capacity, computing machines. (same)

• The development of a machine language for information storage and retrieval. (J. W. Perry and Allen Kent, School of Library Science, Western Reserve University, Cleveland, Ohio)

• Study of mechanical aids in special classification systems. (Allen Kent, J. H. Shera, Western Reserve University, and Classification Committee of the Special Libraries Association)

• The encoding of classification systems for mechanized searching and correlation. (Rosella Busemeyer, in collaboration with Center for Documentation and Communication Research, Western Reserve University)

• The encoding of subject indexes for mechanized searching and correlation. (same)

• The indexing and coding of metallurgical literature for testing the possibility of searching by means of computer-like devices. (Perry and Kent, same)

• Comparative evaluation of coding schemes for mechanized information storage and retrieval systems. (W. J. Turanski, Remington Rand Univac, Philadelphia, Pa.)

• The design of mechanized storage and searching system for agricultural chemical information. (W. M. Waldo, Monsanto Chemical Co., St. Louis, Mo.)

*Equipment for Information Storage, Retrieval, and Reproduction*

• The design of mechanical searching devices suitable for patent searches. (S. Alexander and M. E. Stevens, U.S. National Bureau of Standards, Washington, D.C.)

• The development of a device for the selection of specific frames on a microfilm reel, and the development of a code for identifying and searching frames. (L. M. Bohnert, Federal Telecommunications Laboratories, New York, N.Y.)

• The development of a "data-taking" and "data-retrieving" mechanism which duplicates the perceptual, motor, and mental function of the human nervous system. (J. R. Bussey, Sandia Corporation)

• The design of a mechanized searching and correlating device for medium-sized collections of literature or data. (S. Herner and R. S. Meyer, Herner, Meyer & Co., Washington, D.C.)

• The development of the Minicard system of information storage and retrieval. (Eastman Kodak Co., Rochester, N.Y.)

• The development of a microimage data storage and retrieval device that provides rapid access to information-containing frames recorded in miniature on a 10-inch square sheet of microfilm, automatically searching the microfilm, and printing out one frame every two seconds. (M. L. Kuder, U.S. National Bureau of Standards, Washington, D.C.)

• A high-speed printer, utilizing ferromagnetography. (Robert D. McComb, General Electric Company, Schnectady, N.Y.)

• The testing of commercial data-processing machines for the storage and retrieval of information. (A. Opler and T. R. Norton, Dow Chemical Co., Midland, Mich.)

• The design and construction of an experimental computer-like machine for testing mechanical searching codes. (J. W. Perry and Allen Kent, School of Library Science, Western Reserve University, Cleveland, Ohio)

• Study of automatic correlation of recorded information for purposes of commercial intelligence. (Staff, Center for Documentation and Communication Research, same)

• Development of an association of ideas machine. (Mortimer Taube, Documentation, Inc., Washington, D.C.)

• The development of a combination of a "Peek-a-Boo" searching system using microfilm. (W. A. Wildhack and J. Stern, Division of Basic Instrumentation, U.S. Bureau of Standards, Washington, D.C.)

*Indexing, Cataloging, and Classification*

• The conversion of manipulative indexes, such as punched cards, into non-manipulative indexes in book or catalog card form. (Charles L. Bernier, Chemical Abstracts Service, Columbus, Ohio)

• A study of the syntax and morphology of subject headings. (J. E. Daily, School of Library Service, Columbia University, New York, N.Y.)

• The indexing of publications in psychiatry, psychoanalysis, and mental health. (A. Grinstein, M.D., 18466 Wildermere Ave., Detroit, Mich.)

• The compilation of a subject heading code for library cataloging. (D. J. Haykin, Library of Congress, Washington, D.C.)

• A study of the use of the Library of Congress Classification in libraries in the United States. (A. L. Hoage, School of Library Service, Columbia University, New York, N.Y.)

• The drafting or adaptation of a classification scheme suitable for the arrangement of entries of bibliographies in the Social Sciences. (Barbara Kyle, Social Science Documentation, London, W.1, England)

• An analysis of the index to the *Canadian Labour Gazette* to determine the use to be made of it, the user's needs, and means for improving the Index. (B. Land, Library School, University of Toronto, Toronto, Canada)

• A critical analysis and revision of the *A.L.A. Cataloging Rules*. (S. Lubetsky, Library of Congress, Washington, D.C.)

• The design of indexing and classification systems for the storage and retrieval of church music manuscripts. (R. S. Meyer, Herner, Meyer & Co., Washington, D.C.)

• A study of the cataloging of publications in microfilm form. (S. Ross, Library School, Florida State University, Tallahassee, Fla.)

• Development of an indexing abstracting system for Development and Proof Services, Aberdeen Proving Grounds. (J. W. Perry and Allen Kent, Western Reserve University, and Madeline Berry, National Science Foundation, Washington, D.C.)

• Revision of subject headings for *Dissertations Abstracts*, University Microfilms, Inc., and Association of Research Libraries. (Robert Booth, School of Library Science, Western Reserve University, Cleveland, Ohio)

• Association of ideas in indexing. (Mortimer Taube, Documentation, Inc., Washington, D.C.)

• A study of the principles of classification and indexing. (B. C. Vickery, Imperial Chemical Industries, Akers Research Laboratories, Welyn, Hertz, England)

*Mechanical Translation*

• A study of codes necessary for mechanical translation. (E. Dostert, Institute for Language and Linguistics, Georgetown University, Washington, D.C.)

• The development of a memory device to be used for a mechanized Russian-English dictionary. (G. W. King, International Telemeter Corporation, Los Angeles, Calif.)

- The design of a mechanical translating process which will make possible the translation of foreign language material into precise stylistically current English without human editing. (A. Koutsoudas, Project Michigan, University of Michigan, Ann Arbor, Mich.)
- The automatic encoding of terminology. (Staff, Center for Documentation and Communication Research, School of Library Science, Western Reserve University, Cleveland, Ohio)
- The development of a machine memory for the automatic translation of Russian into English, and the preparation of an index to a Chinese dictionary, to serve in the future for machine translation projects. (E. Reifier, University of Washington, Seattle, Wash.)
- The analysis of German for mechanical translation. (V. H. Ingve, Massachusetts Institute of Technology, Cambridge, Mass.)

*Production and Dissemination of Published Information*

- The distribution of meteorological data on Microcards. (O. M. Ashford, World Meteorological Organization, Geneva, Switzerland)
- A study of publications stemming from defense-related reports. (Dwight E. Gray, Technical Information Division, Library of Congress, Washington, D.C.)
- A study of the need for preserving primary scientific records in anthropology and psychology. (B. Kaplan, National Academy of Sciences, National Research Council, Washington, D.C.)
- Canadian Library literature indexing project. (Irene McAfee, Canadian Library Association, Montreal, Canada)
- The bibliography of Newfoundland and Labrador. (Agnes C. O'Dea, study being conducted under a grant from the Carnegie Advisory Committee for Newfoundland Historical Research, Memorial University of Newfoundland)

*The Use of Information and User Requirements*

- A feasibility study to determine the possible application of operations research methods and techniques to devising means for the improvement of scientific information. (R. Ackoff, under grant from the National Science Foundation, Operations Research Group, Case Institute of Technology, Cleveland, Ohio)
- A study of public library reference services including an investigation of the types of use made of such services. (Frances N. Cheney, Library School, George Peabody College, Nashville, Tenn.)
- A study of the use of technical information by small and medium-sized manufacturers. (S. Herner and R. S. Meyer, Herner, Meyer & Co., Washington, D.C.)

- A study of the use of domestic and foreign information by American medical scientists. (same)
- A study of user language, viewpoints, and information requirements by means of the analysis of reference questions. (same with S. Herner)
- A questionnaire survey of the use of the library catalog. (S. Jackson, Brooklyn Public Library, Brooklyn, N.Y.)
- A survey of the ways that industrial and governmental organizations obtain access to recorded information to support the decision-making processes in the planning and administration of business and research. (Allen Kent, Center for Documentation and Communication Research, School of Library Science, Western Reserve University, Cleveland, Ohio)
- Survey of centralized vs. individual information processing, abstracting and indexing, in the United States. (same with Robert Booth)
- Study of documentation needs of members of American Chemical Society. (same with Division of Chemical Literature of the American Chemical Society)
- An analysis of the variety of services offered to scholars in the development of special collections, use of interlibrary loans, utilization of microfilm and other media, as well as the problems of availability and accessibility of research materials. (M. Kroll, Library School, University of Washington, Seattle, Wash.)
- A survey of the documentation resources available to social scientists in the libraries of London, and possibly elsewhere in the United Kingdom. (Barbara Kyle, Social Science Documentation, London, W.1, England)
- An investigation of possible relationships between creativity and information-seeking patterns among a group of chemists in an industrial research laboratory. (R. D. Maizell, Olin Mathieson Chemical Co.)
- An interview analysis of the flow of information among scientists in chemistry, biochemistry, and zoology. (H. Menzel, Bureau of Applied Social Research, Columbia University, New York, N.Y.)
- An operations research analysis of library operations and library use. (P. M. Morse, Massachusetts Institute of Technology, Cambridge, Mass.)
- A study of the literature resources in psychiatry, with the objective of defining research problems in this area. (T. H. Rees, Jr., Center for Documentation and Communication Research, School of Library Science, Western Reserve University, Cleveland, Ohio)
- A study of the possibility of diary methods to ascertain the information-gathering habits of scientists. (Ralph R. Shaw, U.S. Department of Agriculture, Washington, D.C. now with Graduate School of Library Service, Rutgers University, New Brunswick, N.J.)
- A study of the sources of information in the British iron and steel industry and of the use made of information in the industry. (I. M. Slade, British Iron and Steel Association, 11 Park Land, London, W.1, England)

*Theoretical Studies*

• A study of the theories of information search systems. (Y. Bar-Hillel, Hebrew University, Jerusalem, Israel)

• Development of a general theory of documentation and the development of searching strategy. (J. W. Perry, Allen Kent, and the staff of the Center for Documentation and Communication Research, School of Library Science, Western Reserve University, Cleveland, Ohio)

• The development of a glossary for machine literature searching. (T. H. Reed, Jr. and Allen Kent, same)

• The study of the morphology and development of the semantic code. (Perry, Kent, *et al.*, with John Melton, John Carroll University, Cleveland, Ohio)

• The systematization of rules and procedures for the preparation of telegraphic style abstracts. (Center for Documentation and Communication Research, with Jessica Melton, Cleveland, Ohio)

• Development of a glossary for ordnance terminology. (Center for Documentation and Communication Research, with Margaret E. Egan)

• The development of a generalized information theory including storage and retrieval theory and communication theory. (Mortimer Taube, Documentation, Inc., Washington, D.C.)

• A study of methods for indicating relations among index entries, and for copying with interrelations of meaning, in searching systems. (Phyllis M. Williams, Washington, D.C.)

*Education and Training of Documentalists*

• The training of documentalists, a portion of the study of education for librarianship. (J. H. Shera, and faculty of the School of Library Science, Western Reserve University, Cleveland, Ohio, under grant from the Carnegie Corporation of New York)

Probably no aspect of librarianship is more amenable to research than is the field of documentation. The ends which it purports to serve are particularly receptive to research. The requirements of the user whom the documentalist serves and the ways in which he employs graphic records are more subject to analysis and scientific generalization based upon observable facts than are, for example, the uses to which the so-called "general reader" puts books from the public library. The pathway by which the former threads his way through the swelling morass of print is, perhaps, less idiosyncratic than that of the casual reader, or even the "serious" user of books. The task of research in documentation is further facilitated by the fact that a majority of its practitioners are trained in the stern discipline of scientific method. Research is not, or certainly should not be, alien to their nature. The documentalist, if he is to be a scientist, should not cringe before the relentless verdict of valid evidence, nor shrink from an unpalatable conclusion.

Yet both the depth and the volume of research in documentation still remain disheartening. There are many areas which are still inadequately explored. Far too little is known about the use of graphic records by the scholar and about the possible effects upon our society of failure in recorded communication. The basic theory of documentation has suffered from excessive speculation. Systems have been devised recklessly and promoted with an abandon that disregards any evidence of their effectiveness or efficiency. Automation, which has brought such impressive technological advance in many fields, is often decried by documentalists; conversely, "machines" have been foisted upon a naive public with little evaluation of their capabilities and limitations. Classification, as a fundamental tool of documentation, has suffered neglect and, often, disparagement. In the face of an acute shortage of trained documentalists and the demand for new skills that are certain to follow in the wake of automation, there has been but slight attention to the professional education of the documentalist. Perhaps worst of all, the entire field is sicklied-o'er with the pale cast of bias, prejudice, "huckstering," and polemics. Documentation is wallowing in a sea of claims and counterclaims that have no foundation in solid fact.

Further, the documentalist cannot live alone. He must, quite literally, draw his sustenance from many disciplines and a variety of technical developments in a great cluster of related fields. Thus, the contribution that can be made to documentation by information theory, by symbolic logic, by switching theory, by operations research, and by communication theory, to name but a few, must be carefully explored. One may properly assume that each has a contribution to make toward improving the utilization of recorded knowledge, but until a program of research far more extensive than any yet undertaken is carried through, the nature of the contribution each has to make can be but dimly perceived.

Of all the criticisms that may be brought to bear against research in documentation, however, the most serious is the neglect of fundamentals. As a profession, documentation is threatened with a potential exhaustion of its store of fundamental knowledge; lacking such a reservoir of new theory, its literature becomes repetitious, its techniques sterile, and its progress attenuated. There may soon come a time when documentation can no longer advance for the simple reason that it has no idea what direction such advance should take, and only a well-defined program of fundamental research will restore the sense of direction.

The reasons for this neglect of the fundamental are not difficult to discover. The swelling flood of recorded information has brought outcries of desperation from those threatened with inundation. There is an ever-increasing and often irresistible demand for immediate and practicable solutions that promise hope of rescue. Often those who suffer most are least patient with the theoretical, and it is difficult to convince them that the only true solution to their difficulties lies in greater attention to, and support for, fundamental research. As the present writer has previously said:

> ... only through such fundamental research will those who seek to advance the science of documentation be free to explore wherever or whatever their best judgments dictate. The great fountainheads for the support of research—industry, government, the foundations—must recognize that pure research seldom emanates from immediate practical needs. They must not always ask to see the end foreshadowed in the beginning; they must not always demand immediate and tangible results. They must have courage to invest in the future, fortitude to withstand occasional failure, patience to await results, and faith in the ability of fundamental research to discover the best path. Where there is no vision a profession cannot prosper. A sedulous dedication to the exploration of fundamentals is vital to documentation, and indeed it is this that distinguishes the true profession from the craft.[3]

Fortunately there is some evidence of an awakening awareness of the importance of research, especially fundamental research, to the future of documentation. Admittedly, mere talk does not solve many problems, but interests and concerns that become vocal have greater opportunity for serious consideration than those which remain unarticulated. The size and character of the audiences that participated in the two recent Cleveland symposia (Conference on the Practical Utilization of Recorded Knowledge, January 1956; Symposium on Systems for Information Retrieval, April 1957) eloquently testify to the diversity of interests with a vital stake in documentation, and where there is general concern the probabilities for constructive action are immeasurably increased. In short, perhaps the most significant feature of these conferences was the simple fact that so many people came to them—people from many fields and with a wide variety of needs. It is heartening, too, that so much energy and so many resources are being expended in the promotion of the International Conference on Scientific Information, planned for autumn, 1958, and to be held under the auspices of the National Academy of Sciences, the National Research Council, the American Documentation Institute, and the National Science Foundation. If this conference fulfills its promise, it should be a powerful force in promoting research in scientific documentation. In this connection, one should also mention the renewed vitality of the Committee on Research and Development (under the chairmanship of Saul Herner) of the American Documentation Institute, the expanding program of the Division of Chemical Literature of the American Chemical Society, and the increased interest in documentation evinced by the Special Libraries Association and its newly formed Documentation Division.

Through the efforts of the participants at the first Cleveland conference, there was formed in the early autumn of 1956 the Council on Documentation Research, composed of representatives from over 30 professional, governmental, industrial, and educational organizations that have already recognized the inadequacy of today's techniques for the storage and retrieval of recorded knowledge. The organization has a four-fold objective:

1. To promote understanding and cooperation among those who produce, organize, and use recorded knowledge of all types and in all fields.
2. To assist in the identification and clarification of problems common to those who produce, organize, and use information in diverse areas.
3. To promote research and development in documentation.
4. To encourage exchange of information concerning developments in principles, systems, and equipment for the effective organization of graphic records.[4]

If the American Documentation Institute expands its concern with research, one may anticipate that it will consolidate with the Council, but at the present time the two organizations appear to meet somewhat different needs.

Without financial support, research in any field can make little progress, however enthusiastically it may be championed; documentation is no exception to this. Harassed by the growing need to use efficiently the essential body of recorded information, industry and business are increasingly making funds available for the development of palliative measures. At the present time, unfortunately, little of this is available for fundamental research, but it may prepare the way for more theoretical exploration. Enlightened management's growing awareness of the importance of the documentation problem gives reality to the prognostication of a time when a vice president in charge of information may be an essential officer in every major commercial and industrial enterprise.

Government, especially the federal government and its agencies concerned with the armed forces and intelligence is generally even more alert to the importance of documentation than industry and trade. It is increasingly making substantial amounts of money available for documentation research, with considerable regard to the need to support fundamental research as well as development.

Most important of all, however, are those agencies created specifically to disburse funds supporting activities that are dedicated to improving man's knowledge. The many benefactions of the Carnegie and Rockefeller Foundations are well known to librarians, and there is now some evidence that they may be turning their attention to the more specialized field of documentation. More directly concerned and more immediately active, however, is the Division of Scientific Information, under the leadership of Alberto Thompson, of the National Science Foundation. This division supports a number of projects in documentation applied to the science field. In May 1956, the Division sponsored a conference at Endicott House in Cambridge, Massachusetts, which brought together some 30 representatives of varying scientific disciplines, in the hope of formulating a research program in documentation that would enlist contributions from electronic engineering, information theory, linguistics, and other fields. Exploratory discussions like this are of great value, if they are supplemented by a program of activities that will carry forward their recommendations.

Most important of all, perhaps, was the creation, about a year ago, of the Council on Library Resources, Inc., supported by a five-year grant from the Ford Foundation, and under the directorship of V. W. Clapp. At the time this is being written the initial grants of the Council have not yet been announced, but one of its stated objectives is "through grants-in-aid to institutions and individuals, to identify the problems which now present obstacles to efficient library service, and seek to find methods for overcoming these impediments through the development of new procedures and the application of technological developments."[5]

The responsibility of the documentalist to perfect his techniques and methods may be far more urgent than even he himself realizes. In Eastern Europe a great giant has, at long last, shaken off the shackles of feudalism and put scientific and technical knowledge to work with all the power of dictatorship. Today the English-speaking peoples of the earth face a new threat of world economic conquest and the domination of men's minds. Much has been heard of late concerning the growing superiority of Soviet science and the extent to which it may be outproducing ours, not only in the manufacture of instruments of war, but also in the development of peaceful applications of scientific research. The American press has issued alarming reports of Russian preeminence in the training of scientists and engineers, and the alleged success of Soviet planning in its relentless drive toward world leadership.

At least partially in substantiation of these claims there have recently appeared three publications prepared by members of the Academy of Science of the USSR and issued in Moscow. These indicate that Soviet documentalists have, by the application of documentation theory originally developed in the United States, devised experimental equipment for mechanized literature searching. Admittedly this equipment is still a prototype, or was when these publications were issued, and so far as is known here it lacks many of the capabilities that American documentalists believe to be possible for mechanisms of this sort. But it is well to be reminded that no secret is being made of this achievement, and one leaves to conjecture the amount of such Soviet progress that has not as yet been publicly reported.[6-8]

On our ability to prosecute fruitful research and development in documentation may rest the very future of our civilization and the perpetuation of our cherished way of life. We are today engaged in a grim game; we may not long hold all the high cards, if indeed we do now. Research in documentation is more than an intellectual game pursued for the love of the sport and the intellectual excitement that it may engender. The documentalist of today bears a burden of responsibility far heavier than any known to his predecessors; he may even hold the key to the future of mankind.

## FOOTNOTES

[1] J. H. Shera, "Documentation: Its Scope and Limitations," *Library Quarterly*, Vol. 21 (January 1951), 13-26.

[2] American Documentation Institute, Committee on Research and Development, *Report of the Chairman of the Committee, 1955-56*. (Unpublished.)

[3] J. H. Shera, Editorial, "Fundamental Research—A Few Fundamentals," *American Documentation*, Vol. 7 (July 1956), ii.

[4] Council on Documentation Research, *Minutes of the Meeting*, September 14, 1956.

[5] Council on Library Resources, Inc. (press releases dated September 18, 1956), *College and Research Libraries*, Vol. 17 (November 1956), 469-73+.

[6] V. P. Cherenin and B. M. Rakov, *The Experimental Information Machine of the U.S.S.R. Academy of Sciences* (Moscow: U.S.S.R. Academy of Sciences, 1955).

[7] V. P. Cherenin, *Some Problems of Documentation and the Mechanization of Information Searches* (Moscow: Institute of Scientific Information, Academy of Sciences, U.S.S.R., 1955).

[8] L. I. Gutenmakher, "New Type Statistical and Information Machines," *Vestnik Akademii Nauk SSSR*, Vol. 10 (October 1956), 12-21.

**18**

# Librarians Against Machines

"And further, by these my son, be admonished: of making many books there is no end; and much study (or reading ) is a weariness of the flesh." Thus wrote the author of Ecclesiastes in a passage that has so often been quoted that it has become trite, but that still stands as eloquent, not to say biblical, testimony to the burden of literature searching that has plagued every scholar since the days of the great Alexandrian library, and perhaps as early as the time of Assurbanipal's royal collection of clay tablets at Nineveh. The proliferation of recorded knowledge has been a matter of concern to scientists as well as librarians for many centuries. One cynic, now unhappily forgotten, expressed disquietude over the growth of libraries and cemeteries and proposed cremation as a solution for both. It was not, however, until Fremont Rider published *The Scholar and the Future of the Research Library* that concern changed to alarm. Rider's main purpose, of course, was to promote the use of microcards (micro-opaques) as a form of relief for the library's growing problem of book storage. Such micro-opaques have indeed become popular, even commonplace, since he wrote, but it was his extrapolation of the exponential growth of libraries and their bibliographic instruments that shocked the world of scholarship. Rider, who was writing in the early 1940s, showed that the major university and college libraries had been doubling in size every 16 years, and that if this rate of increase were projected into the future, the Yale University library, which throughout its history has approached very closely the statistical norm of all the institutions Rider studied, would "in 2040 have approximately 200,000,000 volumes, which will occupy over 6,000 miles of shelves. Its card catalog file—if it then has a card catalog—will consist of nearly three-quarters of a million catalog drawers, which will themselves occupy not less than eight acres

Reprinted by permission from the September 1967 issue of the *Wilson Library Bulletin*. Copyright © 1967 by the H. W. Wilson Company.

of floor space. New material will be coming into it at the rate of 12,000,000 volumes a year; and the cataloging of this new material will require a cataloging staff of over six thousand persons."[1]

Rider's statistical projections were eagerly seized by administrators, especially those concerned with the management of academic institutions and industrial research installations, and there was much loose talk about the growing costs of literature searching—even to the point of assuming that if a particular experiment costs less than $x$ thousands of dollars it would be more economical to repeat it than to invest in the costs of an exhaustive literature search to make certain that the experiment had not previously been done. In a widely publicized essay entitled *From Fright to Frankenstein*, Ralph R. Shaw, then librarian of the U.S. Department of Agriculture, attempted to allay all such apprehensions by challenging Rider's acceptance of the exponential curve as being descriptive of future library growth,[2] but only in the more conservative segments of the library profession did his reassuring words have any substantial impact, and the fright continued whether or not it led to Frankenstein. Indeed, proposals for the mechanization of literature searching, particularly through the adaptation of computers to library operations, were only intensifying the panic.

Rider's prognostications were picked up by, among others, Derek J. de Solla Price who saw in the exponential growth of recorded scientific knowledge one of the diseases of science that could lead to eventual suffocation of innovation through the proliferation of its own recorded achievements.[3] Recent expansion in library growth may prove Rider's estimates to have been conservative. On the other hand, a recent study of the mathematics literature suggests that it may be increasing at a rate of only 2.5 percent annually, thus doubling in volume approximately four times a century.[4] But even such a rate of growth will pose a serious problem to librarians.

The miniaturization of the printed word proposed by Rider now seems crude compared to the refinements that have recently been introduced. The National Cash Register Company of Dayton, Ohio, has effectively produced readable text at reduction ratios of over 48,000 to 1 in area.[5] But such microscopic printing approaches only the optical limits of textual reproduction. In Germany, the physicist G. Mollenstedt demonstrated the possibility of etching on a thin metal film with an "electronic pencil" 80 angstroms in diameter letters one to two millionths of an inch in height; and Professor Richard P. Feynman of the California Institute of Technology conjectured that if organic life is able to store its genetic information at the ultimate molecular level by "printing" it in the form of long "coded" chains in the chromosomes, it should also be at least theoretically possible to approach such a level with man's intellectual information.[6] For the foreseeable future, at least, there would appear to be always room at the bottom, and the problem of library storage, however much it may inconvenience the reader, will not prove serious.

The serious problem of information storage and retrieval, then, is not the storage but the retrieval; for what will it profit a man if he has the entire collection of the Library of Congress on the corner of his desk if he cannot effectively and efficiently gain access to its intellectual content? Possession may be nine-tenths of the law, but that proportion does not hold for scholarship. The difficulties of information retrieval arise, not so much from the swelling body of material as from the complexities of its content. The interdependence of those disciplines which comprise the sciences is destroying the lines of demarcation that once defined the conventional areas of study. Isolationism is no more valid for today's scholarship than it is for international policy. Yet there is a paradox in these interrelationships that finds expression in Price's "Diseases of Science": the more difficult it becomes for scholars to master the records of science the more vital it is to the welfare of science that such mastery be realized. For generations, the scholar has dreamed of a Utopia in which he would have access to the total store of potentially useful materials and the ability to choose from it only the best documents for his immediate need. The advent of the Hollerith machine and its subsequent refinements made possible by the introduction of powerful electronic computers opened the possibility of storing huge collections of recorded information from which pertinent segments, correlated as the user desires, could be retrieved through the simple typing of requests on a console.[7]

Though the majority of librarians, for very good reasons, have been skeptical of this new technology, and some have been reluctant to accept the basic premise that machines could be made that are "smarter than men," enthusiasm for mechanized information retrieval spread rapidly during the late 1950s and the 1960s, especially among the engineers, whose vision of automation was unlimited; among scientists, who were bedeviled by the burden of bibliographic search; and among executives, who were eager to reduce the mounting costs of libraries and library service. When the federal government and other sources of research funds began to provide quite substantial support for the exploration of automated information retrieval, the trend of the future became reasonably clear. It also became evident that many scientists were coming to believe that librarianship was much too important to be left to the librarians.

As Ben-Ami Lipetz has shown, these automata have not yet realized the promise of their adherents. Thus, he writes:

> The difficulty of handling analytical problems has so far limited the use of mechanical techniques in information storage and retrieval work to applications that never required much analytical judgment on the part of the humans who formerly did the work. Savings in clerical activities have been great, and performance has been accelerated in such applications. But the human indexer, translator, evaluator, and abstractor are still very much needed—more than ever in view of the increasing rate of production of new records. There is great need for machines to take over significant portions of the intellectual work. Faster, larger,

cheaper computers are not the complete answer, although they will certainly be necessary. The major contribution will probably come from enlarged understanding of how human evaluations are made and from increased effort to design improved programs of instruction that will endow machines with analytical abilities simulating human abilities. In a real sense the problem is one of learning how to educate machines efficiently.[8]

Or, to state Lipetz' point another way: the problem is one of learning what it is that we want the machines to do and then designing machines and the appropriate software that can do it efficiently. Lipetz is optimistic about man's ability eventually to develop computers that will be capable of learning human analytical powers. Herbert Simon, who is a cautious student of the role of automation in our society, believes that "insofar as we understand what processes are involved in human creativity—and we are beginning to have a very good understanding of them—none of the processes involved in human creativity appear to be beyond the reach of computers."[9]

But we are here not primarily concerned with the future of the computer in the storage and retrieval of scientific information. Let us assume, and there appears to be very good reason for such an assumption, that machines can be built that will relieve the scholar of much of the burden of bibliographic search, and that they will eventually be able to provide the precise information the user needs when he needs it, in response to a very simple operation on his part—say, pushing a button on a remote console. If this is what we want done, then the engineers can eventually be expected to do it.

Our primary concern here is with the impact of a technological revolution, or threatened technological revolution, upon an activity that has begun to think seriously about its professionalization—the occupation of librarianship. "No less certainly than the civilization of an armed force is based on its weapons system is the civilization of our society based upon the instrumentation of the industrial process," writes Elting Morison. "All our economic and social arrangements—how we feel about what we do, which is all that culture is—are founded upon the way our industrial energy is organized. How large a part and what kind of part do we want the computer, with its overriding skill in the analysis of measurable data, to take in the decisions that determine the way this energy will be organized? This is worth thinking about."[10] If one looks at Morison's assertion from the standpoint of an occupational group that is experiencing a rather drastic and potentially far-reaching change, his question is, indeed, worth thinking about.

Robert D. Leigh, writing in the late 1940s in his official capacity as chairman of the Public Library Inquiry, took the rather cautious position that librarianship is a "skilled occupation on its way to becoming an organized profession," and added that "like other occupations the librarians have accepted professional status as a goal."[11] Whether or not one believes that the credentials the librarians have submitted for acceptance as a profession are valid is here irrelevant. The important fact that librarians as an organized group aspire to become a profession has direct bearing upon their reaction to the technological revolution now taking place in their sphere of social endeavor.[12]

Many writers, from a variety of disparate disciplines, have, over the years, identified a formidable list of attributes that define a profession—autonomy, organizational or associational structure, possession of a body of theoretical knowledge, sources and size of financial rewards, service or dedication, possession of special social privileges or sanctions, and many others depending upon the profession or professions taken as a standard.[13] But perhaps all of these can be subsumed under the two accepted by Goode,[14] because they seem to be socially central to the basic concept and are founded in all definitions: 1) a collectivity or service orientation, and 2) prolonged specialized training in an abstract body of knowledge.

The role of the library throughout history has been to maximize the social utility of graphic records for the benefit of society. Hence the librarian stands as a mediator between man and his records, and librarianship is fundamentally an act of mediation. To this end the librarian must select, or "screen" the "best" materials for his clientele, and organize and otherwise order the flow of information to meet the needs of his patrons. In a very real sense he is, and always has been, an information specialist. Thus, the concept of service, even devoted service, is indigenous in librarianship, and it is difficult to see how, in this respect, he would fail to meet the qualifications of a professional.[15] Four of Ranganathan's "Five Laws" of librarianship (every book its reader, every reader his book, books are for use, and save the time of the reader) are all eloquent testimony to the "library faith" of service.[16] The American Library Association has long been dedicated to the principle of the best books for the most readers, even to a point that approaches the zeal of the missionary. Collectively, librarians have also formulated their own code of ethics insisting upon the rights of intellectual freedom, the integrity of their book collections, and the freedom to read—and have in a variety of ways defined standards of professional conduct and behavior. Admittedly many of these standards are not sanctioned by law, as are those of such professions as medicine or public education, but that is largely because the body politic does not feel a sense of urgency about the need for information and does not see the inherent harm in either misinformation or the absence of adequate knowledge. As the dean of a leading medical school once told the present writer, "We all die of a lack of information." But in the eyes of the layman it is cancer, or heart disease, or some other ailment that gets the blame. There is a certain irony in the fact that a culture like ours, which places great emphasis upon science and extending the frontiers of knowledge, should view with such indifference the importance of organizing and servicing that knowledge in the most effective and efficient ways possible. There is irony, too, in the fact that though the public is at long last beginning to recognize the utility of information, librarians are often rejected as proper administrators of it. Therein lies the crisis that confronts librarianship at the present time.

Perhaps the reason for this paradox is to be found in the second point raised by Goode—the failure of librarians to develop a substantial body of theoretical knowledge and a system of graduate education that is truly professional in its orientation and content. The conventional techniques of bibliographic organization used by librarians have been slowly developed over a relatively long period of time, and are based on quite unsophisticated assumptions about the ways library patrons use the card catalog, classification schemes, and other bibliographic apparatus that characterize the majority of library installations today. Though the techniques of bibliographic description have been codified and standardized, largely through the work of the Library of Congress, the subject analysis of library materials, except for refinements in classification and more precise technologies, have received surprisingly little attention since the days of Charles Ammi Cutter.[17] Personal assistance to the reader (reference work) dates only from 1876 and the pioneering efforts of Samuel Swett Green of the Worcester, Massachusetts, Free Public Library.[18] Thus the sudden upsurge in the production of scientific literature and the complexities that characterize its use, together with the growing dependence of science upon recorded knowledge, have caught the librarians professionally off base and quite unprepared for the intrusion of a new technology that has been known variously as documentation, information science, automation, and information storage and retrieval, despite the obvious fact that the storing and retrieving of recorded knowledge had been the librarian's unique responsibility for many centuries. That librarians were thus caught was largely due to the unfortunate fact that they had neither given much consideration to the theoretical foundations of their procedures, nor developed a research program that would advance such theory or explain and improve its applications. Librarians know very well *how* to do what they do, but they never concern themselves to any great extent with *why* they do it. They understand the *Können*, but the *Wissen* has escaped them. Their discipline is a vast accumulation of technical details rather than a body of organized abstract principles that can be applied in concrete situations—a body of knowledge known and understood by all members of the guild and one that the librarians themselves have created.

Because librarians have not devoted sufficient attention to the theoretical considerations of their work, and because they are not truly professional, they have largely failed to grasp the meaning of the dilemma in which they find themselves. As Philip Ennis has shown, the library is a part of the total communication system in society, particularly that part which relates to communication among scientists and other scholars and communication between the scholar and the general public. At the same time, the library is itself an organization that encompasses a variety of physical entities, human beings, and social relationships. All of the library's relationships are subject to technological change and are interdependent. Thus a technological innovation that may well meet the needs of one may not necessarily be beneficial or acceptable to the other.[19] Microfilm, for example, which might effectively solve the librarian's difficult problems of acquisition and storage, might also result in serious inconvenience to the patron; and a computer, which might admirably solve the patron's searching problem, might bring about serious dislocation of functions within the library staff.

As an occupation drives toward professional status, a substantial amount of attention is devoted to education and the establishment of professional schools, and accrediting bodies are created to watch over standards of educational performance. Too frequently these standards are more concerned with the outward manifestations of academic achievement than with the intellectual content of the discipline to be taught: the amount of study required beyond the baccalaureate degree, the number of the faculty who hold the doctorate, the extent of "research" activity as indicated by faculty publication, and other considerations that can be reduced to statistical quantification. Lip service is given to creativity and innovation, but excessive departure from traditional course content is likely to be regarded with considerable suspicion.

For almost a century librarianship has been struggling to divest itself of its training-class and apprentice origins. In 1923, C. C. Williamson urged that library schools should be integral parts of universities in order to enrich the intellectual content of their curricula, but the change brought little marked improvement.[20] Library schools remained largely isolated units in the university complex, and their faculties were not in the mainstream of academic life. In 1926 the University of Chicago established, with the support of the Carnegie Corporation, a graduate library school with the first doctoral program in librarianship. This school has made a major contribution to the improvement of professional education for librarians, though it has always been a target for the conservatives. Nevertheless, many of its graduates introduced the "Chicago philosophy" into librarianship, and its program of study, superficially at least, was widely copied. Slowly and painfully library education has been scrambling upward; certainly it has more intellectual content than it possessed when Williamson wrote, but it has not yet achieved a true synthesis between *Wissen* and *Können*.

Into the librarians' comfortable and tidy world of rules, techniques, and standardized procedures there burst, following the close of World War II, the spectre of automation, with its band of nonlibrarians. These engineers and other scientists brought with them a strange new vocabulary and a vision of computers as push-button libraries that could master the rising flood of paper record. The librarians had always been Utopians in the conventional sense that they were concerned with people, with service to the book needs of the individual from the preschool child to the aging adult. Librarians, then, were people-centered. But these "New Utopians," to use Boguslaw's phrase, were "concerned with non-people and with people-substitutes. Their planning [was] done with computer hardware, systems procedures, functional analyses, and heuristics. . . ."[21] Moreover, the librarians were strongly humanistic in their point of view. The humanities had long been the gate of entry into librarianship, and indeed many librarians were fearful and distrustful of science. They had turned to librarianship for the very reason that they were self-consciously inadequate in science. Even the statistical approach to librarianship, which at the University of Chicago had received such wide attention during the 1930s, had caused considerable concern. In its initial manifestations automation was received by librarians with little more serious attention than if it had been the scientific fantasy of a Rube Goldberg or a Buck Rogers. But Robert Maynard Hutchins is right when he states in a recent syndicated column that the computer cannot be treated

> as though it were just another invention, whereas it cannot be compared with any mechanical device in history. It adds a new dimension to the powers of man and to human life. To suppose that so fundamental a change can leave the economic system (and, one might add, librarianship) virtually untouched is to ignore the radical nature of the new instrument that mankind now has at its disposal. I believe that whenever the computer establishes itself—and it is rapidly doing so everywhere—it will eventually reduce labor as we have understood it and may reduce it almost to the vanishing point.[22]

The impact of this new mechanism on a branch of organized human activity that is aspiring to professional prestige, then, is worthy of serious thought.

Marshall McLuhan, who welcomes rather than fears or criticizes technological change, holds that, on the evidence of technology's past encounters with human society, cultures are shaped more by the media through which men communicate than by the content of their communication. Along with the historian Harold Innis and most cultural anthropologists and students of evolution, McLuhan believes that it was the invention of hand tools and spoken language that differentiated man from the beasts and that these innovations led to the development of the human brain as distinct from the brain of all other species.[23] Whether this sequence is historically right or not no one really knows; it is the old hen-and-egg mystery and probably the egg theory of hens is potentially as valid as the hen theory of eggs. But certainly McLuhan is right in drawing attention to the relationship between tools and mechanisms and the values held by men in organized societies and their subcultures.

Though Americans recognize that technological change is inevitable, and indeed, welcome and encourage it, they remain in large measure appalled by the possible consequences of their ingenuity. Consciously or unconsciously, men seek refuge in the continuation of old patterns of behavior, even though quite different conditions maintain because of the introduction of new mechanisms. Thus: in the Socratic dialogue, *Phaedrus*, Socrates sets forth the argument that the invention of the alphabet "will create forgetfulness in the learners' souls, because they will not use their memories; they will trust to the eternal written characters and not remember of themselves. . . . You give your disciples not truth, but only the semblance of truth; they will be hearers of many things, and will have learned nothing; they will appear to be omniscient and will generally know nothing."[24] Fear is especially strong among those occupations that are service oriented, or when the innovation comes from without the occupational group or subculture. Thus librarians were especially apprehensive over the invasion by documentalists and information scientists. Their first response was a pretense that it did not exist; their second, logical rational refutation; and their third (and extreme) stage, the resort to *argumentum ad hominem*. Behind all these, of course, lie the fears of loss of professional identity, unemployment, and, to use Schumpeter's term, "the gale of creative destruction." Even in those areas where automation promises almost immediate relief from burdensome detail, the computer is not always accepted with enthusiasm. Resentment can easily replace reason, especially when the benefits come from those who are outside the culture group. The engineers do not really understand library problems, so the argument goes—and it has sufficient validity to delay the benefits that fresh insights from nonlibrary disciplines might bring.

But the technological innovation does not have to be disruptive; it is not necessarily a hostile force dislocating comfortable routines. It can provide the intellectual "kick" that propels librarianship into new dimensions of service. That librarians are deeply troubled by the new technology can be directly attributed to their devoting excessive attention to the techniques of their craft, and to their neglect of the fundamental questions that they should have been asking. The computer could force them, at long last and in self-defense, to examine the philosophical implications of librarianship. It could also condition them for accommodation with areas of inquiry that have not previously been thought to be related to their work.

If librarians, then, are to take advantage of the new technology, they must first extend the boundaries of their thinking, which has been channeled and confined for so many generations, and accept into the body of their professional knowledge ideas that at first may seem alien, if not hostile. The profession must be particularly alert at its margins, and sensitive and responsive to change, in order to insure open and clear communication with all relevant sources of innovation—physiology, psychology, and behavioral science, as well as the humanities. With such infusion librarians will be in a much stronger and more strategic position to ask the right questions and formulate their own body of theoretical knowledge. But as librarians must seek unity with the scientific world, so also must librarianship seek unity within itself. Communication must be established among the several subsystems, the school librarians, the public librarians, the academic librarians, and that multifarious cluster of activities carried out by special librarians, documentalists, and information scientists. Librarianship must also develop a sound research policy that is directed toward the solution of fundamental problems, not a series of statistical exercises in which counting and tabulating masquerade under the guise of scientific inquiry. Quantification and research are not synonymous, and the slavish following of a methodology, however good the design, does not guarantee valid results. Today, librarianship is not research-oriented, but it must become so if the *why* is properly to be related to the *how*. "We have all the answers," Archibald MacLeish once told his staff at the Library of Congress. "It's the questions we do not know."

Finally, practice must be made more responsive to theory. By its very nature innovation begins by destroying traditions, patterns of thought, and habits of behavior, that people have long cherished and to which they have become accustomed. This period of stress engendered by the destructive force of innovation can probably never be eliminated, but it must be decreased to the minimum by increasing the absorptive power of the profession, by intensifying the professionals' hospitality to change.

In simulating and promoting all of these professional needs of the librarian, the computer and the intellectual forces that it represents can be a powerful ally and effective catalyst. It should neither be feared as a competitor nor condemned and ridiculed because it has not yet achieved the intellectual capabilities of the human being. Whether the computer can ever be "taught to think" is not a matter of concern here; the important point is that it can compel the librarian to ask the right questions about what he really should be doing, and it can direct his thought to the right answers to those questions. Alfred North Whitehead sees society as a proper balance in the conflict between conservatism and innovation: "There are two principles inherent in the very nature of things, recurring in some particular embodiments whatever field we explore—the spirit of change and the spirit of conservation. There can be nothing real without both. Mere change without conservation is a passage from nothing to nothing. Its final integration yields mere transient nonentity. Mere conservation without change cannot conserve. For after all, there is a flux of circumstances, and the freshness of being evaporated under mere repetition."[25] On the other hand, Professor Platt sees society moving toward a new unity: "We have been isolated human beings, selfish, combative, ignorant, helpless. But now for several hundred years the great evolutionary hormones of knowledge and technology have been pressing us, almost without our understanding it, into power, prosperity, communication, and interaction, and into increasing tolerance and vision and choice and planning—pressing us whether we like it or not, into a single coordinated humankind. The scattered and competing parts are being bound together."[26] Librarians should not belittle or inveigh against the new Utopians and their machines. To say that science is not the sum of human culture is not the same as saying that it is unimportant or alien to culture. Librarians must not emphasize conservation at the expense of change; they dare not forget that the Luddites eventually were put to death. "The fault, dear Brutus, is not in our machines, but in ourselves. . . ." Or, to quote that eminent social philosopher of our own day, Pogo: ". . . on this very ground, with small flags waving and Tinny blasts on tiny trumpets, we shall meet the enemy, and not only may he be ours, he may be us."[27]

## FOOTNOTES

[1] F. Rider, *The Scholar and the Future of the Research Library* (New York: Hadham, 1944), p. 12.

[2] R. R. Shaw, *D.C. Libraries* 24, 6 (1953).

[3] D. J. de Solla Price, *Science Since Babylon* (New Haven: Yale University Press, 1961), p. 104; *Little Science and Big Science* (New York: Columbia University Press, 1963), p. 59; C.F.J. Overhage, *Science* 155, 802 (1967).

[4] *See* K. O. May, *Science* 154, 1672 (1966).

[5] This reduction process is known as the Photo-Chromic Image (PCMI). The manufacturer has put the entire text of both the Old and New Testaments on a 2-inch plastic square.

[6] J. R. Platt, *The Step to Man* (New York: Wiley, 1966), p. 4.

[7] F. J. Keppel, in *The Library of Tomorrow*, E. M. Danton, ed. (Chicago: American Library Association, 1939), p. 5; V. Bush, *Atlantic* 176, 106 (1945); L. N. Ridenour, *Bibliography in an Age of Science* (Urbana: University of Illinois Press, 1951), p. 5; R. S. Casey and J. W. Perry, *Punched Cards, Their Application in Science and Industry* (New York: Reinhold, 1951; 2nd ed., 1958); J. W. Perry, *Machine Literature Searching* (New York: Interscience, 1956), J.C.R. Licklider, *Libraries of the Future* (Cambridge: M.I.T. Press, 1965); C.F.J. Overhage and R. J. Harman, eds., *INTREX, Report on a Planning Conference on Information Transfer Experiments* (Cambridge: M.I.T. Press, 1965).

[8] B. Lipetz, *Sci. Amer.* 215, 242 (1966).

[9] H. Simon, quoted in E. E. Morison, *Men, Machines, and Modern Times* (Cambridge: M.I.T. Press, 1966), p. 77.

[10] E. E. Morison, *Men, Machines, and Modern Times*, p. 78.

[11] R. D. Leigh, *The Public Library in the United States* (New York: Columbia University Press, 1950), p. 192.

[12] William Goode agrees with Leigh that librarianship is moving along the professionalization continuum, but doubts that it is likely to achieve the status of a profession because the general public will probably not permit librarians to

attain the degree of collective self-control demanded of truly professional groups. *See* W. Goode in *Professionalization*, H. M. Vollmer and D. L. Mills, eds. (Englewood Cliffs, N.J.: Prentice-Hall, 1966), p. 33.

[13] Everett C. Hughes takes the position that professions apply an esoteric skill, or body of esoteric skills, to the giving of a service; that professions are practiced in complicated organizational structures that are complex forms of group or associational activity; that the clients are drawn from society at large; and that the profession is concerned with the distribution of its services as well as with their production. *See* E. C. Hughes, *Library Quarterly* 31, 336 (1961); *see also* M. L. Cogan, *Harvard Educ. Rev.* 23, 33 (1953).

[14] W. Goode, in *Professionalization*, H. M. Vollmer and D. L. Mills, eds., p. 36.

[15] Goode's argument (*ibid.*, p. 41) that the librarian is not a professional person because he gives his patrons "what they want" instead of what they "need" is a mere playing with semantics.

[16] S. R. Ranganathan, *The Five Laws of Library Science* (Madras, India: Madras Library Association, 1957). The expression "The Library Faith" derives from O. Garceau, *The Library and the Political Process* (New York: Columbia University Press, 1949).

[17] C. A. Cutter, *Rules for a Printed Dictionary Catalog* (Washington: Government Printing Office, 1876); Vatican Library, *Rules for the Catalog of Printed Books* (Chicago: American Library Association, 1948), p. 249; D. J. Haykin, *Subject Headings, A Practical Guide* (Washington: Government Printing Office, 1951); M. F. Tauber, ed., *The Subject Analysis of Library Materials* (New York: School of Library Service, Columbia University, 1953).

[18] S. Rothstein, *The Development of Reference Services* (Chicago: Association of College and Reference Librarians, 1955), p. 21.

[19] P. H. Ennis, *Library Quarterly* 32, 191 (1962).

[20] C. C. Williamson, *Training for Library Service* (New York: Carnegie Corporation, 1923), p. 86.

[21] R. Boguslaw, *The New Utopians* (Englewood Cliffs, N.J.: Prentice-Hall, 1966), p. 2.

[22] R. M. Hutchins, Cleveland *Plain Dealer* (August 7, 1966), p. 6AA.

[23] M. McLuhan, *Understanding Media* (New York: McGraw-Hill, 1964), Chap. 1.

[24] Plato, *Dialogues* (London: Oxford University Press, 1924, new ed.), I, 484.

[25] A. N. Whitehead, *Science and the Modern World* (New York: Macmillan, 1929), p. 289.

[26] Platt, *Step to Man*, pp. 202-203.

[27] Walt Kelly, *The Pogo Papers* (New York: Simon and Schuster, 1952), Introduction.

# 19

# Of Librarianship, Documentation and Information Science

When Otlet and La Fontaine laid their plans late in the 19th century for a great world bibliography of all recorded knowledge, they reaffirmed and gave new impetus to a movement dating at least from the days of Johann Tritheim and Konrad Gesner, and probably earlier.[1] The two acquaintances, who first met in the rue de Florence, Brussels, probably did not themselves realize how deeply their roots ran, nor the magnitude of the movement which, despite all of its subsequent vicissitudes, they had revitalized. Though they saw as their objective the organization and indexing of the universe of recorded knowledge in whatever form it might appear, they turned to librarianship for their basic techniques and strategy. They began to build their world bibliography from conventional library catalogs, and they chose the Dewey Decimal System as the foundation for their classification scheme. But they were striving not only for comprehensiveness, but also for a more penetrating subject analysis of bibliographic materials than had been used in conventional librarianship and, to differentiate their activity from that of the librarians, they therefore called it "documentation." Thus was begun a schism within librarianship whose end has not been reached.

Less than two decades after La Fontaine and Otlet began their work, John Cotton Dana, who for some time had been preaching the importance of library service to business and industry as a neglected area of librarianship, and who had established the Business Branch of the Newark, New Jersey, Public Library, the first of its kind in the United States of America, led his little band of dissenters out of the ranks of the American Library Association to form the Special Libraries Association. For want of a better term he called his activity "special librarianship." Efforts to unite the Dana movement with the senior organization ended in failure, and the profession of librarianship suffered further fragmen-

From *Unesco Bulletin for Libraries*, Volume XXII, No. 2, 1968. Reproduced by permission of Unesco.

tation. A second unfortunate fracture among the librarians occurred in the 1930s with the formation of the American Documentation Institute.[2] The new association was originally conceived as an organization of representatives of the several learned societies in the country dedicated to the encouragement, development, and promotion of new scientific aids to the bibliographic activities of the scholar.[3] However, because the most vocal and influential members of the institute were deeply concerned with new methods of photographic reproduction, especially microfilm, documentation on this side of the Atlantic soon became virtually synonymous with microphotography, just as in Europe it was closely associated with the promotion of the Universal Decimal Classification.

Organized documentation activity was largely held in abeyance during World War II but experimentation in crude forms of mechanized information retrieval was attempted by some of the intelligence services of the American armed forces. The rebirth of the ADI (now the American Society of Information Scientists) brought with it a strong and growing interest in what was then called "machine literature searching." During the decade of the 1950s the threads of the bibliographic skein became more and more tangled. The Special Libraries Association formed its Documentation Division; the chemists, intrigued by the rapidly growing literature problem, founded the Chemical Literature Division of the American Chemical Society; the microfilm interests, which felt themselves adversely affected by the shift in emphasis within the ADI, formed their own independent group which became known as the National Microfilm Association, with a membership made up largely of commercial organizations manufacturing and marketing microfilm equipment. The technical writers and editors also seceded from the ADI, while the several science abstracting services formed their own group. Most recently, the American Association for the Advancement of Science formed its information sciences section, and the American Library Association created its Information Science and Automation Division (ISAD), which was an outgrowth of the original Interdivisional Committee on Documentation. This listing is not complete, but it is of sufficient length to indicate the growth of specialized organizations concerned with "the new librarianship," and the extent of proliferation that characterizes the field even today. It is important to note, too, that in many of these organizations a very substantial proportion of the members were not librarians but scientists, or at least men with scientific training who turned to documentation because they were interested in the literature problem; indeed, many were openly contemptuous of the librarians.

## THE TWO LINES OF DEVELOPMENT

Historically, two major lines of development have characterized the library movement, and it is these which have ideologically been responsible for the fragmentation. In the beginning, librarianship was a scholarly pursuit devoted, from the time of the great Alexandrian Library established by the Ptolemys in

Alexander's city at the mouth of the Nile, to the systematic collection and organization of recorded knowledge, the "transcript," as Kenneth Boulding calls it, of the human adventure. The librarian as scholar-bookman dominated the profession until the early decades of the 19th century brought the rise of popular concern with the common man, the faith in human perfectability, and the growth of democracy which depended for its success upon an enlightened and educated electorate. With the emergence of the public library came the beginnings of the ideal of community service and the efficacy of education in elevating man to new levels of self-improvement. Thus the public library became aware of its public relations and so turned the corner which a church does when it begins to proselytize. Today there are many who fear that the desire to move ALA headquarters from Chicago to Washington means that the association is becoming little more than a political pressure group.

This change in viewpoint from scholarship to service, which was latent in the Librarians' Conference of 1853,[4] became clearly evident in 1876, when ALA was founded at the Philadelphia Centennial. From that point on, the advocates of expanded library service, supported by the generosity of Andrew Carnegie and the corporation which bears his name, became increasingly powerful at the expense of those whose primary concern was bibliographic. It was at this time that the path of librarianship began to branch in directions that have become increasingly diverse. The one led toward the state associations (ALA chapters) and other local and regional groups, the other toward the FID, SLA, ADI, and related organizations. This change might best be illustrated graphically (see Fig. 1).

The widening split in librarianship was accompanied not only by growing institutional complexity and a serious questioning by the "invading" non-librarians, of library goals and objectives, but also by an open contempt for librarianship itself. The invaders wanted no part of library education as a preparation for their work, and this rejected the techniques of the librarian despite the fact that they themselves reinvented methods that had long ago been either adopted or discarded by the librarians; under no circumstances did they want themselves to be stigmatized as librarians. Over the years, the conflict in which the documentalist-information specialists would rather fight than switch engendered more emotional heat than intellectual enlightenment. The phenomena is especially interesting to the student of the sociology of professionalization as an example of the desire of an alien group to change the terminology of the invaded, and thus present at least the outward manifestations of a new discipline. Changing the terminology, it was believed, changed the character of the practice; "descriptors" somehow endowed "subject headings" with scientific respectability and made them acceptable in good society. In terminology, especially, familiarity breeds contempt. So the scientists in their white aprons rejected the sweet little old lady behind the circulation desk and all her works,

**FIG. 1. LIBRARIANSHIP AS BIBLIOGRAPHIC SCHOLARSHIP**

Ancient libraries
Medieval libraries
Renaissance
Beginnings of science
Enlightenment

The scholarly library

*The popular library*
Private library clubs
Social libraries

*Eighteenth century*

*Library scholarship*
Great research libraries of Europe

*Nineteenth century*

Public library movement
Adult education

Boston Public Library
Librarians' Conference of 1853

Beginnings of research
    libraries in U.S.A.

Popular culture
Free public schools

Documentation movement
Otlet and La Fontaine
Bibliographic activity
Poole's index

Public Library Act, United Kingdom
American Library Association
Carnegie grants

*Twentieth century*

Local and regional
    library associations
State associations

Council of National
    Library Associations

Special Libraries Association—Chapters
Special library movement
ASLIB
American Documentation Institute—Chapters

International Federation of
    Library Associations

Chemical Literature Division
American Chemical Society
American Association for the Advancement of Science,
    Information Science Division

Education for librarianship

Conventional

Documentation

Information science

National Microfilm Association
Association of Technical Writers and Editors
National Federation of Science Abstracting and
    Information Services
Special bibliographic services
Chemical abstracts
Biological abstracts, etc.
Research in library automation and information science

Associations of special
    types of libraries:
Medical, music, law, Catholic,
    college and university

without stopping to inquire whether the gray-haired bearer of the torch of learning was herself anything more than an anachronism in conventional librarianship. Because the letter killeth, one is brought squarely up against the problem of definition.

## THE PROBLEM OF DEFINITION

When the furor over documentation was at its height, someone whose name regrettably has not come down to posterity defined the term as "librarianship practiced by amateurs." The verbal caricature was not entirely invalid, though as a definition it is scarcely worthy of an entry in the Oxford English Dictionary. Otlet defined the term as "a process by which are brought together, classified and distributed, all the documents of all kinds of all the areas of human activity,"[5] a definition which has the virtue of placing the emphasis upon process and procedure. S. C. Bradford closely followed Otlet, but insisted that it was not a science but an art—"the art of collecting, classifying and making readily accessible the records of all kinds of intellectual activity . . . the process by which . . . is . . . put before the creative specialist the existing literature, bearing on the subject of his investigation, in order that he may be made fully aware of previous achievements in his subject, and thus be saved from the dissipation of his genius upon work already done."[6] Bradford has thus emphasized acquisition and organization, and limited the clientle to the scholars. Katherine O. Murra provisionally accepted the definition of the *Schweizer Lexikon*, which called it the "handling and organization of library materials."[7] Mme. Briet, however, is perhaps most comprehensive of all; she says that even animals in the zoo are documentation.[8] In 1951, the present writer stated that documentation was that part of bibliographic organization which served the needs of scholarship, and its function was to expedite the flow of recorded information "within a group of specialists or among various groups of specialists. It is not concerned with the flow of communication at the popular, non-specialist, or lay public levels."[9] Such a distinction is probably too restrictive to be acceptable today. If documentation is a system or method for the application of librarianship, its techniques could be applied to children's literature as well as to monographs in molecular physics.

But the meaning of documentation poses a problem that is now virtually academic, for in the United States, at least, it has come to be regarded as being still more obsolete than librarianship, even by many of those who a few years earlier were its most ardent advocates and practitioners. At the conference on the training of Science Information Specialists held at the Georgia Institute of Technology in the spring of 1962, the assembled delegates agreed that the terms of documentation and documentalist should be avoided, "because of the wide variation in their use and in the numerous interpretations of their meaning. We suggest, therefore, that if anyone should wish to use these terms he should state his particular definitions."[10] As an alternative to the vague comprehensiveness of documentation, the Georgia conference identified five categories of workers: librarian, special librarian, science librarian, technical literature analyst, and information scientist, of which the last was used to refer to those engaged in research rather than service. Whether this categorization is valid or not cannot be considered here, except that it should be pointed out that the terms are far from being discrete and mutually exclusive. Be that as it may, the final demise of documentation seems to be signified by the ALA's rejection of it for its new division of Information Science and Automation, and by the proposal now before the American Documentation Institute for a constitutional revision that would change its name to the American Society of Information Scientists.

## INFORMATION SCIENCE IN THE LIBRARIAN'S WORLD

When Shannon and Weaver evolved their "information theory," they, too, were guilty of an unfortunate use of terminology. They were concerned, of course, not with a theory of information but a theory of signals, the message-carrying capacity of a symbol, a telephone wire, or any other medium or channel of communication. But the term is attractive, and those concerned with improving access to recorded knowledge were not slow in seizing upon it for their own purposes. Thus information science soon became the accepted term for non-conventional librarianship. Perhaps the tenuous relation between information theory and the utilization of recorded knowledge is best expressed by an anonymous limerick writer in the July 1962 issue of *Behavioral Science* (Vol. VII, p. 395):

> Shannon and Wiener and I
> Have found it confusing to try
> To measure sagacity
> And channel capacity
> By $\Sigma p_i \log p_i$.

The Georgia conference defined an information scientist as: "One who studies and develops the science of information storage and retrieval, who devises new approaches to the information problem, who is interested in information in and of itself." Thus, the problem shifts from the distinction between librarianship and documentation to the interface between information science and the library profession.

To understand this new relationship it is first necessary to inquire into the nature of librarianship itself. Librarianship in the generic sense, as a professional activity, is concerned with all of these agencies, operations, techniques, and principles that contribute to the objective of making graphic records as useful to society as is humanly possible—i.e., of maximizing the social utility of graphic records for the benefit of mankind.

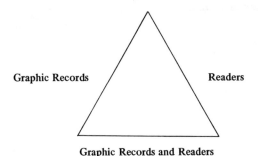

Graphic Records and Readers

Documentation, therefore, as indicated above, is nothing more than a form, or aspect, of librarianship; it is, as the present writer said on another occasion, "librarianship in a high key."[11] Librarianship, admittedly, is a service profession, and its internal variants are shaped by the nature and character of the group served. Librarianship is librarianship whether it serves the bibliographic needs of the scientist surrounded by his test-tubes and retorts or the child pouring over his first picture-book.

By contrast, "information science," Rees and Saracevic told an audience at the 1967 convention of the Special Libraries Association, "cannot be equated with documentation, information retrieval, librarianship, or with anything else. Information science is not souped-up information retrieval or librarianship any more than physics is supercharged engineering."[12] In the view of these two writers, information science is an area of research which draws its substance, methods, and techniques from a variety of disciplines to achieve an understanding of "the properties, behavior and flow of information. It includes systems analysis, environmental aspects of information and communication, information media and language analysis, organization of information, man-systems relationships, and the like." Thus they arrive at a definition of information science as the "investigation of communication phenomena and the properties of communication systems."

The present writer could argue with Rees and Saracevic when they deny to the pursuit of information science the status of a profession, because "it satisfies no social need and is not concerned with operational services." They also charge that "it does not have a theoretical base." But it does satisfy the need of society to understand man in relation to himself and his environment. To say that a profession must be concerned wtih "operational services," denies the status of professionalism to all branches of pure science and other forms of theoretical inquiry. It may not have a theoretical base as yet, but it is striving to derive one from its contributory disciplines, and it is the theoretical base for the practice of librarianship.

Debate over professionalism is, however, not very fruitful; more to the point is the spectrum of librarianship devised by Rees and Saracevic, reproduced in slightly modified form as Fig. 3.

**FIG. 3. THE SPECTRUM OF LIBRARIANSHIP**

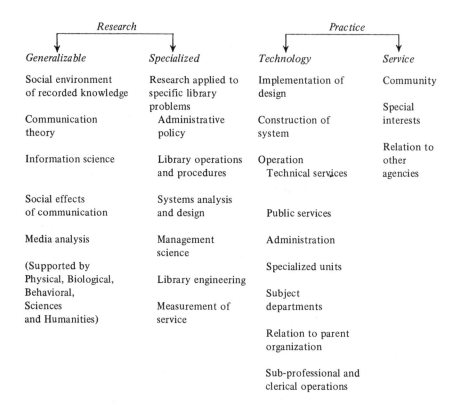

| Research | | Practice | |
|---|---|---|---|
| Generalizable | Specialized | Technology | Service |
| Social environment of recorded knowledge | Research applied to specific library problems | Implementation of design | Community |
| Communication theory | Administrative policy | Construction of system | Special interests |
| Information science | Library operations and procedures | Operation Technical services | Relation to other agencies |
| Social effects of communication | Systems analysis and design | Public services | |
| Media analysis | Management science | Administration | |
| (Supported by Physical, Biological, Behavioral, Sciences and Humanities) | Library engineering Measurement of service | Specialized units Subject departments | |
| | | Relation to parent organization | |
| | | Sub-professional and clerical operations | |

The several constituent elements in Fig. 3 are, quite obviously, not mutually exclusive, but are interrelated and interdependent in a variety of ways. Practice identifies areas where research is needed, or where research shapes and otherwise influences practice. The assumptions and *ad hoc* methods of the older librarianship will no longer suffice in today's complicated world of recorded knowledge. Moreover, to a very great degree, the associational structure represented in Fig. 1 can be identified with the elements in Fig. 3. Because there is no unifying principle in the former, however, it represents fragmentation while the latter depicts unity. That such an unfortunate dichotomy, or disparity, does not exist in other professions such as law or medicine is doubtless due to the fact that the surgeon or other specialist begins his professional education as a doctor and hence does not forget that his specialty is part of a larger whole. Similarly the legal specialist is founded in the general principles of the law. Librarianship, by contrast, is not yet sufficiently mature to have evolved a common generalized discipline that all librarians and information scientists must master before they embark upon their respective specializations. The identification of this common body of theory and practice is the peculiar responsibility of library education, working in concert with the practitioners.

## THE RELATION OF INFORMATION SCIENCE TO LIBRARIANSHIP

Robert S. Taylor, in a recent study supported by the National Science Foundation, has identified five areas in which information science and technology interact with librarianship and library education:

1. Systems analysis, which is concerned with the design and development of models and simulation techniques in the study of the library, or parts thereof, or of large configurations such as library nets.
2. Environment consists of the study of the social context in which the library operates, the social processing of knowledge, and the intellectual requirements of various segments of society or of various types of societies and levels of intellectual and technological development.
3. Information channels encompass all the media of communication through which knowledge is transmitted and received. Such channels are not confined to books or materials in codex form, but encompass any medium including the library or information center itself.
4. The fourth category might be called bibliographic organization or analysis, since it treats of the naming, labeling and classifying process, and it must rely more heavily than it has in the past upon the work of linguists, logicians, psychologists and mathematicians.
5. Finally, there is the man-system interface, which is concerned with the totality of interactions that takes place between the user and whatever bibliographic services or devices are available to him. Such "instrumentalities" may be either human or mechanical, the reference librarian, a card catalog, an index, a computer, or even a book.[13]

Taylor himself admits that these categories overlap at many points, and that any one study can cut across several lines, but they do demonstrate rather clearly the structure of the intellectual base that information science provides to librarianship, and suggest the ways in which modern librarianship has failed to inquire into the why of what it is doing.

Information science, then, is not antithetical to librarianship; on the contrary, the two are natural allies, and librarians should not reject this new intellectual relative, nor should the information scientist discredit the librarian. Both have made and will continue to make mistakes, and if the librarian is the more guilty it is only because he has had more time in which to err. The laws of chance prohibit innovation without error. For the moment, at least, the librarian and the information scientist may speak with different tongues—new concepts require a new terminology—but eventually a consensus and a common understanding will be achieved. Rees, Saracevic, and Taylor all represent a new generation of librarians, a generation that can lead librarianship back to the scholar-librarian. He will be a new kind of scholar-librarian (and the scholarship will be totally different from that of the Ancients) but he will be able to give the profession the intellectual enrichment and depth for which it has for so many years been searching.

## FOOTNOTES

[1] S. C. Bradford, "Fifty Years of Documentation," in *Documentation*, 2nd ed. (London: Crosby Lockwood, 1953), pp. 132-43; Theodore Besterman, *The Beginnings of Systematic Bibliography* (Oxford University Press, 1935), pp. 6-20; Ernest A. Savage, "Co-operative Bibliography in the Thirteenth and Fifteenth Centuries," in *Special Librarianship in General Libraries* (London: Grafton, 1939), pp. 285-310.

[2] Jesse H. Shera, "Mirror for Documentalists," *D.C. Libraries* c, 27 (April 1956), 2-4; Vernon D. Tate, "Introducing American Documentation," *American Documentation*, Vol. 1 (January 1950), 3-7.

[3] Robert C. Binkley, *Manual on Methods of Reproducing Research Material* (Ann Arbor: Edwards Brothers, 1936), 307p.

[4] George B. Utley, *The Librarians' Conference of 1853* (Chicago: American Library Association, 1951), 189p.

[5] Paul Otlet, *Traité de Documentation: le Livre sur le Livre, Théorie et Pratique* (Bruxelles: Editiones Mundaneum, 1934), pp. 6-8.

[6] *Ibid.*, p. 11.

[7] Katherine O. Murra, "Second interim report of the Unesco Library of Congress Bibliographical Planning Group," Appendix to the *Library of Congress Information Bulletin* (September 13-14, 1949), 6. *See also* Leo M. Kern, *Grundfragen der Dokumentation* (Bern: Buchler and Co., 1948), pp. 3-5.

[8] Suzanne Briet, *Qu'est-ce que la Documentation?* (Paris: EDIT, 1951), p. 7.

[9] Jesse H. Shera, "Documentation: Its Scope and Limitations," *Library Quarterly*, Vol. 21 (January 1951), 13-14. Reprinted in the author's *Documentation and the Organization of Knowledge* (London: Crosby Lockwood, 1966), pp. 2-3.

[10] Unpublished definitions.

[11] Jesse H. Shera, "Librarianship in a High Key," *ALA Bulletin*, Vol. 50 (February 1956), 103-105.

[12] Alan Rees, and Tefko Saracevic, *Education for Information Science and Its Relation to Librarianship*, Unpublished paper presented before the annual conference of the Special Libraries Association, New York, 1967. p. 2.

[13] Robert S. Taylor, "The Interface Between Librarianship and Information Science and Engineering," *Special Libraries*, Vol. 58 (January 1967), 45-48.

# 20

# The Sociological Relationships
# of Information Science

My good friends, both new and old, it is indeed a great pleasure to return to the organization which will always remain for me the ADI. As I was winging my way from Austin to Philadelphia, I could not but recall the first time this organization met in Philadelphia. It was, I think, in 1957 or 1958, and there were all of 75 in attendance. Exhibitors numbered about three, and at the banquet there were only about 35 diners. The attrition is easily explained. My old friend Scott Adams was program chairman and the ADI was then experiencing rather serious financial difficulties. He needed a cheap banquet speaker so he got me. That was the low point, I think, in the history of the association.

It is, therefore, a great source of satisfaction to me to see the organization grow to the position it holds today; but for me personally the greatest satisfaction of all is the progress that my old squalling infant, *American Documentation*, has made during the past decade. In my final report as editor of that journal, I expressed the hope that the future of the publication would be such that the lean years of my stewardship would pale into insignificance and be forgotten. Happily that wish has come true, and the current editor and his supporting referees are to be congratulated on their success in making of their enterprise one that, in the quality of its contributions and attractiveness of format, does not need to yield to any scientific publication either here or abroad. If I allowed my membership in ASIS to lapse a year ago, it was, I assure you, entirely for economic reasons. I find that the title emeritus is much more honor than profit in the academic world.

Address delivered at the 33rd annual meeting of the American Society for Information Science, Philadelphia, Pa., October 14, 1970; later published in the *ASIS Journal*, Vol. 22 (March-April 1971), pp. 76-80.

Now I hope you have all listened carefully to what I have just said because this will be the last time this morning that I intend to compliment you. Indeed, my laudatory preamble leads quite naturally into my main theme. You call yourselves a society of information scientists. This desire to be identified as scientists and support a new scientific discipline is quite in character with our national psyche, for if the United States can be said to have a national religion it is most certainly Science, with a capital S. We have always had a sublime faith in science. I can remember as a boy in 1917, when we entered World War I; an old Irishman, Mr. Hooper, who drove a milk wagon for my father's dairy, said, "I'm lookin' to Tom Edison, he'll come up with something." But this faith in the scientist, the inventor, the engineer, goes back much further than my youth. Cotton Mather was among the first to support inoculation for smallpox at a time when it was scarcely popular to do so, especially for a man of God; and he was, I believe, the first American to be elected to the Royal Society, an affiliation in which he took much pride.

From the very beginnings, America has identified its national character in terms of a pastoral idiom inherited from the European Utopians, expressed on this side of the Atlantic in such experiments as those at New Harmony, Indiana, Oneida, New York, the Transcendentalist movement, and Thoreau at Walden Pond. Machines were to be implanted in, and humanized by, an idealized landscape. Through machines, through scientific invention, society would create an harmonious unity of eternal bliss from the union of the rural setting and the industrial city, in which technological power and democratic localism could comprise an ideal way of life. The building of the Erie Canal opened the West to the pioneer. But it was the steam engine, both on water and on rails, that occupied a particularly important place in the pantheon of technologies because of its ability to link country and city. Thus, intellectual awe of technology generated a confusion of engineering fact with spiritual symbolism to produce what has been called "the technological sublime."

Yet, industrialization turned the cities into slums, made labor even more burdensome than it had been, and created new class and race warfare. Despite Harriet Martineau's enthusiasm for what she called "mind among the spindles" the lot of the mill girls of Lowell and Lawrence, Massachusetts, stands as a vivid example of the havoc that steam power and mechanization of industry did to the lives of those who left the rural life of northern New England for the lure of the cities to the south.

With the advent of electric power, hope sprang anew in the minds of the Utopians, and the electrical sublime replaced the mechanical. Any number of authors wrote with a religious fervor of the benefits of electricity, which, unlike steam, did not need to be utilized close to its place of origin. Edward Bellamy wrote *Looking Backward; A.D. 2,000*, whose socialistic thesis has been obscured by his prognostication of radio. It remained for Henry Adams and Samuel

Clemens, two of the most unlike writers one could imagine, to see this new source of energy as a spectre of disaster and to speak out against the new electric ethos. Adams, that magnificent interpreter of the spirit of the Middle Ages, as you know if you have read *Mont-Saint-Michel and Chartres*, was obsessed by the laws of thermodynamics and the entropic menace, and he filled the pages of his *Education*, and especially the chapter on "The Dynamo and the Virgin," with disillusionment. Similarly, Mark Twain's Connecticut Yankee, who in the beginning saves himself through his knowledge of eclipses, eventually realizes that the electrical fence erected at his own command actually entraps him.

But, as those of you who have lived through the 1930s know, the public utilities industry only increased the concentration of power in the hands of a few, a trend that even Franklin Roosevelt's rural electrification program and the formation of cooperatives did little to attenuate. Again, the blinding flash that fused the sands of Alamagordo seemed to illuminate a new world in which the peacetime uses of atomic energy would herald a better life for everyone, but in its wake came increased world tension and terror of "the bomb." Today, as Carey and Quirk have said, "An increasingly prevalent and popular brand of the futurist ethos may be regarded as being that which identifies electricity and electrical power, electronics, and cybernetics with a new birth of community decentralization, ecological balance, and social harmony."[1] Thus there has arisen a new optimistic school of thought that has been articulated and reiterated over many decades and that still has many spokesmen in our time. But the use of electronic technology has recently become biased toward the concentration of power in computer centers and energy grids, and once again the voice of protest, not confined to the young, is being heard. In the pages of such prestigious journals as *The Atlantic, Harper's, The New Yorker*, and a host of lesser publications appear warnings that there may be something seriously wrong with science in general and with the new electronic age in particular. It is, perhaps, significant of a changing spirit even in the scientific community itself when such a distinguished figure as Vannevar Bush has recently entitled a collection of his essays *Science Is Not Enough*.

Much of the same cycle of action and reaction, of faith in the machine followed by distrust and disillusionment, has characterized the field in which we are engaged. When the ADI was revived, following the close of World War II, many, and I certainly include myself among them, inspired by Frederick Keppel's vision of Hollerith machines, which would mechanize library service, and Vannevar Bush's Memex, the personalized information retrieval device, saw automation as solving all the problems of organizing recorded knowledge for effective use. The 1950s brought the burgeoning of such mechanisms as the Rapid Selector, Recordak's Minicard, the Western Reserve Searching Selector, and numerous other devices launched with high hopes by IBM, Univac, and others. But the mechanization of information retrieval poses problems that have still not been adequately solved, and there are many who are disturbed by the extent to which the computer is beginning to dominate and shape our lives. Vannevar Bush has written an essay appropriately entitled "Memex Revisited," which he has included in the collection of papers mentioned above; though he has not lost faith in his personal information retrieval device, he admits that it will probably be a long time in coming.

What we failed to perceive in the 1950s and early 1960s was that we had fallen into the error that Abraham Kaplan calls the Law of the Instrument. Simply stated, his principle holds that the machine makes its own ends; the device determines what we shall do. Stated another way, the principle is entirely behavioristic: the invention and fabrication of a particular instrument immediately fix the conviction that it is exactly what is needed to do whatever we think needs to be done. The marketing of a Xerox machine, for example, promotes the notion that everything must be reproduced in multiple copies and widely distributed, whether or not such distribution is needed; or, a boy given a hammer suddenly discovers that everything needs to be pounded. What we also failed to perceive was that information retrieval is a child of information science, not an independent discipline in its own right, and that information science itself is an aspect of the communication process. And communication is a social phenomenon.[2]

Information transfer, whether expressed in mathematical equations or in engineering, is still a product of society, of men working together in groups to achieve certain ends. Indeed, the anthropologist cannot conceive of culture without communication, without the information transfer necessary to carry on the group's activity, to transmit belief, and to bridge the generation gap. We have been transferring information all our lives without knowing it, like Molière's bourgeois gentleman. A culture is a tri-partite system of social organization, mechanisms or machinery, and belief; if any one of the three advances at the expense of the others, the society is in trouble. Today we have permitted science and the products of science to outrun our social organization and our body of belief, and we may be in serious difficulty. Science, indeed, is not enough.

For a number of years we have all been talking glibly about the "information explosion," but it is neither an explosion nor information. An explosion is spherical, it exerts its force in all directions simultaneously, whereas the so-called information explosion is linear; it turns out mainly in one direction only—the direction of the mechanism of our culture. Neither is the explosion concerned with information; it is a paper explosion. It is not knowledge, but paper that is increasing at an exponential rate. The major problem, then, is the control of paper, not the control of knowledge, and Everyman wants to control others' paper output, but not his own.

There have been those who have suggested that man now has too much knowledge, that he has more knowledge than he can use, and that there should be a moratorium on the knowledge industry. Such observations are, of course, nonsense. The problem is not that man has too much knowledge, but that he does not have enough knowledge of the right kind. The only remedy for too much knowledge is more knowledge—knowledge of how to use the knowledge we have. Perhaps this seeming paradox can be best expressed by a Venn diagram of two overlapping circles, as in Fig. 1.

FIG. 1.

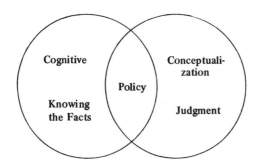

The cognitive sphere is "telling it like it is"; it is Francis Bacon wringing from Nature her secrets. Conceptualization is putting it all together, synthesis, understanding the meaning of the facts. Policy, then, is, or rather should be, the product of the two. The Germans have two words for it—*kennen*, to know about, and *wissen*, to understand, and let us not forget that the German noun for science is *Wissenschaft*, and that it derives from wissen, not kennen. It is not enough that we know what information science *is*, we must understand what it can *do* and how it can be used for the betterment of mankind. "Society is our trustees," Frances Peabody told the medical profession, "it is to society that we are responsible." His statement accords with the notion in general that when a subsystem fails to perform as the system believes that it should, that is, if it fails to produce effectively and economically in terms of the system's orientation— the subsystem is rejected or destroyed. If we forget that it is to society that the information scientist must be accountable, the information scientist will follow the great American bison into the setting sun. Elting Morison, in that provocative little book, *Men, Machines, and Modern Times*, has set forth the thesis that the engineer can do nearly anything; the problem is that man has not told the engineer what it is he is to do. Morison quotes Thomas Huxley's famous query, "What are we going to do with all these new things?" and adds that Huxley should have asked, "How can we organize society so that we can take full advantage of all these new things?" I hope that from your exploration of information science you will gain some insights that will improve the communication process in society. This may sound very utilitarian; I have no patience with science for its own sake. I am certainly not rejecting theory;

theoretical research is, in the broadest sense, perhaps, the most utilitarian of all.

On last Monday evening I attended, as did many of you, an invited panel on of all things, "The Futurology of Information Science," which represented the new futurist ethic gone completely to seed. I have not heard so much unmitigated drivel spoken in one evening since I last attended a conference of the American Library Association. By Tuesday afternoon I was ready to "scotch" the whole conference. So I sought out the companionship of a very dear and trusted friend, and together we walked over to the adjacent park, sat on a bench, and watched the pigeons. You should watch pigeons more often. They are very perspicacious creatures; they know exactly what to do to the human race, and if you know pigeons you know what I mean! For some two hours we watched the pigeons while my friend, who is very wise, perceptive, and has no illusions about some of my own particular brand of drivel, chewed me out about a course I am giving at the University of Texas. I had it coming to me; my friend is always a very wholesome antidote for my innate sense of ego. So, as I sat there listening to her and watching the pigeons, I thought of Emerson in the woods near Fresh Pond. Thus he writes in his journal for April 11, 1834:

> Went yesterday to Cambridge and spent most of the day at Mount Auburn, Got my lunch at Fresh Pond, and went back again to the woods. After much wandering and seeing many things, four snakes gliding up and down a hollow for no purpose that I could see—not to eat, not for love, but only gliding.

But I realized that it was not then, but on the night before at the panel on "The Futurology of Information Science," that I was like Emerson at Fresh Pond, watching the little snakes gliding up and down, "for no purpose that I could see."

The futurology of information science, indeed! An old gypsy with a deck of cards or a cup of tea leaves could probably have done as well. We now have, I am told, "Professors of Futurology" in some of our universities. In the small southwestern Ohio town where I grew up, we had a man who vulcanized and otherwise repaired old tires, who called himself a "Tireologist"; we thought it was funny—we would have thought "futurology" was funny, too. So now we have as more or less respectable disciplines not only information science (when no one knows what it is) and futurology (when no one can see the future), but, heaven help us, even "sensitivity training." We had sensitivity sessions, too, when I was a boy, but we didn't call it that, and we didn't practice it in groups, only in pairs usually under the benign and discreet cover of darkness, and it never occurred to us that we should have academic credit for it. The point I am trying to make is that today everything must be expressed in terms of science. Thus, we live by computer. Our behavior, whether rational or erratic, must be explained in terms of scientific laws. We communicate through channels and over networks, and our lives are governed by Kaplan's law of the instrument. What has become of the little lady librarian in the high-necked dress who probably practiced all of these disciplines, except possibly the sensitivity sessions, without even knowing it—and did quite a respectable job, too?

A library, or an information system of any kind, is a trinity of a) the atomistic, b) content, and c) context. By the *atomistic* I mean the technology of the operation; it can be machines, catalog cards, classification schemes, or any hardware or software that will contribute to the effectiveness of the system. By the *content* I mean simply that which is transmitted—a book, a picture, a sound transcription, a message, or whatever it is that appears to meet the needs of the user and is transferred from the store to the receptor. By *context* is meant the social environment in which the system, or the act, takes place. It is this social environment, the state of scholarship and social organization of the culture at any given time, that defines the setting and determines the character of the other two.

I believe we have done fairly well with the atomistic; we have gone up many blind alleys and followed many false leads, but that is inevitable in a technology that has been changing as rapidly as has ours during the past several decades. After all, we must not forget that chemistry began as alchemy, astronomy as astrology, biology and medicine as superstitious belief. There was a time when the Egyptians sought to cure a headache by drilling a hole in the skull to let the evil spirit out. We should not be impatient if our technology has not developed as rapidly as some wish it might. Nor should we complain if Vannevar Bush's Memex is not yet a reality, or likely to be one in the near future.

With the content we have done much less well. We do not yet know the impact of the message on the receptor, or understand the psychological process of learning, much less comprehend the effect of reading on the individual. Language itself is still largely a mystery to us. Though librarians have for centuries been dedicated to providing the "best" books to their patrons, we do not yet know what a "best" book is in any given situation.

With the context we have been virtually complete failures. We do not know how a message is communicated through society or what its impact upon social behavior is. We say confidently that the role of the library—or the information center, if you prefer—is to maximize the social utility of graphic records, or the graphic message. But what I have called "social epistemology" is still a mystery. The answers to some of these questions we may think we know intuitively; the lady librarian in her high-necked dress thought she knew them, and perhaps she did. But the chaos in which society finds itself today suggests, at least, that we do not know what we really are about. If there ever was a time when society needed constructive action based on valid information, it is most certainly now. The problems of our society are mountain-high, they reach to the skies— over-population, war, the devastation of the environment, drugs, pollution; one could go on and on, but you know them all. It is small wonder that youth is in revolt or that pigeons display their contempt for the human race in a dramatic, if not very elegant, way.

"The proper study of mankind is man," said Auguste Comte, the father of modern sociology, and James Thurber replied, "Says man." But who but man is there to say it? There is *no* science—"Es gibt *keine* Wissenschaft"—wrote Heinrich Rickert more than a half a century ago. "There is *no* science, which, *as a science*, tells man what he ought to desire or what he ought to do."[3]

I am not rejecting science; I am not turning my back on it. Science has many achievements to its credit, and that part of the world that is doing even moderately well is doing it at least partly because of the scientist quietly working in his laboratory or writing equations on paper. I would not for a moment suggest that you cease your explorations of the scientific aspects of the information problem. But I am a humanist, have always been one, and at my age I am not likely to change. I think it is time for the humanist to speak out, to urge that in your work with equations you do not forget the human equation, which is the most important one of all. Cognitive man does not live by the bread of science alone. The purpose of knowledge is to facilitate adaptive behavior. Listening to a symphony, enjoying a poem, or studying a painting may give a scientist as sudden a flash of insight as reading a scientific report that bears directly on his field of inquiry. Information science is, or should be, involved with the whole concept of knowledge in whatever form its manifestations may take.

In my introduction I mentioned that our meeting this morning was, for me at least, a kind of happy reunion, and so I have sought to celebrate it with a bit of poetic insanity, but this is all right, because madness is no stranger to this organization. I have entitled this epic *Consule Watsoni*, the days of the consulship of Watson Davis, that distinguished early leader of this organization who was recognized, even by those who often disagreed with him, as a man of stature.

### Consule Watsoni

In Watson's day, when life was slow,
We dwelt in peace in Dewey's glow
Before Doc. Inc. was ever built,
Or Peek-a-Boo, sans sense of guilt,
Was added to the scholar's woe.
Then, low-reduction ratio
In microfilm was all the go,
Or filing cards that would not wilt.
In Watson's day.
We had no I.S. then, you know;
Still hidden lay *that* unknown foe.
No Xerox spewed, no ink was spilt,
No poet got upon his stilt,
To write these Frenchified rondeaux,
In Watson's day.

All that is in the past now, and I have had my sport with the futurologists for some of their absurdities, but the fact still remains that we *must* look to the future. The Red Queen, you will remember, in *Through the Looking-Glass*, told Alice that it was a great advantage to have a memory that worked both ways, but Alice said she was afraid that her memory didn't work in that fashion. She said she couldn't remember things before they happened, to which the Red Queen observed, "It must be a very poor memory that works only backward." It has been popular to call the library the "memory" of society, but it, too, must be a memory that works both ways if we are to meet our social responsibilities as we should.

John Milton, you will recall, wrote *Lycidas* as a memorial to a friend who had died by drowning, and after he had eulogized his friend at the beginning of his poem he launched into a rather savage attack upon the British clergy, which at that time had sunk to a low state of moral decay. He likened these clerics to hypothetical shepherds presiding over their emaciated flocks—not shepherds with crooks, but shepherds *and* crooks. Thus, of the flocks that were the parishioners, Milton said, "The hungry sheep look up and are not fed." This metaphor, in language not entirely symbolic, but to be taken with a certain degree of literalness, may be applied to the position of society today with respect to the unfulfilled promise of information science. The hungry sheep look up and are, indeed, not fed; and there comes echoing back to us that old familiar refrain, "God have mercy on such as we, baa! baa! baa!"

## FOOTNOTES

[1] He has reported this theme in his recently published *Pieces of the Action* (New York: Morrow, 1970).

[2] Subsequent to the presentation of this address Scott Adams pointed out to us that the Russians have already made information science subordinate to social science. He has provided us with the following quotation: "Information science is a discipline belonging to Social Science, which studies the structure and general characteristics of scientific information, and also general laws governing all scientific communication processes." Council for Mutual Economic Assistance, *Information on the Activities of the Bodies of the Council for Mutual Economic Assistance in the Field of Scientific and Technical Information during the First Part of 1970.* Prepared for the Fifth Session of the Central Committee to Study the Feasibility of a World Scientific Information System, convened by UNESCO-ICSU, 30 September–1 October, 1970 (Moscow, September 1970), p. 7.

[3] We have taken some liberty with the translation; the original German is "Es gibt *keine* Wissenschaft, die *als Wissenschaft* des Menschen sagt, was er

wollen oder tun soll." Henrich Rickert, *Die Grenzen der naturwissenschaftlichen Begriffsbildung* (Tuebingen: Mohr, 1929), p. 708.

## BIBLIOGRAPHY

Berrier, F. K. *General and Social Systems.* New Brunswick, N.J.: Rutgers University Press, 1968, p. 28.

Carey, James W., and John J. Quirk. "The Mythos of the Electronic Revolution." *American Scholar*, XXXIX (Spring 1970), 219-20.

# V.

# The Academic Library

# 21

# Handmaidens of
the Learned World

"There is too much cheap help in the library." This, according to
Dr. Works,[1] constitutes one of the major criticisms brought against the libraries
of educational institutions by others in the learned world; and, though ardent
librarians will differ markedly in their conceptions of the extensiveness of such a
condition, the statement is at least significant. That we, as members of the
library profession, are stamped with the stigma of mediocrity there can be no
doubt, and it is useless to blink the fact that the outstanding students among the
graduates of colleges and universities are not entering the library field. Truly
may it be said of the candidates for degrees in our schools of library service,
"These are not the salt of the scholastic earth." Adequate statistical data in
substantiation of this have not been forthcoming, though Dr. Works' admirable
chapter on "The Status of the Professional Staff"[2] has paved the way. But in the
final evaluation the problem is not one to be interpreted in terms of
mathematical analysis, for the quantities involved are not to be measured on
such a basis. It remains for only a single comparison to make the situation clear.

One has but to contrast the *Bulletin* of our own American Library
Association, essentially trivial in content and superficial in treatment as it is,
with the publications of other learned societies. One has but to mention the
publications of the Modern Language Association, the American Sociological
Society, the American Chemical Society, and the American Statistical Association, not to exclude a host of others equally important—all accepted by the
academic world for the soundness and scholarliness of their content—to show
how utterly and completely we have failed. Nor is it the intention to throw the
major share of the responsibility for this upon the ALA *Bulletin*, for it is only

one symptom of many. The American Library Association, boasting a membership of 12,000, a total far surpassing that of most other learned societies, issues a publication list of some 250 titles, ranging from sizable volumes to pamphlets and broadsides. Yet of all this voluminous mass of print it is possible to count on the fingers of one hand those volumes that will stand as authoritative contributions to the literature of their field; and probably only one, Mudge's *Guide to Reference Books*, is of definitive and permanent value.

For some it may seem a far cry from the "wee slip of a girl" handing out books at the circulation desk at the beck and call of the scholars of the world, to the inadequacy of the publications issued by the ALA. But throughout the various ramifications intervening between these two extremes, there runs the thread of causality; and though one cannot be said to be the direct outgrowth of the other, the relation between the two is reciprocal, mutually productive, and interdependent—like Kipling's law of the jungle, the cause "runneth forward and back."

The question of the cause of this situation, then, naturally presents itself. Nor is the answer to be sought in the curricula of the professional library schools. That the students emerge from these institutions with technical training that is generally satisfactory is beyond dispute. But something that transcends technical skill is necessary if librarians are to be more than automatons trained to "fetch and carry." The problem is one of personnel. A John Cotton Dana and an Isadore Gilbert Mudge were born, not made; and the inability of mere technical training to create the mythical silk purse from lowly porcine origins is as true here as everywhere else. Yet, though the names of Dana and Mudge loom large on the library horizon, they are not unique among mankind, for others such as they are being and will be produced. The problem that squarely confronts us all is to induce a goodly proportion of them to enter the library field.

The obvious solution that presents itself is, of course, increased monetary reward. Though this is of major importance as a remedial factor, it is by no means a panacea. For, as its absence was not the sole cause of the present situation, so its presence cannot be the entire remedy. One must not forget that each graduation day sends forth a generous quota of superior young men and women into other types of academic life which, when compared with the lot of the librarian, do not yield a pecuniary return commensurate with the additional expenditures of apprenticeship and preparation involved.

Nor should the masculine-minded seek the explanation in the predominance of the opposite sex. The current issue of *P.M.L.A.*[3] lying upon the writer's desk at the moment contains a liberal sprinkling of women authors. Nor is the writer likely soon to forget that the name of the outstanding scholar among his colleagues in graduate school was Dorothy; and as final proof there appears once more the monumental *Guide to Reference Books*. This is not the place to argue in defence of the overt truth of the intellectual equality of the sexes; to do so would be supererogation.

The true solution is much less obvious than either of these, and, though in essence it is simple, in actual practice in its constructive aspects it is much nearer the other extreme. For a solution, then, one must return to the critique of the second paragraph of the above, for it is only through adequate intellectual stimulus, and through opportunity to express the results of that stimulus, that one can hope to attract to librarianship the talent that it so sorely needs.

Granting the important and essential place of detail in the library scheme, clerical minutiae must be subordinated to larger ends if the library profession is to survive. The opportunity for individual expression in research must receive more, much more, than mere casual encouragement. The media for all this are not far to seek, and the problems—technical, administrative, bibliographical, all insufficiently cultivated—exist in abundance. What is needed is the development of a constructive program under the auspices of the American Library Association that not only points out, to its members, the need for this research, but that offers the opportunity for its tangible expression through publication in authoritative professional channels. No library service can possibly be better than its personnel. But the personnel of a library staff will not draw unto itself the talent that is so essential as long as the publishing board of its national professional association directs its efforts toward issuing ephemeral trivialities designed solely to increase the annual circulation figures of the libraries concerned.

The obvious reply, of course, will be that the new *Library Quarterly*, as announced by the University of Chicago, will fill this need. One hopes that this is true, and gladly admits that the outlook is encouraging. But, successful as it may be in filling this need, the significant fact still remains that the project had to be undertaken by an agency totally removed from the American Library Association, to which the real obligation belonged; and further, that the way had to be shown by an institution that, though it does more than any other single organization to raise bibliographical standards, for some unaccountable reason is still without the hallowed pale of accredited library schools.

Finally, the problem is not one to be dismissed lightly as concerning only those in charge of the publication policies of the ALA. Had librarians pushed their needs more enthusiastically they would doubtless have found acceptance at the hands of those in authority. In no truly democratic organization can there be a shifting of responsibility to the administration: the failures and shortcomings rest squarely upon the shoulders of the individual members. If librarians cry for academic recognition, they must do something to merit it. These are problems well worth pondering by all who would have the librarian be something more than a handmaiden in the learned world.

## FOOTNOTES

[1] George A. Works, *College and University Library Problems* (Chicago: American Library Association, 1927), p. 84.

[2] *Ibid.*, pp. 80-98.

[3] *Publications of the Modern Language Association.*

# 22

# The College Library of the Future

Faust: *Wohin der Weg?*
Mephistopheles: *Kein Weg! Ins Unbetretene.*

Ever since the fitful winds first made sport of the prophetic leaves of Cumae and Delphi, inquisitive man has endeavored to reconstruct the sibylline messages that they bore. In this human eagerness to project one's vision into the future, librarians have had their share. But apart from the sheer pleasure derived from speculation of this sort, such forecasts may be of real value in focusing attention upon the library as a product of contemporary social and economic forces, in aiding in the reevaluation of current library practices, in helping to project the library and its functions upon the background of the particular community it serves. In short, these mental forays into the future can render a major service in the complete reanalysis of the position of the library in relation to its own unique *Weltanschauung.* Obviously, such generalizations as these would hold for any type of library in any given environment, but attention in the present series has been limited to the small and middle-size college, so that it is with these that this discussion will be ideal.

Nor is the place of the small college an insignificant one in the educational *mise en scène,* for it is more than likely that the future will witness a marked continuation of the revolt against bigness as a virtue in itself, with a resultant elevation of the college to a new level of scholastic importance. As the child admires the greater bulk of the adult as a mark of superiority, so our nation in its infancy sought to find inherent virtue in physical growth—a spirit that has been so delightfully epitomized in Dr. Lounsbury's epigram, "An easterner who

Address before the College and University Section of the American Library Association, Midwinter meeting, Chicago, Illinois, December 1935. Originally published in the *ALA Bulletin,* Vol. 30 (June 1936), pp. 495-501.

hasn't sufficient money to found a college goes west and establishes a university." But already the American megalopolis has reached the point of rapidly diminishing returns: industry is discovering the values of decentralization; Big Business itself is beginning to fall from the sheer weight of its own intricate bulk; and it is reasonable to suppose that educators, too, will soon realize that many of their functions, especially as related to undergraduate life, can best be carried out in smaller units. Thus the college will be recognized, not as a diminutive counterpart of the large university, but as a valid unit in the educational scheme, working to carry out its own peculiar functions.

This rising importance of the smaller colleges will have significant and far-reaching repercussions upon their libraries, and these same libraries have had placed within their grasp in recent years one scientific development that can help tremendously to speed this very trend. In the past, despite the major advantage of the smaller, more efficient unit, the great handicap to the college has been a poverty of source material in its library collections; but it is in the newly developed photo-technical processes that the answer to this dilemma is to be found. For as the gift of Gutenberg brought many books within the reach of many men, so any book may come to any library through the medium of the microphotograph. In the fields of the physical sciences the smaller colleges may still suffer from a paucity of laboratory resources, but in the humanities, at least, the college can compete on even terms with its larger colleagues. In this one element alone the library can do much toward the elevation of the college to a position of new and greater importance in the academic world.

If this rise in significance of the college be accepted as a rather certain development of the future, its implications for the library logically fall into two major categories—that is, *technical* and *philosophical*—in turn united and correlated by a third which, for want of more accurate nomenclature, shall be denominated *investigatory*. By this is meant those surveys and classificatory standards through which the library attempts to measure the intangible elements of the world it serves, elements that may dictate changes in library policy or indicate effectiveness of results. Janus-like, the *investigatory* looks toward both the *technical* and *philosophical*, so that schematically this tripartite division might be presented as in Fig. 1:

**FIG. 1.**

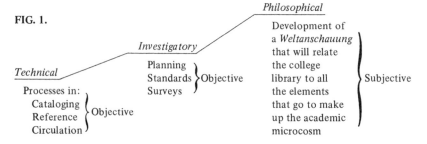

The technical division needs but brief consideration, not because it is lacking in significance, for it certainly is not, but rather because it has reached a high point of development and has already received more than its share of attention in training for library service. With the exception of the above-emphasized photographic processes, it seems unlikely that the immediate future will produce any marked developments in the mechanics of library service. Little fault can be found with the trained librarian as a technician; he is thoroughly familiar with the materials at his command, and he knows how to use them. This is not meant to imply that technical perfection has been attained—far from it. Our classification systems, for example, as Dr. Bliss has so ably shown, leave much to be desired, and we can ill afford the maintenance of an ostrich-like complacency in regard to their improvement. But by and large the profession as a whole is reasonably proficient technically; the future should produce, not so much improvements in the bibliographical processes themselves, but rather an extension of these perfected processes into that vast number of college libraries whose technical equipment, despite modern advances, is still lamentably inferior to the best contemporary practice. Though we may permit the profession in general a reasonable degree of pride in their bibliographical achievements, the colleges cannot be permitted to be complacent when such a large percentage of their number is content with antiquated methods. Nor can college libraries render distinctive service to their respective communities when college administrators regard them as reservoirs for the genteel disposition of widows and orphans, and the librarianship itself as a suitable reward for some obsolete pedagogical wheel-horse no longer sufficiently alert for classroom duty.

## CRITERIA OF MEASUREMENT

Turning to the *investigatory*, the librarian finds himself on much less familiar ground. True, as early as 1919, Dr. Bishop, in an address before the Ohio College Association,[1] was lamenting the inadequacy of the average college library and setting forth in rather sketchy form measures for improvement. But as is so often the case when educators talk about the improvement of professional standards, the emphasis is almost entirely upon physical plant. Similarly, the criteria formulated by the Committee on Standards of the American Council on Education, and adopted by a number of voluntary and regional cooperative educational associations, are confined almost exclusively to the size of the book collections and the physical condition of the library building itself.

Important as these criteria may be, they, of course, fail to tell the whole story, and in addition suffer greatly from being couched in the vaguest of terms. Little wonder that Robertson in his "The College Library"[2] paints a rather sorry picture of library conditions in our smaller educational institutions. Dr. Works' important study,[3] while it erected no specific standards itself, merits inclusion for its valuable contribution in directing attention to hitherto neglected aspects of college library service and the need for their more accurate measurement.

Further progress was recorded by the Advisory Group on College Libraries of the Carnegie Corporation, in its three-year survey resulting in the erection of five criteria: buildings, staff, book collection, classification and cataloging, and the training in the use of the library.[4] This represents progress, in that at least an acknowledgment is made of the importance of training in library use, yet even here, from the social point of view, the vision of this group was still emphatically myopic. By far the most significant work that has yet been done is that of Dr. Waples' report for the North Central Association of Colleges and Secondary Schools.[5] The seven criteria here set forth represent the first thorough attempt to describe accurately the basic needs of the college library. Very wisely the committee has placed emphasis upon the qualitative rather than the quantitative standpoint. Instead of being merely concerned with the book collection as a unit numerically measured, there is real attempt to ascertain its value for educational purposes, and to determine to what extent a particular collection is used by students and faculty. One may search in vain through the seven criteria for any emphasis on plant *per se*. Obviously, the criteria deal with qualities that are much less tangible.

## DISTINCTLY A SOCIAL PHENOMENON

Librarians are rapidly beginning to realize that their work cannot be measured in terms of mere mechanics, but rather that the college library is a distinct social phenomenon, and that for the accurate measurement of its results an entirely new set of techniques must be developed. Admittedly this work is but a beginning, for only time can determine whether these criteria are valid in developing a systematic evaluation of the library's influence upon student reading. But at least it is a definite step in the right direction; should later experience prove some of the judgments invalid, they will still remain of service in encouraging additional investigation. Here, indeed, is the very groundwork for all future college library development—its significance is difficult to over-emphasize.

Closely allied to this trend is the increased emphasis on measuring student and faculty use of the library. Similar reader interest studies, like those of Waples, Tyler, and Carnovsky, of Chicago, applied to the college, should be of considerable value in indicating future lines of development, in regard to both building the book collection itself and administering library services. Here is virtually new soil whose fertility and potentialities have yet to be accurately ascertained.

## COOPERATIVE REGIONAL PLANNING

In the final analysis all of these investigatory trends lead to the ultimate goal of cooperative regional planning for college libraries, which will affect the entire field of college library practice. Small beginnings have already been made. These are primarily union lists of holdings, designed to help lift the excessive and rapidly growing burden of interlibrary loans from the shoulders of the larger universities, to make the smaller institutions more self reliant and mutually independent, and above all to lay the foundations for more highly developed cooperation and sympathetic understanding.

With this accomplished, it is not far to the next significant step—cooperative purchasing, which has many blessings for libraries with limited financial resources, especially as related to the acquisition of expensive foreign serials. Other forms of cooperation immediately suggest themselves, in cataloging and classification, reference, research, and perhaps even the interchange of staff members to the mutual advantage of all concerned. Regional groups of colleges would do well to unite in projects such as these, to appoint commissions for studying local conditions, and to suggest lines of approach and points of departure. Again, the all-important photo-technical processes enter the picture to lend their valuable aid in smoothing out difficulties and facilitating research. With so much of importance to be gained through cooperative planning of this sort, one cannot but be astonished at the human stupidity that permits our petty jealousies and rivalries to prevent us from attaining the rewards that cooperation can give. Let it be hoped that the future has much to offer in stimulating cooperative planning, and that it is a future that is not far distant.

## A PROFESSIONAL CREDO

Having seen that technologically librarianship has made significant progress, and that investigatory activities have already achieved impressive beginnings, we now turn our attention to a field of which the past can ill be proud. As Pierce Butler has shown, librarians have been singularly uninterested in the theoretical aspects of their profession.[6] Satisfied by a simple pragmatism, they are content with a rationalization of each immediate technical process, without any intellectual interest in attempting to generalize these rationalizations into a professional philosophy. From this indictment of the library profession as a whole the college librarian is not exempt. He has been as indifferent as the rest toward the development of any professional credo that might guide and direct his several processes, and give meaning to their results. J. Periam Danton has cut squarely to the heart of the matter when he asserts that:

> When the library profession becomes thoroughly conscious of precisely what it is trying to do and why it is doing it, we may hope to see a very significant change affecting not only libraries and librarians but also the society which they serve.

The bewildered groping which characterizes so much of our activity is largely the result of lack of a definite conception of our purposes.[7]

Φιλοσοφία Βιοῦ Κυβερνήτης! Lacking this guiding power of a valid philosophy, how, it may be asked, are the college librarians prepared to answer the host of questions that beset the academic world today? We boast of tolerance, but can we afford to be tolerant of intolerance? With academic freedom threatened on every hand, does the profession dare maintain a detached point of view? "There are times when silence is not neutrality but assent." In a day when a drugstore demagogue can command a legislative investigation into alleged "subversive activities" in one of our great institutions of learning, it is not absurd to fear that some power-crazed dictator of the future could repeat the holocaust of Alexandria.

Assuredly, there has been much glib talk among librarians concerning the ideals of the profession, its tolerance, its detachment, its objective point of view with regard to the problems that beset mankind—ideals which have seen their fullest realization in the building up of the respective book collections. College librarians cannot justly be accused of deficient idealism; in many ways they have exemplified the scholastic virtues of tolerance, objectivity, and breadth even more fully than their colleagues in the classroom. The fault lies in their failure to organize for the defense of these ideals in some future crucial hour. They would do well to remember William James' pragmatic judgment:

> The more ideals a man has, the more contemptible, on the whole, do you continue to deem him, if the matter ends there for him, and if none of the laboring man's virtues are called into action on his part—no courage shown, no privations undergone, no dirt or scars contracted in the attempt to get them realized. It is quite obvious that something more than the mere possession of ideals is required to make a life significant in any sense that claims the spectator's admiration.

## A UNITED FRONT

What bulwarks have college librarians erected against encroachment on academic freedom? They should form a united front with other professions for the protection of civil liberties. Plans for the future should include laying the foundation for close cooperation with groups such as the American Association of University Professors (committee A), and organizations with similar aims. If we fail in this, we face the future unprepared—

> ... the sin I impute to each frustrate
> ghost
> Is, the unlit lamp and the ungirt loin.

Here, indeed, is a problem that bids fair to rock the profession to its very foundation. Can the future, then, afford to concern itself solely with the trivia of charging system detail or the technical minutia of reserved book administration?

## TO CREATE SOCIAL CHANGE

Much has been written of late concerning the importance of economic and social changes in our society and their implications for the library profession. Well enough, librarians should adapt their practices to meet changing public needs. But the college librarian has an additional duty—that of himself affording the stimulus to *create* social change. If the library is to become the cortex of the academic body politic, librarians must not be content to follow—they must lead. There may be those who will stand aghast at the vision of the college library as an agent of "propaganda" for a new social order. Even the ancient specter of "indoctrination" may once more glide squeaking and gibbering through our cloistered world. But they who in the past have so prided themselves on their objectivity and detachment, what have they done to prevent the growth of those very forces that now threaten civil liberties and academic freedom?

> You of the virtue (we issue join)
> How strive you? *De te, fabula!*

There is nothing startling in such a view of the college library. If a paradox does exist it is only apparent, not real. The difficulty arises from the inability to realize that librarianship can never be innocent of social presuppositions, but must ever be the resultant of a people's conceptions of social welfare. We must realize that the real choice before us is between a college library program based on our traditional social philosophy of *laissez-faire* capitalism and individualism, and a program based upon a social philosophy whose central doctrines are formulated in terms of the needs of society as a whole. Obviously, any proposal to change the social philosophical basis of our educational system will be looked upon as an effort to indoctrinate youth, because the traditional philosophy is so thoroughly rooted in all our daily activities that it is imparted to college students as a matter of course. In either case, the educational system is based upon a social philosophy. The pertinent question is, which philosophy will guarantee to the academic world the maximum of liberty to pursue truth?

## REMAKING THE ACADEMIC WORLD

Librarians are wont to lament the passive role that they are compelled to play on the academic stage, and in many ways they have no one to blame for this but themselves. Yet the fault is not entirely theirs. It represents the logical result of an educational system that has very sadly lost its way. What is the function of education anyway? When we look at the sport pages of our daily press we begin to wonder! One could scarcely bring the charge of inefficiency against so competent a librarian as Dr. Keogh, but it must not be forgotten that the Yale Bowl and a top-heavy athletic program preceded by over a decade the Sterling Memorial Library and the dormitory book collections. Librarians have their faults, many of them, but in a mad academic world, blindly seeking distinction through athletic glory, led by fascist-minded administrators who have completely forgotten the meaning of education, there seems to be little hope for any very important role for the librarian. This is not said, however, to excuse the librarian for his inactivity—for his manifest indifference toward his social obligations to the community he serves. Again, the charge that I would bring against the librarian is that by united action he has not fought to overcome these menacing trends. If his condition is to be greatly improved, we must begin by completely remaking the academic world.

These are problems rife with implications, pregnant with meaning, for the future of the college library. Today we can ill afford to stand mutely behind our circulation desks, calmly handing out reserved books at the beck and call of an endless stream of students, blandly reaffirming our convictions of our own "academic detachment." We may be rudely awakened some morning with the realization that we are the hapless and unwilling guardians of the propaganda of a fascist *régime*.[8] Here, then, is the challenge that the future flings to the college librarians of today: that they make the fullest use of technical advances placed within their hands; that they unite themselves more firmly in cooperative undertakings; that they study more intensively and learn to measure more accurately the results of their work; that they band themselves together to preserve their rightful heritage of academic freedom against the ever-growing forces that menace it so severely; and that to achieve greater unanimity of action they formulate an adequate philosophy of their profession that will integrate their activities with the academic microcosm, giving direction to their efforts. And having done these things, be not content with the achievement thereof, but in this age of social *Sturm und Drang* be ever watchful to keep an eye to the future—an ear to the ground.

## FOOTNOTES

[1] W. W. Bishop, "Our College and University Libraries, A Survey and A Program," *School and Society*, Vol. 13 (September 18, 1920), 205-14.

[2] D. A. Robertson, "The College Library," *Educational Record*, Vol. 10 (January 1929), 3-28.

[3] G. A. Works, *College and University Library Problems* (Chicago: American Library Association, 1927).

[4] Carnegie Corporation, Advisory Group on College Libraries, *College Library Standards* (New York: Carnegie Corporation, 1932).

[5] North Central Association, *Quarterly*, Vol. 9 (October 1934), 207-10.

[6] Pierce Butler, *An Introduction to Library Science* (Chicago: University of Chicago Press, 1933).

[7] J. Periam Danton, "A Plea for a Philosophy of Librarianship," *Library Quarterly*, Vol. 4 (October 1934), 545.

[8] For a striking example of the effects that losses in freedom under a fascist *régime* have upon libraries, *see* W. Munthe, "The Annual Meeting of the German Librarians in Tubingen," *Library Journal*, Vol. 60 (September 15, 1935), 711.

# 23

# College Librarianship and Educational Reform

*I admit that the aims, methods, and subject matter of American education are so ill defined that anybody might think that he could do better with it. Still one shudders to note that every citizen entertains the conviction that he is an educational expert of the most significant variety.*   —Robert Maynard Hutchins

It was grizzly-headed dyspeptic Thomas Carlyle, was it not, who was the authority for the assertion that a "true university is a collection of books"? Mark you well, this austere Scot did not add: a collection of books administered by a trained librarian. But even the most sanguine librarian knows that Carlyle's definition is incomplete. Hence has arisen that hydra-headed problem of integrating the library's functions with the other activities of the college—a problem that has sought solution again and again, only to energe indissoluble as ever. Why, then, have we failed so completely to achieve an adequate synthesis between the library and the academic world? There is nothing intricate, elusive, or involved in that quadrilateral relationship between librarian, faculty, students, and administration. Their lines of approach to common problems must ultimately converge, their respective goals must eventually be identical. Hence they should never work at cross purposes—but they all too frequently do! We rejoice in the library as the heart of the university, but are compelled to admit that all too often its beat is not synchronized with the academic pulse.

A brief retrospective glance may be clarifying. We have seen the college library begin as a mere adjunct to the classroom, a position slightly analogous to the laboratory of today, administered by a part-time professor or retired member

Address before the College and University Section of the American Library Association, Midwinter meeting, Chicago, Illinois, December 1936. Originally published in the *ALA Bulletin*, Vol. 31 (March 1937), pp. 141-46.

of the faculty. Emerging from this chrysalidic stage, the library achieved maturity with the coming of the professional librarian and his trained staff. Expansion followed expansion; exhibition cases lined the corridors; the reserved book department was inaugurated; college students became incunabula conscious; graduate reading lists appeared; courses in the use of the library were added to the curriculum; readers' advisers helped the student to orient himself in the complicated world of books.

Then someone, now happily forgotten, envisaged a stalwart college youth sprawled in a luxurious arm chair, a volume of *Elia* propped upon his heaving, numeral-encrusted breast, avidly absorbing the wisdom of the ages, and the browsing room was born—the browsing room replete with all its paraphernalia of pseudo-bibliophilism, the overstuffed furniture, the paneled book cases, the blazing fireplace, not to mention, of course, the Sunday afternoon lectures on the lure of books, by members of the English department. No one stopped to consider that college students had not the slightest idea how to browse, that browsing as an art in itself is the child of a well-spent leisure, that there can be no leisure in the mad hurly-burly that is college life today. Rather, the typically American procedure was followed in the belief that the mere presence of the physical attributes would somehow instill the spirit that gives life.

All this was, of course, expensive, so there came into being the "Friends of the Library" movement—friends whose friendship could be interpreted in terms of "checks and balances." Thus the library reflected the feverish activity and diffuse expansion that characterized all academic life.

Scant concern was manifest over the results obtained, and few techniques were developed for their accurate measurement. No one ever completely answered Guy Lyle's question as to whether these were merely "costly fads." Wishful thinking was galvanized into incessant activity until ingenuity began to exhaust itself and librarians found themselves confronted by professional stalemate.

Relief was sought in speculation as to the future of college librarianship. We began to seek underlying basic principles only to discover that we had no guiding professional philosophy. So busy had we been with the decoration of our bibliographical wagon that we had forgotten that we had no star to which it could be hitched. Efforts to supply one have failed—failed, as we said at the beginning, because of our inability to correlate the functions of the library with the objectives of the college in its entirety. But what are the objectives of the college? We get only confused answers in reply. We will agree with Randall and Goodrich that "the functions of the library will depend directly upon the aims of the institution which it serves," and that "these aims must be the beginning of any consideration of the library itself." But what are the aims of education "at the college level"?

Seven years ago, in the pages of the *New Republic*, a recent college graduate was finding comfort in the fact that the "race between education and catastrophe is being run by tortises, and not by jack rabbits; education may still save civilization." Today the velocity of catastrophe has been accelerated to an unbelievable degree, while education lags far behind. It is not idle inquisitiveness, then, that prompts the librarian to speculate as to the goal of our collegiate system; upon it depends the whole future of educational librarianship.

## "ILLITERATES WITH A DEGREE"

E. C. Kyte of Queens University, Kingston, Ontario, has recently told a group of Eastern librarians that students emerge from college "illiterate, having no acquaintance with letters, but illiterate with a degree," and that though the university has given them its mark of approval, librarians know that mark "to be a lie."

These are indeed stern and uncompromising words, but the fact remains that the outstanding characteristic of our higher educational system is the universal lack of enthusiasm for it on the part of both students and faculty. Yet, students are entering college in ever-increasing numbers, not because of parental duress, and certainly not because they believe it particularly advantageous economically (the depression with its hosts of unemployed college graduates ended all that), but because the supposed necessity for a college education has so completely and ineradicably fused itself into our social *mores*. So the baccalaureate degree becomes a mere shibboleth in our schizophrenic societal ideology. Not for the love of learning or intellectual adventure, but from fear of social conspicuousness does the undergraduate consent to swallow the academic pill, provided that it be small and sufficiently sugar coated. But despite its infinitesimal size and saccharine exterior a surprisingly large number gag at its administration or disgorge it completely.

## TRUSTEES SCORED

If, then, higher education be the colossal and expensive disappointment that it is, what are the elements that make it so? They are, indeed, legion. Because of ever increasing enrollment, classes are growing larger and larger; thus more and more instructors are forced to retreat to the lecture method with consequent destruction of the vital personal relation between student and teacher. The pathological emphasis is on grades with its unlimited abuses, hand-shaking, course-picking, and plain dishonesty. The result in most colleges is loss of the liberal tradition and the substitution of more and more subjects to the course of study until the "course" itself became the core of the curriculum. The perennial examinations have ceased to be periods of intellectual inventory and have degenerated to mere exhibitions of mental gymnastics; stripped of any appeal as challenges to growth and development, they are feared by students and dreaded by the teaching staff. Higher education itself is lost as to whether its true aim is the instruction of the young or the promotion of furibund research—research sanctified as "pushing back the frontiers of knowledge." Permeating the system is the influence of the university corporation or governing board of trustees, that nondescript agglomeration of big business men, lawyers, prelates, and politicians, obsessed with money, destitute of any qualification for the offices they hold. Until the weight of their stultifying influence is lifted, there can be small hope for marked educational advance. Above all rises the eternal hubbub from the alumni, its importance inversely proportionate to its volume, concerning itself with everything about the educational system except what really matters.

What are the results on the student body? Intellectual curiosity and enthusiasm are almost negligible. Reading is confined to textbook assignments and many boast of doing little of that. Campus conversation is replete with sex, sports, dates, and small talk, the more ungrammatically expressed the better. Serious magazines are ignored while the *Saturday Evening Post*, *Popular Mechanics*, *College Humor*, and the "wood pulps" are worn to shreds. Any attempts at serious discussion quickly degenerate into puerile exhibitions of ignorance, sophistry, credulity, and prejudice. Extracurricular activities with any real educational value—honors work, forensics, music, dramatics, college publications—interest only a limited few.

## AN ASTOUNDING PRONOUNCEMENT

Bad as are the results of the present system on the student body, the influence on the instructional staff may be even worse. Advanced degrees are sought and "research" engaged in, not because of any sincere intellectual drive but for the opportunities they offer for promotion. Young instructors emerge from graduate school without the slightest preparation for that profession which they are to practice. At its best this faculty gives us the occasional great teacher, a Bliss Perry or a "Billy" Sumner. As its too frequent worst we get such an astounding pronouncement as those unctuous words of Nicholas Murray Butler: "An educated proletariat is a constant source of disturbance and danger to any nation."

In this mad, chaotic academic world that we have pictured it is most pertinent to ask: "What price librarianship, now?" The assumption that the not far distant future will produce a complete revolution in American higher education seems not unjustified. By this is not meant the continuous process of half-hearted tinkering with the system that is going on about us. American education must be razed to the ground and built anew, built anew upon a solid philosophy, a philosophy which sees clearly the true objectives of education and follows them relentlessly.

Many questions, however, must be answered first. If we assume that education can have a liberal purpose, and that the college can be a fountainhead of ideas; if we say tentatively that the college exists for the purpose of acquainting young men and women with functional knowledge and the methods by which such knowledge is created and criticized, is this knowledge to be general or esoteric? Is the curriculum to be adjusted to the many or the few? Are we all capable of education in terms of ideas? Finally, if the ideal curriculum is found, what of the issue between freedom and compulsion? We have heard much about the evils of compulsion and the virtues of academic freedom. Can we ask students to accept unquestioningly an educational process that the philosophers think best for them?

The answers to these questions will dictate the future form of the new learning. Hope that they can be answered springs from those sporadic radical experiments in reorganization that are being developed at such centers as Wisconsin, Yale, and Chicago. What sort of new academic phoenix will arise from the ashes of the old order is yet far from certain, but whether it be the experimental college of Meiklejohn or the general education and higher learning of Hutchins, one thing seems clear: there will be a greater and greater emphasis upon the use of books. Are librarians equipped to assume those added responsibilities? Are they capable of meeting the challenge that the future of education flings to them? I submit the obvious fact that they are not!

## A GLORIFIED ARTISANSHIP

We have, I believe, reached the point in our analysis where it is time to confess that the practice of librarianship which we have been endeavoring to dignify by the name of science is at best little more than a glorified form of artisanship. Only pseudo-professional in its approach, it is degenerating into a form of master craftsmanship that, given the rules of the game, almost any individual of reasonable intelligence and aptitude for bibliographical mechanics can adequately perform. We have yet to establish conclusive proof that the rules of the library trade can any better be learned in the classroom than in actual practice; this we tacitly admit when, for one reason or another, we accept years of experience in lieu of professional training in librarianship. We are seeing the library school submerged in wave after wave of vocationalism, a vocationalism not only bad for the library schools but bad for the profession as a whole. Every true profession requires for its continuous development the existence of centers of creative thought; the extent to which library training schools abandon creative thought and degenerate into trade schools determines the extent to which librarianship itself must degenerate into a trade.

But what are the creative aspects of librarianship and the intellectual content of its discipline? Are they to be found in the minute descriptive bibliography of a Wilberforce Eames or an A. W. Pollard, in Lester Condit's microscopic examination and measurements of type specimens from the pages of incunabula? Or will we find them in the newer concept of scholarship which concerns itself with the social implications of the library? Or are they to be found at all?

## EXPERIMENTATION ONLY ANSWER

Only experimentation can answer this agnosticism—experimentation that may have to begin with the complete demolition of our present library schools, at least so far as training for college and university librarianship is concerned. For these schools have been breeders of mediocrity even as have the colleges and universities to which they, like barnacles, have been attached.

In the beginning there must be a complete divorce between training for public librarians and that for library workers in the educational fields. Their approach, their content, their *materia bibliographica*, are so unrelated that any attempt to combine the two must end in chaos—they have little in common but the books they handle and the pen and ink they use. This must in turn be followed by further breaking down of training for college librarianship into subject-matter fields. It is well and good that college librarians be required to make extensive study of college administration and general educational methods in their present state of flux. Surely every college librarian should keep at his elbow for constant reference Hutchins' slender but pregnant volume on *The Higher Learning in America* and read it religiously once a week. But this does not go far enough. We must recognize that the minutiae that are our present library techniques are but means to a higher end, a mere skeleton that must ever be subordinate to subject specialization. As new forces in education grow and expand, it may very well become as absurd to think of the librarian administering to all branches of the university as it now is to suggest that one professor teach all subjects. We must have library specialists in botany, chemistry, sociology and all the other major fields of learning. One example will suffice. When Yale University sought for a keeper of its rare books, did it go to an accredited library school, spread its desiderata before them and ask, "What have you?" It did not. Rather it went to its own faculty and chose one who probably knows very little about library techniques but a great deal about the scholarly approach to bibliography. In short, it chose that eminent Boswellian, Chauncey Brewster Tinker, and no one can condemn the choice. This is the direction that librarianship must take under the impetus of the new movements in educational reform. Library schools as we know them today, then, should disappear, but library training will recrudesce as departments of library science within the main subject divisions of the university.

Finally, college and university librarians in their professional associations should unite unequivocally with those courageous and advanced leaders in the educational field, and work with unmitigated zeal for a revitalized spirit in higher education. This is no invitation to an easy and pleasant task. It will require forthright and venturesome leadership, which, unfortunately, the profession does not now seem to possess. It will mean challenging intellectual dishonesty and sham in high places even when those high places control our purse strings. Worst of all there can be no guarantee of success. We do not know how close to the brink of catastrophe our civilization stands. In our fumbling efforts we may help only to push it over. But should we, by uniting our efforts with those of our progressive colleagues, help to salvage education the reward would be very great indeed.

This, then, is the choice that lies before us. We can either continue to tinker with and polish our well-learned techniques as we have been doing for so long or, with no assurance of success, we can demolish the old defunct system and build anew. Consciously, by deliberate action, or unconsciously, by continuing to drift as we have been drifting, we are going to make that choice. There is little doubt as to which we shall choose. But so long have we been mistaking shadows for realities that one cannot suppress the wish that we might, like the prisoners of the Platonic cave myth, cast off the shackles of our indecision—and face the light.

# 24

# The Changing Role of the College Library— A Reappraisal

Thomas Carlyle's now famous characterization of "a true university" as "a collection of books," may have been the result of a kippered herring for breakfast or the product of ill-considered thought, but whether its origins were gastronomic or cerebral, there can be little doubt that it has warped the philosophy of the academic librarians for generations. Librarians, especially academic librarians, are by tradition a modest, not to say a timid, breed, and they fastened upon this epigram of the dyspeptic Scot with all the eagerness of desperation. With a few notable exceptions, whose names scarcely need to be cataloged here, the typical college librarian of the 19th century in America was an "academic cast-off," and the library was an Elysian field in which a deserving and faithful pedagogue could be "put out to graze." In an atmosphere so impregnated with the spirit of inferiority, it is not surprising that the librarians cherished these words of hope with even greater avidity than they husbanded the books of which they were the "keepers."

The history of the professional rise of the college librarian is a narrative of a long struggle for academic respectability. Certainly no one will begrudge him the laurels that he has so laboriously won, but it is regrettable that, in this process, the true objectives of the college library and its relation to the community of which it is an important part have been so badly misinterpreted. The true relation of the college library to the educational institution it serves is the subject of our exploration today.

From the earliest times, the library has been closely identified with its

Address before the annual conference of Eastern College Librarians, New York City, November 27, 1954. Originally published in *Library-Instructional Integration on the College Level* (Chicago: Association of College and Reference Libraries, American Library Association, April 1955). *A.C.R.L. Monographs*, No. 13, pp. 6-13.

coeval scholarship. The custodians of the clay tablets in the valley of the Tigris and Euphrates, the librarians of the great Alexandriana at the mouth of the Nile, the monks in the monastic libraries and the cathedral schools of the Middle Ages, all were men of learning who held their offices in some cultures even by hereditary succession, but always by the inherent right of their proved ability to use the records entrusted to them in the advancement of human knowledge. Why, then, did the college librarians of 19th-century America fall from so exalted a position?

To this question no one really knows the answer, but I suspect that it was the result of a complex of forces. In part it was probably precipitated by the proliferation of print that began in the early decades of the 1880s. This flood of material tended to make of the librarians mere "book handlers," and in its mediocrities the librarians lost caste. But perhaps even more important in this decline was the fact that during this period education itself sadly lost its way. Confronted by a rising spirit of seemingly limitless optimism, and a growing belief that an education was the right of every citizen in a democracy, the educators of Horace Mann's generation, and those who followed him, inherited a classical concept of education that had its origins in a slave-master society—a society in which physical labor was the responsibility of the workers, and philosophical speculation was the prerogative of an aristocratic leisure class.

This concept of education was, almost without alteration, imposed upon a democracy which, in itself, was based on quite a different form of social organization. Such an attempt to prepare an entire national population for active participation in the control of its political system was an educational revolution that was surpassed only by the organizational changes in society itself—changes that democracy had created. The librarians shared in the ensuing confusion over educational ideas and ideals, and this confusion has not yet been clarified by any means. Following the leadership of the educators, the librarians, too, went astray. In the resulting turmoil, the library soon came to be regarded as little more than an extensive reserved-book collection, and the librarian as only a caretaker in a "storehouse" of books.

To say that a true university is a collection of books has no more validity than to say that a school is "Mark Hopkins on one end of a log." Both assertions contain elements of truth, but both, also, are serious oversimplifications. A university, and even a small college, is a complex unity of many elements: the faculty, the student body, the physical plant (classrooms, libraries, laboratories, residence halls), yes, even the alumni, the administration, and the janitors. But more important still, it is a center of exciting intellectual activity, where conflicting ideas, beliefs, and assumptions can find complete expression and can compete on a basis of equality for acceptance and survival. But from Carlyle's aphorism it was a simple and logical transition to the proposition that, if a university is a collection of books, then the librarian must be a teacher, and the prestige-hungry librarians were quite ready and eager to reach the conclusion from the premise. But the premise was a half-truth, and therefore the conclusion could not be anything more.

A librarian, though admittedly a part, and a very important part, of the total educational system, is not a teacher—at least, he is not a teacher within the formal definition of the term. When he acts as a librarian, he does not meet classes, he is responsible for no segment of the formal curriculum, and he can exercise no control over the intellectual progress (or lack of it) that the students may experience. As a librarian, he cannot compel attendance at classes, impose penalties for incomplete work, or assign grades as symbols of accomplishment.

Of course, there are many instances in which librarians do actually serve as members of the faculty and do meet certain classes within the curriculum; but in those cases they are not acting as librarians, they are acting as teachers. It is a case of a single individual cast in two separate roles, just as distinct as that of the teacher who leaves his office at five in the afternoon and, upon arriving at home, steps into the role of parent. This does not imply that the position of the librarian is of either greater or lesser stature than that of the teacher; it is merely different. And it is so different that the attempt to force the one into the pattern of the other has actually worked to the disadvantage of the librarian.

What, then, is the function of the academic librarian? To answer this, one must first inquire into the function of the library itself. I believe that one cannot improve upon the definition of a library as a social instrument, or agency, created to maximize the social utility of graphic records. Utilization is, of course, impossible without the availability, or retrievability, of any document or record, for any given purpose, at any time. Once one accepts the implications of such a statement of purpose, the objectives of the academic librarian *vis-à-vis* his constituency fall quickly into line.

Now availability, in its larger aspects, is bidimensional. It includes a) acquisition, and b) organization, and from these two attributes derive all library operations, at whatever level and for whatever purpose.

Acquisition is founded in subject knowledge. For this reason it has, in the college or university library, long been traditionally a responsibility of the faculty, on the assumption that the faculties of the several subject departments were the true bibliographic experts of their respective disciplines. Within the last decade, however, there has emerged an increasing conviction among librarians that the library itself must assume greater responsibility for the development of its collections. A recent informal survey of the book funds of some 38 college and university libraries in Ohio reveals that in no fewer than 11 institutions, no allocation of the book funds is made to faculty departments, but the entire amount is placed at the complete disposal of the librarian. Again, in 21 institutions, half or more of the funds were allocated to the librarian. Unfortunately, comparable figures are not available for an earlier period, but there can be little doubt that this is a rather drastic reversal of previous procedures.

In part, this is a manifestation of a trend that has been in evidence for at least half a century, for the history of college librarianship shows a steadily increasing concentration of administrative authority with the librarian and away from the library committee and the college administration. The decline in the authority, and even in the prestige, of the library committee is graphically presented in a study conducted at the Graduate Library School of the University of Chicago in 1950 by Elizabeth Kientzle of the John Crerar Library. This study of 103 midwestern colleges with libraries of more than 50,000 volumes each showed fairly conclusively that the value of the library committee was in direct proportion to the degree of its inactivity.[1]

The trend away from the library dependence upon the faculty, especially with respect to book selection policies and procedures, has been encouraged in part by the improved professional training of librarians themselves and the library schools' increasing emphasis on subject competence. But even more, perhaps, it is the almost inevitable result of increasing specialization among the faculty. For, with the growth of each subject area, in bulk and complexity, the individual professor must necessarily limit his competence to a smaller and smaller perimeter of specialization; as he does so, his value as the librarian's advisor on collection development is correspondingly diminished. Since the academic community is in a constant state of warfare against the forces of atomization and fragmentation, it is a major responsibility of librarians to provide one of the strong cohesive forces that will make the university the unit it should be. Admittedly this is "a large order," but it is one that cannot be neglected.

Academic librarians, therefore, cannot afford to leave the development of their acquisition programs to fortuitous circumstances or to shift the responsibility to less competent hands. As the rising flood of recorded information necessitates increasing selectivity, acquisition policies must be formulated that are the product of an awareness and understanding of the book requirements for scholarship and their relation to the potential supply of graphic records. This means that librarians in the future must not only be specialists in subject bibliography in the traditional sense, but they must also understand the uses to which recorded information is put by the student, by the teacher, and by the research worker at all levels of intensity and academic sophistication.

The librarian as bibliophile, as bookworm, as authority on watermarks, typography, and the history of the papyrus roll is a picturesque concept that will die hard, for it is deeply rooted in a nostalgic longing for a quaint and romantic past. But it must die, or at least be drastically restrained, if librarianship is to be saved from intellectual dilettantism. This transfer of responsibility for implementing the acquisition program and its formulation from faculty to library staff cannot succeed if librarians continue to insist that they are teachers, or if library schools insist on filling the heads of their students with a romantic "love of books." The profession is passing, albeit not without *Sturm und Drang*, from the attitudes of adolescent dilettantism to the maturity of a genuinely professional outlook from which its problems and materials are objectively and impersonally viewed.

Developments in the second half of our dichotomy, the organization of library materials for retrieval at any given time for any given purpose, are just as revolutionary and perhaps even more spectacular. Probably the most striking feature of our traditional methods in subject cataloging and classification is the widespread and growing lack of enthusiasm for them. As the subject categories of Dewey became foggier and foggier, as the UDC was revealed as being neither universal nor decimal, as the schematism of the Library of Congress proved less and less effective (however carefully it had been hammered out by Charles Martel), as we have discovered that all bibliographic classification is not necessarily Bliss, as Ranganathan began to experience some complications with his Colon, and even as the logical structure of coordinate indexing was revealed as being infected with "Unitermites," it became increasingly apparent that Jevons was not very wrong when he condemned library classification as "a logical absurdity." Today this feeling has grown so strong that the John Crerar Library has discarded book classification almost entirely, and the Lamont Library has devised its own scheme to facilitate the extracurricular reading of Harvard undergraduates.

This realization of the inadequacy of traditional bibliographic organization was stimulated by World War II and its aftermath of accelerated inquiry into the pure sciences and the technologies. Traditional methods of organizing information were revealed to be hopelessly inadequate to meet these demands for the retrieval of precise and exact information, especially considering the tremendous economic and national interests dependent upon the ability to produce at a moment's notice the one and only correct answer. As a consequence, the documentalists and the special librarians began to explore the applicability to a variety of library materials, of symbolic logic, of new methods for organizing information, and of new and intricate electronic machines for the high-speed manipulation of this organization information.

Concurrently with these developments came the discoveries of Shannon, at the Bell Telephone Laboratories, that information carried over a noise-laden channel exhibited mathematical properties analogous to entropy in thermodynamics. He also found that these could be related to certain statistical procedures. At about the same time, Norbert Wiener at M.I.T. began to explore the problem of communication between man and machines and between machines and machines (cybernetics), and at Harvard and elsewhere scientists sought to analyze communication and information theory with certain practical ends in view. Thus it soon became apparent that it was possible to construct electronic computers (giant brains) that could retrieve specific information with incredible speed from vast storehouses of graphic records. Where this revolution will eventually lead, and what transformations it will make in the bibliographic organization of the future, no one can now foretell. All that can be said at the moment is that mankind is only on the periphery of a totally new era in the arrangement and organization of recorded information, and that libraries must be prepared to exploit these new inventions, when they become available, or their social responsibilities will be lost to others with more technological competence, but with less social and cultural vision.

In both acquisition and organization, then, new forces are at work. Their exact nature is as yet but dimly understood, but they carry within themselves the power to remake completely the old familiar pattern of the librarian and his library which has become so familiar to us during the past half century. In short, librarians are confronted by movements and developments arising largely from the profession, which they must be prepared to understand and to meet. Such understanding, and the adjustments which will follow in its wake, are not easily mastered. The difficulties of this mastery inhere in the obvious truth that librarians—all librarians, and not merely those serving institutions of learning— have failed to meet the tests imposed by the responsibilities that were socially theirs. These are strong words, but they are true. To understand fully, then, the proper role of the academic librarian, one must look for a frame of reference to the larger problem: the librarian's function in the total social pattern and in the culture in which the library exists today.

One might logically assume, I think, in view of the long history of the library as a mediator between society and its graphic records, that librarians, if anyone, would be the experts in the uses to which society puts these records. It seems not too much to ask that the librarian know and understand *why* people use books (recorded information), *how* they use books for whatever purpose, and the ways in which this use of books influences the behavior both of the individual and of society. How else can we acquire materials and organize them effectively if we remain ignorant of the precise uses of graphic records and the social consequences of such uses? Yet we have not made even a substantial beginning toward answering such fundamental questions as these, and the reason for our failure is that, as librarians, we have in a sense been untrue to our calling.

Lacking a communication system, no culture can exist; of this we are reasonably certain. We also know that the several types of social organization, and the varying patterns of human behavior, are influenced in one way or another by variations in the communication process. Likewise, it seems apparent that there is direct, or person-to-person, communication, and indirect communication, with an intermediary (a printed book, for example) between the transmitter and the receptor. We can distinguish, too, between mass communication, which is transmitter initiated (e.g., the radio and the newspaper), and individual communication, which may be receptor initiated and which is highly personal, for the promotion of which the library is one agency. But we are yet unable to describe, with any degree of accuracy, the role of these many types of communication in contemporary society and the part that each plays in determining the configuration of our present-day culture and our social behavior. How can we expect the college librarian to choose his books effectively and arrange them physically, or analyze their contents efficiently, if he has only vague notions of why the students and faculty use books, how they use them, and in what manner this use influences their attitudes and their decisions?

It immediately becomes apparent that we are concerned here with the extension of knowledge about knowledge itself. To be sure, the epistemologists have long studied the origins and development of knowledge, how it is coordinated and integrated, how it is accumulated and transmitted from generation to generation. The philosophers, too, have for centuries studied the limits and nature of knowledge, its sources, and the methods by which it may be augmented. But all such studies have been confined to the intellectual process of the individual. Even when the psychologists carried the speculations of the philosophers into the laboratory and subjected their theories to "scientific" scrutiny, the approach was still centered about the individual, and they have ignored any comprehensive inquiry into the intellectual differentiation and integration of knowledge within a complex social structure.

Conversely, the sociologists, who have been concerned with the behavior of men in groups, have paid but scant heed to the intellectual forces that are shaping society. True, a small group (Mannheim, Sorokin, Maquet, et al.) have been concerned with developing the "sociology of knowledge," which attempts to discover how the social status of an individual or group affects the content and form of accepted ideas; but this is only one strand in the complicated pattern. Thus has arisen a need for a new science of communication—which we have for the past several years referred to as "social epistemology"—that will provide a framework for the effective investigation of the whole complex problem of the intellectual processes of a society where the individual mind can no longer grasp all of the relevant reality. It is a study of the ways by which society as a whole seeks to achieve a perceptive and understanding relation to its total environment; the focus of such a discipline will be upon the production, dissemination, integration, and utilization of all forms of communication throughout the entirety of society. From such a discipline should emerge a new knowledge about, and a new synthesis of, the interaction between social activity and the totality of human knowledge.

Obviously, this discipline will have its own body of theoretical knowledge, but for the librarian, especially, it will have very practical applications; the effective practice of librarianship rests solidly upon it. The library, especially the academic library, is probably the oldest and perhaps the most efficient mechanism for facilitating interaction between the individual and the accumulated body of recorded knowledge. Because the librarian is in such desperate need of the wisdom that this discipline can give, he must, and should, take the initiative in its promotion. He must make himself the "expert" in "social epistemology," and he must pioneer both in promoting the development of its theoretical framework and in applying it practically to immediate social ends, for without it he can no longer claim to be an effective mediator between man and print. Thus librarians must be at once research workers and practitioners, pure scientists and engineers. They must develop their own body of theory and translate that theory into effective action. There is no hierarchy of respectability here—both are of equal importance, and both are essential to the advance of librarianship.

Admittedly, the strain that this new discipline will impose upon education for librarianship is very great, but however heavy the burden, it is the responsibility of the library schools to be prepared to meet it. In all honesty we must admit, I think, that education for librarianship has failed; this failure has expressed itself in five fundamental and important ways:

1. It has not established a clear distinction and a proper relationship between the fundamental and the technological in library matters, with the result that a necessary knowledge of practical aspects has been completely ignored, or the theoretical has been overshadowed by an excessive emphasis on technological detail.

2. It has failed to evaluate all the uses to which society puts graphic records, and hence has never really come to grips with the problem of the role of the library in this "use" process. It has emphasized numbers of users, rather than insisting upon an understanding of all of these uses and their proportional importance in society.

3. It has not achieved a proper synthesis between the general and the special. Yet this is one of the most important problems confronting society today. By "general" is here meant that common body of knowledge, beliefs, and attitudes that gives unity and stability to a culture and rational direction to social change; the "special," on the other hand, is the ever-increasing number of areas where knowledge and skills that may be in the possession of a relatively few individuals are used for the benefit of all. But librarianship has over-emphasized one aspect of the general—or what is common to *all* readers—which has led to an excessive attention to mere numbers of users, has confused the library with the mass media of communication (one of which it certainly is not), and has overburdened library education with a preoccupation with public library service at the level of the "general reader."

4. It has failed to recognize the essential unity of the library process in all

types of use and the social importance of preserving that unity. But if we maintain that all knowledge is unitary, then it logically follows that the academic community must exhibit a parallel unity, and the library within the educational system must assume responsibility for being a great cohesive and unifying force.

5. Finally, education for librarianship has failed to identify the really important problems for its own area of research, which is, perhaps, the most damaging failure of all.

By this time you may suspect that I am preaching revolution in education for librarianship, but I am striking at the very foundations of the library schools as we have known them for the past half-century—and you are right! We cannot afford half-way measures of reform, if librarians are to become anything more than glorified slaves in a bibliographic "lumber yard," taught only to fetch and carry in response to faculty commands. A quarter of a century ago I urged college and university librarians not to make of themselves "handmaidens of the learned world." That plea still stands, but I now realize that if we are to be something more than hewers of wood and drawers of water, we must begin by reconstructing the theoretical framework of education for librarianship from the very bottom. Such a reorientation must proceed, I believe, along the following lines:

1. Revitalization of education for librarianship must begin with a profound and, insofar as it is possible within the framework of our existing knowledge, thorough study of the place of the library in the social pattern, with particular emphasis on the role of the library in the total communication process. The basis for this must be a recognition of the library as an *individualizing* agency that is founded in diversity in the use of graphic records—an agency fundamentally different from the mass communication agencies, which tend to promote conformity and uniformity.

2. We must provide for the study and the evaluation of the indirect services that reach society at large only through the intermediary activities of groups of specialists.

3. We must relate the social functions of the library as an instrument of communication to the growing body of knowledge about information theory.

4. The elements common to all branches of librarianship must be isolated and incorporated into a basic core curriculum, which must include a comprehension of the process as a whole.

5. We must isolate the elements common to groups of libraries or to particular library functions and incorporate such elements into a well-integrated program at the level of specialization, founded upon subject specialization in an established discipline.

6. We must develop a basic research program that will relate a significant body of knowledge about librarianship to the larger body of knowledge about

man in general, for this relationship between knowledge about librarianship and the larger knowledge about man and society must be the frame of reference for all future investigation into the professional training of librarians.

7. Finally, we must recruit for librarianship able young men and women who are not only thoroughly trained in the elements of a general education, but who have also demonstrated competence in the mastery of some subject field or cluster of related subject fields. This would seem to come first, but it has been placed last for the simple reason that librarianship cannot attract the qualified personnel it so desperately needs unless the prospective candidate can be convinced that there is in librarianship a body of intellectually exciting professional knowledge, and that librarianship offers economically rewarding opportunities.

What is here envisaged cannot be accomplished overnight, and the road to achievement is well strewn with a variety of barriers. Growing up, for the group as well as for the individual, means recognition of self as a separate entity, casting off the status of dependence and accepting the responsibilities of self-sufficient status, with full knowledge that these responsibilities are many and heavy. But I submit that this is the only honest and forthright approach to the solution of our professional problems; in fulfillment, we can achieve pride in the knowledge that by improving man's understanding of himself both as an individual and as a social being, we have made a unique and lasting contribution to the scholarship of our culture. Here certainly is a really dynamic role for the college librarian—an opportunity to extend, through constant inquiry and research, our knowledge of how the scholar, as pupil and as teacher, makes use of graphic records. Let us, then, cease trying to be what we are not and should not want to be. Let us forget this silly pretense of playing teacher, of asking ourselves such rhetorical questions as, "Are college librarians academic?"

In short, let us be librarians—where librarianship is defined as that branch of scholarship that treats of the acquisition, organization, and use of graphic records for the improvement of society. If we develop the scholarship of our profession to the limits of human knowledge, we will soon discover that librarianship is just as rewarding, just as academically respectable, and far more intellectually satisfying, not to say stimulating, than teaching six sections of freshman composition or, for that matter, conducting a graduate seminar in the liturgical drama of the Middle Ages.

## FOOTNOTES

[1] Elizabeth Kientzle, "The College Librarian and the Library Committee," *Library Quarterly*, LI (April 1951), 120-26.

# VI.

# Of Library Education

# 25

# In Defense of Diversity

American library education today needs a National Plan like it needs a cerebral orifice. Such a verdict may sound strange, coming as it does from one who, since the days of the New Deal, has recognized the merits of and has supported economic and social planning. But the principles that govern educational theory and economic behavior are very different if they are not, indeed, quite antithetical. Thus, any attempt to interpret education in terms of economic ends leads inevitably to Beardsley Ruml's conclusion that "the Board of Trustees has in fact final responsibility under its charter for the educational program as well as for the property of its institution. Having final authority and responsibility, it also has accountability. . . . The Trustees, therefore, must take back from the faculty *as a body* its present authority over the design and administration of the curriculum."[1] Not only would Ruml deprive the faculty of its traditional prerogative to determine the instructional pattern, but also his insistence upon managerial efficiency has led him to propose certain organizational structures as models for higher education. "Centralized leadership is essential," he writes. "A college is a diverse institution, and the typical curriculum is incredibly complex. Sound planning for change requires central direction."[2] Admittedly, this centralized structuring (Ruml has characterized it as a "mechanism") must be imaginative, but the authority upon which it rests must be sufficiently great to guarantee the "implementing of its plans."

Nevertheless, the fact remains that an educational institution, Ruml to the contrary, is very far from being an economic enterprise, and its success is not to be measured solely, if at all, in terms of managerial efficiency. The relentless search for truth is the only *business* of the scholar, and the aim of education is

---

Originally published in the *Journal of Education for Librarianship*, Vol. 4 (Winter 1964), pp. 137-42.

to foster the intellectual development—self-determination—of youth. The academic ethic is rooted in a late 19th-century liberal faith in variety, in unprogrammed initiative. "Looking at the nation as a whole, educational variety verges on anarchy," said President Kingman Brewster, Jr., of Yale recently in addressing a Butler University audience.

> Differences in purpose, in tradition, in organization, in sources and methods of financial support make the higher educational scene a crazy quilt which defies the statistician and the planner. . . . You and I cannot *prove* that this is a more vital and stimulating and innovative system of education than any minister of education could devise; but we can say we believe it to be so from experience as well as from faith. It is *within* the academic institution that we can affirm with even more insistence the validity of untrammeled initiative in preference to conformity to the dictates of a master plan. Perhaps one reason for this preference is a sense of man's fallibility; a feeling that no person, no group, no generation is wise enough to be given the power to tell others what they may and may not think, or value, or believe.[3]

We emphatically share Brewster's predisposition toward a dispersion of power and initiative as opposed to centralized authority and planning in a single all-embracing design, and for variety and individuality rather than uniformity and equality. This predisposition, call it prejudice if you will, colors our whole attitude toward the philosophy that underlies the projected National Plan for Library Education and the research center for its development so laboriously hammered out by Richard Logsdon and his Drafting Committee. The advancement of library education is the responsibility of the library schools themselves, and, though they would do well to enlist the assistance of the wisest minds in the profession, they cannot abrogate to a superior bureau the task of doing their thinking for them, even if it is to be disguised as research.

If there is a royal road to progress in education certainly it has not yet been found, and at the present time, at least, there is no substitute for the empirical approach to the problem of education. Horace Mann, Charles W. Eliot, Robert Maynard Hutchins and other great innovators in American education did not seek the solution to educational problems through any recommendations of a national planning commission. The great strength of the Graduate Library School of the University of Chicago during the 1930s arose from the fact that the school sheltered a group of highly intelligent and strong-minded individuals who knew what they wanted to so and were given the freedom to do it. They emphatically did not agree among themselves, and they certainly did not search for a common denominator that would reconcile their points of view into a unified system. They fought each other tooth and claw, and from that conflict came a rich and exciting educational experience that compelled the student to make his own decisions by the light of his own best judgment.

We, too, in our immodest way, are convinced of the rightness of our ideas; were we not so persuaded, we would not espouse them. But it would doubtless be catastrophic if we were permitted to force down upon the brow of library education our own private laurel crown. We also acknowledge that in the final analysis it may be best for the profession that there are those who disagree with us, for time and experience may prove that they are right. If our beliefs cannot win acceptance in the competition of the marketplace of educational philosophy (a phrase that Ruml should like) they will not have earned the right of survival. We want no national planning office, however representative it may be, to do our thinking for us, and we ask of no other man that he blindly accept our opinions. Lacking any valid tests for prognosticating the success of an educational system, there is no alternative but to wait until experience has established the worth of the product. The Albany school proved its worth in the early years of the present century, as did Chicago in the decade of the 1930s, but we doubt that a national plan can succeed today. More likely, progress will come from intelligent experimentation and inquiry in a variety of places under a diverse array of conditions, for therein lies the essençe of the educational process. Again to quote Brewster: "Over the long pull innovation's progress is more likely when many centers of initiative are working on an unsolved problem in a variety of ways than when all must conform to a master plan."

Today the educational process is so complex and so imperfectly understood that the work of a national commission, particularly when it is structured to provide a voice for all segments of the library profession, will almost certainly end in a welter of compromises that satisfy no one and leave unsolved the problems to which it was supposed to address itself. When the proposal of the Drafting Committee was laid before the Joint Committee on Library Education of the Council of National Library Associations, there developed emphatic insistence from the practicing librarians that the program be insulated against domination by the library educators. One could scarcely find a more dramatic example of the practitioner's distrust of the educator who has "never met a payroll." Who knows what is best for library education? The answer is obviously relative to the person of whom the question is asked.

By turning our back on a national commission and its comprehensive plans we are not, of course, suggesting that there is no need for standards of excellence in library education, the definition of educational objectives, or the pursuit of research. Standards that are derived from verified knowledge and focused upon objectives that are well understood, the profession most certainly must have. We would not even object to a national body that restricted its activities entirely to large-scale or massive fact-finding and other research whose magnitude is beyond the limits of local resources. We have long argued for the importance of a national manpower survey, and we deeply regret the rejection by the Council on Library Resources of any concern for library education. Faith in variety, in unprogrammed initiative, in freedom for heterodoxy, does not imply irresponsibility. Freedom to experiment bears no guarantee of approval of the results.

Because one does not forbid a course of action does not assert its commendation. Freedom is a means, not an end. The end is the achievement of wisdom by the individual and, through the individual, by society; and the end is best served by the creation of an atmosphere that promotes freedom to experiment. Library education must be allowed to make its own mistakes in its own way, and it is a sad commentary on the profession that library educators have grown so timid, so lacking in initiative and imagination that the practicing librarians now believe that professional salvation lies only in the creation of a supreme authority to guide the educators through the underbrush of possible error. We are not yet ready to agree that library education has become so divorced from reality that it needs a parachute to escape from its mythical ivory tower.

The greatest need of library education today is for resources that will bring to its academic corridors a new generation of highly intelligent and imaginative young men and women who, inspired by an awareness of the potentialities of librarianship, will give to the profession a dedicated, venturesome, and self-reliant spirit. The hope of librarianship, like the hope of society itself, lies in its youth, and there will be little reason for optimism if the young minds of the profession are stamped out in the giant presses of some national plan. "We have a horror of creative intelligence congealing into too-good teaching—static ideas," said Alfred North Whitehead.

> '*This* is the correct thing to know.' Teachers should be acutely conscious of the deficiencies of the matter taught. . . . They should be on their guard against their materials, and teach their students to be on their guard against them. Once learning solidifies all is over with it. . . . The danger is that education will freeze, and it will be thought, 'This and this are the right things to know'; and when that happens thought is dead. I am immensely annoyed by the smugness of a certain kind of talk which goes on among my colleagues, scornful talk about no theory being good that is 'only half tested,' and the meticulous assembling of facts. . . .[4]

We view with alarm the recent introduction of educational programs for training documentalists and information scientists that are divorced from the basic courses in librarianship and bibliographical theory. We are equally disturbed by the proliferation of undergraduate instruction in the elementary techniques of library practice, which threaten the general education so necessary to the librarian's adequate performance of his responsibilities. We have vigorously fought the growth of these tendencies in the past, and until we have been convinced of our error we intend to continue to fight them in the future. But we acknowledge that Ruml is quite right (though it weakens his own case for planning) when he says that "no one can predict where [educational] leadership will arise"; that those institutions "which are now regarded as the strongest may not in fact be the source of this leadership."[5] "*Wohin der Weg?*" asked Goethe's Faust, and Mephistopheles replied, "*Kein Weg; ins Unbetretene.*"

Library education does not need a supreme authority to "research" it, or dictate the direction that its research should go, much less to formulate a master plan to shape its future course. Soul-searching must come from within. We would not see library education prostrated upon the psychiatrist's couch. We like to recall the words of Henry Adams, who was so excited by the seminar of the 19th-century German universities as an instrument for stimulating learning, that he set his students "to burrowing like rabbits all over the historical terrain." American library education, too, needs the freedom, the resources, and the intellectual competence to burrow all over the library landscape. It certainly does not need a ready-made blueprint to chart the pattern for the warrens it should dig. Rather, it needs a benign Mr. McGregor to provide it with quantities of lettuce to give its Peter Rabbits the strength and the resources to pursue their excavations.

The right of the teacher to teach the truth as he sees it in his own way has indeed been the essence of academic freedom ever since the youth of Athens followed their masters in the Peripatetic School and the young monks followed the wandering scholars of the Middle Ages. Educational uniformity is incompatible with academic freedom, but diversity is not to be understood as a euphemism for uneven quality. There must be pluralism. There are no short-cuts; there is no one right way. The problems of education are never solved, for society itself is always in flux, so let us have a lively and fruitful exchange between students and teachers, with the faculty doing their share of the listening.

## FOOTNOTES

[1] Beardsley Ruml, *Memo to a College Trustee* (New York: McGraw-Hill, 1959), p. 13.

[2] *Ibid.*, p. 68.

[3] Address by President Kingman Brewster, Jr., of Yale at the inauguration of President Alexander E. Jones of Butler University, Indianapolis, Indiana, February 7, 1964. (Quoted from manuscript copy.)

[4] A. N. Whitehead, *Dialogues of Alfred North Whitehead, as Recorded by Lucien Price* (Boston: Little, Brown, 1954), p. 63.

[5] Ruml, *Memo*, pp. 75-76.

# 26

# Changing Concepts of Classification: Philosophical and Educational Implications

To the traditional needs of man for air, water, food, and shelter, Professor Platt of the University of Chicago has added a fifth essential to physical survival, the need for novelty. Every prisoner who has undergone solitary confinement has known the meaning of "stir crazy," but recent experiments in sensory deprivation have shown that men placed in an environment from which a maximum amount of sensory variation had been removed soon came close to the brink of madness. The human being, in both his physical and mental attributes, has not been made to operate in a vacuum. The human brain not only organizes, it exists in order to organize, and it becomes seriously deranged if it is denied the opportunity for organization. The fifth need of man, writes Professor Platt, "is the need for what can be called—in a mathematical sense—"information for a continuous, novel, unpredictable, nonredundant, and surprising flow of stimuli."[1] This input information constitutes the raw material for organization of sense perceptions into meaningful patterns. This activity of organizing input information not only characterizes the sane mind but also is necessary to maintain its sanity. Without organization into meaningful patterns, sense perception becomes chaos and insanity.

Similarly, Leonard Meyer, in *Emotion and Meaning in Music*, sets forth the thesis that formal music is dominated by an inherent intellectual meaning, a meaning that is based on a combination of pattern recognition that alternates between familiarity (repetition) and innovation (surprise). Thus the Occidental is unsatisfied by Oriental music when first exposed to it, because in it he can discover no pattern of familiarity and hence no possibility for surprise. But to

With James W. Perry. Originally published in P. N. Kaula, ed., *Library Science Today; Ranganathan Festschrift. Vol. I, Papers Contributed on the 71st Birthday of Dr. S. R. Ranganathan, 12 August 1962* (New York: Asia Publishing House, 1965), pp. 37-48.

one reared in Western culture, Mozart's genius was, as has been said, that he combined the maximum of surprise with the maximum of certainty.[2] Music, therefore, cannot be the "universal language" that it is popularly alleged to be. We of the Western world may find the music of India, the Far East, or the Islamic world "interesting," or even pleasing or enjoyable, but it would be rash indeed to say that we *understood* it. Music, like any other form of communication, is a product of its culture.

This need of the brain constantly to process new information is not confined to the aesthetic world. It is an inherent characteristic of the nervous system of at least the higher animals, and is part of the process of intellectual growth and learning. A major part of the nervous system is not predetermined at birth but grows continuously under the impact of stimulation and experience—through the organizing and processing of information. Puppies reared as far as possible in isolation from external stimuli were found to be perceptibly more stupid than dogs raised under "normal" conditions. The brain must constantly process some kind of information; attention may wander but it does not cease. The total capacity for handling information, though it varies from individual to individual and is sharply differentiated between man and the higher mammals, is roughly constant for each individual, like the capacity of a water pipe through which only a given amount of flow can be forced. Moreover, the brain of man and the higher mammals not only structures, classifies, or organizes, the information it receives; it searches for and creates structure and pattern in the environment. The brain, as the psychologist says, has "closure"—the ability to fill in the gap in a pattern—so that a conclusion can be reached despite a missing fragment of evidence. Thus, events can be anticipated without having been previously experienced. The lion is in hot pursuit of the antelope, because he perceives in the creature that which is edible, though he may never have seen such an animal before. But to the lion he is "like" that which is known to be edible, hence he anticipates a hearty breakfast. Conversely, nature in the struggle for survival has deliberately used deception to confuse and promote false analogy and misclassification from fragmentary evidence. Thus, crypsis among the insects is a form of camouflage used to deceive the enemy into classifying a potential victim as a leaf or twig. Certain defenseless moths may assume the physical attributes and even the behavior of a wasp to protect themselves from predation.[3]

Thus the brain "reasons" by clues and analogies, and "solves" problems by their fragmentation into parts sufficiently "familiar" to admit of separate solution. Man uses symbols that are the essence of analogy, and indeed the very nature of man himself as man is this highly developed ability to organize, process, and *learn* information. As this need for information, for something upon which the brain can feed, drives individuals, so also with equal force it drives societies and cultures. It is the basis of all collective behavior, for the collective mind operates in the same way as the individual brains of which it is composed. It may learn more slowly, adjust itself less quickly—in short, be less efficient in its processing of information—but it is stimulated by the same drives and it operates in the same way. A society, therefore, that is to avoid stagnation and decay must provide for the introduction of new information with which the collective mind can nourish itself, just as the individual needs a steady accretion of new information for his mind to process. Hence, one achieves the paradox that the only stability is in instability, and the only permanence in classification is reclassification.

But the mind cannot weave its patterns of information that the senses, through the nervous system, have communicated to it, unless that information is communicated in some form that the brain can manipulate. One may question whether every process of thinking involves language, but to conceive of thought without some form of symbolization is difficult if not impossible, and the discussion here can at least be limited to symbolized thinking—to thinking formalized in language. Symbols, says Hans Reichenbach, are "first of all, physical bodies, like all other physical things,"[4] whether they be words of a printed page, air waves capable of producing the sensation of sound when they strike against the human ear, movements of the human hand or head, or artifacts employed to symbolize a nation, a religious faith, or any form of social organization or concept. But symbols are more than physical entities; they are things with *meaning*. Meaning, therefore, still following Reichenbach, is a quality imposed on and possessed by symbols. The physical things called symbols have a function that they acquire by being put into a certain correspondence with observed facts—a function through which the symbol "operates." This function, or quality, is called meaning. In animals, meaning, as the function of symbols, may depend directly upon the correspondence between symbol and the fact for which it stands; at such a stage symbols become essentially signals. But in man, and possibly in the higher apes, whether a symbol has the function of meaning does not depend merely on the symbol and the facts in question but also on the use of certain rules called the rules of language. The structuring of symbolism into language intensifies the function of meaning. Language then becomes a structured body of knowledge symbolized in ways that permit its manipulation by the human nervous system.

The system of rules that is the structure of language is not a closed class; man frequently invents new rules, when there are special purposes for which new symbols are needed. The signs and lights employed for the regulation of motor traffic form a "language" different from ordinary language in its symbols and rules. Thus, not only is language being constantly enlarged or reshaped to meet the requirements of life, but new languages are being invented for special purposes for which existing languages are inefficient or inappropriate.

Language, then, is more than a symbolized structuring of knowledge or information: language and knowledge are inseparable. If knowledge were not expressible through language so that the human brain could receive it, interpret it, and otherwise manipulate it, the achievement of knowledge would be impossible for man.

Because language as symbol epitomizes knowledge, and is the instrument by which the brain is able to comprehend knowledge, language largely determines conduct and behavior. Even among primitive races the power of symbols to influence and control action is very great, and as the accumulated body of human experience (knowledge) grows, the role of its structuring becomes increasingly important, making possible both the assimilation of increasingly intricate bodies of knowledge and more complex forms of social organization. Because of man's ability to use symbols to control action, language (or, more precisely, words) has been endowed with certain supernatural powers. Thus incantations and other magical formulas have been employed in an attempt to influence future events; and man has resorted to mystical jargon to exert his will not only upon other individuals but also upon natural forces, physical phenomena, and inanimate objects.

## STRUCTURE OF KNOWLEDGE

The internal structure of knowledge is the system of connections patterned in the process of thinking. But the psychological operations involved in thinking are fluctuating processes which, under certain conditions, skip entire groups of operations. They do not always keep to the ways prescribed by logic, and man in his search for the interconnectedness of ideas cannot bind himself to formalism because the brain itself will not be bound to the narrow steps and prescribed courses of so-called logical reasoning. Logic itself is a man-made system of connectives and relationships that has evolved from human experience with observed phenomena. And it may be said to inhere in nature only because man chose to put it there. The structuring of knowledge that is so essential to the operation of the human brain may have nothing whatever to do with formalized "logic." Indeed, psychologically, logic may be quite illogical; and who is to say, in our present imperfect understanding of nature, which is more logical, or more natural—the operations of the nervous system itself, or the patterns that man has woven with it?

## SCIENTIFIC KNOWLEDGE

Man first found in his environment a heap of disorganized facts or observations. Whether system inhered in it is a matter of debate, but certainly there was no system apparent to him. From this rubble he created structure—and eventually science—which at least has utility, for it provided guidance in attacking the problem of survival, and eventually of controlling the environment.

The structuring of knowledge serves as a frame of reference, as a means for grappling with situations. It does this by interpreting them as problems that can be attacked in two ways: by applying previously generated knowledge and by conducting experiments to fill in gaps.

It must be recognized, however, that knowledge, including scientific knowledge, is not a system of certainties or well-established statements that steadily advance toward a state of finality. Moreover, such scholars as Karl Popper argue that we can never claim to have attained truth, "or even a substitute for it, such as probability."[5] Whether Aristotle was convinced that there is an inherent order in nature discoverable by man, and that this order may be expressed as a permanently valid classification system, is a matter for debate. But certainly such views were widely held for centuries, although the orientation shifted as classicism and scholasticism gave way before an evolving science. The fact that philosophic contemplation and logical reasoning, as the best approaches to an understanding of nature, yielded to experimental observation and the correlation of results is of less importance to the epistemologist in his search for the understanding of the growth of knowledge than the fact that each age must create its own scheme of classification in terms of its own understanding of human phenomena. Thus understanding, or knowledge, itself must create a system, a scaffold, around which it can place the building blocks of experience, inference, and conjecture.

## ORDER OF CLASSIFICATION

Cassirer has criticized Linnaeus for having devised an "artificial" rather than a "natural" classification, a "binary nomenclature" that moves in "the realm of mere names," rather than "in the realm of things," a "mere verbal cloak."[6] But until man has achieved ultimate truth, can a classification be anything but "artificial," or at least relative to the existing state of knowledge? What is meant by a "natural order"? Man, himself, is a part of nature; therefore, one could argue with equal validity that any order which man has created to expedite his pursuit of knowledge is a "natural" order. Hence, Cassirer's statement that "an artificial order cannot be treated as knowledge" is essentially meaningless.[7] Under scrutiny it crumbles apart in the fingers. To insist that a classifier is moving toward a classification of "names" rather than of "things" is to miss the point both of classification and nomenclature. Obviously, to be useful, a classification must have an *inherent* order, but this has nothing to do with its "naturalness" or "unnaturalness." Of necessity, a classification is an ordered list of terms, or names, for only in a very limited way can we manipulate objects; and concepts or ideas have no physical existence at all and must be given names. The important fact is that the name is the verbal correlate of the class for which it stands; it is the symbolic expression of the class and the members of which that class is composed. Classification can no more escape nomenclature than language can escape symbols.

As Ledger Wood points out, the peculiar characteristic of all knowledge is "that it is always *of* or *about* an actual or supposed object other than itself."[8] Referential transcendence, then, according to Wood, is an indispensable feature of all knowledge; therefore, cognitive transcendence always is inherent in the knowledge-situation. Classification, if it is to be useful in the development of man's knowledge, must reflect, in a variety of ways, this referential element. The concepts with which it deals must refer to each other in ways that are in harmony with or contribute to this knowledge-situation. Only thus can classification be useful to the scholar, and the proper object of study of the epistemologist.

## VALUE OF CLASSIFICATION

"The value of classification," writes Jevons, "is co-extensive with the value of science and general reasoning. Whenever we form a class we reduce multiplicity to unity, and detect, as Plato said, the one in the many. The result of such classification is to yield generalized knowledge."[9] Perhaps no one has more vigorously stated the importance of classification to epistemology than did Professor Bowen, almost a century ago: "The first necessity which is imposed upon us by the constitution of the mind itself, is to break up the infinite wealth of Nature into groups and classes. . . . Perhaps it will be found . . . that classification is not only the beginning, but the culmination and the end, of human knowledge."[10]

In one sense Cassirer's critique of Linnaeus is valid, for it is a protest against the extent to which, beginning in the 18th and particularly during the 19th centuries, classification became identified with taxonomy. At about the same time, it also became something of a plaything of the logicians, who, under the influence of Aristotelian logic, saw it as an instrument for the exercise of man's powers of "reason." To criticize these developments does not deny the contribution that classification can make to scientific description, or the role that reasoning plays in the organization of human knowledge. But they did place both science and classification in something of a straightjacket. For science is much more than Jevons' "detection of identity," and classification transcends the mere "placing together, either in thought or in actual proximity of space, those objects between which identity has been detected."[11] With the shift in philosophic thought, which is the foundation of science, away from logical contemplation to experimentation, there was not—perhaps because of a curious form of hysteresis that frequently plagues human thinking—a corresponding change in the role of classification. Taxonomy and Aristotelian logic had fastened upon classification the notion of a fixed array of specimens that reveals the inherent order in nature and that, once discovered, remains valid for all time. Thus science supposedly supplied the building-blocks with which taxonomy erected a permanent structure.

But there is no permanence in science—no ultimate truth in the absolute sense. Of the revolution in scientific thought that has taken place in the first half of the 20th century, Alfred North Whitehead could say:

> Fifty-seven years ago, it was when I was a young man in the University of Cambridge, I was taught science and mathematics by brilliant men and I did well in them; since the turn of the century I have lived to see every one of the basic assumptions of both set aside ... the most fundamental assumptions of supposedly exact sciences set aside. And yet, in the face of that, the discoverers of the new hypotheses in science are declaring, 'Now, at last, we have certitude'—when some of the assumptions which we have seen upset, have endured for more than twenty centuries.[12]

## RANGANATHAN'S UNIQUE ANALYSIS

One cannot condemn the taxonomists for building their structures with bricks of straw; these were all that science gave them. But they should not have deceived themselves with the illusion of permanence merely because they had erected a pretty pyramid in which each block had its "proper" place. This "logic of taxonomy" has been doubly unfortunate, not only because it has tended to ossify classification into a rigid and supposedly permanent hierarchy, but also because it has obscured the larger and far more important contribution that classification can make to epistemology. To the librarian, this double misfortune has been particularly deplorable. Taxonomic classification, by providing him with an array of pigeon-holes into which he could conveniently slip his books or cards, has given him a false sense of security with respect to the retrieval of information. At the same time, he has been led away from epistemology, which is the true foundation of library science as the management of recorded knowledge. Of all librarians, only S. R. Ranganathan has attempted to build a bibliographic classification upon epistemological principles. By demonstrating the ways in which knowledge grows—by "denudation, dissection, lamination, and loose assemblage,"[13] he has clearly shown the relation between bibliographic classification and the patterns of man's cognitive growth.

## REFERENTIAL CLASSIFICATION

Thus, through the influence of this distinguished Indian scholar and those who have followed, or been inspired by, his teachings, librarianship is entering a new era in classification, a transition in which the old rigidity and assumed permanence of taxonomic grouping is yielding to what Whitehead has called a "referential" classification—a dynamic and flexible system, or more specifically a network of interrelated systems, that will give new dimensions to the organization of recorded knowledge. No longer will bibliographic classification be tied to the linearity of the book shelf or the catalog tray, but in time there will emerge systems that will be capable of indefinite expansion, which will make possible an unlimited variety of correlations and provide for a much more minute analysis of the materials classified than has ever been possible before. The old dichotomy between a classification of books and a classification of knowledge will disappear, and in its place there will be thought patterns that simulate the mental processes or channels of the library user. As man's understanding of the growth of knowledge increases, and as he learns more about the operation of the nervous system, especially the brain, and the ways in which we "think," he may even be able to provide for serendipity.

## FACET ANALYSIS

Librarianship has not consciously assumed a static state of knowledge, but its conservative adherence to traditional techniques has resulted in such an orientation. Excessive preoccupation with form—often, it must be admitted, for its own sake—has laid a heavy hand upon the librarian and rendered him immobile in the face of scientific (*Wissenschaftliche*) progress. To a world bound to the formalized structure and the growing obsolescence of the Decimal Classification, a world that had not been liberated as it should have been by the even less flexible system designed for the Library of Congress, faceted analysis came as a breath of fresh air. So great was the significance of this innovation that its potentialities were not—perhaps could not be—immediately realized. At the time of its introduction the librarians were not ready for it, but its importance is becoming increasingly recognized by those who are seriously concerned with the retrieval of information. In library practice, facet analysis has opened the door for the introduction of electronic technology, popularly known as machine searching. This has made possible a far greater depth of literature searching than could ever be achieved with a traditional card catalog of manageable proportions. The faceted approach has expanded to almost limitless boundaries the range of questions that the reference librarian can ask, questions for which answers can be achieved with speeds that an earlier generation would have thought beyond belief. The opportunities for mechanization revealed by the faceted approach have revolutionized the total cost structure of library service, they have made possible an intensity of literature search that previously would have been beyond the limits of economic practicability even for the largest libraries. Far from making the librarian an automaton, a "slave to the machine," it promises him a new freedom and a mastery over his materials that he has never enjoyed before.

But important as these practical ends are, the great contribution of Ranganathan's methods lies in the theory of librarianship itself. As was suggested above, facet analysis derives from Ranganathan's investigations into the way in which knowledge grows; in his work, librarianship, as the science of the management of knowledge, merges for the first time with epistemology. This distinguished Indian philosopher found librarianship little more than a bundle of techniques, a rather simple technology. He and his followers have raised it to an intellectual discipline in its own right. Thus he has laid the theoretical foundations upon which others can build. Important as the Colon Classification is as an exemplification of his theories, one may hazard the not unreasonable guess that it is the theory upon which the scheme is based that will survive and stimulate the minds of future generations long after the ingenious scheme itself has been superseded. Epistemology decrees that each age must fabricate its own classifications, but the epistemological foundations of those classifications are constant.

"The One remains, the many change and pass." Philosophy is still the "pilot of life."

The implications of these changing concepts in the organization of knowledge are no less important for the education of the librarian. That library education has so long remained at the vocational level is due to a misunderstanding of librarianship and a misuse of education. The failure to see librarianship as anything other than a technology has made its training programs little more than the communication of vocational skills. This has been intensified by the failure to see education as anything other than compressed experience. But librarianship can be an intellectual discipline in its own right, and education is not a substitution for experience, but a preparation for it. There is no substitute for experience, and the only way to obtain it, in a specific activity, is to engage in that activity. Hence professional education is particularly vulnerable to the encroaches of apprenticeship and practical training. Librarianship, if it is ever to become anything other than a vocation, must abandon the practice of putting its students through what Robert M. Hutchins has called, "little fake experiences in the classroom."[14] We must teach our pupils theory, not techniques; principles, not practice.

The practitioners who set themselves up as authorities in professional education—and every practitioner does—constantly cry for initiates into the profession who know *how* to do this or that, never *why* they do it. If one elects to spend two years of professional "study" learning how to classify by the Decimal system, then suddenly finds himself employed in a special library for which the DC is completely unfitted, he will be lost. But if he has spent his years of education preparing himself to comprehend the theory of classification, he will be able to work out his own formulas for either the Decimal system or any other that he might encounter or fabricate. Similarly, the teacher who teaches only "facts" or techniques, may one day awaken to the *fact* that the world has gone on without him, and that his students have passed him by. But we are less concerned with the personal tragedy of the individual teacher than the greater tragedy of the profession. For a profession that pins its hopes on a technology is not truly a profession—it is a vocation, and a very ephemeral vocation at that.

Librarianship stands in such a perilous position at this very moment.

336 Changing Concepts of Classification

Because it has put its faith in a technology, it rejects innovation, recoils from self-scrutiny, and babbles incoherently of "fright and Frankenstein," when confronted by "a machine." This fear of the machine is a normal reaction against what Robert M. Hutchins has called "the cult of scientism,"[1][5] a cult that has done great disservice to science, and one which few good scientists follow. At the beginning of this essay, we spoke of man's need for information, and because the world presents itself to us as a mass of incomprehensible items, we are led to the worship of information by the simple process of collecting facts and subjecting them to examination. This, according to John Dewey, is still the curse of education, particularly in the social sciences. But man cannot understand the environment merely by looking at it. One of the primitive assumptions of science is that we live in a universe of order, an order that is determined by and controlled through the operation of certain fundamental principles that admit of reasonably exact definition and yield ultimately to elucidation. Thus man reaches the conclusion that there is a body of universal laws that can be grasped by the human intellect and utilized effectively in the solution of human problems. One cannot quarrel with this view, for it emphasizes anew the need of education to deal with these basic metaphysical problems, rather than with facts alone. But, at the same, this intensive inquiry into the nature of the environment had led to a blind devotion to the fact for its own sake. Thus has arisen the cult of scientism, which holds that everything that is not science is antiquated and irrelevant, for science is modern, enlightened, and progressive. Paradoxically, this has also led to an equally irrational rejection of science, because "science cannot tell us where to go." Because men can use science for evil purposes as well as for good, there has grown up a popular distrust of science, a belief that science itself will lead man to destruction, an anti-intellectualism that holds that too much knowledge, like a little knowledge, is "a dangerous thing." If a government exists by the consent of the governed, a society or a profession will become subservient to the machine only when it places a higher value on a technology than it does on creative thought. The goal of education is not the assimilation of facts or the building of a machine, but the training of the intellect. Therefore, the aim of education for librarianship is the training of the intellect in matters pertaining to human knowledge. Librarianship is not a trick of finding a particular book on a particular shelf for a particular reader. Of all the disciplines, it is the broadest and richest—the most interdisciplinary. It reaches to the very center of man's intellectual achievements, and seeks to understand the relations of the parts to the whole of human knowledge. If librarians fear technological advance it is because they have been schooled in a vocational technology that seeks not the understanding of man's intellectual achievements but the manipulation of a set of skills.

Librarians are wont to lament the failure of their profession to attract "bright" young people into its ranks. But, far too often, "the sheep look up and are not fed." Two hours in the library school classroom are ample to demonstrate how serious this intellectual starvation can be. One does not nourish an active mind by stuffing it with rules. Man needs not only novelty—information—but improvement. He seeks not just a different society but a better one. Only those who recognize the important place that librarianship holds in the wisdom of the race can hope to contribute to the proper education of the librarian. Only such as they will be able to attract to the profession those "bright" initiates who see in librarianship an important role in the improvement of mankind and who want to share in it. The sheep look up and must be fed.

## FOOTNOTES

[1] John Rader Platt, "Fifth Need of Man," *Horizon*, Vol. 1, No. 6 (July 1959), 106.

[2] Leonard Meyer, *Emotion and Meaning in Music* (Chicago: University of Chicago Press, 1956), p. 307.

[3] H.B.D. Kettlewell, "Brazilian Insect Adaptations," *Endeavour*, Vol. 18 (1959), 200-210.

[4] Hans Reichenbach, *Experience and Prediction* (Chicago: University of Chicago Press, 1938), p. 17.

[5] Karl R. Popper, *Logic of Scientific Discovery* (New York: Basic Books, 1959), p. 278.

[6] Ernst Cassirer, *Problem of Knowledge* (New Haven: Yale University Press, 1956), pp. 127-28.

[7] *Ibid.*, p. 128.

[8] Ledger Wood, *Analysis of Knowledge* (London: Allen and Unwin, 1940), p. 9.

[9] W. Stanley Jevons, *Principles of Science* (New York: Dover, 1958), p. 674.

[10] Francis Bowen, *Treatise on Logic, or the Laws of Pure Thought* (Boston: Sever and Francis, 1866), p. 315.

[11] Jevons, *Principles of Science*, pp. 673-74.

[12] Alfred North Whitehead, *Dialogues of Alfred North Whitehead as Recorded by Lucien Price* (Boston: Little Brown, 1954), p. 131.

[13] S. R. Ranganathan, "The Colon Classification and Its Approach to Documentation," in Graduate Library School, University of Chicago, *Bibliographic Organization Papers Presented at the 15th Annual Conference of the Graduate Library School, July 24-29, 1950* (Chicago: University of Chicago Press, 1951), p. 97.

[14] Robert M. Hutchins, *No Friendly Voice* (Chicago: University of Chicago Press, 1936), p. 127.

[15] Hutchins, *Education for Freedom* (Baton Rouge: Louisiana State University Press, 1947), pp. 33-34.

# 27

# The Problem of Finance

"Where but in education," President Kirk of Columbia University once asked an audience of university administrators, "can one buy a product for one-half of the cost of its production?" To this rhetorical question he added that the situation was as it was because education is subsidized by those least able to afford it—the faculty. John Ruskin, in *The Crown of Wild Olive*, expressed much the same point of view when he wrote, "No nation ever made its bread either by its great arts, or its great wisdom ... but its noble scholarship, its noble philosophy, and its noble art were always to be bought as a treasure, not sold for a livelihood." Yet money motivates education, even as it does the mare, and the university administrator cannot escape the dismal science of economics, free himself from finances, or be rid of the burden of the budget. A university is not an economic enterprise, but it is forced to exist in a world in which men live by taking in each other's washing, and the university has no tangible laundry.

In a very real sense every institution in society is economic—it must have some means of acquiring an income if it is to survive in our system of specialized production. In our contemporary society there are but three principal methods through which income is achieved. The first is through the sale of a product or a service. This is the method of the marketplace, in which goods or services compete with each other for their share of the total gross product. This method is the foundation of capitalism, and a derivative of it is the use of money, through investment (or lending), to earn more money. The second method, which is the prerogative of government, is through the taxation of the earnings of the marketplace, whether those earnings are the rewards of enterprise or

Originally published in Sarah R. Reed, ed., *Report of an Institute, April 14-15, 1965, Washington, D.C.* (Washington, U.S. Office of Education, Department of Health, Education, and Welfare, 1966), pp. 33-45.

income from investment. The third is through gifts or loans, which themselves are the result of either enterprise in the marketplace or the taxing power of the government. (The actual fabrication of money, either legally or illegally, does not come within the scope of the present discussion.) All three of these methods of achieving economic survival, then, depend upon the seller's capacity to satisfy a human want or need. In the Garden of Eden, presumably, there was no economy, for in it there was neither want nor need until man first tasted the forbidden fruit of the tree of knowledge and became aware of his boredom.

But the groves of academe are no Garden of Eden; rather, they are a nursery for trees of forbidden fruit. To the extent that higher education sells a product or a service, it partakes of the nature of an economic enterprise operating in the marketplace. To the extent that higher education receives, either directly or indirectly, income derived from tax support, it is an agency of government and essentially a socialistic institution. And to the extent that it receives gifts for its support, it is an object of charity. Although a university is not an economic enterprise, to the degree that higher education contributes to the intellectual advancement of society, it is an essential part of the economic system. Theodore W. Schultz argues that education is an investment in human capital just as a factory is an investment in physical plant capital, and the one is no less a real contribution to the growth of the marketplace than is the other.[1] Similarly, the studies of Machlup, Harbison, and others have shown a direct correlation between a society or region's expenditures for higher education and economic growth.[2] Thus, though higher education is a part of, and cannot be understood without reference to, the national economy and the system it represents, higher education is a very special kind of enterprise, an undertaking established not to earn or save money, but to *spend* or invest it intelligently and efficiently for the production of an intangible good.

## DIRECT INCOME FROM STUDENT CHARGES

Conventionally, the economics of the marketplace are based on direct charges for products sold or services rendered, and the "mark-up" provides the margin of profit—the rewards. In an earlier day this system prevailed even in education. At the great Medieval universities, and perhaps even earlier in the peripatetic schools of Greece, the student in effect dropped his quarter in the turnstile at the door of the classroom, and the professor pocketed the "take." This system of direct reward to the teacher was eminently profitable to an Abelard or a Duns Scotus, who could "empty Paris," but we can only speculate about the economic status of the average academician. With the increased institutionalization of the university, the federation of autonomous units that characterized its Medieval ancestry was eventually lost to the highly structured academic commonwealth of the present day. As the costs of education rose (to almost astronomical heights in the present century), the share that could be charged directly against the student declined proportionately.

Professor Seymour E. Harris points out that in 1958, charges to students accounted for about 25 percent of the total educational revenue, and that by 1970 this figure will likely rise to some 40 percent.[3] John D. Millett, who has probably studied the financing of higher education more deeply than any other single individual, observes that in 1960 the total operating expenses of higher education were 5.6 to 6 billion dollars, and adds, "It seems likely that nearly 40 percent of this total amount was derived from student charges, since almost all auxiliary service income results from charges to students."[4] The figures cited by both men pertain to all higher education. The student in the private or independent[5] college or university bears a significantly larger proportion of his educational costs than does his counterpart in a publicly supported institution; but in no situation does the student begin to pay for the full cost of his education.

Professor Harris insists that an increasing proportion of the costs of higher education must be borne by the student. Schultz believes that all three of the major sources of income must advance in a more or less constant ratio. Sidney Tickton of the Fund for the Advancement of Education is of the opinion that the student's share of costs will continue to increase, but that it can and will be met "with the aid of scholarship money, if the education provided is distinctive, has a high degree of excellence, and is sufficiently differentiated from that provided by other types of higher educational institutions to be worth the higher price."[6] Such optimism may be justified, especially if personal income keeps pace with educational costs. But Tickton has "cheated" somewhat by introducing scholarships and other forms of financial aid into his argument, for he is only saying, in effect, that students could pay the entire cost of their education if someone else picked up the bill. One finds it difficult, however, to suppress the haunting concern that higher education, particularly private and independent higher education, may be dangerously close to the point at which it must price itself out of the market. Despite all the impressive statistics that have been marshalled to prove that education is a richly rewarding investment for the individual and that college and university degrees return their costs to the graduate manyfold in increased earning power, the fact still remains that the majority of the population will not sacrifice the present or mortgage even a small piece of the future to buy a share of higher learning. A distinguished scientist once remarked, not entirely facetiously, that he was "not impressed" when he was repeatedly told that the United States spends more money annually for tobacco, movies, and liquor than it does for education. He asserted: "I like to smoke, drink, and go to the movies, and that has nothing to do with my concern for education." But in a capitalistic society, money is the index of value, and if society is unwilling to pay the price of education, then there is something wrong with society or with education, or possibly with both. But wherever the fault lies, the economic crisis that education faces is very real, and it is not likely to be solved by the direct methods of the marketplace.

## GOVERNMENTAL SUPPORT

"For the institution of higher education as a whole in the United States," writes Millett, "about 50 percent of educational income and about 35 percent of all operating income are being provided by government. In terms of social purpose, our national security, and financial support, higher education has begun to assume more and more the appearance of an agency of the government."[7]

Governmental concern for higher education dates back to the late Middle Ages and the beginnings of the Renaissance. As the universities began to challenge the cathedral schools and divest themselves of their monastic associations, royal charters for new universities were granted, and many institutions founded under church auspices enjoyed patronage from the nobility and the crown. On this side of the Atlantic, state and federal concern for higher education began long before the passage of the Morrill Land Grant Act of 1862. Following the Northwest Ordinance of 1785, which provided lands for the support of public elementary and secondary schools, an act of 1787 provided lands for the support of public higher education. Jefferson's proposals for the University of Virginia are a landmark in the movement for state support.[8] Today every state of the union has at least one state-supported institution of higher education, and many have a complex network of state colleges and universities. With the passage of the Morrill Act and subsequent legislation, federal aid to higher education became really massive, and at the present time virtually no college or university, public, private, or independent, is lacking some form of federal investment. Such subsidization is a natural outgrowth of the conviction, which dates back to colonial times, that the education of youth is a public concern, and that the opportunity for universal education is essential to a democratic society and to the social mobility and economic well-being of its citizens.

There is no need to dwell at length upon the financial situation of state-supported institutions or those universities, colleges, and junior colleges that have been established by municipalities; we need only point out that they must compete with similar institutions and other services in their respective governmental units for their share of the revenues. Although they can be, and have been, embarrassed by legal restrictions, local accounting procedures, and the intellectual limitations of those who directly or indirectly control their purse-strings, in general they are more responsive to the upward thrusts in the economic cycle and perhaps somewhat slower to feel the pinch of deflation than are their privately supported counterparts. The public till is an economic buffer even when legislative bodies are most dollar-conscious. In many ways, the financial position of these public institutions is to be envied, even when they think their lot is hard.

Federal and local government has also assisted private and independent educational institutions by exempting them from taxation, principally from real property and gift taxes. Especially since the close of World War II, the federal government has provided loans or gifts, often on a matching basis, for plant construction, the purchase of equipment, and the stocking of libraries. Also, the so-called GI bill provided scholarship aid to students pursuing the baccalaureate or advanced degrees, and in recent years a number of federal assistance programs have been inaugurated, particularly in science and medicine. Perhaps, however, the most spectacular government funding has come in the form of grants or contracts for research, of which the Manhattan Project was a dramatic example. It has been estimated that today almost one billion dollars are poured annually by the federal government into the research resources of academic institutions.[9] Daily the faculties and administrators of colleges and universities beat upon the doors of such fund-granting agencies of the federal government as the National Science Foundation, the National Institutes of Health, the U.S. Office of Education, the Atomic Energy Commission, and other offices; and many institutions employ specialists whose major responsibility is to seek out support for research and assist in the preparation of proposals geared to the psychological orientation of any one of a number of government agencies. With the passage of the National Defense Education Act of 1958, and its legislative descendants, a whole new array of academic activities have received financial assistance from the federal government in a variety of ways. This is not the place to debate the question of the relevance of research to the objectives of higher education; but in most cases, contract research—underwritten by committed funds—generally contributes only peripheral support to teaching programs.

Such largesse has developed mainly because of the importance of higher education to the national security, and especially the research responsibilities of higher education. Nor do these contributions seem likely to diminish in the future. "On the contrary," writes Millett, "governmental financial assistance to colleges and universities to educate needed talents and to perform vital research will unquestionably grow.[10] Bruner has written that an "almost inevitable consequence of the national security crisis is that there will be a quickened flow of federal funds in support of education. . . . The National Defense Education Act is only a beginning."[11] Indeed, one might say with considerable accuracy that federal funds are beginning to take the place of private philanthropy in support of private and independent higher education.

That support of colleges and universities is a proper function of government has been not only accepted, but even welcomed, by the great American public. But government funding is not without its dangers. This warning does not imply fear that the bureaucracy will interfere with academic freedom or impose its ideology upon the teacher. But the availability of government money has, up to the present time, led to an overemphasis upon government interests, especially science, both in teaching and research, and it has tended to channel research to the extent that, all too often, proposals are shaped to please the bureaucrats instead of the investigators. Moreover, governmental regulations and accounting procedures can tie up administrative offices and personnel until, like Gulliver enmeshed in the Lilliputian web, the educational giant could be immobilized. All too few administrators have the courage to refuse a handsome subvention even when it threatens to distort or reshape their educational or research objectives. President John S. Millis of Western Reserve University has acknowledged the existence of the dangers to the university which lie, often concealed, in excessive dependence upon government grants, particularly grants for sponsored research. "I wish to devote a portion of this report," he wrote to the Trustees of the University in 1963, "to a discussion of questions which are being actively debated both inside and outside of the universities. The questions are: What effect is the rapidly growing emphasis upon research having upon the university? Is the university being diverted from its historic purpose? Is it becoming unbalanced? Is it in danger of losing its freedom because of increasing dependence upon outside sources of support, particularly upon government support?"[12] Millis did not answer any of these questions. He concluded only by insisting that they must be dealt with seriously and soon, for they are "coming upon us with great rapidity," and they are "becoming more insistent each year."[13]

Not only are the universities threatened with the unresolved problem of the extent to which government funding should be permitted to dictate the profile of higher education, but also there is the obvious fact that federal money, unlike endowment, is "soft" money. It is not, in itself, income-producing or self-perpetuating. It must be sought annually or biennially. It comes, often, at the whim of a capricious bureaucracy, and there is no guarantee that it will not evaporate whenever there is a change in the policies or programs of the sponsor or when Congress becomes frightened of its own prodigality. Nevertheless, the stern fact remains that someone is going to have to bear the escalating costs of education if its intellectual standards are to be preserved. In a democracy, the education of the citizenry, at all levels, is a proper—even inevitable—concern of government, and it is the responsibility of the citizenry to make as certain as possible that its elected officials exercise their powers in the nation's best interest.

## ENDOWMENT

Patronage of the scholar by men of wealth dates at least as far back as the Golden Age of Greece, and a generous endowment still remains the nearest we know to the ideal method for the support of education. Endowment wisely invested provides stability to the budget; it is "hard" money that acts as buffer against violent swings in the economic cycle. A properly balanced portfolio of investments will respond relatively quickly to inflationary pressures and retard the effects of deflation. Because education is always something of a gamble, because there are no accurate means for predicting success either in teaching or in research, the quality of an educational system does not become apparent until long after the student has left the halls of ivy. "Patient money" is higher education's great need, and "patient money" is exactly what unrestricted endowment can provide. It frees the academic community from dependence upon the "buyer," from the hand-to-mouth existence of government contracts, and from the matrix of bureaucratic domination. To the independent or private institution it stands as does tax support to public colleges and universities. It is their life-blood.

Excessive hunger for endowment can, of course, make higher education subservient to the potential donor. "Education," writes Millett, "is a dangerous business," for, he continues,

> it is committed to change. It expects first of all to change individuals by augmenting their store of knowledge and by developing their ability to reason. Beyond this, the educated person may become an instrument of social change. . . . Creative change is the province of a higher education which is a part of society rather than an escape from it. Higher education by its activity appears to threaten the positions of leadership in the established institutions of society. Higher education may question the ways and means by which men produce goods and services, the ways and means by which men live together, the ways and means by which men govern themselves and others, the ways and means by which men express their ultimate concern for the Ultimate. Higher education may declare that what is thought to be knowledge is no more than folklore and convention.[14]

All this may be repugnant to the potential donor, or the trustee, both of whom are likely to have a strong vested interest in the maintenance of the *status quo*. One need not be an octogenarian to recall the too-often repeated aphorism that America has replaced "the little red school house with the big red university," or Robert Maynard Hutchins' rejoinder to the industrialist who wanted to know whether communism was being taught at the University of Chicago College: "Yes, communism in the College and cancer in the Medical School." But university faculties are not nearly as radical as some people seem to think, and the tradition of academic freedom, which is well entrenched in the *mores* of American culture, has been a strong deterrent to interference with the right of the teacher to his own convictions. In actual practice, the pressures against academic freedom have been exercised more by state and local governing bodies than by the wealthy patrons of education.[15]

But the day of large personal philanthropy would seem to be over. Modern tax laws have taken their toll of such huge private fortunes as those of the Rockefellers, the Dukes, and the Stanfords. The private foundation has largely displaced the individual as the dispenser of spectacular largesse, and corporate and committee decisions have replaced those of individuals. Increasingly, benefaction is becoming institutionalized. One finds it difficult to say whether this change is good, bad, or only different. Certainly it has introduced more "machinery" into the process of benefaction. It has freed philanthropy from the individual whim, but has substituted the idiosyncracies of the corporate mind. Value judgments as to which entails the lesser annoyance to the applicant probably rest on one's personal experiences.

## FINANCES AND ACADEMIC ORGANIZATION

In higher education, absolute authority is as abhorrent to the American as is absolute power in business, government, or even the church. Though the modern university has structured the loosely associated federation of its Medieval forerunners, nevertheless a pluralism of substantially autonomous units has always been regarded as a safeguard against excessive control from the top. As a consequence of its inherent distrust of authority, higher education has built up a community, rather than a hierarchy, of colleges and schools within each institution. As has been said, within a university the forces of diversity are stronger than those of unity.

The tenuousness of administrative controls over the university components has brought much criticism from without the academic world and a demand that higher education be put "on a more business-like basis." This relatively loose administrative control is reflected in academic budgetary procedures. As Henry Wriston has said:

> The relationship of the president to the budget is a strange mixture of delegation of authority and personal control. It would be beyond human power for him to 'make' the budget all by himself. . . . Decentralization is the first necessity; only by such methods can the vast mass of requisite data be gathered and put in reviewable order. Delegation is the second essential; the business office must collect, organize, calculate, and predict. Advice is the third step; without help no president can know enough to make the enormous range of decisions required to arrive at wise conclusions. This assistance must come from department chairmen, from deans who are responsible for the first review of sections appropriate to their realms of action, from officers dealing with the maintenance and operation of the plant. How orderly and rational that sounds![16]

But the position of the university president is not like that of his counterpart at the head of a business or industrial corporation, and he is not entirely to be blamed if his institution's budgetary procedures are not as tidy as managerial theory holds that they should be. In a corporation, those to whom budgetary responsibility is delegated have, in general, the same objectives and point of view as the president and may differ from him only in degree of boldness. But the great danger to the president of a university lies in the delegation of excessive authority to those whose business it is to "run" the financial operations of the institution, people who are not educators in the strict sense of the word and who see the university only in terms of assets and expenditures. He who pays the fiddler calls the tune, and in this case it is the comptroller who issues the salary checks and calls the tune.

President Wriston could have made an even stronger case for the uniqueness of the position of the college or university administrator. As John Fischer has recently written,

> Professors grumble constantly, as we all know, about academic administration—but in fact most universities have less administration per square yard than any other institutions in American life. Typically the president is a sort of Merovingian king, presiding nervously over the savage and powerful barons who run their separate schools, departments, laboratories, and institutes like so many feudal fiefs. He has only very partial command over the university's budget; because of the tenure rule, he cannot fire an incompetent or lazy professor; and his control over what happens in the classroom is marginal.[17]

No one would deny the faculty their right to security and academic freedom, but it is purchased at a price to the institution. The AAUP and the accrediting agencies are powerful organizations, and no president runs afoul of them without imperilling the public relations of his institution. Moreover, even if the president had a great deal more authority than he does, he probably could not expedite reforms however necessary he thought them to be. Though higher learning is dedicated to change, and the faculty hospitable to innovation in the resolution of political and social issues, when it comes to the world of education the professor is almost always as conservative as Barry Goldwater. As Hutchins has written,

> The reasons which make it almost inevitable that the professor should be right about the world, the country, or other people's business, have no application to his own. The professor is not always right about education, because there he has vested interests, personal ambitions, and ancient habits, all of which he wishes consciously or otherwise to protect. Every great change in American education has been secured over the dead bodies of countless professors. In education the professor is a practical man. . . .

And Hutchins defines practical men as those who "practice the errors of their forefathers."[18]

But of all the handicaps under which the academic administration labors in safeguarding the efficient use of its funds, perhaps the most vexing is the inability to assess with any degree of accuracy the excellence of its product. Business and industrial management can establish quality controls, balance sales against inventory, and measure with a high degree of precision the contribution that each segment of the organization makes to the efficiency of the whole. Not so the university administration. No one has yet devised an objective impersonal method for quantitatively measuring degrees of excellence in teaching. There are not even any valid tests for the prognostication of success in teaching, nor any identification of characteristics by which the good teacher can be reliably defined. Good teachers are distinguished from poor ones mainly on the grounds of such rather dubious evidence as hearsay, student gossip, and a kind of campus osmosis. There is no solid safe yardstick by which a dean or department head can justify his recommendation to raise the salary of one instructor or recommend the discharge of another. He is generally forced to work from a negative position. As Hutchins told an audience in Rockefeller Chapel at the University of Chicago some 20 years ago, "Almost every decision an [academic] administrator makes is a decision against somebody. This is true even of decisions that look as though they were for somebody, like a decision to raise a man's salary. The administrator quickly learns that such a decision is really a decision not to raise the salaries of other men in the same department. In a university the administrator must appeal for support to those he has alienated in the course of his duty."[19] The situation has not changed since Hutchins spoke. In the end the administrator must rely on his own personal judgment; but if he depends too heavily upon himself, or if he overrules the considered opinions of his advisors too often, he is in danger of being charged with favoritism, recrimination, or incompetence.

Because there are so many ways for the administrator to lose and so few to win, he almost inevitably shores up his decisions with things that can be measured quantitatively: research productivity, consultant jobs undertaken, research contracts awarded, prizes won, pages published in learned journals, books authored. Yet the validity of such counting is always open to question for, though the administrator is not expected to judge the actual value of such activities, he equates them all as being quantitatively equal—and subconsciously denies their validity as true tests of educational achievement anyway.

In the topsy-turvy economics of the academic world, it is probably pointless to belabor the administrator for not finding "a better 'ole"—if he knew one, he would doubtless run to it. "On many occasions," writes Millis, "we have had to make a quantitative decision based on moral judgments." Qualitative answers, Millis points out, must be given to such quantitative questions as: How many students should the university undertake to educate, and in how many, and in what, fields of knowledge? What quantitative limit, if any should be imposed on the research program? In making such quantitative determinations, the university administration must make "judgments of the moral responsibility of the university to its society. . . ." All such decisions must be based on "the consideration of quantitative data of financial and physical resources, an assessment of human potentialities, but always measured against the moral responsibility of the university to assume its full share of the task of furnishing our society with educated men and women."[20] "Moral judgment" is a fine euphemism for informed opinion or educated hunch, but it does not engender objectivity in the assessment and decision-making processes.

## THE FINANCIAL PROBLEMS OF THE LIBRARY SCHOOL

The preceding pages have dealt with the problems of academic economics as a whole for the simple and obvious reason that a graduate (professional) library school is a part of a larger community, and it is in the light of its academic setting that the financial problems of the library school must be viewed. Moreover, the financial problems of the library school may be considered as a microcosm of the whole university budget. If the substance of librarianship is interdisciplinary, so also are its finances. The administrator of a library school must argue for his share of the university's resources, but he cannot argue effectively if he does not understand how those resources originate, are allocated, and are expended. If library school deans have failed to get what they believed to be their fair share of the university's funds, if their schools have seemed to be academic poor relations, it could well be (at least in part) because their schools have not been in the main current of the academic community. And if university administrators have not thought of library schools as integral parts of the university, it may be because the deans have not thought of themselves or their schools in that way either. The first task of the library school administrator, as a responsible budget officer, is to understand the position of his school in the intellectual as well as the fiscal program of the parent institution.

But, though the administrator of a library school must be concerned with financial matters, he is much more than a budget programmer. As a university is first and foremost an educational instrument, so the library school administrator is first and foremost an educator. An institution of higher education does not exist for the purpose of maintaining a neat set of financial records nicely balanced between income and expenditure. A budget is not an end in itself; it is created to improve, whenever possible, the efficiency and effectiveness of the institution it is made to serve. The task of the administrator is to align means with ends, and for the academic administrator this requires knowing what the objectives of his school are, the means by which they may be achieved, and the resources, both human and fiscal, needed to achieve this educational goal. The great weakness in most library school fiscal operations is their absence of plan. The administrator works from year to year, from budget to budget, arguing each year as best he can for his share of the university's income, but without any real sense of direction, purpose, or ultimate end. He is like the chess player who thinks only of capturing the nearest pawn, without concern for any strategy that will lead him to a checkmate of his opponent's king. The preparation of the budget, then, should be a form of strategy, not a series of maneuvers to outwit the university administration—a well-ordered, long-term campaign to align resources and goals, viewed always in the context of what library education should be. A budget is a means, not an end; and form follows function in financial matters as much as in architecture.

A clear sense of priorities measured in the light of ultimate objectives, then, is the basic budgetary responsibility of the dean. If he and his faculty are alert to their educational needs and opportunities, it is unlikely that any institution, however wealthy, will have enough money to meet their demands. As Wriston has said, "Any time a president boasts that, 'our resources are adequate for our program,' you can be certain that the program is impoverished. With all that needs to be accomplished ... money will always be short."[21] Budget preparation may be almost as much a process of elimination as of innovation. Again to quote Wriston, the president (and one might add, by extension, the dean)

> must spot the program that is 'living on its legend,' and balance its continuance against new proposals which may offer greater promise of educational advance. If he does not do this the educational program will rapidly ossify, and all the work of a curriculum committee, all the insights of some alert professor cannot stop the process. If every new idea must wait upon increased resources so that it may be piled atop all the old procedures, the situation soon becomes hopeless.[22]

Admittedly, library schools are usually spread so thin, and they are so likely to be lacking in program depth, that there is little opportunity to eliminate one educational endeavor, even when it is "living on its legend," to make room in the budget for another; and it is often next to impossible to add any new activity without some sort of compensatory adjustment. Nevertheless, it is the responsibility of the dean to make certain that his budget is as nearly educationally watertight as he can make it, and that every item in it can be defended.

Finally, if it is the obligation of the dean to interpret and defend his budget to the university administration, so also it is his responsibility to make certain that his faculty comprehends the educational program of the parent institution and the financial circumstances within which it must be carried out. A faculty is a sensitive organism, both intellectually and emotionally; if it is not a little taut, intense, edgy, it is probably not taking its work very seriously. But if it is made up of intelligent and reasonable men and women, as indeed it should be, it will either accept a rational explanation of financial stringency, or seek jobs elsewhere. Acting as the channel of communication is not always easy, for not always do the beliefs, procedures, and objectives of the dean coincide with those of the administration; but somehow he must come to terms with both the administration and his faculty or he faces very unhappy, and even disastrous, consequences.

In the final analysis, when the dean deals with the financial problems of his school (as with all administrative matters) there is no substitute for what Hutchins has identified as the characteristics of the administrator—courage, fortitude, justice, and prudence or practical wisdom. We would not attempt to assign a position of preeminence to any of these, but it is, perhaps, notable that

Hutchins has placed courage and fortitude first. Certainly, courage and the fortitude to "carry through" are essential in dealing with the budget. We emphasize them here because they are probably the elements most lacking in library education in its pursuit of adequate financial support. An administrator who administers is bound to cause trouble for the budget officer. "If a university has a deficit of two million dollars, as every well-run university has . . ." we once heard Hutchins say, and the key word was "well-run." The Rockefeller Brothers Fund report stated the same idea more elaborately:

> It will not be enough to meet the problem grudgingly or with a little more money. The nation's need for good education is immediate; and good education is expensive. That is a fact which the American people have never been quite prepared to face. At stake is nothing less than our national greatness and aspirations for the dignity of the individual. If the public is not prepared for this, then responsible educators, business leaders, political leaders, unions, and civic organizations must join in a national campaign to prepare them.
>
> But first our national leaders will themselves have to grasp the true scope of the task. Perhaps the greatest problem facing American education is the widely held view that all we require are a few more teachers, a few more buildings, a little more money. Such an approach will be disastrous. We are moving into the most demanding era in our history. An educational system grudgingly and tardily patched to meet the needs of the moment will be perpetually out of date. We must build for the future in education as daringly and aggressively as we have built other aspects of our national life in the past.[23]

Alfred E. Smith, when he was still the Happy Warrior and governor of New York, said "The trouble with 'pay as you go' is that you don't pay and you don't go." There was never a better guide for education—in librarianship, or out.

## FOOTNOTES

[1] Theodore W. Schutz, "Education and Economic Growth," in National Society for the Study of Education, *Social Forces Influencing American Education*, Sixtieth Yearbook, 1961, Pt. 2 (Chicago: University of Chicago Press, 1961), p. 46.

[2] Fritz Machlup, "Education," *The Production and Distribution of Knowledge in the United States* (Princeton: Princeton University Press, 1962), Chap. 4; Frederick Harbison and Charles A. Myers, *Education, Manpower, and Economic Growth* (New York: McGraw-Hill, 1964); and Seymour E. Harris, ed., "Economics and Educational Values," *Higher Education in the United States: The Economic Problems* (Cambridge: Harvard University Press, 1960), Sec. 6.

[3] Seymour E. Harris, "Financing Higher Education: Broad Issues," in Dexter M. Keezer, ed., *Financing Higher Education, 1960-1970* (New York: McGraw-Hill, 1959), p. 36.

[4] John D. Millett, *The Academic Community: An Essay on Organization* (New York: McGraw-Hill, 1962), p. 48.

⁵Independent is here used to mean those institutions that have no church or other affiliation—e.g., Harvard, Yale, the University of Chicago.

⁶Sidney G. Tickton, *Letter to a College President* (New York: Fund for the Advancement of Education, 1963), p. 27.

⁷Millett, *The Academic Community*, p. 53.

⁸Freeman Butts and Lawrence A. Cremin, *A History of Education in American Culture* (New York: Holt, 1953), pp. 198ff.; Clark Kerr, *The Uses of the University* (Cambridge: Harvard University Press, 1963), pp. 51-52; Marjorie B. Smiley and John S. Diekhoff, "Schools for All," *Prologue to Teaching* (New York: Oxford University Press, 1959), Pt. 2; Richard Hofstadter and Wilson Smith, eds., "The Nation, the States, and the Sects," *American Higher Education: Documentary History* (Chicago: University of Chicago Press, 1961), Vol. 1, Pt. 3.

⁹Millett, *The Academic Community*, p. 52; *The Mighty Force of Research*, by the Editors of *Fortune* (New York: McGraw-Hill, 1953), pp. 16-17; Machlup, *The Production and Distribution of Knowledge*, Chaps. 4-5.

¹⁰Millett, *The Academic Community*, p. 52.

¹¹Jerome S. Bruner, *The Process of Education* (Cambridge: Harvard University Press, 1960), p. 76.

¹²John S. Millis, *Research . . . How Much? Report of the President, 1961-62* (Cleveland: Western Reserve University, 1963), p. 1.

¹³*Ibid.*, p. 4.

¹⁴Millett, *The Academic Community*, p. 55; Robert M. Hutchins, "The Professor Is Sometimes Right," *No Friendly Voice* (Chicago: University of Chicago Press, 1936), pp. 155-61.

¹⁵Robert M. MacIver, *Academic Freedom in Our Time* (New York: Columbia University Press, 1955); also, Richard Hofstadter and Walter P. Metzger, *The Development of Academic Freedom in the United States* (New York: Columbia University Press, 1955).

¹⁶Henry M. Wriston, *Academic Procession* (New York: Columbia University Press, 1959), pp. 167-68. It is odd that Wriston gives the deans no authority to initiate "sections appropriate to their realms of action."

¹⁷John Fischer, "Is There a Teacher on the Faculty?" *Harper's Magazine*, Vol. 230 (February 1965), 18.

¹⁸Hutchins, *No Friendly Voice* pp. 156, 157.

¹⁹Robert M. Hutchins, "The Administrator," in Robert B. Heywood, ed., *The Works of the Mind* (Chicago: University of Chicago Press, 1947), p. 141.

²⁰Millis, *The Academic Community*, p. 4.

²¹Wriston, *Academic Provision*, p. 168.

²²*Ibid.*, p. 169.

²³Rockefeller Brothers Fund, Inc., *The Pursuit of Excellence: Education and the Future of America* (New York, Doubleday, 1958), p. 33.

# 28

# The Self-Destructing Diploma

When we were very young there was current in the library profession a cynical aphorism that "the librarian who reads is lost." By contrast a good friend of ours, who has had many years of experience in the administration of higher education, was wont to observe that every diploma, whether for an undergraduate or advanced degree, should be so printed that in 10 to 15 years it would fade to a blank sheet of parchment and the recipient would be compelled to return to school to renew his education. Such a proposal probably strikes terror to the heart of most of us, but in a day when knowledge and skills are undergoing such rapid change, the idea—painful though it is to contemplate—has merit. Education, professional or otherwise, does not, or should not, end with the granting of a degree. No piece of parchment, even inscribed in Latin, can guarantee competence for the future. Indeed, it is doing well if it accurately testifies that the recipient is educated or professionally competent on the day of graduation.

In the June when we graduated from high school there appeared in a local newspaper a cartoon showing a metaphorical picture of the world, a little man with a huge globe for a head, taking a sweet girl graduate, dressed in cap and gown, by the hand and saying, in response to her musing observation, "Matilda Jones, A.B.," "Come on, little girl, and I'll teach you the rest of the alphabet." It is with the rest of the alphabet that we as practicing librarians should be concerned, for ourselves as well as for others. "Never seek the advice of the practitioner on professional education," a university president once warned us, "for he will always think in terms of his own professional preparation which will probably be 10 to 20 years out-of-date."

Originally published in the *Bulletin of the Ohio Library Association*, Vol. 42 (October 1972), pp. 4-8.

Such a reaction may seem overly cynical, yet we have found it to be all too frequently true. Continuing education is a subject about which there have been more pious pronouncements and good intentions than constructive action, and when even limited programs have been provided they do seem to have been "more of the same," rather than innovative. That there is latent demand for solid and pedagogically sound educational recycling cannot be denied. Last April at a conference in New York, on "Access to Knowledge and Information in the Social Sciences and the Humanities and Implications for Library Education," sponsored by Queens College of the City University of New York, we discovered an intense enthusiasm for formalized continuing education, and distress that it was not being adequately met. We contend that the first responsibility of the librarian, if he is to fulfill his professional responsibilities effectively, is to be an educated person, where being educated, as John Diekhoff has written in an essay on John Milton, means not "approaching the encyclopaedic goal of mastery of all knowledge. It never was quite possible. . . . What gives depth and meaning to general knowledge is the specialized knowledge upon which it impinges. What we sometimes describe as the 'narrow specialist' is not only narrowly expert. He is also broadly ignorant. And his broad ignorance may often make him an inadequate specialist. To combat such inadequacy in himself, any man may well devote a lifetime. For an educated man is not one who knows but one who is learning."[1]

Everyone, of course, must learn for himself, but this obvious statement does not imply that learning is exclusively an individual matter. Learning is also a social process, a process, as Diana Crane[2] and other students of the sociology of knowledge have shown, that is also the product of social diffusion.

Since the environment of learning is social as well as cognitive, one can anticipate that there will exist in a learning group a kind of "contagion" that will sensitize the individual members to innovation and the assimilation of new knowledge. Indeed, the studies of William Goffman and his associates have indicated that the dissemination of knowledge and information bears striking resemblances to the way epidemics originate, attain maximum strength, and eventually subside.[3] In the total complex of events that contribute to the learning process, and they are of course many, there is no substitute for the interaction of mind on mind in an environment conducive to reflective inquiry.

The voluntary association of individuals for a specific purpose is certainly not new to librarians; the modern American public library may well be said to have begun with the library societies of the 18th century, and librarians themselves have in a variety of organizational forms come together to improve themselves in their profession. Perhaps the annual institutes inaugurated in 1936, at the Graduate Library School of the University of Chicago by Louis Round Wilson, may be regarded as the first major pioneering effort to establish continuing education for librarians. The original pattern was to formalize these institutes in a two-week series of lectures and discussions supported by specialized library service and prescribed reading with which the registrants were expected to be familiar. In time, however, the library service and prescribed readings were dropped, the duration of the institutes shortened to one week, and subsequently to no more than three or four days. But after more than 35 years the program, even in its attenuated form, still flourishes; the contributions that the published proceedings have made to library literature are substantial and reach an audience far beyond the fortunate few whose finances permit attendance. No other library school can boast of such an achievement, and the Chicago institutes have undoubtedly stimulated less ambitious undertakings in the decades that followed.

To enumerate here the many attempts throughout the country to promote continuing education for librarians would be neither relevant nor possible. It is important to emphasize, however, that the role of continuing education is being increasingly recognized. At the Detroit convention of the ALA, the Council of the Association approved as association policy a statement on library education and manpower that emphasized the desirability of both formal and informal programs.[4] The following year Dr. Margaret Monroe, then president of the Association of American Library Schools, appointed a study committee, under the chairmanship of Dr. Elizabeth W. Stone, to investigate the role that the AALS should be playing in this area of educational activity; the report of that committee has just appeared in the official journal of the association.[5] Librarians, thus, like other professionals, are becoming increasingly aware of the need for a variety of learning experiences that extends or builds upon previous experience in the same general area of knowledge and the specific goals of which are not intended to terminate all study in that area. Thus, continuing education implies that the learner has previously studied some related body of knowledge, that he is carrying the process further, and that he proposes to continue such study in the future. One should also note that efforts are now underway to promote an interest in continuing education on the part of the National Commission for Libraries.

Ohio's record in continuing education for librarians is not unimpressive. Shortly after the close of World War II, the library of the Case Institute of Technology held an annual one-day conference on some current development, or developments, in librarianship relating generally to the needs of the scientist and engineer. In the 1950s and early 1960s, the School of Library Science at Western Reserve held at irregular intervals three- to four-day conferences on the emerging field of documentation, information retrieval, and information science. Much more recently the Ohio State Library, in cooperation with Miami University, and with the assistance of federal funding, held a series of week-long, more or less formalized workshops in scientific management for librarians, which have proved to be conspicuously successful. One could, of course, mention other examples, such as the annual three-day workshop at Case Western Reserve for alumni of the library school and others, and the annual two-day event at the library school at Kent, but enough has been said to indicate that a precedent has been set in Ohio for such activity. Yet, good as these activities have been, and many have been quite successful, they lack coordination and the unified formalized structure that would establish them firmly as an important part of the practicing librarian's professional life.

To think constructively, rather than to engage in emotional polemics or sentimentalizing about continuing education, one should first inquire into the environment in which it flourishes. History seems to indicate that it is stimulated by crisis, or assumed crisis—periods of rapid change and professional stress when the old order and its paradigms, to use Thomas Kuhn's term, are threatened.[6] Louis Round Wilson inaugurated the institutes at Chicago at a time when librarianship was shifting away from a traditional emphasis on the humanities and toward the social and behavioral sciences. Indeed, the theme of the first institute was the implications for the library of changing social trends.[7] The conferences at Western Reserve were a response to the rise of documentation and the incipient information science, which emphasized the new role of the computer in information retrieval and the problems it would raise. The workshops at Miami were an expression of the librarians' need for a better understanding of the benefits to be derived from the study of scientific management generally. One may also suggest that these programs seem most useful when they emphasize presentations by non-librarians, people who are experts in a field outside conventional librarianship, leaving to the librarians the problem of relating these specialties to library theory and practice. Such programming is particularly true of the conferences held at Western Reserve in the 1950s, while the Miami workshops were staffed exclusively by scholars in administration, especially public administration and management. Success of these conferences, then, seems directly related to the degree of "outside" participation offered. Librarians are too prone to replow already well-cultivated ground. Librarianship has suffered too long from excessive emphasis upon "state of the art" elucidations when the "art" is librarianship or some aspect thereof.

Also it would appear that successful continuing education programs are most likely to result if they are cumulative, each building upon and being more advanced than the one that precedes it. In the past there has been too great a tendency for meetings to "flit" from topic to topic without ever considering any one in depth. The butterfly may attract attention, but all it accomplishes is to lay eggs and to make other butterflies to flit about and lay more eggs.

The programs should demand of their participants something more than passive listening; librarians get enough of the latter at their national, state, and regional conferences, to say nothing of staff meetings in their own libraries. Man learns best that which he does for himself; ideally, exercises, reports, even tests or examinations should be required to give the participants a goal toward which to work and a sense of accomplishment when the program is ended. In addition, time should be provided for participants to meet and talk informally with each other and with the program staff. "We learn more from each other than we do from the faculty," we were wont to say when we were students at the University of Chicago; though the statement was hyperbole, there was more truth in it than the faculty would have liked to admit.

An effective program must be a cooperative undertaking, involving the libraries, the library schools, the state library, and the state library association. Since we have mentioned library schools, let us emphasize, albeit parenthetically, that continuing education is just as important, if not more important, to the faculty of the library school as it is to the practicing librarian. It is a poor teacher indeed who does not raise his eyes from notes that are 20 years old. We believe that the state library is, perhaps, in the strongest position to assume leadership,[8] as is now being planned in Illinois, but leadership there must be even though no one agency should be expected to carry the entire burden. The system concept is as applicable to continuing education as to any other major human undertaking. If the end is worthy, there must be some sacrifices on the part of all involved. To say that the participants should contribute something from their own time does not mean that they should be expected to carry the entire load, for the library that employs them must give something too, and this failure has, in the past, been responsible for indifferent success in many undertakings. The ALA educational policy statement cited above is specific on this point:

> Library administrators are responsible for providing support, funding and opportunities in the form of in-service programming, including leaves, sabbaticals, and released time for the continuing education of their staffs.[9]

One would think that such a warning, or admonition, would be unnecessary, and that library administrators would rejoice at every display of enthusiasm for new knowledge by those who labor in the vineyards. But we all know that there are administrators who are indifferent, if not hostile, to the staff member who is eager for growth. Perhaps one of the reasons for the outstanding success of the Miami program was that it was aimed at the administrators themselves. They were quite willing to grant themselves released time.

But we must emphasize that we are not arguing for the creation of "ninety-day wonders." The mention of the sabbatical in the statement just quoted is significant and important. Every library administrator should make certain that his budget provides financing for those staff members who can qualify for, and profit from, advanced formal study at the graduate level—and preferably, we might add, in a substantive field rather than in librarianship. Advanced subject knowledge is far more important to the good librarian than "more of the same" in library school. Nor are we saying that every librarian, or even a substantial proportion of them, needs a doctorate. Too much emphasis over the years has been placed on degrees rather than on knowledge.

Adequate financing is, of course, essential. Good education is expensive, and good education we must have if librarianship is to survive. Nor should we look always to Washington to "pick up the tab"; there must be support, and more than token support, at the state and local levels. When Cleveland, for example, decided to have a great symphony orchestra and a great art museum, the community was willing to provide it. The same principle must be true for education.

Finally, continuing education must be understood as an integrated whole, not a cluster of sporadic and isolated instances. Again we return to the concept of *system*, for librarianship, along with education, faces a crisis the magnitude of which none of us can really foresee. If we are to survive that crisis, we must unite. Librarianship has many achievements to its credit, but it has been "isolationist" in many ways, too. Continuing education, life-long professional improvement, is not a panacea for all our ills, but neither is it a decoration, nor icing on the cake. The state library, the state library association, and the libraries of the state must stop playing around the edges of the problem. A self-destructing diploma may not be needed, but few will deny that that venerable parchment would be enhanced if it were periodically reset in a new frame of reference.

## FOOTNOTES

[1] John S. Diekhoff, "The General Education of a Poet," *Journal of General Education*, Vol. 14 (April 1962), p. 21.

[2] Diana Crane, *Invisible Colleges* (Chicago: University of Chicago Press, 1972), Chapter 2, "Scientific Communication and the Growth of Knowledge."

[3] William Goffman and Vaughan Newell, "Communication and the Epidemic Process," *Proceedings of the Royal Society*, Section A, Vol. 298, pp. 316-39.

[4] *Library Education and Manpower: A Statement of Policy* (Chicago: Office of Library Education, American Library Association, 1970).

[5] Elizabeth W. Stone, "The Role of the AALS in Lifetime Learning for Librarians," *Journal of Education for Librarianship*, Vol. 12 (Spring 1972), pp. 254-66. Dr. Stone's major study in the area of continuing education is, of course, her *Factors Related to the Professional Development of the Librarian* (Metuchen, N.J.: Scarecrow Press, 1969). *See also* her "Continuing Education in Librarianship; Ideas for Action," *American Libraries*, Vol. 1 (June 1970), pp. 543-51. *See also*, L. E. Bone and F. R. Hartz, "Taking the Full Ride; A Librarian's Route to Continuing Education," *Library Journal*, Vol. 95 (October 1, 1970), pp. 3244-46.

[6] Thomas S. Kuhn, *The Structure of Scientific Revolutions* (Chicago: University of Chicago Press, 1971).

[7] Louis Round Wilson, ed., *Library Trends* (Chicago: University of Chicago Press, 1937).

[8] Continuing education, especially for staff members and consultants of state libraries, was given special emphasis at the Allerton House conference on the state library, held in 1970. Guy Garrison, ed., *The Changing Role of State Library Consultants* (Urbana, Ill.: Graduate School of Library Science, University of Illinois, 1968).

[9] *Library Education and Manpower.*

# Two Messages as President of Beta Phi Mu

In the Phi Beta Kappa *Key Reporter* for the summer of 1970, the late Ewart K. Lewis, who was at the time of her death a member of the department of history at Oberlin College, addressed herself to the fundamental question: "What is the point of Phi Beta Kappa?" The question is, I think, highly pertinent to Beta Phi Mu. Her answer, which, as she admits, is highly personal, is that the essence of that distinghished fraternity is to be found in its local chapters. Yet the local chapter, as she observes, is a very strange organization: it administers no property, it lobbies for no policies, it holds almost no meetings. She likens Phi Beta Kappa in one respect to a butterfly; it exists only to perpetuate the species. From the long winter months when it was only a dry chrysalis it emerges in the spring for a brief moment of intense and glamorous life for no reason other than that of reproduction.

Mrs. Lewis has voiced many of our own uncertainties about Beta Phi Mu. We conventionally say that our fraternity exists to reward scholarship, but scholarship is its own reward, and it does not need a secret society to add to its laurels. Moreover, scholarship leads to many other rewards than mere membership in our organization, to the rewards of service, of leadership, of opportunity to benefit in some way the harrassed lot of mankind. Beta Phi Mu requires a stipulated grade average for admission to membership, but rewards are not to be measured mathematically.

If membership in Beta Phi Mu is not a reward for scholarship, then one may properly ask, "What is it?" I think it is a symbol, a public affirmation, sanctified by ritual if need be, that scholarship is honorable, that scholarship is good. In short, Beta Phi Mu *is* very like the butterfly; it exists for what it is, for what it

Reprinted from the *Beta Phi Mu Newsletter*, No. 30 (November 1970), and No. 31 (April 1971), respectively.

represents. It announces to the library profession that its initiates are like every other library school graduate, but with something added—a dedication to the highest scholarly ideas of librarianship. I have long been concerned with our society's seeming preoccupation with the publication of "pretty" books, "keepsakes"—as if those trappings of scholarship somehow proclaimed our scholastic virtue in an unquestionable way. I would not deny the value of high artistic standards in publishing, but such activities are not our *raison d'être*, at least not in my opinion. I would much rather see our fraternity dedicated to the *encouragement* of scholarship than to the *rewarding* of it. I have no real objection to "pretty" books, but far too often they are like the conventional "Arrow Collar Man," impeccable in every detail, but somehow unacceptable in good company.

The value of Beta Phi Mu is a subtle thing. It is not something that can be touched, or heard, or seen. It may be no more than the flash of a golden key in the sunlight. It is the affirmation of a faith that springs from the grass-roots of the local chapters. It proclaims that scholarship is something very precious, something that needs to be cherished. I have not attended a meeting of the Society of Phi Beta Kappa since my initiation, and that was more years ago than I would like to think, but I do not feel any sense of loss or any sting of neglect. Phi Beta Kappa is there and I am a part of it. That is quite enough for me, and I have never received any indication from my chapter or the national office that they felt otherwise. Beta Phi Mu does not need always to be "doing things." Our profession is overburdened with organizations that are constantly "doing things," and most of it is a preoccupation with being very busy doing nothing. Beta Phi Mu is, indeed, very like a butterfly; it has no visible "business" than that of procreation. But we would not want a world without butterflies, and I would be most unhappy to see the library world without Beta Phi Mu.

\* \* \* \* \*

Every writer probably lives as much for praise as for royalties. We, being no exception—the royalty checks aren't very large anyway—are pleased to acknowledge the receipt of a tidy little batch of fan mail in response to our presidential message of last November. But of all these letters two stand out as especially memorable and welcome. The first came from a young woman who, a few years ago, was one of our students, and who, because she has been our most forthright and uncompromising critic, has remained a particularly cherished friend. We anticipated that, if we heard from her at all, it would be a carefully reasoned, logical, and completely devastating rejoinder, but to our surprise and delight, she approved of the little piece. She could not, however, resist one delicately feathered shaft—she admired, she said, the modest subtlety with which we let it be known that we are also a member of Phi Beta Kappa! The second letter came from a young woman who is completely unknown to us. She wrote to say that when she was initiated into Beta Phi Mu she decided against the purchase of a pin, but after reading what we had written she wanted the little gold dolphin and anchor of Aldus Manutius and forthwith ordered one. Both of these missives were received with a warmth that was tempered only by the thought that it may have been the butterflies, rather than our prose, that touched these feminine hearts.

Man lives by symbols; symbols are the adhesive that binds the culture and proclaims authority. One customarily thinks of symbols as representations of good, as promoting the highest ideals of human behavior—like the star, whether of David or the one over Bethlehem, the flag, or the *Holy Bible*, square, and compasses of Freemasonry. But symbols are like Humpty Dumpty's use of language; they mean what the user intends them to mean, and they can exert their power on the side of evil as well as of good. They can stifle as well as inspire creativity. "Put a uniform on a man," says one of the characters in Sanche de Gramont's *Lives to Give*, "I don't care whether he's a bell captain or admiral of the fleet, and you smother the tiny flicker of awareness in the brain that passes for conscience."

We who are librarians are particularly conditioned by symbols, for we live and do our work in a world of recorded words, which themselves are only symbolic marks on paper. It is our task as librarians to search out the pertinent symbols from the sea of print, and when need be, to convey their meaning to those we serve. The key of Beta Phi Mu is especially appropriate, for we are indeed fishers of words. " 'The question is,' said Alice, 'whether you can make words mean so many different things.' " " 'The question is,' said Humpty Dumpty, 'which is to be master—that's all.' " Like Humpty Dumpty, we must be nominalists; we must be masters of the symbol.

We believe that the founders of Beta Phi Mu were wise in holding ritual to a minimum. It has no ceremonial robes, no paraphernalia other than a small gold lamp, and its rites are simple. Each member is "the master"; each must identify for himself the meaning of the symbolism.

This absence of ritualistic trappings probably creates, in the mind of the outsider, the misleading impression that Beta Phi Mu is an intensely practical sort of association instead of the poetic thing that it actually is. This error is strongly substantiated by the fact that one can say of librarians, as Professor Ewart Lewis said of academicians in her Phi Beta Kappa address, that as a class they are "prosaic and practical. They have a high rating with credit bureaus and automobile insurance companies. They do not, typically, indulge in crime. Their holy wars, however vehement, inflict no other social casualties than a general round of insomnia."

It is not love of books but the patient and relentless search for truth that should motivate the librarian even as it should the academician. The values that we as a society cherish are the quick intelligence, accurate knowledge, precise and logical thought, and the disciplined pursuit of wisdom; these each member must either have or search out in his own way. *Aliis inserviendo consumor.* In dedicating ourselves to the service of others through books, in deriving our symbolism from the Greek *Biblioteki froneos medeontes* (librarians are the guardians of knowledge), we implicitly proclaim that bibliographic scholarship— not machines, nor systems theory, nor managerial practice—is central to our profession. Perhaps never in its history has our culture been so desperately in need of bibliographic scholarship as it is today. There are many forces that are eroding the conventional character of the library: the loss of cohesive social values; changes in the life styles of the population; the weakening of family and community continuity; the rising demand for change in education, especially higher education; the fragmentation and ephemeralization of the learning experience as reflected in the fleeting shadows on the television screen; the proliferation of "things" made possible by the burgeoning of scientific and technical innovation augmented by pressures from the marketplace for "progressive obsolescence" in a throw-away age; and many more that all of you can name.

In this uncertain world, balanced precariously between menace and promise, the library must prepare itself for the possible coming of a new "Dark Age," when it may be required to succor the world of learning and relate itself to the elite as did the monastic libraries of the Medieval world. Can we who are members of Beta Phi Mu be trusted to carry the flickering lamp of learning into the winds of a barbaric storm? I believe we can, and I am convinced that we must.

* * * * *

It was Dr. Johnson who once said that no one ever does anything consciously for the last time, no matter how unpleasant the task, without a feeling of sadness. When the task has been a particularly pleasant one the regret is even keener. We have enjoyed our last year as your president and we hope that we have left Beta Phi Mu just a little stronger than it was when we assumed the badge of office—at least we seem to have helped the jewelery market. The annual meeting and initiation will take place on the afternoon of Sunday, June 29th, and we hope to see there as many of you as can possibly come. These convocations bring us together in a much-needed renewal of unity, and this common bond in the promotion of bibliographic scholarship is especially important to a fraternity such as ours. The solidarity of Beta Phi Mu is not unlike that expressed in Kipling's Law of the Jungle:

All this is the Law of the Jungle,
    As old and as true as the sky;
And the wolf that will keep it may prosper,
    But the wolf that will break it must die.
Like the creeper that girdles the tree trunk
    The Law runneth forward and back:
"The strength of the pack is the wolf,
    And the strength of the wolf is the pack."

So we began with butterflies and ended with wolves, and there were stars, and flags, and uniforms in between—one *does* have to be careful with symbols!